Between Two Countries:
A History of Coronado National Memorial 1939-1990

Between Two Countries:
A History of Coronado National Memorial 1939-1990

by

Joseph P. Sánchez
Bruce A. Erickson
Jerry L. Gurulé

© 2007 by Joseph P. Sánchez
Published by Rio Grande Books
www.nmsantos.com

All rights reserved.
Printed in the United States of America

Book design by Paul Rhetts and Barbe Awalt

No part of this book may be reproduced or transmitted in any form, or by any means, electronic or mechanical, including photocopying, recording, or by any information retrieval system, without the permission of the publisher.

Unless otherwise credited, all illustrations are reproduced courtesy the author's private collection.

ISBN 10 1-890689-41-6
ISBN 13 978-1-890689-41-4

Library of Congress Control Number: 2007925292

Cover: Coronado National memorial, looking eastward, from Montezuma Canyon toward San Jose Peak, Mexico. *(Coronado National Memorial)*

For Loretta Sánchez, Genoa Erickson, Suzanna Gurulé,

In Memory of Luis Gastellum and Al Schroeder
who left indelible marks in the history of the
National Park Service

Contents

Preface xv

Part I—Historical Background

Chapter I
In the Eye of the Storm: The Creation of the Coronado International
"Monument," 1939 to 1941 1

Chapter II
"At the Point on the International Border where Coronado crossed
into the United States:" Bureaucrats, Historians and the Search for
Coronado's Route into Arizona, 1872-1990 25

Chapter III
The United States-Mexico Conundrum and the Change from "Coronado
International Memorial" to "Coronado National Memorial" 37

Chapter IV
A Memorial to Mr. Coronado? A Monument to Misunderstanding:
The View from Cananea 61

Chapter V
From Master Plan to Mission 66 Accomplishments: Early Development of
Coronado National Memorial, 1952-1966 77

Chapter VI
The "keen interest of...the people of Cochise County and elsewhere:"
Grassroots Support for the Memorial 97

Part II—Land Acquisition

Chapter VII
Early Peoples, Settlers, and Speculators: The Land before the Memorial 123

Chapter VIII
Private Development and "Boundary Adjustment —
a Radical Proposal,"1952-1978 137

Chapter IX
Resources Made Available for the Enjoyment of the Public:
1978 to the Present..151

Part III—Contemporary Issues

Chapter X
The Border: Mexican and American Issues, 1940—present 169

Chapter XI
The Memorial's New Direction: Ecology and Biodiversity along
the U.S. and Mexican Border..179

Chapter XII
Epilogue: The Development of Coronado Memorial and its Interpretive
Program..191

Appendix A
Land Acquisitions and Transfers with references to Associated Structures ..217

Appendix B
Grazing...252

Appendix C
Mining..256

Bibliography of Published Sources 261

Footnotes..266

Index 325

Prologue

Much has been written about the Expedition to Cíbola (1540-1542) led by Francisco Vázquez de Coronado.[1] In 1940, Coronado's *entrada, or* reconnaissance, caught the imagination of Americans as an opportunity to commemorate the 400th anniversary of Spain's exploration of the American Southwest and northwestern Mexico. Earlier, in 1935, Congress had created the Coronado Cuarto Centennial Commission to spearhead the commemoration of that historic event.

The Expedition to Cíbola is part of the Age of Discovery that followed Columbus's First Voyage in 1492. Rumors, forged by ancient myths about rich civilizations, abounded throughout the Americas and spurred a number of European expeditions to explore in all directions. At least two great civilizations were found. Tenochtitlan, in Mexico, gave rise to the possibility that the myths could be true. Peru confirmed that more than one such civilization was possible. Meanwhile, Spanish officials in Mexico City pursued the idea that another could be found. To that end, Francisco Vázquez de Coronado was commissioned to lead a large expedition to find it. Thus, Coronado sought the Seven Cities of Cíbola or Quivira, thought to be another rich civilization located somewhere far to the north. With a force of 285 Spaniards, several missionary priests, and about 800 Indian auxiliaries supported by a large supply train, Coronado moved northward. Finally, mythical Quivira was disproved, and Coronado found neither mineral wealth nor rich civilizations.

The expedition began at Compostela, moved north to Culiacán, crossed northwesterly through Sonora and entered present United States somewhere in southeastern Arizona. From there, the expedition proceeded northward to Zuni Pueblo. A detachment of the expedition explored the south rim of the Grand Canyon, which was seen and described by Europeans for the first time. From Zuni the expedition traveled eastward to Tiguex on the Río Grande where Albuquerque now stands. The expedition wintered there, explored as far north as Taos Pueblo and south, probably to Socorro. Other pueblos such as Jemez and Zia were visited by the expedition. By springtime, Coronado and his men had moved eastward to Pecos Pueblo and out to the Great Plains reaching as far northeast as present Lyons, Kansas. Soon after reaching a place they thought was Quivira, Coronado suffered a serious head injury after falling off his horse in a race. Injured, depressed, and disappointed, Coronado returned to Mexico following the same route through Arizona and Sonora. In two years the expedition traveled over 4,000 miles from Compostela to the plains of Kansas and back.

The expedition's reports gave Europeans their first glimpses of places and people in the interior of North America. Among the marvels seen by Coronado's men were the Grand Canyon, the southern Rocky Mountains, the Continental Divide, the Río Grande, and the many Indian pueblos along it from Taos to Socorro, and others from Zuni and Jemez to Pecos. Other places included Cañon Blanco and Palo Duro Canyon, in the Texas Panhandle, and the Great Bend of the Arkansas River in Kansas. On the Great Plains they saw buffalo numbering in the thousands and, Plains tribes, who lived off the land, seasonally following the herds from sunrise to sunset.

The significance of the expedition is based on the vast lands explored and the people with whom contact was made a mere forty-eight years after Columbus's First Voyage. The expedition began a literary history of the area explored along with the first ethnological descriptions of tribes from Plains to Pueblo Indian Peoples. Scientifically, they wrote about the flora and fauna as well as other marvels they saw. The reports of the Coronado expedition by Juan de Jaramillo and Pedro de Castañeda, in particular, as well as letters to the king by Coronado form the earliest literary descriptions of the greater Southwest and are part of the national stories of the United States and Mexico.

At the same time, between 1539 and 1543, two other explorations sallied forth. The first, led by Juan Rodríguez Cabrillo, explored the California coast from Baja California by sea reaching the southern coast of Oregon. Far to the east, Hernando de Soto led the second expedition from Georgia to the Mississippi River crossing through states known today as Florida, Alabama, Mississippi, Tennessee, Louisiana, and Arkansas. Some of Soto's men crossed into eastern Texas. As a result of their efforts, Europeans grasped the large extent of the continent measuring at least 3,000 miles across. Coronado's expedition inspired subsequent exploration of the interior inclusive of the founding expedition of New Mexico by 800 settlers led by Juan de Oñate in 1598.

Some of the contacts made by the three expeditions were friendly others were antagonistic. For Native Americans, those expeditions left another legacy. In New Mexico, the pueblos at Tiguex along the Río Grande took the brunt of warfare against Coronado's Expedition that had intruded upon them with demands for food and other items that, given their limited resources, they were not prepared to share. Coronado, on the other hand, had extended his supply line and the expedition was in desperate need of food. Zuni Pueblo was the first to experience the impact of the Spanish *entrada*. The belligerency of the expedition affected Spanish-Pueblo relationships throughout the latter sixteenth century, when other expeditions visited New Mexico.

Coronado is chiefly remembered as the leader of the expedition to Cíbola. Yet, little is popularly known about the man and his life. Francisco Vázquez de Coronado (1510-1554) was born in Salamanca, Spain, the son of the nobleman Juan Vázquez de Coronado and doña Isabel de Lujan. He was the youngest of six brothers and two sisters, and under the laws of primogeniture, the entire *mayorazgo*, or entailed estate, went to the eldest son, Gonzalo, when their father died. The younger brothers received substantial financial settlements, and endowments were made to convents where the two sisters had become nuns. Francisco and his younger brothers were forced to seek their fortunes elsewhere. One brother, Juan Vázquez de Coronado became an *adelantado* (governor-general) in Costa Rica. Similarly, Francisco sought his fortunes in the viceroyalty of Mexico.

Coronado arrived in New Spain in October 1535 as a member of Viceroy Antonio Mendoza's entourage. As a favorite of Mendoza, Coronado gained prominence in Mexico City. In 1537 the viceroy sent him to Amatepeque in western Mexico to quell a rebellion by African slave miners, which Coronado quickly suppressed. With his star on the rise, Coronado was appointed to the city council of Mexico City in 1538, a post he held for the remainder of his life. He also became a member of the *Hermandad del Santísimo Sacramento de la Caridad*, a lay charity society founded in 1538 to help the needy and educate orphan girls in Mexico City. In 1538 Coronado's land holdings expanded when he purchased the privately held half of Teutenango (thirty-one miles southwest of Mexico City) and Cuzamala (122 miles southwest of Mexico City). In August 1538, Mendoza appointed Coronado as governor of Nueva Galicia, which today comprises a large swath of land north of Guadalajara to Chihuahua and Coahuila. During his governorship (1539-1544), Coronado acquired more land in Mexico.

In 1537 Coronado married a wealthy heiress, Beatríz de Estrada, daughter of the deceased Alonso de Estrada, the royal treasurer in New Spain. In dowry from her mother doña María Gutiérrez Flores de la Caballería, Beatríz de Estrada received half of Tlapa (140 miles south-southeast of Mexico

City), which contained 6,802 tributaries in 1548. Coronado and doña Beatríz had five children. In 1597, forty-three years after Coronado's death, doña Beatríz was still listed as encomendera of half of Tlapa.

In 1540 Coronado embarked on his most famous undertaking, the Expedition to Cíbola. Upon their return to Mexico in 1542, the Crown investigated the conduct of the expedition after charges of mismanagement and cruelty to Indians were brought against Coronado and several of his lieutenants. The abuse of burden bearers on the expedition, the attack on Zuni Pueblo as well as pueblos on the Río Grande, and the mistreatment of certain Indian headmen were among allegations investigated by the commission under Judge Lorenzo de Tejada. Between the conquest of Tiguex and the investigation of it in 1544 by Spanish authorities in Mexico City, the inescapable conclusion was that Spanish-Indian relations in New Mexico had been damaged. In the end, the board of inquiry absolved Coronado of all charges against him. His second in command, García López de Cárdenas, however, was not as fortunate. He served seven years in prison, six of them in the fortress at Pinto, Spain, and one year at Vélez, Málaga, Spain.

After the expedition, Coronado's life returned to that of a socialite, politician, and landowner. He lived in Mexico City and served as *regidor* (alderman) in the *cabildo* of Mexico City. Coronado died in 1554 and was buried in the Iglesia de Santo Domingo in Mexico City.

The story that follows is about legacy and an historical process that came full circle. To be sure, the history of the expedition was written centuries later by a modern generation that wrote with its own twentieth century cultural values. In a Euro-centric sense, Coronado's Expedition, like those of Sir Walter Raleigh and Jacques Cartier were part of the historical process that evolved into countries known today as Canada, Mexico, and the United States. Thus, in 1940, the United States looked back on the Age of Discovery as a part of the legacy of its origins. The Coronado Cuarto Centennial Commission was established by the U.S. Congress with two major chapters in New Mexico and Arizona. At that historic moment, a plan to commemorate the expedition emerged. This study presents the story of that commemorative event. In New Mexico, Coronado State Monument, near Bernalillo and, in Arizona, Coronado National Memorial resulted from the commemorative efforts of the commissions in both states.

Notes

[1] Regarding Coronado' life and expedition, see George P. Hammond and Agapito Rey, editors,. *Narratives of the Coronado Expedition 1540-1542* (1940). Arthur Grove Day. *Coronado's Quest: The Discovery of the Southwestern States* (1940). Herbert E. Bolton, *Coronado on the Turquoise Trail: Knight of Pueblos and Plains* (1949).

Between Two Countries:
A History of Coronado National Memorial 1939-1990

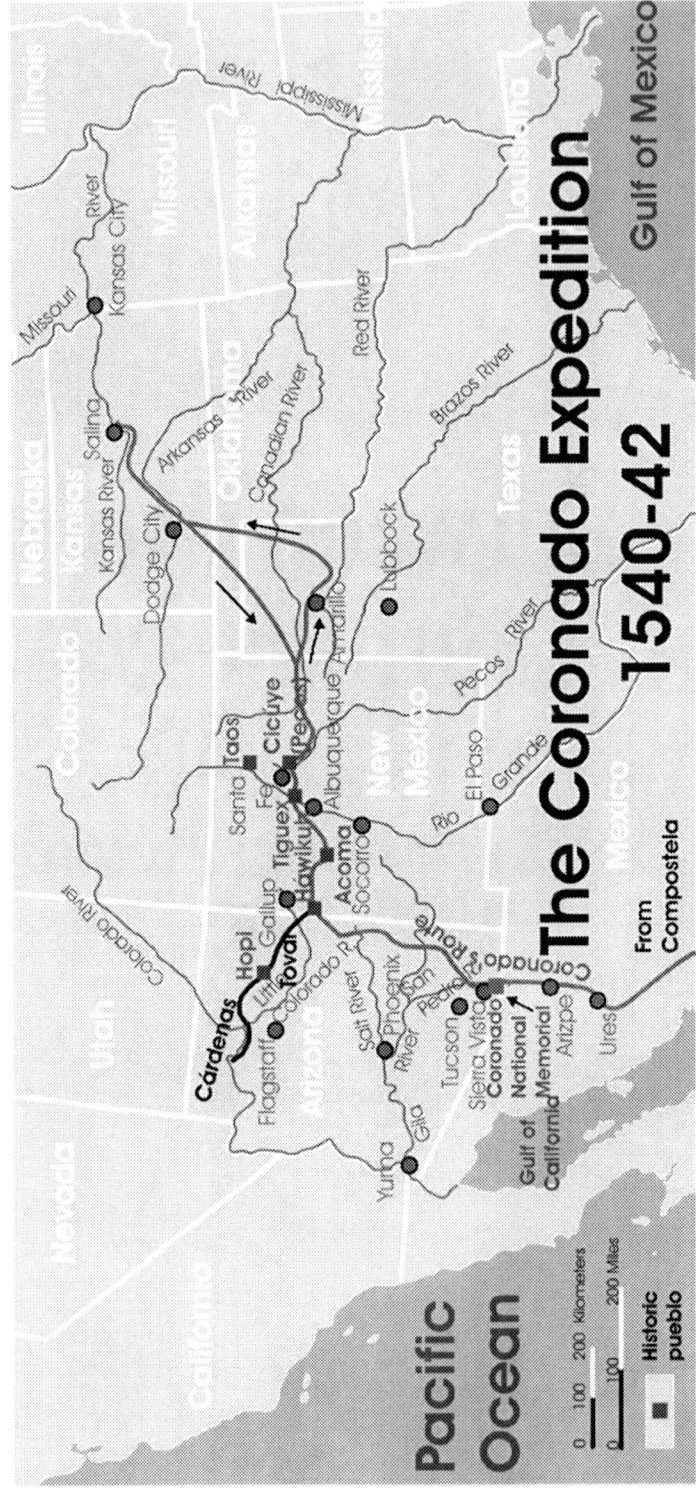

Francisco Vázquez de Coronado's route across what is today Mexico, Arizona, New Mexico, Texas, Oklahoma and Kansas. (Map by Mario Millones, 2006)

Preface

The past is out of reach, buried deep—Who can discover it?-
-Ecclesiastes 7:24

Why a history of Coronado National Memorial? In some ways, history is the recording of events in a formal and factual way in order to gain an understanding of the past and present and, perhaps, to ascertain trends leading to the future. In that same manner, the present history of Coronado National Memorial reveals underlying trends, practices, and themes that have, since 1941, gained, at least, in venerability, and others, more ancillary, that have long since disappeared.

The creation of the Memorial left in its wake many lessons about the process of establishing an international park. On its face, the proposal for establishing a park on the U.S.-Mexico border between two friendly countries appeared to be a simple matter of getting both parties to agree to the proposition. Yet, the historical complexity upon which the relationship is based is profound. In the first place, the historical experiences of the two nations resulted in disparate political practices and institutions; disparate cultural or world views; and, disparate historical traditions resulting in how each would define their public policies. In the political and cultural contexts of relationships between Mexico and the United States during the last half of the twentieth century, the concept of an international memorial was, at least, improbable, as it turned out. Still, hope springs eternal in certain circles today as it did for the National Park Service representatives in the 1940s who wished that Mexico would respond to their proposal for a Coronado International Memorial. In the end, the National Park Service settled for a National Memorial that would commemorate the eventful Coronado Expedition of 1540 and the harmonious relationships between Mexico and the United States. The historical question continues to beg for an answer: Will there ever be a reciprocal Coronado National Memorial on the Mexican side?

The establishment of Coronado National Memorial, on the other hand, offered the usual procedural challenges of starting a National Park area. First, issues regarding size and location had to be resolved; then questions about budget and staffing needed to be answered; and, finally, institutionalizing Coronado National Memorial into the National Park Service system as a full member followed. The latter occurred more fully when Mission 66 became policy for the development, restoration, and maintenance of National Park Service infrastructures. Coronado was the direct beneficiary of Mission 66, for it advanced the slow developmental process that had already begun to languish in the bureaucratic web of the 1950s. Without Mission 66, the development of Coronado National Memorial would have been ponderous.

With the travails of developing Coronado, came the growing pains involved in the evolution of its interpretation program. The most galling issue revolved around how to tell the Coronado Expedition story. Along with the struggle to identify the primary theme, the self-identity of the park suffered somewhat. The usual question is: If Coronado did not pass through the park area, what is the Park Service doing here? From the beginning, the creators of the Memorial considered the possibility that the Coronado Expedition passed near the area. The viewshed offered from Montezuma Peak certainly covered the possibility that if one had stood there in 1540, the likelihood of catching a glimpse of the expedition would have been highly probable. On that point, the consensus of most historians who have studied the expedition is affirmative. Yet, from point of view of park staff, explaining that to the visiting public, in time, became less clear, and the park sought, in the 1970s to reaffirm that premise. During that period, Coronado National Memorial stressed the legacy aspects of the Coronado Expedition by emphasizing the cultural heritage of the area and its relations with Mexico and by instituting the Coronado Historical Pageant, that eventually evolved into the Borderlands Festival, which ran for several years. Additionally, the interpretation program at the Memorial has been developed to stress the history of the Coronado Expedition of 1540, relate its importance to the heritage of the area, and stress cultural, political, natural, and scientific relationships with Mexico.

Visitation at the Memorial is another trend that is continuously monitored. Today, the Memorial receives nearly 90,000 visitors. During the years 1972 to 1988 when the Festival and similar programs ran their course, visitation received a varying boost ranging from roughly 800 to 13,000 people. In the past, tourism in the area aided in the visitation at the Memorial; and, it was generally noted that visitation numbers increased when Fort Huachuca, Sierra Vista and other neighboring developments were on the upswing. Conversely, visitation seemed to decline when the aforementioned population centers underwent stress. Times have changed the dynamics of the relationship between tourism, population upswings/downswings and increases or decreases in visitation. At present, southeastern Cochise County is one of the fastest-growing areas in Arizona, yet, visitation at Coronado National Memorial seems to be decreasing.

The history of Coronado National Memorial as told in this narrative is about three generations: the generation that actively worked to get legislation passed to establish a commemorative place for this important legacy of our national story; the generation that implemented the establishment of the area inclusive of developing its structures, interpretive programs, roads, and infrastructure; and, the generation that currently maintains, protects, and continues the work of the Memorial. It is the latter who holds the key to the future of Coronado National Memorial, for it is they who will pass the torch to those who will come after them. In that regard, the early chapters of this study attempt to establish the narrative, chronology, and trends as the United States National Park Service wended its way through the bureaucratic course in attempting to establish Coronado International Memorial. Similarly, the middle chapters deal with the acquisition of land for Coronado National Memorial; and, the concluding chapters discuss evolution of activities of the Memorial. Thus, what follows is dedicated to all who have worked to make Coronado National Memorial what it is.

Collectively, the sources housed in various institutions amount to thousands of pages of correspondence, reports, news clippings, minutes of meetings, land transaction records, telegrams, and telephone notes. In writing this history, the authors encountered variations of the same information repeated in the different types of documentation. That phenomenon affected the organization of materials in this work. For example, the chapters dealing with Mexico utilize many of the same descriptions used in chapters dealing with land acquisition, for in many ways both topics interrelate. Similarly, the history of the founding of the Memorial crosses over into relations with Mexico and the many land transfers that occurred. Thus, the topics tend to build on one another. The result is a fascinating account of the history of Coronado National Memorial from its incipient stages to the culmination of its establishment and beyond.

In writing this history, the authors are indebted to many people whose assistance is greatly appreciated. Special thanks to Mrs. Agatha Gastellum and Steve Gastellum for allowing us to use a period picture of the late Luis

Gastellum. Dr. Robert Spude of the National Park Service's Intermountain Systems Support Office in Santa Fe, New Mexico, deserves a special acknowledgement for initiating this important history of Coronado National Memorial. The staffs at the National Park Service's Western Archeological Conservation Center (WACC) in Tucson; the Special Collections Library at Arizona State in Phoenix; the Center for Southwest Research at the University of New Mexico; the Arizona Historical Society in Tucson; at the Cochise County Assessor's Office and the Recorder's Office in Bisbee; and, the Lands Office of the National Park Service's Intermountain Support Office in Santa Fe, New Mexico. In particular, the authors gratefully acknowledge the staff at Coronado National Memorial, particularly former Superintendent Jim Bellamy, Barbara Alberti, Scott Sticha, Henry Ruiz, Fred Moosman, and Nancy Wilcox for their assistance gathering much needed information.

Joseph P. Sánchez, Ph.D
Albuquerque, New Mexico

Part I—Historical Background

Chapter I

In the Eye of the Storm: The Creation of the Coronado International "Monument," 1939 to 1941

> *I can assure you that any more land withdrawals in Arizona are going to be mighty unpopular*—G.M. Butler to Carl Hayden, 1940

> *The Secretary of the Interior is not going to withdraw six thousand acres for a Coronado Monument....Such a proposal was made by the acting Regional Historian of the National Park Service at Santa Fé....I have no difficulty in putting my foot on it*—Senator Carl Hayden to G.M. Butler, 1940

> *I do feel that the National Park people are so much more capable of a decision than I am that I have followed their proposals and given them my general support*—Clinton P. Anderson to Senator Carl Hayden, 1940

I had a good deal to do eleven years ago in getting the original bill passed—Arizona Congressman John Robert Murdock, 1952

When, in 1941, the Coronado International Memorial (the predecessor of the present Coronado National Memorial) was authorized, many issues emerged that at any given point could have tolled the death knell for its establishment. Although the opportunity to create an international monument had presented itself in the 400th anniversary of the Francisco Vázquez de Coronado Expedition, it would take the collective optimism of supporters for an international monument to bring it to fruition. Indeed, impetus for the international monument grew from the work of the Coronado Cuarto Centennial Commission that had been created by the United States Congress in 1935.[1] As Arizona had not yet established its own chapter of the U.S. Coronado Cuarto Centennial Commission, Odd S. Halseth, a Phoenix archaeologist, was the Arizona representative on the National Advisory Committee of the New Mexico Commission.[2] Four years later, the Arizona Coronado Commission was created by the Gubernatorial Proclamation of July 27, 1939.[3] Working together, the supporters of the international monument on local, regional, national and international levels wore down the tired and weary obstacles in their paths. The story of the creation of the Coronado National Memorial is one of community spirit, a hallmark of our national character.

On August 30, 1939, the Coronado Cuarto Centennial Commission of Arizona adopted a resolution proposing that an international monument and a museum be established on the U.S.-Mexico border, specifically between Arizona and Sonora, Mexico. The monument's purpose would be to commemorate the 400th anniversary of the Coronado Expedition that had explored from western Mexico, through Arizona, New Mexico, western Texas, Oklahoma, and central Kansas. If any doubts existed concerning the clout the Commission enjoyed to make such a proposal, it was dispelled quickly by Charles M. Morgan, Executive Secretary of the Coronado Cuarto Centennial Commission. Transmitting a copy of the Commission's resolution to the President of the United States, Morgan boldly, but firmly, stated his position. He wrote, "I am directed to request official action, by the President of the United States and by the necessary departments and agencies of the United States Government, in conjunction and cooperation with the President of Mexico and the necessary departments and agencies of the Mexican Government, to set aside and create said International Monument, at the place and in the manner and for the purposes set forth in the Resolution."[4]

Additionally, the Resolution carried the endorsement of R.T. Jones, Governor of Arizona, who urged his old friend, U.S. Senator Carl Hayden, to use his influence on this matter. "I trust," wrote Governor Jones, "that you will write the President, the secretaries of State and Interior, and any others, who, in your judgment, will be able to help expedite action on this proposal. It is important that it be pushed through as rapidly as possible, since 1940 is just around the corner."[5]

Throughout September 1939, Senator Carl Hayden from Arizona, taking his lead from the Resolution, worked to establish the proper channels to communicate, diplomatically, with Mexican officials as well as with members of the American President's cabinet, regarding the proposed international monument and museum. In exploring ways and means to create the international monument, Hayden wrote to Cordell Hull, Secretary of State, saying, "I presume that such an international monument could only be established by joint proclamation of the Presidents of the United States of America and of the United Mexican States."[6] Hayden then requested that the Secretary of State contact the American Ambassador to Mexico so that he could present the proposal to the proper Mexican officials.

With his request pending, Hayden, in early October wrote the Secretary of the Interior asking for the involvement of the National Park Service in this effort. "I realize" he wrote, "that you can reach no final decision in respect to the proposed cession of public land for this purpose until after the attitude of the Mexican Government is ascertained, but I shall be glad in the meantime if you will ask the National Park Service to investigate the feasibility of the land cession and of the monument erection along the lines proposed by the Coronado Cuarto Centennial Commission of Arizona."[7] Along another line, Hayden reminded the Secretary of existing legislation aimed at establishing a monument to commemorate the historical event. "You will recall," he recounted, "that Public Law No. 186 of the 76th Congress, approved July 17, 1939, authorizes the sum of $10,000 to be spent for the erection of a monument of this type, but does not, of course, specify that such a monument shall be of an international character."[8]

Meanwhile, on October 10, 1939, Secretary of State Hull replied to Hayden's missive: "I take pleasure in informing you that I have recently sent instructions to the American embassy at Mexico City with the view of ascertaining the general attitude of the Mexican Government towards this matter. However, I am still awaiting a report from the Embassy. You may rest assured that I shall be glad to give every possible consideration to the international aspects of the Cuarto Centennial celebrations and render all appropriate assistance in that connection."[9] Hull, nevertheless, was quick to point out to Hayden that the proposed domestic activities would be the responsibility of the Secretary of the Interior.

Not long afterwards, John W. Finch, acting Assistant Secretary, the Department of the Interior, replied to Hayden. Finch informed him about the Cuarto Centennial Commission's Resolution, and the pending response from the U.S. Embassy in Mexico. "I am asking the National Park Service," he wrote, "to consider the feasibility of the plan, to determine, if possible, the point where Coronado crossed into what is now the State of Arizona, and, if this point can be located to recommend appropriate boundaries."[10] Exuberantly, Hayden wrote his friend R.T. Jones about his success in getting the National Park Service involvement in the international monument. Cautiously, he added, "You will note of course, that no final action can be taken by the Interior Department until the attitude of the Mexican Government is ascertained."[11] Within five days, Hayden was again in communication with Hull concerning the status of his request for information regarding Mexico.

Meanwhile, the Cuarto Centennial Commission and Governor Jones' office had been in contact with Mexican officials in Mexico City. On October 19, Jones informed Hayden that in a dispatch from the Associated Press in Mexico City dated September 29, the Mexican Government "will send a delegation' to take part in the Coronado Cuarto Centennial Celebration." Jones continued, over-optimistically, saying that Mexican officials "will cooperate in the establishment of a suitable monument to Coronado on the border, which is our Commission project for the establishment of the International Monument and the erection therein of a Coronado Memorial Museum at such suitable monument."[12] Hayden later learned that U.S. Ambassador Josephus Daniels could not confirm the Associated Press' story.

In the same missive, Jones informed Hayden that the United States Coronado Exposition Commission member states of Arizona, New Mexico and Texas had adopted a resolution to send a delegation to Mexico City to arrange "the details of Mexican Government participation."[13] Jones asked Hayden's assistance on this matter.

Meanwhile Secretary of State Hull informed Hayden that the American Embassy had been unsuccessful in acquiring "an expression of views of the Mexican Government concerning this matter, but so far the Mexican Government has not made a definite statement on the subject to our representative in Mexico City."[14] On November 26, 1939, Hull informed Hayden that the Mexican Government had requested additional information regarding the proposed international monument.[15] By year's end, Hull reported to Hayden that no word had been received on the Mexican Government's position on the international monument.[16] Perhaps the New Year would bring more optimistic tidings.

Months later, in February 1940, the Mexican Government responded to the U. S. Embassy in Mexico City. Clinton P. Anderson, Managing Director, United States Coronado Exposition Commission in New Mexico, learned of the response from a copy of a letter from the U.S. Embassy. Writing to G.C. Dickens, Executive Officer, United States Coronado Exposition Commission in Washington, D.C., Anderson quoted a portion of the letter. "The American Ambassador to Mexico," it stated, "informs the United States Coronado Exposition Commission that the Mexican Government will accept the invitation to cooperate in the Exposition, and will later discuss the plans of participation."[17] Still, the Mexican Government's response fell short of a commitment. Nonetheless, it stirred in Anderson a need to do something to draw Mexican interest.

Surely, Anderson's proposals must have raised eyebrows. Anderson suggested that the Department of the Interior take the lead. He claimed that when, in April 1939, the Commission had met with the President of the United States, he was pulled aside and instructed by him that he wanted the Commission "to take an army of CCC young men or National Youth Administration boys and march them over the road which Coronado traveled."[18] Recognizing that the Mexican Government did not have the money to participate in the event, Anderson went a step farther. He wrote:

> I have in mind specifically this: rather than use NYA or CCC boys it will be far more colorful if we selected seventy-five young men from Mexico. I would like to have these young men selected from the descendants of members of Coronado's expedition, but if that involves too much of a difficulty we could go on down the list and take them from the high school at Hermosillo if need be, which is only 150 miles below the border.[19]

At first, Anderson thought the idea to be feasible and began to think up grandiose plans for its implementation.

Anderson suggested, depending on available funding, that the United States transport the young men from Mexico to points visited by Coronado such as Hawikuh, the Grand Canyon, Tiguex, Palo Duro Canyon (near Amarillo, Texas), Oklahoma, and Kansas. He even suggested that the U.S. Government acquire cavalry horses and have the young Mexican men ride "a substantial portion of the trip on horseback."[20] All this, pondered Anderson, could include a meeting of the two presidents from each country. Then he questioned whether the invitation to the American President "be conditional upon the willingness of the President of Mexico to meet him there?"[21] Having brainstormed in his letter, he explained "You can see from the above that I am trying to determine how much of this sort of expense the Federal government would be willing to assume in order to carry out what the President regarded as the proper part of the celebration."[22]

On February 15, Anderson received an answer from Hayden regarding the cavalry horses. Hayden wrote that the Secretary of War advised that it would not be practical to furnish either cavalry horses or army trucks for use in the Coronado celebration.[23]

As Mexican participation floundered, so too, did the Commission's hope for international cooperation. Hayden took a wiser route. In a telegram to Anderson, he wrote I "believe it to be advisable to withhold further action--looking toward general meeting until we can secure an expression of views from these individuals."[24] Turning to a more serious matter, Hayden sought an answer to Anderson's query. That is, Anderson had raised two questions. The first question concerned the ability of the National Park Service or the Department of the Interior to indicate by February 20, whether a favorable recommendation could be submitted to Congress regarding the creation of an international monument at or near the point where Coronado first entered what is now the United States. Secondly, he asked if an international museum within such an international park would be looked upon with favor by the United States?[25] At that point, the questions were rhetorical. No one had a clear answer to either question.

Meanwhile, Oscar L. Chapman, Assistant Secretary of the Department of the Interior, informed Senator Hayden that the National Park Service's investigation of the feasibility of the proposed international monument had been made by a representative of the National Park Service's Region III Office in Santa Fe. The report, when written, would be communicated to him.[26] The field investigation team, led by Dr. Aubrey Neasham, the Regional Historian for the National Park Service in Santa Fe, and a committee, had visited Arizona in mid-December. His head spinning with ideas about the international monument, Neasham met with the committee several times to formulate their reports and recommendations.

Among his consultants was Dr. Emil Haury, Head of the Department of Anthropology at the University of Arizona, Tucson. In December, Haury wrote Neasham and expressed his views on the international monument. Haury explained that he supported the idea of the Coronado International Monument, and he urged the cooperation of the Mexican government toward that endeavor. "Soliciting the cooperation of the Mexican government," he wrote optimistically, "should, it seems to me, be accomplished without too much difficulty. Apart from the objectives that such a monument would endeavor to reach, there would also be tangible evidence of a feeling of good neighborliness between our and the Mexican government."[27] Haury obviously did not know the difficulty Hull and Hayden had already experienced in their attempts to get a response from the Mexican Government.

By February 1940, Neasham had generated a series of reports dealing with the prospect of an international monument commemorating the Coronado Expedition of 1540. The consultants to these reports included Jerome C. Miller, associate landscape architect, and W. Ward Yeager, associate forester of the National Park Service Region III, as well as Dr. Haury and Dr. Russell Ewing of the University of Arizona. In mid-December 1939, they had met with a team to survey the international border between Nogales and Naco to determine the location of an international monument "at or near the point where Coronado crossed from Mexico into what is now Arizona."[28] Indeed, A.J. Wirtz, Under Secretary, the Department of the Interior, wrote Hayden and identified the survey team as Neasham, Herbert E. Bolton, and George P. Hammond, all distinguished historians. Wirtz apologized that the report had been delayed by the need to identify Coronado's route. The team had spent several weeks tracing the route of the Coronado Expedition, he wrote, and the survey was presently nearly completed.[29]

Their reports made some interesting observations and recommendations regarding the establishment of the international monument. They stressed, moreover, the importance of Mexico's cooperation in the establishment of an appropriate commemorative site. Neasham's report, nonetheless, reflected the hopes of those on the United States side who worked to establish the Coronado International Monument.

Neasham clearly understood the significance of establishing the international monument. "It is believed," he wrote, "that the creation of an international monument…in which can be established an international museum to commemorate the explorations of Coronado…is desirable and feasible, provided the Governments of Mexico and the United States cooperate fully to bring about the establishment and maintenance of such an area…."[30] Throughout his report, Neasham stressed that "cultural understanding" was the pillar upon which the international monument would be built.

Ahead of his times, Neasham foreshadowed that cooperation between the two nations in regard to scientific endeavors would eventually take place. On that point, he reported, "It is believed that an international monument established in the area indicated will be of great value in advancing the relationships of the United States and Mexico upon a friendly basis of cultural understanding. Furthermore, such an area with its international museum would serve as a common clearing ground for scientific endeavor between Mexico and the United States."[31] The museum was, indeed, an integral feature of the international monument as in it could be displayed important artifacts and documents demonstrating the history and culture of that area.

Next, Neasham added another enthusiastic point for the justification for the international monument. In his conversations with a certain "Señor Gonzales" who was the Mexican consulate in Phoenix, Neasham explored the meaning of a proposed international highway that would be completed in two years. The highway, running from Guadalajara, Mexico, would straddle the Pacific Coast before turning inland and terminate in Nogales, Arizona, thus stimulating increased tourism. Neasham pointed out that the international "parkway or freeway" would eventually connect the proposed international monument and Nogales on the United States side. Neasham saw many possibilities growing out of the international freeway that would pass along "a scenic border country."

Unabated in his enthusiasm, Neasham wrote, "The area of Bisbee and Douglas, Arizona, could tie in with that parkway without difficulty. The War Department, too, may be interested in developing such a parkway, because of its close proximity to the Mexican border and Fort Huachuca. It is believed that the people of Arizona would enter wholeheartedly into the development of an international monument, museum, and parkway along the international border."[32] To that end, he recommended that an international survey party comprised of representatives from the United States and Mexico investigate the possibilities for the creation of an international monument, museum, and parkway. "Mexico," he wrote, " has indicated that she will cooperate fully with this government in celebrating this year's Coronado Cuarto-Centennial, of which the establishment of an international monument is an important phase."[33]

Neasham was optimistic along other lines. For example, should an agreement be reached between the United States and Mexico to create the international monument, he speculated that funding by Congress for the commemoration of the Cuarto-Centennial would be matched by Mexico in 1940. Pointing out that the Civilian Conservation Corp would establish a camp; and, Mexico would set up "a similar labor unit;" he cautioned that a "joint administration of the two National Park Services of Mexico and the United States would, of course, have to be provided."[34] Neasham, needless to say, did not fully understand the Mexican bureaucracy, for a Mexican National Park Service did not exist, but his meaning was well taken.

Neasham's report recommended an international advisory board be formed to further such interests on both sides of the border. Three citizens from each country would make up the board, hopefully headed by Dr. Herbert E. Bolton of the Advisory Board on National Parks, Historical Sites, Buildings, and Monuments. That committee, read the report, would "do much to insure the success of the international monument, in view of the sympathy, contacts, and cultural understanding of such an individual."[35]

In context, it would be unfair to characterize Neasham's enthusiastic report as a product of naivete, for a genuine feeling on the part of the United States—through the Cuarto Centennial Commission and the National Park Service—was based on the hope that all could ride on the coattails of interest engendered by the opportunity presented by the 400th anniversary of Coronado's Expedition. Neasham's report expressed the hope that "international travel, advancement of good will, and cultural relationships with Latin America"[36] could be spurred by this effort. Indeed, it was an interesting time in the history of the United States, as war clouds burst into the violence of World War II.

In his transmittal of Neasham's report to Hayden, Harold L. Ickes, Secretary of the Interior, clarified the position of the Department of the Interior. The Department, he wrote "is not in a position to give approval to a proposal for an international project of this character prior to receiving an expression of the views of the State Department. If the State Department favors the creation of an international project, the Department of the Interior will interpose no objection, provided the development conforms to sound park practice."[37] Ickes, moreover, stated that Interior policy prohibited the creation of an international park, but would permit an international monument or memorial.

Expressing concerns about the amount of land involved and any mineral or grazing privileges attached to the land within the monument, Hayden, on Thursday, February 29, 1940, responded that an international monument would be "highly desirable." Incidentally, he informed Ickes "it occurs to me that more land is proposed to be taken for the Monument within the United States than would seem to me necessary. I am particularly interested in the fact that the land involved shows at least two existing mines, the Grubb Stake Mine and the Texas Mine [sic]."[38] Hayden suggested that the proposed area of the international monument be reduced "to eliminate therefrom any land, which contains potentially valuable minerals, or that a careful and complete geological and mineral survey be made so as definitely and finally to determine that no minerals exist in whatever area is selected."[39]

Over a week later, Hayden revisited the question regarding the size of the monument and suggested that "eleven sections of land are vastly more than is needed for a monument of this type. I should assume that an acre or two would be ample."[40] The eleven sections were to be taken from the Coronado National Forest for the monument. Given that grazing privileges existed on that land, they too would be taken into consideration. Hayden recommended that the Secretary of the Interior deliver a copy of the proposal for the monument to the Secretary of Agriculture so that the Forest Service could study and reach an agreement regarding the boundaries. Evidently, some discussions between Hayden and his constituents had taken place over the size of the proposed monument, grazing privileges, and any subsurface minerals that could exist within the projected boundaries.

To Hayden's concerns, Arno B. Cammerer, Director, National Park Service, responded that once the State Department informed Interior of the possibility of an international monument, the National Park Service would make "further studies…to insure the exclusion of mineral lands from the proposed area."[41] The issue of the size of the monument would resurface several times in the next few weeks.

Meanwhile, Clinton P. Anderson had been moving the question of an international monument before the Department of State. Pressing the issue, he informed Hayden that Ickes had requested the Cuarto Centennial Commission to present the "matter of the international monument"[42] to the Secretary of State. The urgency for Anderson concerned April 14, 1940, as the date that if the Commission hoped to "have a celebration…as planned, it will be necessary for the State Department to act promptly."[43]

Imposing if not bold, Anderson made a request of Hayden. "Will you," he writes, "be good enough to get in touch with Mr. Dickens and attempt to expedite action by the State Department, so that we may notify a representative of this Commission who is now in Mexico and who is awaiting definite action by the American Government, in order that Ambassador Josephus Daniels may immediately present the subject to the Mexican Government?"[44]

The pressure to propose legislation for the monument grew in Hayden's mind. On March 18, he received a letter from E.K. Burlew, First Assistant Secretary of the Interior, repeating that Interior could not approve a proposal for an international monument unless it received a favorable expression from the Department of State. "Until such an expression has been received," wrote Burlew, "the Department of the Interior cannot submit a proposal to establish an international monument to the Department of Agriculture. It is understood, however, that the Coronado Cuarto Centennial Commission is presenting the above-mentioned proposition to the Department of State for its consideration. If that Department favors the proposal, the Department of the Interior will submit it to the Department of Agriculture for study."[45] About the same time, Ickes formally requested an opinion from the Department of State concerning the feasibility of an international monument.[46]

The Department of State moved slowly. In a telegraph to Stuart M. Bailey, Chairman of the Arizona Coronado Cuarto Centennial Commission, Hayden advised him that the Department of State would not be able to present the proposal to the Republic of Mexico by April 15. Meanwhile, he suggested that the National Park Service make an additional study regarding the boundary and mineral possibilities on the proposed land. In his telegram, Hayden enlarged his suggestion:

> THE ENTIRE PROPOSAL WILL ALSO HAVE TO BE PRESENTED TO THE DEPARTMENT OF AGRICULTURE SO THAT THE FOREST SERVICE CAN MAKE AN INDEPENDENT STUDY AND SUBMIT A REPORT THEREON STOP THIS LATTER STEP IS NECESSARY SINCE THE LAND PROPOSED TO BE TAKEN FOR THE MONUMENT IS LOCATED WITHIN THE CORONADO NATIONAL FOREST STOP….[47]

Much to Hayden's chagrin, he discovered, in a conversation with Fred Winn, Forest Supervisor in Tucson, that the Forest Service "apparently has never received any information from the Park Service" regarding the proposed international monument.[48] To that, Hayden instructed Frank C.W. Pooler, Regional Forester in Albuquerque to send "one of your men… to Santa Fe and discuss the proposition with representatives of the Park Service there, who have under study…an international monument which will embrace approximately eleven sections of land within the Coronado National Forest near the Montezuma Pass."[49]

Two weeks later, Pooler reported to Hayden that he had met with National Park Service Regional Director Hillory Tolson in Phoenix and discussed the matter. Soon after, Tolson met with Forest Service personnel at the proposed site and walked through the land in question. On March 21, Tolson and Neasham met with Pooler in his downtown Albuquerque office in the Post Office Building to discuss the proposal further. Pooler summarized the National Park Service position. "There are several patented mining claims and water rights," he informed Hayden, "which the Park Service would wish to avoid."[50] After he and Park Service officials examined the site for the monument and museum and reviewed the international aspects of the proposal, Pooler concluded, "we will then be in a position to submit joint recommendations."[51]

Having attended a public meeting regarding the Catalina Highway Bill, G.M. Butler, dean and director of the Arizona Bureau of Mines and the College of Mines and Engineering at the University of Arizona, advised Hayden that he feared public reaction against any project that suggested land withdrawals in Arizona. "I can assure you" he wrote, "that any more land withdrawals in Arizona are going to be mighty unpopular."[52] Butler voiced a concern that the Secretary of the Interior "contemplates withdrawing 6,000 acres near the point where Coronado is supposed to have entered Arizona and setting it aside as a monument to Coronado." To that Butler opined that he thought there was an abundance of "mineralization in the area involved, and I hope that you will watch this movement like a hawk."[53] Squashing that rumor, Hayden promptly and somewhat tersely, responded that the Secretary of the Interior "is not going to withdraw six thousand acres for a Coronado Monument....Such a proposal was made by the acting Regional Historian of the National Park Service at Santa Fé, but I have no difficulty in putting my foot on it."[54]

Hayden, of course, could speak with authoritative bravado, for he already had a part of his answer. The day before he made his response to Butler, Hayden had received word of the joint proposal from the National Park Service and the U.S. Forest Service submitted by Pooler to his boss, the Chief Forester, in Washington, D.C. Dated April 5, Pooler's letter explained that he had met with NPS Regional Director Tolson, Historian Neasham, and a certain Mr. Ritchie of the National Park Service along with Clinton P. Anderson of the Coronado Cuarto Commission and Mr. Dickens, the Washington representative of the Commission. Both Anderson and Dickens were in direct contact with Hayden, for they hoped to move the establishment of the international monument as soon as they could to coincide with celebrations of the Coronado Expedition anniversary. "Accordingly," wrote Pooler, "I advised Mr. Tolson and Mr. Anderson that they were authorized to state that the Region would recommend favorably on the proposed monument and that we would forward the report promptly."[55]

By consensus, they agreed to reduce the amount of land originally requested by 50% equalling 2,750 acres. They justified the request by explaining the need for an international monument that would represent the desired relationships between the two countries. "The purpose of this monument on the international boundary," stated Pooler, "is...to include a sufficient area which, with that to be provided by the Mexican Government, will furnish a national monument of real international aspect."[56] In his conclusion that the Mexican government would support the monument, Pooler, in hindsight, appears misinformed.

Based on the report's findings, Pooler explained that "forest values," that is, minerals and other natural resources, were negligible in the "small" area under consideration[57] and that "grazing use will not be disturbed except for the small plots immediately around the structures. He concluded that "any opposition...by the stockmen [regarding] future use of the area for grazing can be worked out on a cooperative basis." He surmised that "the Park Service will recommend the establishment of the national monument on the lines shown subject to all valid existing rights which would include valid mining claims already of record and outstanding grazing permits for the remainder of the contract term."[58]

Arguing that time was of the essence, as "the dedication ceremonies are desired at the earliest possible date," Pooler, urging his boss to acquiesce to the compromise in the joint proposal regarding the 2,750 acres, ventured an explanation. "I do not think," he wrote, "the Forest Service should place itself in the position of arguing acreages but rather should, in an instance of this kind, cooperate fully while considering all the interests involved." Besides, Pooler already had gone out on the limb by advising Tolson and Anderson that the region would "recommend favorably on the proposed monument."[59]

The resulting report, dated April 4, was signed by John A. Adams, Regional Forest Inspector, Division of Recreation and Lands, in Albuquerque. The proposed Coronado International Monument, wrote Adams, "is located in the Huachuca Division of the Coronado National Forest, approximately thirty miles west of Bisbee, Arizona. The area contains 2,745 acres in T. 24 S., Rs. 20 and 21 E., adjoining and north of the International boundary."[60] A survey of the area had been made by Forest Service personnel on March 12 and 13 to determine the location, land status, range use, range improvements, and forest products.

Range use, on the other hand, posed complications. There were three grazing allotments within the area. Two permittees had prescribed privileges to the Lone Mountain allotment. H.D. Lee had a yearlong term permit to graze 650 head of cattle as well as a temporary permit that covered a short period for any natural increase to his herd. His neighbor, Alex D'Albini also had a yearlong term permit for 88 head of stock, and another yearlong term permit for 42 cattle on the Grubstake allotment. Meanwhile, Joe Zaleski continued his yearlong term permit on the Montezuma allotment for 30 head of cattle which was the portion that he would later consider donating in Section 18.

As there were other accessible areas to Bisbee, Warren, and Lowell for forest products such as fuel wood and fence posts, the report included an observation that they would not be inconvenienced by the withdrawal of public land for the establishment of the Coronado International Monument. Oddly, the volume of this use was unknown, and there was no public outcry against the withdrawal of that land. Additionally, lands adjoining the north boundary of the proposed monument included homesteads controlled by Zaleski and the popular Border Guest Ranch, both of which would be unaffected by the alienation of lands to the monument. Indeed, the report suggested that the Chamber of Commerce of Bisbee and other towns in southern Arizona as well as the State Coronado Commission would support the establishment of a monument.[61]

Beyond location, land status, range use, range improvements, and forest products, there were other amenities. Perhaps, the panoramic vistas afforded from the highpoint offered the best vantage point from which to commemorate the Coronado Expedition. The writers of the report aptly observed:

> The lookout or observation point is located half a mile south where the road crosses the saddle in the southern part of Sec. 11. From this point an unexcelled view is had of the country north of the Sonora Valley, as well as the Cananea Mountains in Mexico. To the west is seen the Patagonia Range across the San Rafael Valley. From the Sonora divide following north viz. The San Pedro Valley is the probable route of Francisco Coronado during the year 1540.[62]

The land offered the best vantage point for interpreting the historical event and the geography of the area.

Having reviewed the report, Senator Hayden responded to Cammerer, director of the National Park Service. In his letter dated April 8, 1940, Hayden "objected most vigorously to the size of the tentative international monument" that totaled less than 13 sections or nearly 6000 acres. He reasserted that notwithstanding the presence of grazing privileges and mineral wealth within that acreage, the proposed size was unjustified. He wrote, "I assumed...that the only reasonable justification for requiring as much land...proposed was that the Park Service desired to build a new highway within the monument and to protect its right-of-way against mineral and grazing development."[63]

To Hayden, the size of the Coronado International Monument worked against his presentation of a bill before Congress to establish it. Despite the fifty percent reduction of land proposed, Hayden told Cammerer "I cannot see any conceivable purposes in having even this much land."[64] He pointed out that beyond the need to construct a highway, if the land contained scenic or historical features suitable for development as a national monument, it would support justification for that much land. His objection revolved around value the 2,750 acres had for its grazing and mineral development. He argued that the report of the Regional Forester indicated that the land in question "is covered with unpatented claims and...three grazing allotments."[65] Virtually lecturing the director of the National Park Service, Hayden remarked, that while Mexico would contribute "artifacts and relics" related to the Coronado Expedition, "one acre would be ample land upon which to place such a museum." Fifty acres, he opined, would be enough land for a park boundary with parking and other facilities for visitor purposes. "On the Forest Service map," he added, "there is marked in the north half, northwest quarter, sec. 20., T. 24 S., R. 21 E., a small square which is designated as the probable museum site.[66] Although Hayden felt strongly about his stance, he would later modify his argument. After a long recitation of the sections, townships, and ranges involved, he proceeded to tell Cammerer what he was willing to support. In no uncertain terms he suggested that a total of 160 acres be withdrawn for the international monument. He wrote:

> The Monument would be adjacent to an existing dude ranch and apparently a right-of-way to it from the proposed highway along the north side of the dude ranch would be preserved.... If you want to have a proposed circle road from the proposed northern road, skirting the guest ranch down to the monument and around into Mexico and back up to join the existing road coming up Copper Canyon, there can certainly be no objection to such construction....So far as that goes, if later on additional recreational facilities are felt to be necessary in any of the forest land adjacent and to the west of the monument area, a regulation of the Forest Service governing recreational permits should be ample to protect the interests of the United States.[67]

Tauntingly, Hayden suggested that Cammerer should certainly agree that no conceivable justification existed for "the elaborate proposals jointly submitted by the Regional Offices of the Forest Service and the National Park Service. Hayden believed that the interests of the United States Government would be better served by setting aside only 160 acres he proposed. He ended with the admonition that "I cannot consent to any monument land acquisition on a more grandiose scale."[68]

Cammerer responded that the position of the regional representatives of the Forest Service and the National Park Service was that the monument should contain approximately 2,750 acres. So as to mitigate that statement, Cammerer quickly and diplomatically added, "I agree with you that the area of the monument should be limited to a minimum, and I have advised Regional Director Tolson of your letter. He reminded Hayden that the Department of State had yet to respond to the international aspects of the monument. Meanwhile, he and Tolson, who was being transferred from Santa Fe to Washington, D.C. as NPS Chief of Operations, would review all the plans of the projected Coronado International Monument within a week.[69]

Leaving no stone unturned, Hayden, let loose a flurry of correspondence regarding the proposed international monument. Within a few days, he had written Colonel John R. White, the newly appointed Regional Director of the National Park Service's Santa Fe office, to inform him about the Coronado International Monument proposal.[70] Apparently, the project was too important for Hayden to let drop, for he kept tight control over it. In a letter to Pooler, he commented that "Mr. Cammerer agrees with me that the area of the proposed International Monument to Coronado should be limited to a minimum and that he has so advised Dr. Hillory. A. Tolson, the former Regional Director of the National Park Service at Santa

Fé."⁷¹ Apparently other correspondence or telephone calls had been made, for Hayden confided to Pooler that upon Tolson's arrival in Washington, Cammerer would set a new boundary.⁷²

It would take a Herculean effort to bend the mind of the stalwart Senator Hayden who was convinced that 160 acres sufficed for the international monument. Apparently, he believed that private lands would be required, and that would not set well with his rancher constituents.

In this dark moment, tall, lanky, charming, Clinton P. Anderson stepped forward. Sitting at his desk, he looked over a copy of Hayden's letter that called for limiting the acreage of the proposed international monument. With a twinkle in his eye, Anderson began his response. Diplomatically, Anderson waxed eloquent expressing to Hayden how he appreciated his thoughts on the proposed size of the international monument. "I wish I could discuss this with you intelligently," he wrote, "But I do feel that the National Park people are so much more capable of a decision than I am that I have followed their proposals and given them my general support."⁷³ Anderson reminded him that private lands were not involved. Applying logic to the situation, Anderson posited:

> I wish that before they reach a final decision you could take a look at it. I think that would help you to appreciate the suggestion made by the Park Service. Their lookout is back a short distance from the border. It is at a very excellent location and I really feel that it would be very much worth while to connect the lookout point with the museum site. If you do that you stretch the area quite a little distance along the border I admit, but the land is not of great value for any purpose other than a park area. It is rather sandy at the bottom and rather steep on the grades which go up toward the lookout. It would be one thing to transfer this much acreage from private ownership to Federal ownership, but it is quite another thing to transfer it from Forest Service land to Park Service land.⁷⁴

The last sentence surely caused Hayden to raise his eyebrows and tilt his head in approbation. Clearly he grasped Anderson's meaning: the land in question was largely, if not entirely, being transferred from one government agency to another.

Astutely, Anderson pointed out that the Senator had short-changed the proposal by addressing the space requirement "only for the museum itself.... but at the same time if you look over the land I feel you will be inclined to say that it would serve as useful a purpose in the international monument as it does now in the Forest Service."⁷⁵ Using salesmanship skills, Anderson wrote, "I believe it will be a splendid national attraction." He described the historical landscape and ended by saying "All the rest is wilderness looking just as it did when Coronado crossed it 400 years ago. There are very few areas in the United States of which that can be said....I know of no place along the border which serves as well as the lookout point selected by the Park Service."[76]

Hayden got the point. "I thank you for your letter of April 11," he responded to Anderson, "in which you ask that I reconsider my suggestion that the proposed Coronado international monument be restricted insofar as the American portion thereof is concerned to no more than 160 acres."[77] He stated that Director Cammerer and Chief of Operations Tolson had recently made the same request. Hayden repeated that he could not consent to any proposal that called for a withdrawal of any considerable area of land in Arizona that restricted mineral and grazing operations. After they had suggested that legislation could be drawn reflecting that position, Hayden sat back and made a recommendation. "I asked them," he wrote Anderson, "to be good enough to prepare the draft of such a bill and promised that when it was presented to me, I shall be very glad to give it my most sympathetic consideration. I shall let you know what is determined at that time."[78]

Meanwhile, Hayden received a confidential, hand-written letter from Fred Winn, the Forest Supervisor in Tucson, stating that he opposed Pooler's agreement with the National Park Service. Winn felt that 160 acres was ample. Not wishing to embarrass Pooler, Winn stated that the grazing "permittees" and the small mine owners had not been consulted. Closing, he asked "Again, please do not mention this letter. It is for your information only."[79] Hayden assured him that he would not introduce any legislation unless its purpose was understood and approved by "all local interested parties."[80]

Returning to the lack of response from Mexico, Hayden transmitted a copy of Anderson's letter to Cordell Hull. "I assume," he wrote," that if legislation establishing the proposed international monument is to be sought, there will be no great point in your presenting any proposals along these lines to the Republic of Mexico, at least until the legislation has been formulated and introduced."[81] Hull quickly responded. He mentioned that State Department officers working on the "Coronado matter" would be able to meet with Tolson in Washington. Beyond that, Hull astutely reiterated the desire of his office to assist in the "Coronado matter" in any way. He had instructed Ambassador Josephus Daniels in Mexico City to act "as soon as the [Coronado] Commission presents to the Department [of State] a definite proposal with regard to the international monument...in honor of Coronado."[82] Still, Mexican officials, apparently cool to the idea, had not responded.

Whatever transpired to change Hayden's mind on presenting a bill to Congress establishing the Coronado International Monument is not clear in the record. On Monday, April 17, 1940, Tolson informed Hull that "he was now in a position to make recommendations to the United States Coronado Commission on the basis of which the Commission could present a definite plan to the Department of State."[83] Possibly after a few telephone calls, he decided to move forward with his proposal.

On Monday, April 22, 1940, Hayden informed W.E. Clark, clerk of the Cochise County Board of Supervisors, as well as a selected group of people, mostly leaders of associations in Arizona, that he would present a bill providing for the creation of the Coronado International Monument in Arizona to the Committee on Public Lands and Surveys. In his correspondence, he provided a print of a bill dated April 20, 1940, to set aside an area for "a Coronado international monument."[84] The bill called for the establishment of the international monument with the prerogative to grant grazing privileges as well as prospecting and mining privileges within the monument area as consistent and appropriate with public uses.[85] Despite his earlier objections to the contrary, Hayden's bill called for 2,960 acres! It was the first legislative step in the creation of the monument. The bill remained in committee until May 28, when a new draft was presented. Section 2 of the new bill read, "The National Park Service, under the direction of the Secretary of the Interior, shall promote and regulate the use of the Coronado International Monument for the benefit and enjoyment of the people of the United States."[86] Slowly, legislation that would establish the Coronado International Monument under the administration of the National Park Service emerged.

Costs associated with the Coronado International Monument were discussed in terms of the $10,000 given the Cuarto Centennial Commission which were authorized to be used for monument purposes. Additionally, it was hoped that "$35,000 or $40,000" would later be donated. In his letter to Anderson, Director Cammerer estimated that "Approximately $150,000 to $200,000 will probably have to be expended in the monument area before the development program has been completed." The annual administration and maintenance costs were estimated to be another $10,000.[87] Aside from the size of the land being an issue, so were the costs of developing and maintaining the site.

Once the bill was introduced, the response from Hayden's Arizona constituency was cautiously supportive and emotionally mixed. Charles F. Willis, State Secretary of the Arizona Small Mine Operators Association, for example, endorsed the bill on the premise that those "already having mining property in that area are fully protected," and that the opportunity for future prospecting in the area is maintained.[88] Others, such as the Arizona Cattle Growers' Association, registered their outcry in such a way as to threaten the progress of the bill. Their concern dealt mostly with the size of the monument and fears that their grazing privileges would be curtailed.

Mrs. J.M. Keith, Secretary of the Arizona Cattle Grower's Association, expressed a guarded opinion about the effect of the Coronado International Park on her constituency. She noted that, while from a historical viewpoint setting land aside to commemorate Coronado's passage through Arizona was desirable, "Experience has shown that once lands are withdrawn they can never be fully utilized by the stockmen."[89] D'Albini's handwritten letter echoed a similar tone. Recognizing that the land upon which he grazed his stock was already under Forest Service control, he reported that he had spent much money within the tract of his permit to build a water catchment for his stock. Furthermore, he expressed fears that the creation of the Coronado International Monument on U.S. Forest land would lead to the devaluation of his water improvement actions and would create "a natural refuge for lions and wolves due to the dual authority in administration." He worried that the "dual administration" would "provide a relay station for the border renegades as it is on the national border at what is known as 'smuglars (sic) Gap'. Although D'Albini believed the land would have "value only as a monument site," he felt it would only require a few acres not "the high acreage proposed."[90]

Speaking for other permittees, Henry Davis Lee announced he was "unalterably opposed" to the transfer of nearly five sections of land that would result in "jeopardizing existing capital investment." He asked, "what public good would be done with extra acreage entailing expenditures of tax payers money"?[91] W.E. Clark, however, reported the protests from certain stockmen based on their fear that the monument would fence the area. Expressing their concerns, Clark stated that the Board of Supervisors "stands on [its] former telegram to you concerning this matter."[92] State Land Commissioner William Alberts expressed that his office would support the bill provided that the Board of Supervisors of Cochise County did not raise any objections to it.[93] They had earlier affirmed its support and remained steadfast in its decision.

Meanwhile, Mrs. J.M. Keith softened her tone. On May 11, she responded to Hayden's letter in which he had explained the intent of his bill. "We appreciate your understanding of the cattle industry," she wrote, "and feel sure that an International Monument can be worked out without too great an injury to our stockmen in Southern Arizona....We want to be helpful in all projects that will be a benefit to Arizona as a state, and cattlemen are especially interested in historical lore in Arizona."[94] Hayden had managed to assuage the anxious feelings of a major constituency that could have raised a considerable opposition to the passage of his bill.

Actually, Hayden put in more time thinking about and consulting the National Park Service regarding the cattle grower's objection to fencing the area. Hayden explained to Mrs. Keith that he had made two proposals to the National Park Service and had created wording to place in his bill reflecting them. His first proposal concerned the western boundary of the monument, which he suggested be moved one section to the east. The National Park Service objected to that proposal because of the proposed loop road which the topography of the countryside allowed. He explained that it was the "only suitable location for such a loop road going into Mexico and returning, and my suggestion was, therefore, not acceptable to the National Park Service."[95]

Regarding the second proposal, Hayden had better success. Hayden spoke with Tolson about National Park Service plans to fence the exterior boundaries of the monument. Tolson responded that "the only portions of the Monument which might ever be fenced would be the look out point, the museum site, and the rights-of-way of any roads which were built within the Monument and that no fences would ever be built along the boundaries of the Monument."[96] Hayden then suggested that "a prohibition against such fencing be placed in the bill, and the National Park Service agreed to it. Hayden asked the Arizona Cattle Growers' Association to review his new provision which would be inserted to the end of Section 2, page 2, line 23 of the draft bill. It read as follows:

> *Provided*, That in the administration of the Monument, the Secretary shall not permit the construction of fences except along the International Boundary, beside Monument roads or approach roads thereto, and around Monument areas within which improvements have been located by the National Park Service;
> *Provided further*, That any roads constructed within the Monument by the National Park service shall include necessary cattle underpasses.[97]

Hayden believed that such language in the bill would allay the fears of Lee and D'Albini.

Although issues regarding fencing and grazing privileges had been ameliorated by Hayden's compromises with the National Park Service, the ranchers found a ready ally in the *Arizona Daily Star*. Earlier, on May 5, 1940, the *Star* printed an editorial favoring Hayden's stand to reduce the size of the monument. It argued that 3000 acres was too much for purposes of a monument to Coronado, although the editor agreed that the explorer of yore merited the honor. Instead, the editorial vented its fiery breath against the National Park Service. "However," went the editorial, "in recent years, there has been a bureaucratic mastodon marching across the southwestern states which must have been wearing the fabled seven-league boots as it paced off its own peculiar bed grounds. For national parks created by proclamation, have appeared as if by magic in areas which prior to their dedications were used in part for grazing, usually under lease from the U.S. Forest Service."[98] Henry Davis Lee, owner of the Lone Mountain Ranch, read the editorial and, in a self-implicating way, remarked to Mrs. Keith in a letter, "Where the *Arizona Star* got its dope is an untruthful flattery to me, I wish it were true."[99]

On a more serious note, Lee wrote to Hayden expressing his view that some people, ignored in the process, had not been heard. Regarding the size of the monument, Lee said that if the monument were to occupy more than 100 acres, the rights of permittees would be secondary. "If," he wrote, "a greater acreage is deemed necessary…then we feel: first, that the National Park Service is not a sympathetic service to grazing interests, second, that the proposed bill would give little or no protection to our existing grazing and water rights and investments."[100] Recalling the establishment of Saguaro National Monument east of Tucson when Forest Service permittees lost their grazing privileges, Lee noted that establishing an NPS international monument would adversely affect cattlemen in the area. He proposed that the Forest Service "supervise the Monument in its entirety (it is our feeling that the Forest Service is competant [sic] to do so)."[101] Basically, Lee, speaking in behalf of D'Albini, Zaleski and other ranchers, felt that the National Park Service would be insensitive to the needs of cattle growers and unsympathetic to their grazing privileges. Working in unison, D'Albini helped Lee draft his letter to Hayden.[102] Don Smith, executive secretary of the Santa Cruz County Chamber of Commerce in Nogales, endorsed their sentiment regarding the excessive size of the monument.[103]

Hayden assured Smith that he would not take any action that would hurt Lee, Zaleski and D'Albini and hoped to reach a compromise with them. He knew that Lee was "entirely opposed" to the creation of any national monument and that D'Albini worried about the fencing issue. He thought that Zaleski was approachable on the issues as he had offered to donate a piece of land to the National Park Service "to straighten out the boundary."[104] As Hayden had predicted, D'Albini, having read the amendment, wrote, "Your Proposed fence provision to the bill creating the Coronado Monument removes all my objections to same."[105] After conferring with the Secretary of the Interior, Hayden suggested to Regional Director John White in Santa Fe that he and Neasham visit D'Albini and explain the process of establishing the monument and the prescribed rights of the appropriate cattle growers.[106]

Lee was not so trusting. He wanted Hayden to make a similar proposal to protect the water rights of the permittees. Still in opposition to the large acreage proposed in the bill for the monument, Lee wrote:

> It appears…that unless a great deal of money is…spent on roads, water development, public camp sites, etc., the Monument and Museum should be put in some place readily accessible to the public. My suggestion would be near where the main Bisbee, Fort Huachuca highway crosses the San Pedro River, which is actually following the footsteps of Coronado. It is my impression that the Bisbee Chamber of Commerce had such a site picked for the Marcos de Niza Monument which finally got away from them and was located in the San Rafael Valley near Lochiel.[107]

Lee hoped to convince Hayden that the monument idea was badly conceived and that the costs of running the monument were not justified.

By late summer 1940, the Committee on Public Lands and Surveys submitted its report recommending that the bill pass and attached supporting letters from the Acting Secretary of Agriculture and the Acting Secretary of the Interior. Additionally, the report included a printed invitation to Mexico from the United States Coronado Exposition Commission. The invitation, addressed to Mexico's Minister for Foreign Relations, expressed the hope that Mexico would join the United States in developing Coronado International Monument as a bi-national effort.[108]

Word spread quickly that Hayden had introduced the legislation. From Bisbee, W.E. Clark, Clerk of the Cochise County Board of Supervisors, sent him a telegraph saying that the Board of Supervisors was pleased that private interests were adequately protected and that they had received only two protests from two holders of National Forest Service grazing permits. "We believe they are not injured," he added.[109]

On September 30, an elated Hayden announced the passage of his bill by the Senate. With subdued enthusiasm, he sent a telegram to Charles F. Willis, State Secretary of the Arizona Small Mine Operators Association in Phoenix and copied eighteen other supporters of the bill. In it he expressed the following: "VERY GLAD TO ADVISE SENATE TODAY PASSED MY BILL S4130 PROVIDING FOR THE ESTABLISHMENT OF THE CORONADO INTERNATIONAL MONUMENT IN COCHISE COUNTY STOP BILL NOW GOES TO HOUSE OF REPRESENTATIVES WHERE I HOPE EARLY ACTION CAN BE HAD." Hayden personally thanked his eighteen principal contacts, some of whom opposed the Memorial. Recipients of Hayden's telegram included Stuart M. Bailey, William Alberts and Mrs. J.M. Keith from Phoenix, G.M. Butler and Fred Winn from Tucson, Grace M. Sparkes from Prescott, Frank Pooler from Albuquerque, Henry Davis Lee from Patagonia, Alex D'Albini and Joe Zaleski from Hereford, W.H. Hathaway and Don Smith from Nogales, Mayor W.K. Caley, W.E. Clark, M.J. Cunningham, C.C. Beddome, Folsom Moore, and S.S. Shattuck from Bisbee.[110] Meanwhile,

Senate Bill 4130 returned to the House of Representatives shortly thereafter. It seemed that the tempestuous rapidity with which the bill had taken form had left a swirl from Arizona to Washington, D.C.

The House did not take up the bill until mid-November 1940. Arizona Congressman John Murdock defended his House version of the bill and responded to questions from Congressman Church from Illinois regarding its appropriateness. Clarifying his support of the bill, Murdock responded that "My bill is identical with the Senate bill. The Senate bill has already passed the Senate."[111] Murdock went on to explain that $10,000 had been appropriated to establish the monument "at the point on the international border where Coronado crossed into Arizona 400 years ago this spring."[112] He specified that no further appropriation would be required, unless for maintenance. Asserting his support of the bill and its protection of grazing, prospecting and mineral development rights, he stated: "This is not a new principle. We have extended the right of grazing and mineral prospecting on other public lands and national forests and Indian reservations. The idea has my concurrence. I believe in it."[113]

Congressman Church from Illinois, who had raised objections, but was now quieted by Murdock's responses, stood and announced. "I ask unanimous consent that the bill be passed over without prejudice."[114] Another hurdle had been surmounted as the bill progressed through the legislative processes. One more stop, the Oval Office, and the bill, with the President's signature, would become law. Finally, the Coronado International Memorial received official confirmation with the Act of August 18, 1941 (55. Stat. 630).

In view of the bill's supporters, there was still time to commemorate the four hundredth year of Coronado's famed expedition into the heart of North America. By October, members of the Arizona Coronado International Memorial Commission had preliminary sketches of the Memorial that were drawn by the National Park Service.[115] The Commissioners quickly reviewed the plans in anticipation that the Coronado International Memorial would soon be developed on both sides of the border. Time was of the essence.

Signature of Francisco Vázquez de Coronado, 1541. (Intermountain Spanish Colonial Research Center, National Park Service)

Chapter II
"At the Point on the International Border where Coronado crossed into the United States:" Bureaucrats, Historians and the Search for Coronado's Route into Arizona, 1872-1990

The exact spot where Coronado entered the territory of what is now the United States has long been a matter of controversy— Congressman John M. Houston quoting the *Washington Post* to members of the House of Representatives, March 26, 1940

We feel certain that we know almost exactly the spot which was entered by Coronado in 1540—Arizona Congressman John Robert Murdock, 1952

Though this area was set aside as a memorial to commemorate the first large scale Spanish expedition into the Southwest, no physical remains of historic features or trails pertaining to this event exist within the area…from high on the southern end of the Huachuca Mountains, one looks over the San Pedro and Santa Cruz Valleys, either one of which, depending on the historian consulted, may represent the actual route of travel over which Coronado passed….—National Park Service Master Plan, 1954

It is rather doubtful whether Coronado chose a mountain to cross over when there were valleys on either side—Nogales taxpayers against funding a Memorial near Bisbee, 1955

The Memorial will not only commemorate the Coronado expedition and provide an ideal place for telling the history of the Coronado expedition and the history of the Southwest, but…will play an important part in improving the economy of southern Arizona—Hillory Tolson to the Nogales Protestors, 1955

Throughout fall 1940 and into summer of 1941, the United States Congress entertained the possibility of creating the Coronado International Memorial in Arizona. Regarding the proposed "monument," Congressman John Robert Murdock of Arizona commented that the monument would be established "at the point on the international border where Coronado crossed into Arizona 400 years ago this spring."[116] Earlier, on March 26, Congressman John M. Houston addressed the House of Representatives on a *Washington Post* article entitled "Southwest to Celebrate Four Hundredth Anniversary of Coronado's March"[117] dated two days prior. Quoting from it, Houston read that "The exact spot where Coronado entered the territory of what is now the United States has long been a matter of controversy."

The solution to the controversy fell to the National Park Service. Early in January 1940 a special party of historians, headed by Dr. Herbert E. Bolton, director of the Bancroft Library at the University of California drove to Compostela, Nayarit, Mexico. They retraced, mile for mile, what they believed to be the original route of the Coronado expedition of 1540. They determined that the explorers entered the United States at Naco, Arizona, which is on the east slope of the San Pedro Valley, about 10 miles south of Bisbee, Arizona.[118] In his *Coronado Knight of Pueblos and Plains* (1949),[119] Bolton reiterated his position that the entry point, in the vicinity of Naco, was somewhere south of Benson, Arizona.

The acceptance of the vicinity of Naco as the point of entry by the Coronado expedition gained in popularity among the Arizona proponents of the Coronado International Memorial for a variety of reasons. Some conclusions regarding the Coronado entry point were speculative, and others went beyond reason. For example, in a letter dated May 9, 1940, from Mrs. J.M. Keith to Charles M. Morgan, Executive Secretary of the Coronado Cuarto Centennial Commission, she complained that 2,900 acres "is too large a tract to be effective or practical."[120] Instead she suggested a smaller tract, consisting of one section along the north and one section along the south side of the Arizona-Mexico international line that would include a museum at the "very highest point" along the border. What would be the highest point, and why would it be important? Mrs. Keith explained: "We know, of course, that Coronado climbed the highest peak in order to survey the vast territory to the north and to the south, in his search for the 'Seven Cities of Cíbola.' Nothing lower than the highest vantage point would have satisfied him, and when honoring him we should build at the point that is actually hallowed by his footsteps." Mrs. Keith, undoubtedly, referred to Lookout Peak, which was later renamed Coronado Peak. Still, it would be left to historians, archaeologists, and other researchers to validate the history of the Coronado expedition's entry into Arizona from Mexico.

There was another alternative to the Naco point of entry by Coronado. In his autobiographical notes, Morgan mentions that there was a push to have the Coronado International Monument located in Nogales, Arizona. "For many years," he wrote, "there has been continuous controversey [sic] about where the Coronado Entrada came out of Mexico into what is now Arizona. As a casual student of Southwestern history I was well aware that they went down the San Pedro River—but a lot of very influential people seriously contended that he came down the Santa Cruz, crossing the present line near Nogales."[121] To quell the Nogales proponents, Morgan claimed he influenced a study to be made. "We put a suitable resolution through the commission," he wrote, "…So an imposing historical commission, headed by the famous southwestern historian, Dr. Herbert Bolton, from the University of California at Berkeley, with members from the Universities of Arizona and New Mexico, representatives of the Park Service, photographers, etc. all equipped [sic] with special high-wheeled cars for rough country, carrying all the known data along; took off from Compostela and retraced the route of the Coronado entrada to the border."[122] The Bolton group, wrote Morgan "came out along the San Pedro, any other route would have been quite impossible."[123] Apparently, Bolton had presented his preliminary findings to Congress in November 1939.[124] In his letter to Congressman John R. Murdock in 1939, Clinton P. Anderson, Managing Director of the Coronado Commission, wrote that the people of Nogales raised the question regarding Coronado's route. They did so because, wrote Anderson, they wanted "a monument in that City for Coronado as a step toward the realization of their dream of making Nogales the great International Gateway. I believe that Mr. Morgan feels that Coronado came into the State 160 miles East of Nogales, and that the Park Service will so decide."[125]

Other historians such as R.K. Wyllys at Arizona State Teachers College in Tempe argued in favor of the San Pedro Valley point of entry and against the Santa Cruz Valley route.[126] Renowned, New Mexico historian, J. Manuel Espinosa supported Coronado's entrance along San Pedro River[127] into Arizona near the Palominas-Naco area.

On February 6, 1940, G.R. Michaels, secretary of the Bisbee Chamber of Commerce, announced to Dr. Neasham that the last hurdle toward gathering a consensus about the whereabouts of Coronado's entry into the United States had been overcome. "Needless to say," he wrote, "all of the people in this area were delighted with the announcement from Albuquerque, Sunday. Coronado entered what is now the United States via San Pedro Valley. We…are ready and willing to do everything possible to assist your committee in getting this memorial project under way."[128]

In an undated printed letter to the Minister for Foreign Relations in Mexico, the United States Coronado Exposition Commission appeared ambiguous about Coronado's point of entry. The Commission wrote, "The point at which Coronado's expedition passed into what is now Arizona from Mexico is generally believed by historians to have been in the vicinity of the San Pedro and Santa Cruz River valleys."[129]

Acknowledging the significance of the Coronado Expedition, the Commission appended an "Historical Statement which read: "Coronado's expedition was one of the outstanding achievements of a period marked by notable explorations. It made known the vast extent and the nature of the country that lay north of central Mexico, and from the time of Coronado, Spaniards never lost interest in the country. In no small measure their subsequent occupation of it was due to the curiosity so created."[130]

In 1952, during the Congressional Hearings to change the name from Coronado International Memorial to Coronado National Memorial, Representative Murdock, who had supported the original 1940 legislation, again felt it important to reassert that the location of Coronado National Memorial was correct. "I might say," he remarked, "…there has been some discussion as to where Coronado entered what is now the United States… that…was very definitely determined by a board…headed by Dr. Herbert Moulton [sic], of the University of California, who in my judgment, is the best student on the Spanish phases of American history that we have. We feel certain that we know almost exactly the spot which was entered by Coronado in 1540."[131] The February 1952 issue of the *Arizona Highways* announced it, too, could prescribe the exact route: "Coronado's route from Mexico crossed the southern peak of the Huachucas across the valley and San Pedro where recently an old Spanish spur was found buried in the sand. Their route also trailed over the Bisbee mountain near Lime Peak and across the divide to the valley below."[132] Despite the apodictic quality of such statements, questions regarding Coronado's entry point persisted and would continue to be raised throughout the next fifty years, especially when the 450th anniversary of the expedition rolled around in 1990-1992.

The traditional consensus regarding Coronado's route is that it lies close to that proposed by A. Grove Day and Herbert Eugene Bolton. Both men popularized portions of the route from western Mexico through Arizona, New Mexico, Texas and Oklahoma to central Kansas. Although the entire route they proposed is not the object of this analysis, it plays an important role in evaluating the historical significance of the expedition led by Coronado. Significantly, Day, in 1940, was among the first to propose that the expedition entered Arizona through a point near Naco, not far from the present Coronado National Memorial. The Bolton-Day route is presented herein with the historiographical perspectives of other researchers who have promulgated theories, hypotheses, and issues related to the expedition's travel through a large portion of North America. The collective conclusion about the location of portions of Coronado's route among historians and other researchers has taken the form of consensus. While historians continue their research of Coronado' route, they generally agree with the San Pedro River route, as known in the 1940s and 1950s, which influenced the location of Coronado National Memorial.

Historians agree that the Coronado expedition was the first major European exploration to penetrate the interior of the present United States. Narrative accounts of the expedition describe its many encounters with the native inhabitants and contain a wealth of information about certain societies and cultures while they were still in a pristine state of development. Likewise, the explorers left sundry descriptions of flora and fauna and other natural resources. They were the first Europeans to describe the Grand Canyon of Arizona, and the large herds of buffalo seen on the Great Plains from eastern New Mexico to Texas, Oklahoma, and Kansas. The expedition members noted mountains, valleys, rivers, saltbeds, lakes, forests and other topographical features including the Continental Divide, the watershed that separates rivers flowing toward the Pacific Ocean or the Gulf of Mexico and the Atlantic.

Between 1539 and 1545, two other expeditions, one led by Hernando de Soto, which explored from Florida to Texas; and, the another commanded by Juan Rodríguez Cabrillo, who sailed up the California coast as far north as Cape Blanco in Oregon. With the Coronado expedition, they explored the widest expanse of North America from coast to coast. Overall, the Spaniards were the first Europeans to leave a written record of their deeds in North America. They left a literary heritage about a large geographic area from California to Florida that includes diaries, reports, correspondences, cartography and later historical documentation referencing their expeditions. Related to that heritage is the extensive literature generated by modern writers about the expeditions.

Even before the four hundredth anniversary of Francisco Vázquez de Coronado's expedition, researchers had debated portions of the route subsequently proposed by Day and Bolton. Some of them went as far as to propose new ones. There are reasons for disparities between some of the hypotheses. Day and Bolton dealt with the larger picture of the route. Based on work by previous researchers, they connected known places visited by the expedition with theories explaining how it reached them. Later researchers, focusing on portions of the route, discovered other hypothetical alternatives by concentrating on specific topographical and cultural features in certain areas believed crossed by the expedition.

While Day, Bolton and other researchers tested their hypothetical routes on the ground, other early writers of the route lacked access to the documentation and used translations that precluded certain perspectives about what the expedition had seen. Still, other writers lacked geographical knowledge about the areas traveled by the explorers or did not read carefully the sources available to them. Their search for the route, nonetheless, began with the first steps taken by the expedition upon leaving Compostela on the west Mexican coast.

The singlemost important leg of the expedition runs from Compostela through Sonora. Without a fundamental understanding of that portion of the route, it is impossible to determine where the expedition entered present Arizona and what direction it took beyond that point. The literature suggests two viable points through which the expedition passed upon entering present Arizona: the San Pedro and San Bernardino River valleys. Because Coronado's route from Compostela to either of those two points is vague, a third line of march, one farther east, is possible. A fourth alternative, a western route through the Santa Cruz valley, has been discounted in recent years by scholars. In any case, finding the location of the expedition's entry into the present United States depends wholly on determining the route taken through Sonora.

Although Bolton and Day based their route through Sonora on observation and analogy of their readings of documents and what they perceived to be on the ground, Charles DiPeso, in 1974, utilized available archaeological data and pertinent historical documentation. The historical problem lay in part with the lack of identity of rivers in Sonora for the early Spanish period. DiPeso wrote, "when…historians attempt to correlate present-day names, such as Yaqui or Sonora River, with names used by early explorers who had no maps and often were inconvenienced by a lack of interpreters, and who used such terms as Yaqui and Senora, then distances and travel times are sacrificed, and misconceptions are bound to arise."[133]

By comparing accounts of various sixteenth century expeditions, DiPeso arrived at a certain determination of place-names in Sonora. The variations of place names mentioned by explorers, explained DiPeso, were inconsequential because their singular locations were determined by Indian settlements along them, and their names were constant. Besides, he argued, the distance between them was a controlling factor, for the explorers had given estimated figures of time taken to travel between them and/or measurements in leagues. Additionally, Coronado kept a record of distances by having one of his men count the steps between the expedition's daily campsites.[134]

DiPeso's analysis could very well be a key to the historical conundrum concerning Coronado's route through Sonora. By following the documentation almost to a fault, DiPeso determined that the route of Coronado veered northeastward to the Río Bavispe and its confluence with the Río Batepito, which he followed to the Río San Bernardino that originates in southeastern Arizona considerably east of the San Pedro River. DiPeso made a strong case for the expedition crossing into Arizona at present Slaughter Ranch not far westward from the Arizona-New Mexico border. He concluded that Coronado entered New Mexico crossing into the Animas Valley through Antelope Pass and then straddled the Arizona-New Mexico boundary until reaching Zuni Pueblo.

Earlier, in 1872, Brig. General J.H. Simpson, one of the first to trace Coronado's route in southern Arizona assumed that Coronado had entered present United States through the Santa Cruz Valley, stopping at Chichilticale, which he reckoned to be Casa Grande on the Gila River. There, he turned northeast across the Pinal and Mogollon Mountains to Zuni. Simpson's account, filled with errors, suggested the westernmost theory of the expedition through Arizona. His discussion of the Mogollon Rim route lacks substantive detail.[135] The notion persisted for almost seventy years; however, in 1939, archaeologist Charlie Steen suggested that Fray Marcos de Niza's preliminary expedition in 1539 had entered Arizona through the Santa Cruz River valley and turned northwestward somewhere between Tucson and Phoenix, entering the mountains probably beyond Florence near the Salt River.[136] Later, Niza served as a guide for Coronado in 1540.

Other scholars contended that Coronado entered Arizona through the San Pedro River valley because it was most compatible with Spanish documentation and topography, being the easiest way northward. In 1895, Frederick W. Hodge argued that the expedition traveled north along the Río Sonora and entered Arizona through the San Pedro River valley. Afterwards, he wrote, it crossed the Pinaleño Mountains over Railroad Pass, and followed the San Simeon valley to a point near present Solomonsville and the Gila River, south of the present White Mountain Apache Reservation.[137] Hodge's route took the expedition directly on a northeastward path to the Zuni River. Of this route, Hodge's explanation, likewise, lacks sufficient detail for analysis. The debate over the location of the expedition's crossing into Arizona from Sonora was only beginning. Hodge had raised a point that would cause much speculation concerning the San Pedro River valley hypothesis.

In 1947 George J. Undreiner[138] re-examined Fray Marcos de Niza's journey to Cíbola, that is, New Mexico. He proposed that Niza entered Arizona on April 13, 1539 by following a route north along the Pima road about 15 miles east of Lochiel. Soon after, he reached Quiburi, a Sobaipuri village on the San Pedro River. Three days later, Niza visited Baicatcan, another village on the San Pedro. Herein was the riddle. Pedro de Castañeda, chronicler of the Coronado expedition, stated that after visiting a certain Indian town, the expedition described a four-day *despoblado* (an uninhabited area) north of there. Undreiner argued that in his preliminary expedition of 1539, Niza, probably at Baicatcan, or at least at Quiburi, learned that two more days of travel would bring him to a despoblado which would take four days to cross. He contended that Niza, after two days of travel, had reached the northernmost Sobaipuri village on the San Pedro and that it was probably near Aravaipa Creek.[139]

On that same point, Albert H. Schroeder responded to historians who had suggested that Coronado's expedition went down the San Pedro River in southeastern Arizona. As Juan de Jaramillo, chronicler of the expedition, had indicated that the expedition turned east, Schroeder routed Niza and Coronado either up Aravaipa Creek or east from the Tres Alamos region.[140] Schroeder wrote, "If the former route is accepted it would imply that that portion of the middle San Pedro River, more that two days travel south of the junction with the Aravaipa, would not have been occupied, since it would then be the four-day *despoblado*.

Seeking to validate Niza's descriptions, Schroeder's thesis pointed to the very area where DiPeso, basing his conclusions on archaeological evidence, had suggested. DiPeso argued that "occupation may have been unbroken from late prehistoric into historic (1690s) times. Thus, the old routes appear to be in error."[141] In support of Hodge's hypothesis, Schroeder defends Niza, commenting that "The evidence presented herein not only indicates the good father was telling the truth, but that Coronado and his chroniclers knowingly supported much of his relation pertaining to the trip through this area."[142] Thus, Schroeder, in the end, cast his lot with the San Pedro River valley entrance hypothesis.

The debate surrounding the San Pedro River Valley entrance is tied to the location of Chichilticale (sometimes spelled Chichilticalli). Of Chichilticale, Coronado wrote, "I rested for two days at Chichilticale, and there was no chance to rest further, because the food was giving out."[143] In his account, Pedro de Castañeda reported, "The land changes again at Chichilticale and the thorny trees disappear. The reason is that since the gulf extends as far as that place and the coast turns, so also the ridge of the sierra turns. Here one comes to cross the ridge and it breaks to pass into the plains of the land."[144]

What was Chichilticale? At times the documents refer to it as a valley, other times it appears as a mountain range, a bay, or even a *despoblado*, and finally, as a place or a village. Coronado and Melchior Díaz mentioned the "people of Chichilticale."[145] After careful consideration, DiPeso concluded that it was south of the Arizona-Sonora border closer to the Río Batepito and the San Bernardino valley. He wrote, "Ruins which might be ascribed to those of the 'red house' of Chichilticale occur up and down the San Bernardino Valley, and the Stevens Ranch site contains pottery fragments which indicate a trade relationship with the N[orth] and the Little Colorado."[146] By placing Chichilticale in that area, DiPeso suggested that north of the confluence of the San Bernardino River valley was a fifteen day despoblado.[147]

Schroeder correctly surmised the critical need to define the location of Chichilticale because, for one of many reasons, it determined where the expedition went next. He countered any argument that Chichilticale lay south of the Arizona-Sonora border. Schroeder wrote, "The ethnological traits reported by the early Spanish who recorded their travels of 1539 and 1540 through Arizona point to the Yavapai as the people who occupied the area on the north side of the four-day *despoblado*, where Chichilticale was located. Internal evidence within these early documents also indicates that Fray Marcos and Coronado followed the San Pedro to its mouth, not just to Tres Alamos or Aravaipa on the San Pedro, and that from there they crossed the Gila and went over to the Salt River as Undreiner suggests."[148] Emphatically Schroeder stressed the significance of this point by writing, "Thus, the Yavapai remain as the only possible group, separated by four days' travel, that bordered the Sobaipuri on the north in 1539 and 1540."[149]

In contrast to DiPeso's and Hodge's routes from Arizona to New Mexico, Schroeder proposed that after departing the mouth of the San Pedro River, the expedition proceeded down the Salt River "almost to the mouth of Tonto Creek." Next, he wrote, they went "up Salome Creek and over the north end of the Sierra Anchas and then generally northeast over the Mogollon Rim across to Zuni. There is little or no evidence to indicate they went east from the San Pedro at Tres Alamos or via Aravaipa Creek and then across the present day San Carlos Apache country to Zuni. Such a trail would necessitate a route directed to the north or north-north-east, rather than northeast as the documents state."[150]

Carroll L. Riley and Joni L. Manson concluded, without specifying their argument that Chichilticale was in southern Arizona or New Mexico.[151] Riley, on the basis of historical, anthropological and botanical evidence revolving around linguistics, argued that the location of Chichiltacale was at one of two probable locations: one on the lower Salt River, the other on the upper Gila River[152]

Having crossed the *despoblado*, the anonymous sixteenth century writer of the *Relación del Suceso*[153] cryptically commented that "the entire route up to within fifty leagues of Cíbola is inhabited, although in some places at a distance from the road." This and other commentary by the members of the expedition are open to interpretation. The route to Cíbola from the *despoblado* is fraught with a dearth of information leaving the researcher often with little more than his imagination.

The most accepted route of the expedition through Arizona is that proposed by Herbert E. Bolton. Since 1949, the Bolton route has gained in venerability, partly because of his scholarly influence and partly because his field research almost rivaled that of Coronado's epic march across a large portion of North America. Bolton built on the work of earlier researchers, and was probably influenced, although he denied it, by A. Grove Day's *Coronado's Quest: The Discovery of the American West*, published in 1940.

Day favored the Sonora Valley as a probable point from which Arizona was reached. Opting for the San Pedro River route, he specified that Coronado had entered Arizona through a plain extending to the headwaters of the San Pedro River near present-day Naco. Somewhere near there, he explained, was the point of departure for crossing the despoblado. Day went on to propose that the expedition crossed the Gila and Salt Rivers by means of an old Indian trail, and then proceeded through the White Mountains to the upper drainage of the Little Colorado near St. Johns to the Zuni River. Although Day did not specifically tell how the expedition crossed the area, he deferred to the work by Sauer and Winship for his information.

Just as it is paramount to understand the expedition's whereabouts through Sonora to where they entered Arizona, it is equally important to learn about the route from Arizona to New Mexico. In that way, it may be possible to backtrack to the Arizona point of entry. Each leg of the expedition's trek through a given area links with its previous leg and the one that follows it. Like Day, Bolton relied on Winship and other sources to define his proposed route which he then set out to prove through his fieldwork. Generally, Bolton's route has the expedition leaving the traditionally mentioned Compostela to Culiacán where they followed the coastal plain, veering northeastward between the Gulf of California and the Sierra Madre Occidental crossing rivers until they reached the Sonora River valley. From there, deduced Bolton, the expedition entered Arizona through the San Pedro River Valley. The Bolton route placed the expedition's point of departure through the despoblado near Benson, Arizona, thence northeast through the Galiuro Range and crossed the Arivaipa Valley, passing through Eagle Pass between the Pinaleño and Santa Teresa mountains.

Bolton surmised that the expedition's march through the despoblado ran along the Gila River, crossing it at present-day Bylas, after which it forded the Salt River near Bonito Creek. Next, he proposed that Coronado continued northward, crossed the White River near Fort Apache, ascended the Mogollon Rim by following small streams before emerging on the Little Colorado River near its confluence with the Zuni River. Shortly, the expedition reached Hawikuh.[154]

The route has been accepted by some historians, modified by others and contested by yet another group of researchers who offer their own conclusions markedly different from Bolton's. R.M. Wagstaff, criticized the Bolton proposal by noting that the distances traveled by the expedition do not conform with Bolton's conclusions. Also, Bolton's identification of some rivers, which appear juxtaposed in the narrative are misleading. Although Wagstaff did not adequately support the discrepancies he cited, DiPeso attempted to propose an alternative route in which he accounted for rivers and distances. Employing the same methodology as he had on the rivers in Sonora, DiPeso suggested that the expedition traveled from Antelope Pass to Cíbola, meandering in and out of Arizona and New Mexico until they reached Zuni.[155]

Preceding Bolton, Carl Sauer traced the route through Arizona from the San Pedro River to a point north of Benson, around the Galiuro Mountains into the upper basin of Arivaipa Creek north to the Gila River by way of Eagle Pass between the Pinaleño and Santa Teresa ranges. Following the San Carlos River, the expedition turned northeast crossing the Natanes Plateau and the Black River to a point on the White River near present-day Fort Apache from where Coronado passed near present McNary. From there, they crossed the Colorado Plateau to the Little Colorado River, thence to the Zuni River before reaching Hawikuh.[156]

Historians agree that the San Pedro River served as the passageway to Arizona on the last leg of Coronado's march through Sonora. They mostly agree that from a point along the San Pedro River, the expedition veered northward, entering Arizona somewhere along the present border. Day suggests that Coronado crossed into Arizona where the valley broadens, near Naco, not far from Bisbee. As the exact entry point cannot be ascertained, historians have debated the hypothesis adding their own conclusions. From its strategic location, Coronado National Memorial overlooks the panoramic view of the San Pedro River Valley which, the legislators of 1940 surmised, the expedition crossed in 1540, and commemorates the Francisco Vázquez de Coronado expedition as part of our national story. The wise creators of the Master Plan for Coronado National Memorial in 1954 astutely recognized the purpose of the Memorial. They began the Master Plan Development Outline with the words:

> Though this area was set aside as a memorial to commemorate the first large scale Spanish expedition into the Southwest, no physical remains of historic features or trails pertaining to this event exist within the area…from high on the southern end of the Huachuca Mountains, one looks over the San Pedro and Santa Cruz Valleys, either one of which, depending on the historian consulted, may represent the actual route of travel over which Coronado passed in the spring of 1540 when he with his advance guard, and later his main army, came through this region. There also is a view out over a wide expanse of the Sonora Valley region through which Coronado approached Arizona from the south.[157]

These words ring true today as when they were written.

Chapter III
The United States-Mexico Conundrum and the Change from "Coronado International Memorial" to "Coronado National Memorial"

Provided, that said proclamation shall not be issued until the President of the United States shall have been advised through official channels that the Government of Mexico has established, or provided for the establishment of, an area of similar type and size adjoining the area described herein.— Act of August 18, 1941 (55 Stat. 630)

It is my feeling, Gus, that it will be a long, long time before we can get the Mexican Government to go along with us to establish a joint memorial to Coronado—Hillory Tolson, Acting Director, National Park Service, to G.R. Michaels, February 8, 1946

I understand that Senator Hayden...may discuss with you...and others the feasibility...of establishing the Arizona portion of the proposed Coronado International Memorial as the 'Coronado National Memorial'. To do this, it would be necessary, of course, to amend the act of August 18, 1941, by eliminating the above-quoted provision and by changing the name of the area.—Hillory Tolson to Grace Sparkes, September 15, 1950.

Since that period, interest continued—war retarded action—likewise apparent lack of action and proper understanding in Mexico—Grace Sparkes to Arthur R. Williams, American Consul, Agua Prieta, Mexico, March 19, 1951.

Following the Congressional action of 1940-1941, very little toward the establishment of the Coronado International Memorial occurred. Even though the proposal to establish a suitable monument received a "hearty approval of both President Manuel Avila Camacho and President Franklin D. Roosevelt" in 1940, long term Mexican support for it proved to be lukewarm.[158] On June 1, 3, 5, and 10, 1942,[159] U.S. representatives met with the Mexican International Park Commission in Mexico City to discuss plans for the proposed Coronado International Memorial. The U.S. representatives included Hillory Tolson, chairman; Miner R. Tillotson, Dr. Aubrey Neasham, Mrs. Foster Rockwell, Odd S. Halseth, and Dr. Herbert E. Bolton.[160] The members of the Mexican Coronado International Commission named by Marte R. Gómez, Secretary of Agriculture, were Ingeniero Fernando Romero Quintana, chairman, Ing. Carlos Villas Pérez, Ing. Rafael Fernández McGregor, Ing. Juan Manuel Corona, Ing. José Garcia Martínez, and Ing. Agustín Gómez y Gutierrez.[161] The joint recommendations submitted to Secretary Gómez called for a survey of the proposed site in Sonora that was occupied by the Cananea Cattle Company.

Once the survey was completed, the recommendations provided that the President of Mexico issue "a decree establishing the Coronado International Memorial in Sonora."[162] A copy of the decree, signed and published, would be presented to the United States government. To comply with the recommendations, the surveyor, Villas Pérez, a trained engineer, traveled to the border to "survey and fence the proposed area in Sonora, and to negotiate with the Cananea Cattle Company."[163] As a result of the meeting Mexico City meeting in June 1942, the over-enthused U.S. participants optimistically reported "that they [the Mexicans] would like to see an area of approximately the same acreage [2,800 acres]"[164] on the Mexican side. Unfortunately, World War II intervened and the project lay inactive until 1947.

Among other national priorities affecting the United States, World War II had taken up much of the country's energies, and, during the war years, the Arizona Coronado Commission had been deactivated. Even so, any Presidential Proclamation would have been muted by the Act of August 18, 1941, which effectively put the proposed Coronado International Memorial on hold until Mexico reciprocated with a memorial mirroring the U.S. effort on the border. It seemed that the word "international" required the agreement of both Mexico and the United States to erect the proposed memorial on the border. Meantime, Hayden did not return to his pet project of establishing an international memorial near Bisbee until the late 1940s when the war years were behind him.

In the United States, the embers of hope that Mexico would reciprocate were kept alive during the war years through correspondence and meetings between the Arizona Commission and the National Park Service. Following up on the 1942 meeting, Ing. Emilio Gutierrez Roldán, Mexico's Director General of Forests and Game, wrote, in August 1943, to the NPS Director advising him of an agreement reached with the Cananea Cattle Company. Gutierrez Roldán stated that the Company "had offered to place the land at the disposal of the Director of General of Forests and Game for an indefinite period, subject only to the condition that the Company be allowed to graze cattle on it and to terminate the grant at such time as the land is no longer used as an international park."[165] For a while it looked auspicious. Later, Tolson explained to Hayden that following the National Park Service response of October 11, 1943 from Director Drury to Gutierrez Roldán, communication with Mexico suddenly stopped. A copy of that letter went to Villas Pérez who also did not respond. On April 1, 1944, Tolson asked George Messersmith, American Ambassador to Mexico, to inquire of Gutierrez Roldán the status of the letter and their plans for the International Memorial. On May 3, L.D. Mallory, the Agricultural Attache of the U.S. Embassy in Mexico City, met with Villas Pérez, "who located our letter of October 11, 1943, and found that a reply had not been made to it."[166] He promised a reply, but as of May 27, 1944, none had been forthcoming.

Despite his frustration with Mexican officials, Tolson informed Hayden that tentative plans for development of the site were underway in the event that Mexico would soon reciprocate. As with nearly everyone involved with the Memorial on the United States' side, Tolson continued to hold out hope for a reciprocal agreement with Mexico. Clarifying the implementation of the plans, Tolson explained that they were "tentative" and, given Mexican cooperation, "The final plan for the two areas, however, cannot be developed until an opportunity is afforded after the war, for representatives of the two Governments to confer and agree upon it."[167]

In June 1944, several National Park Service personnel, among them E.T. Scoyen, acting Regional Director in Santa Fe, toured southern Arizona. They made a stop in Bisbee where a meeting between those interested parties took place[168] to discuss the status of the proposed memorial. Everyone agreed that the project was in a holding pattern until the Mexicans could reciprocate.

Mexico City remained silent on the issue of the Coronado International

Memorial. On August 19, 1944, Tolson wrote to Halseth saying "We feel sure that Ing. Villas Perez is still interested in the international memorial project, and has not been in position to get his Department to reply to our communications due to circumstances beyond his control."[169] As a last resort, Tolson was willing to forego an international monument. "If the Mexican Government finally decides that it is not interested in carrying out the recommendations of the Mexico-United States commission which met in Mexico City in June 1942," the Act of August 18, 1941, he wrote, should be amended to eliminate the requirement for an international memorial and instead move for a national memorial within the state of Arizona, [170] Holding out hope, Tolson suggested that they proceed with their plans in a postwar era. Predicting the end of the war and a need for a public works program, he wrote:

> It may be held by some that this is a matter that need not be pressed at this time. However, it is probable that the wars against Hitler's Germany and Japan will be terminated within the next year. If so, active plans, presumably, will be made to handle the resulting unemployment; and funds will probably be made available for some type of public works program. The establishment of the memorial…will involve….reaching agreements with the proper Mexican officials with respect to the developments to be placed in the companion areas of….this splendid international memorial area (which is important because of its great possibilities in the promotion of a friendly relationship between Mexico and the United States in addition to providing a fitting memorial for the Coronado expedition).[171]

Tolson hoped that, this time, things would be different in regard to Mexican participation.

On September 6, 1944, Tolson informed Hayden that Mexican authorities had not responded to his letter of October 11, 1943. Searching for a solution to the lack of communication from Mexico, Tolson asked Halseth to write to his friend Villas Pérez, and he agreed to do so.[172] Still no response. On February 1, 1944, Tolson issued another letter to Villas Pérez asking him about the changing memberships of the Mexican Coronado Commission and the International Park Commission of Mexico. Referencing a letter from Villas Pérez dated May 27 regarding the re-appointment of Ing. Fernando Romero Quintana, and the appointment of Ing. Emilio Gutierrez Roldán to the position of Director General of Forests and Game, Tolson wanted to know whether Gutierrez Roldán would replace Romero Quintana as chairman of the Mexican Coronado Commission.[173] Regarding the unanswered letter of October 11, 1943, Tolson expressed to Villas Pérez that once the Mexican Government had committed to establishing its part of the Memorial, the U. S. President could and would make the necessary proclamation.[174] Apparently, Tolson hoped that the Mexicans would respond if the processes for establishing the Coronado International Memorial did not appear as complicated for them as it actually was politically. By year's end, the response was not forthcoming.

On December 26, 1944, Tolson wrote to Hayden announcing that "it is regretted that no word has as yet been received from Ing. Carlos Villas Pérez, either directly or through Mr. Odd Halseth of Phoenix, Arizona, regarding the proposed Coronado International Memorial Park in Sonora, Republic of Mexico."[175]

Although communications with Mexico were, in 1945, as they had been in previous years, minimal, Tolson continued to make plans in the event that Mexico would respond affirmatively. Aside from making general points about the development that should take place at the proposed site ("small administration building, exhibit room, utility area, custodian's residence, parking area, an observation station, an entrance road, and other necessary facilities"), Tolson wrote to Hayden about unexplored issues:

> It will be necessary for representatives of Mexico and the United States to agree upon and work out a plan for administering the Memorial in view of the fact that important customs and immigration, and perhaps other, questions will arise when the two areas in Arizona and Sonora, Mexico, are set aside as the Coronado International Memorial.[176]

Hoping for a response which, he felt, could come at any moment, Tolson anticipated what steps would have to be taken to plan a joint memorial with Mexico.

As 1945 rolled into 1946, little had been accomplished toward establishing Coronado International Memorial. Disappointed, Tolson, in February 1946, wrote to Michaels saying "It is my feeling, Gus, that it will be a long, long time before we can get the Mexican Government to go along with us to establish a joint memorial to Coronado."[177] By March, Tolson hoped to learn what Halseth had been able to do about the Coronado International Memorial while in Mexico City. Tolson remarked to Michaels, "While it will be helpful to know what Odd Halseth was able to find out about it in Mexico City, I have no confidence that we will be able to do anything in Mexico at this time toward the establishment of the memorial."[178] As secretary of the Bisbee Chamber of Commerce, Michaels continued to have a strong interest in establishing the Memorial and informed Tolson to that end. On November 4, 1946, Michaels wrote to Tolson saying that "nothing could be done until after the first of the year when the new president of Mexico takes office" and he named a new cabinet. In the meantime, he hoped that they could write up a budget in which they would request a small appropriation from Congress for the 1946-47 fiscal year.[179]

As the post-war years set in, a new optimism grew alongside it that things would change for the better. From that parallax view, the Mexican Presidential election of 1946 appeared to bode well. To boost the morale of those involved with the Memorial on the U.S. side, Tolson learned in late November that he and Dr. Jesse L. Nusbaum, a National Park Service Archeologist in Santa Fe, had been appointed to the International Park Commission by Secretary of the Interior.[180] Undoubtedly, Tolson hoped that his appointment would put him in better position to deal with his Mexican counterparts as a peer.

Due to the election of 1946 in Mexico, many governmental departments were reorganized in early 1947. Unfortunately, one of the casualties of the reorganization was the Coronado Memorial Commission of Mexico, which was dispersed. Hoping to reestablish contact, Tolson, Tillotson, Ross Maxwell, Superintendent of Big Bend National Park, and I.J. Castro, also of the National Park Service, went to Mexico City in July 1947 at the urgings of Villas Pérez. They met with Ambassador Walter P. Thurston on July 15 and made arrangements to meet with Secretary of Agriculture Nazario Ortiz Garza and his representatives the following day. Tolson reported that the meeting resulted in the assignment of a "permanent International Park Commission of Mexico."[181]

Its members consisted of Ing. Jesus Merino Fernández Delgado, under secretary of Agriculture and chairman of the Commission. Other members were Lic. Silverstre Aguilar, Director General of Forests and Game; Ing. Villas Pérez, Chief of Office of Department of Agriculture; Ing. Luis de la Fuente, Chief of Development, Forests and Game; and Ing. David Herrera Jordán, Member, Mexican Boundary and Water Commission.[182] That committee would soon change.[183] The upshot of the joint meeting of July 16, however, was a recommendation that a decree be prepared establishing the "Sonora companion area to the Coronado International Memorial."

Almost suddenly, the Coronado International Memorial project received new life.[184] Tolson wrote that the members of the Mexican Commission promised that they would start work immediately on the decrees for both the Coronado International Memorial in Sonora and the international park mirroring Big Bend National Park in Coahuila and Chihuahua. They also agreed to meet in Santa Fe, New Mexico "as soon as practicable after the decrees were issued and printed in the *Diario Official*,"[185] the corresponding publication of the *U.S. Federal Register*.

In July 1947, the Department of State announced that "two decrees" in draft form, that were being discussed in Mexico. One would establish a Mexican park across from Big Bend National Park in Texas, the other a "memorial area in Sonora as a companion area to the proposed Coronado International Memorial in Arizona."[186]

Meanwhile, the National Park Service's efforts were thwarted by the actions of the Cananea Cattle Company. Not long after the promising July 18 meeting in Mexico City, Tolson, much chagrined, received some upsetting news. The most recent information he had "regarding the Coronado Memorial was that Mr. C.E. Wiswall of the Cananea Cattle Company had gotten in touch with the representatives of the State Department of this Country and of the Mexican Government to protest the creation of the memorial."[187] That protest, in large part, led to the decision of the Department of State to demur on the matter.

The following year, on December 21, 1948, Senator Hayden contacted Ing. Villas Pérez advising him that the United States Department of State had informed the Mexican government that it could not insist that Mexico cooperate in the Coronado Memorial project because of "its policy of not pressing the Mexican Government too strongly for action in matters where American interests are involved."[188] The "American interests," revolving around the Coronado International Memorial in Sonora, were those of the Cananea Cattle Company. Having no response from Villas Pérez for a year, Hayden seemed at a loss to find ways to encourage Mexican interest in the Coronado International Memorial.

In January 1949, Hayden wrote to a number of his constituents, responding to a proposed plan by the National Park Service, concerning the Coronado International Memorial. He told them of Tolson's intent to reactivate the Arizona Coronado Commission so that all interested parties could renew plans for the "international monument." Halseth, asked Hayden for his assistance in getting the governor of Arizona involved in the planning as it "will help to bring about a speedy conclusion of negotiations needed to bring the United States-Mexico-Cananea Cattle Company officials together on a plan suitable to all."[189] Perhaps, thought Hayden, the solution to the lack of cooperation by Mexico had presented itself.

Two intricately tied trends had evolved during the interim years to get the Coronado International Memorial going in 1949. One was the ongoing effort to determine Mexico's interest in the project, the other was to reestablish the Arizona Commission chapter of the old Coronado Cuarto Centennial Commission to jumpstart the establishment of the Memorial and Mexico's interest. Halseth put it bluntly to Hayden, "Protocol seems to be a hindrance to the Interior Department, whereas an Arizona Commission could invite participation in meeting and planning."[190] Still, it was Tolson, now Assistant Director of the National Park Service, who earlier had made the proposal to reactivate the Arizona Coronado Commission. Tolson's words were:

> I believe that we can work out a plan which will clear the way for the Mexican government to issue the decree to establish the Coronado International Memorial in Sonora. The Arizona Coronado commission, which became inactive during the war, is, in accordance with my suggestion, being re-activated. It will be composed of prominent Arizona citizens who are interested in the establishment of the Coronado International memorial. Most of them, I understand, are acquainted with the officials of the Cananea Cattle Company, which owns the land (about 2,880 acres) needed by the Mexican Government for the establishment of the Memorial.[191]

Tolson also reported on a meeting that had taken place on December 3, 1948 between him and Charles A. Richey of the National Park Service, and Mr. Reveley and a staff member from the Department of State. At this meeting, Reveley was quick to explain the position of the Department of State regarding the "two decrees." Tolson concluded that "we believe that no further action should be taken in connection with our idea of getting the Department of State to inquire as to the status of the two decrees."[192]

In 1949, it was believed, the time was right, for an international park between the to be established. On February 14, 1949, Hayden wrote to Halseth to say he had asked the National Park Service and the Department of the Interior for their views on Mexico's proposals to establish a Mexican national park opposite Big Bend National Park in Texas and a reciprocating Coronado International Memorial in Sonora.[193]

Hayden expressed to Assistant Secretary Davidson of the Department of the Interior that he felt that Mexico would not support the establishment of Mexican park across from Big Bend National Park because of the heavy investments in the land required of both American and Mexican landowners. On the other hand, he felt that a good possibility existed to establish Coronado international memorials in Sonora and Arizona because only one American concern was involved in the 2,880 acres needed in Sonora for the Mexican portion of the Memorial.

Hayden believed the proposed re-activation of the Arizona Coronado Commission, could continue to push the international memorial proposal forward. In his correspondence with Halseth, Hayden hoped that the reactivated Arizona Coronado Commission would call a meeting with the Mexican International Park Commission, the U.S. International Park Commission, the Cananea Cattle Company in Phoenix, Nogales, or Bisbee.[194] Overconfident, Hayden felt a compromise with Mexico could easily be achieved. All that would be needed, he felt, would be 200 acres on the Mexican side for the necessary structures and the installation of a proposed cactus aboretum that would be fenced.

As for the 2,880 acres held by the Cananea Cattle Company, Hayden believed that as long as their cattle could continue to graze the land, an agreement could be reached. But there were deeper problems. C.E. Wiswall, President of the Cananea Cattle Company opposed the Memorial and suggested that a "shaft of marble or some other material" be sufficient to commemorate Coronado's 1540 expedition "somewhere along the border." Given that previous correspondence with the Cananea Cattle Company had expressed the contrary, Hayden was probably surprised by the attitude expressed by Wiswall. Hayden, believed that the re-established Arizona Coronado Commission members would invite Wiswall to their first meeting and explain to him the purposes of the joint memorials and the reasons why the required tracts of land were important for a more appropriate commemoration of the historical 1540 expedition.[195] Months later, Grace Sparkes, in a letter to Hayden expressed the same sentiment. "I am wondering," she wrote, "why the change of position on the part of the Green [sic] Cattle interests—all back data showed they were for it and only asked that their rights for grazing be protected and in [the] event land was not used for International Park it s[h]ould [sic] revert to them."[196] Hayden must have raised his eyebrows at the scribbled postscript at the bottom of her type-written letter which read: "Has there been any movement to change location of the CIM?"

Meanwhile, Arizona Governor Dan E. Garvey informed Hayden that he fully intended to re-establish the Arizona Coronado Commission with members from Phoenix, Tucson, and Nogales.[197] Reporting to Hayden on the progress made, Tolson wrote that on Friday, March 4, Governor Garvey had officially reactivated the Arizona Coronado International Memorial Commission. The commissioners, wrote Tolson, were former Phoenix mayor, Ray Busey, Phoenix radio commentator, J. Howard Pyle, Phoenix archaeologist, Odd S. Halseth, Tucson newspaper publisher, William R. Mathews, and Nogales Mayor James V. Robins. A new member, Alex Jácome of Tucson was appointed shortly thereafter.[198] Meantime, the new Arizona Coronado International Memorial Commission was instructed to call a meeting on April 1, 1949 and invite members of representatives of the Mexican International Park Commission, the United States International Park Commission, and the Cananea Cattle Company.[199] Did the meeting take place? On April 14, Grace Sparkes wondered if it had as she had not heard any report of it. Neither, had Hayden heard of the meeting taking place, but awaited word.[200] If it did take place, it appears the Mexican representatives did not participate, for it would have been quickly reported to Hayden and Tolson. Their correspondence on the meeting of April 1, 1949, is silent.

On May 3, Tolson informed Hayden he felt confident "that the Mexican Government will go ahead with their part of this program if the Cananea

Cattle Company will withdraw its demand that it be given grazing privileges on the Monument." Tolson hoped that "the Cananea Cattle Company can make some proposal to the Mexican Government to which the Mexican Government will agree."[201] Skeptically, Hayden did not believe that the situation with the Mexican Government had changed. He did, however, believe that the Cananea Cattle Company could donate the 2,880 acres if the land, except for 200 acres for the arboretum, was not fenced. The Mexican Government, however, felt otherwise.[202]

On July 29, Governor Garvey and the Arizona Coronado International Memorial Commission traveled to Tepic, Nayarit, Mexico, to attend a meeting with the governors of New Mexico and California and the Mexican governors of Sonora, Sinaloa, and Nayarit. Garvey hoped that the Arizona commissioners could make a presentation and "reactivate the movement on the part of the Mexican government to cooperate …in…setting up…an international memorial."[203] Although the meeting did take place, Garvey did not report anything until October 28 when Tolson asked him to provide information on it.[204] Two weeks later, Garvey responded that he had visited Mexico with a group of educators and a few members of the Coronado International Monument Commission and that a general discussion had taken place, "however, nothing was done specifically on the memorial."[205] Garvey said the Arizona Commission had deferred action but "I am sure that in the very near future, I can report to you the progress accomplished and whether or not we can get the Mexican officials to cooperate with us."[206] Obviously dissatisfied with Garvey's response, Tolson forwarded copies of his and Garvey's correspondence to Regional Director, M.R. Tillotson, in Santa Fe, and Hayden. The correspondence revealed Tolson's request of Garvey regarding "whether the Arizona Coronado International Memorial Commission proposed to call a meeting of representatives of the international park commissions of the United States and Mexico and of the Cananea Cattle Company for a discussion of ways and means to establish the memorial."[207] Earlier, Hayden, too, had expressed the hope that the governor's meeting could spark an interest in Mexico regarding the proposed memorial.[208] At that time, the governor's meeting with Mexican governors was the only activity that could rekindle Mexican interest in the Memorial, outside of the Department of State, which had backed off in approaching Mexican officials with the proposal.

In late summer 1950, Grace Sparkes invited Hayden to visit the site of the proposed memorial on his next visit to Arizona. Although he agreed, his re-election campaign kept him too busy to go beyond Bisbee to visit the proposed site, much less Montezuma Peak, which Sparkes wished him to ascend to view the panoramic vistas and flavor the ambiance of yore. Apologetically, he wrote Sparkes saying "I regret very much that I was unable to visit the Memorial site while I was in Bisbee just before the election… time just did not permit me to do all the things I would have liked to have done then." Promising to visit the site at another time, he expressed his desire to meet with the "Coronado International Memorial Committee."[209] A few days prior, Sparkes had sent Hayden a telegram to his Westward Ho Hotel room in Phoenix reemphasizing her invitation.[210] Two weeks later, Sparkes, instructed by the Bisbee Chamber of Commerce, which had met on September 13, 1950, issued another invitation to Hayden on his next visit to Arizona. As a friend, she added, "Don't disappoint us."[211]

Unhappy with Hayden's inability to visit the proposed memorial site, Sparkes, as "Chairman of the National Parks and Monuments Committee," turned to Tolson for information on the status of the project. She also invited him to the meeting of September 13.[212] Tolson's lengthy response reiterated much of what was already known to date saying, "Unfortunately, there is very little to add at this time to the information you already have with respect to the establishment of the proposed Coronado International Memorial in Arizona and Sonora."[213] Almost heretically, he proposed a solution to get around the lack of Mexican participation by amending the Act of August 18, 1941. That way the Memorial could change its objectives and its name from the Coronado International Memorial to the Coronado National Memorial.[214]

Tolson's reference to amending the Act of August 18, 1941, appeared to be a new development, but it had been a suggestion that had been fleetingly discussed in the halls of Washington, D.C. On Wednesday, July 5, 1950, D.M. Lyons, a constituent, suggested to "Paul," obviously Paul Eaton, Hayden's Administrative Assistant, that he telephone Tolson and discuss his views. Apparently, Tolson had openly expressed concern that the Arizona Coronado Commission was "inactive" and the Mexican Commission was "doing nothing," and that he had suggested "an amendment" to eliminate Mexican participation.[215] Soon after, Hayden was beset with a number of inquiries regarding the decade-long delay in establishing the Memorial as well as lack of response from Mexico. C. Edgar Goyette, Manager of the Tucson Chamber of Commerce, succinctly cut to the point in his letter to Hayden on July 14. "According to the best information we have," he wrote, "the reason for lack of progress has been due to lack of action on the part of the Republic of Mexico."[216] Pressure mounted as Hayden weighed the possibility of amending the Act of August 18, 1941.

Sparkes's letter to Hayden on September 25, may have renewed his hopes that a compromise between the Mexican government and the Greene Cattle Company was more than possible. She informed Hayden of the September 13 meeting that took place in Bisbee. At the meeting, Hayden's role as a catalyst was discussed, favoring that "you are the one who can iron out the differences of opinion that are necessary apparently between the Government of Mexico and the Greene Cattle Company."²¹⁷ Those in attendance posited the sentiment that "every effort should be made to induce the Mexican Government to initiate its Bill on the same basis as that of our country, wherein those holding legitimate grazing and mineral rights are amply protected."²¹⁸

C.E. Wiswall attended the meeting. He politely answered questions, particularly that regarding whether the Cananea Cattle Company would agree to support the Memorial if the Mexican government guaranteed the protection of grazing and mineral rights. He said, "he would."²¹⁹ With that, Sparkes rested her case with the Senator.

Meanwhile, M.R. Tillotson, Regional Director, National Park Service, Santa Fe, informed Sparkes that new members of the International Park Commission of Mexico included Ingeniero Eulogio de la Garza, Director General, Forestry, Wildlife, and Fisheries Service; Ing. David Herrera Jordán, Mexican Representative on the International Boundary and Water Commission; Ing. Luis Macias Arellano, Chief, Wildlife Division, Forest and Wildlife Service; and, Ing. Humberto Ortega Cattaneo, Chief, Division of Forest Protection. Tillotson informed Sparkes that Tolson expressed the hope that the appointment of the new members meant that Mexico would renew its interest in the project.²²⁰

Coincidental to that small ray of hope showered by the new Mexican committee appointees, Sparkes wrote to Tolson a second time asking him to "comply with Mr. Greene's request for 3 photostatic maps showing the Mexico area proposed for our Coronado International memorial Park. (Please do so. I believe this is very important.)"²²¹ What could it mean? Sparkes added, "I am confident with Carl's insistence with the Greene Cattle Company and the Mexican Park and Forestry Officials, that we do want the international angle kept, the difficulties can be broken and our efforts really worthwhile."²²² Although Tolson denied Greene's request explaining that the Mexicans had not yet produced a map showing their proposed area, he ended his letter optimistically with "It is hoped that the Memorial can be established as an international area in accordance with the terms of the Act of August 18, 1941."²²³

On December 14, Tillotson submitted a trip report of his December 8, 1950 meeting to the National Park Service's director clarifying some changes in the Cananea Cattle Company's organization. "Incidentally," he wrote, "frequent reference has been made in some previous correspondence to the Green [sic] Cattle Company. This, I understand, is the company which operates on the American side of the line and which some three years ago was divorced from the Cananea Cattle Company, operating in Mexico. Also, the Copper Company at Cananea, formerly known as the Greene-Cananea

Copper Company, is now a subsidiary of the Anaconda Cooper [sic] Company and is known as the Cananea Consolidated Copper Company."[224] Tillotson stated that Charles E. Wiswall, Vice President of "La Compañia Ganadora de Cananea, S.A. (The Cananea Cattle Company)" along with his associates, Carl Gutmacher, General Manager, and L.B. Flippen, Ranch Foreman, were in attendance. Apparently, Tillotson made opening remarks outlining the objectives of the Coronado International Memorial, the Act of August 18, 1941, and the position of the Mexican Government in relation to the Greene Cattle Company regarding the Memorial.

Tillotson suggested that "the Mexican Government could not establish such an adjoining area south of the Border until title had been acquired and…the only way for the Mexican Government to secure title would be through the generosity and public spiritedness of the Cananea Cattle Company, since it would undoubtedly be unwilling and without funds to purchase the necessary lands, even if the present owners should be willing to sell and could agree on a price."[225] As he spoke, Wiswall and his colleagues undoubtedly sat menacingly in their chairs. "I immediately sensed that my remarks concerning the possibility of the Cananea Company donating the required lands met with a very cold reception on the part of the company officials present," wrote an observant Tillotson. Not only did Wiswall make known his feeling about "releasing any of their lands but they also objected to any action which would result in bringing Mexican nationals through their property to visit the area. They made a considerable point of probable illegal hunting, wood cutting, and cattle rustling by those who would…visit…the area as an excuse to cross company lands."[226] Wiswall said "the company at this time was not favorable to releasing any land, no matter how small an area."[227] Despite Wiswall's rejection, Tillotson reported his optimistic feeling that the Greene Cattle Company would eventually be willing to offer "the Mexican Government for park purposes…the donation of a reasonable acreage."[228]

Tillotson saw that the size of the "donation" was the problem behind the Greene Cattle Company's reluctance to make any commitment. He recommended "that an effort be made to amend the Act of August 18, 1941, so as to make the size of the area to be established by the Mexican Government a matter of negotiation rather than a matter of law."[229] To that end, he attached a suggested draft of the bill. Tillotson's optimism was buoyed by Wiswall's recommendation that a memorial, somewhere on the border, "be dedicated to the late Colonel William Cornell Greene, founder of the cattle, copper, and other associated companies which bear, or formerly bore, his name."[230] Tillotson saw an opening. Unabashedly, he asked Sparkes that "she might suggest [to Wiswall] that perhaps the United States Government could be persuaded at some later time to place a table in the museum to commemorate this action on the part of the Cananea Cattle Company as a memorial to William Cornell Greene."[231] Meanwhile, Hayden wrote to Wiswall asking him his opinion "whether you think that there is a possibility of an area in Mexico adjoining the American area becoming available for Memorial purposes."[232]

Following up on the December 8 meeting, Tillotson wrote Wiswall hoping to convince him that the donation of land to the Mexican Government would not require 2,880 acres but "an area of considerable less acreage."[233] Explaining the "tentative" plans for the development of the Memorial, Tillotson promised to send him copies of the planning documents. Careful not to offend Wiswall's sensitivities, Tillotson reminded him of their earlier conversation regarding the required size of the donation. Seeking a positive response, Tillotson wrote "If so, I should like to have a statement from you to that effect and, with the full understanding that it would not constitute a commitment on your part, an estimate of the acreage you might be willing to donate for such a purpose. With that as a basis to work on, perhaps we could proceed with the necessary negotiations and with an amendment to the enabling act of August 18, 1941, if such should be necessary."[234] Perhaps realizing the forcefulness of his request to Wiswall, Tillotson, as if softening his approach, told him that he would be glad to meet him in Mexico if Wiswall thought that a written response was not to his liking. The proverbial ball was now in Wiswall's court. The situation was truly "touch and go." Tillotson must have had qualms over his otherwise wishful but obviously manipulative approach toward Wiswall.

Writing to his director, Tillotson said, "I note your…agreement with… Hayden's thought that if the Cananea Cattle Company adheres to the position that it will not donate any acreage for the memorial project, the act of August 18, 1941, should be amended to provide for the creation of a national rather than an international memorial. Personally, I would agree to such a course of action only as a very last resort."[235]

Intuitively, Sparkes sent Hayden a telegram informing him that she would soon be making a presentation on the status of the Coronado International Memorial proposal. She asked him for some up to date information to use in her presentation.[236] Sensing that the Cananea Cattle Company would not make the donation, and that therefore, Mexican cooperation would not be forthcoming, Hayden telegramed Grace Sparkes saying:

> IN EVENT LAND IN MEXICO DOES NOT BECOME AVAILABLE IT MAY BE THAT WE WILL HAVE TO CONSIDER AMENDING PRESENT LAW TO PERMIT ESTABLISHMENT OF NATIONAL MEMORIAL ON AMERICAN SIDE ONLY.[237]

Difficult though it was, no one was ready to fully admit that Mexico was not interested.

Meanwhile, Tolson had been in contact with Hayden's assistant, Paul Eaton, who had a more realistic view of the possibilities that the Cananea Cattle Company would donate any land. Eaton strongly believed that Wiswall "will not agree to his Company transferring any of it holdings in Sonora to Mexico for the Coronado Memorial.[238] Still, hopeful that the "small size" proposal would fulfill the requirements of the Act of August 18, 1941, both Tolson and Eaton hoped to pursue the possibility of the Cananea Cattle Company donation of land.[239]

At year's end, no one had heard from Wiswall, much less Hayden, who had written to him in mid-December. Dated January 31, 1951, Hayden received a letter from Mary Contreras, Secretary to Mr. Wiswall at Ranchos de Cananea. She explained that the reason he had not heard from Wiswall was that he had been in ill health for several weeks and unable to respond to his correspondence.[240] Undoubtedly, Hayden looked forward to a time when Wiswall would be able to respond.

Meanwhile, the newly appointed members of the Arizona Coronado International Memorial Commission, as it was now called, included Grace Sparkes, Margaret Rockwell, Ben Arnold, James V. Robins and the perennial Odd S. Halseth. Their next meeting would take place in Tucson on February 24 at the Santa Rita Hotel. The Commission hoped to take a more active role in the Coronado International Memorial project. They hoped to invite to future meetings representatives of the Mexican Commission, the Cananea Cattle Company, and the National Park Service to participate in that meeting.[241]

At 11 a.m. on February 25, 1951, the Arizona Coronado International Memorial Commission met. The first order of business was to elect Sparkes as chairman. Next they reviewed the already long history of efforts to get the Memorial established. After a lengthy discussion, the Commission adopted several recommendations as follows:

> 1. That the original plans of the Arizona Commission, as approved by the governments of Mexico and the United States, should be pursued to the end that the Coronado International Memorial…be established as an international area, and…if this should fail, plans for a national area should be contemplated.
> 2. That the Governor of Arizona…arrange a meeting with the Governor of Sonora, Mexico, for the purpose of enlisting official support by these two state governments for plans to expedite procedure by the federal governments of Mexico and the United States.
> 3. That members of the…Commission plan and arrange… meetings with the owners of the land in Sonora needed to complete the international area, either in its present proposed

size, or any other size agreeable to the governments of Mexico and the United States.

4. Ms. Sparkes delegated herself to handle the necessary negotiations with the Greene Cattle Company, and appointed Mrs. Rockwell a delegate to deal with Statehouse and Washington matters. Mr. Halseth was asked to prepare a history of the Arizona Commission and the Coronado project from its inception, and Mr. Arnold was asked to contact Senator McFarland in regard to the project.[242]

Halseth sent Hayden a copy of the minutes demonstrating the fresh start of the Commission. Apparently, the Commission hoped to keep the Coronado International Memorial issue separate from the Big Bend International Park proposal. Halseth confided in Hayden that if that happened, "I feel the Mexicans also will act favorably."[243]

Actively pursuing support for their project, the Commission hosted a number of activities between March 5 and 16. On March 10, for example, it sponsored a "horseback trail trip" along the U.S. side of the planned memorial. The seven-hour tour included a hike to Montezuma Peak. During that period, Sparkes hoped to meet with representatives of the Cananea Cattle Company, but, aside from Wiswall being ill, she and "Mr. Greene" missed meeting each other at Bisbee. Sparkes telephoned Wiswall hoping to meet him at some future date.

On March 16th, Sparkes and Brophy, President of the Bisbee Chamber of Commerce, visited Arthur R. Williams, U.S. Consul at Agua Prieta. After two hours of discussion, Williams, agreeing to meet again, informed Sparkes that he preferred his office serve as a "reporting office" whereby he could inform his superiors about the status of the planned memorial.

Beyond that meeting, two, otherwise unrelated, activities took place. On their circuitous way back from Agua Prieta, she and Brophy stopped at Benson to talk to a man "who years ago unearthed a Spanish coin in the Park area." Not long afterwards, Brophy requested that the Arizona Highway Department designate Montezuma Pass and Coronado Peak on official highway maps of Arizona to encourage travelers to visit the area.[244]

Three days later, Sparkes wrote Williams reiterating their discussion of March 16 in Agua Prieta. The letter presented a litany of names and events associated with the Coronado International Memorial proposal from 1939 to 1951 inclusive of the names of the United States International Park Commission members and the International Park Commission of Mexico. The U.S. commissioners were M.R. Tillotson, Conrad L. Wirth, Jesse L. Nusbaum, and Hillory A. Tolson of the National Park Service; Lawrence M. Lawson, U.S. Commissioner of the International Boundary and Water Commission; C. Otto Lindh, Regional Forester, U.S. Forest Service; Moris

Burge, Bureau of Indian Affairs; and John C. Gatlin, Regional Director, Fish and Wildlife Service. The Mexican Commissioners were Ing. Eulogia de la Garza, Director General, Forestry, Wildlife, and Fisheries Service; Ing. David Herrera Jordán, Representative on the International Boundary and Water Commission; Ing. Luis Macias Arellano, Chief, Wildlife Division, Forest and Wildlife Service; and Ing. Humberto Ortega Cattaneo, Chief, Division of Forest Protection.[245] By presenting the facts and names, Sparkes hoped to convince Williams that interest in the Memorial was intense, longstanding, and beneficial to both countries.

Leaving no stone unturned to enlist Williams in the cause and keep the fires of hope burning among the Washington supporters, Sparkes sent a telegram to Governor Howard Pyle who was visiting Washington, D.C. in mid-April. She asked him, while there, to arrange a meeting between Senators Hayden and McFarland, Congressmen Murdock and Patten, Tolson, and Eaton as well as, if possible, a representative of the Mexican Embassy to discuss the Coronado International Memorial. Having spoken to Wiswall, Sparkes felt that he was agreeable to donating a plot of land if the grazing rights of the Cananea Cattle Company could be protected. Also, wrote Sparkes, an additional incentive would go a long way with Wiswall if a small memorial could be incorporated into the plan to commemorate the life of Colonial William Greene, the founder of their company.[246]

Hayden was not as hopeful. Responding to Sparkes request for a meeting, he informed her that it had not been possible to arrange the meeting with the parties aforementioned. Communicating to her that little, if anything had changed, he wrote:

> At the present time help can come only from the Cananea Cattle company or from the Mexican Government. I understand that your Committee is arranging for Governor Pyle and the Governor of Sonora to get together on this problem…. I would…appreciate being advised of the results of such a meeting.[247]

Sparkes and the Arizona Coronado International Memorial Committee members were aggressive. By June, Halseth had met with Governor Pyle and convinced him to write a letter on his behalf introducing him to Mexican officials in Mexico City. Halseth planned to go there in August to convince Mexican officials to move on the project and remove the stalemate caused by the Cananea Cattle Company.[248]

It appears that the Cananea Cattle Company openly played both ends against the middle. On June 18, 1951, for example, Emilio Segura, Jr., Secretary of the Ranchos de Cananea, wrote to Grace Sparkes saying that Frank T. Greene, who had to leave town hurriedly on business, asked him to respond to her letters of May 30 and June 15, 1951. The letter was delivered to Olga M. Reasonover in the Bisbee Chamber of Commerce on June 19, by a "Mexican lad" who insisted that his copy be "receipted," that is, certified in its delivery. Greene's response was that the proprietors of the Cananea Cattle Company had unanimously adopted the following resolution on June 17, 1951:

> RESOLVED, that the use of no graizing [sic] land and of no cattle-watering facilities whatever should be lost by this Company to the Coronado National Park project or to any other similar project, because our ranch is stocked to full capacity and must continue to be, under our program of increased production of beef for the Mexican domestic market and of processed beef for export to the United States, which is a material contribution to the war effort; also because fencing wire is very scarce and expensive at present, with the result that the cattlemen are encountering most serious difficulties in securing, regardless of price, even their minimum requirements of such wire for current repairs and maintenance of their ranch fence lines. A project such as the Coronado National Park would consume a large amount of fencing wire. Furthermore, it is considered that, in the present situation of international emergency, the proposed spending of money and use of scarce materials, for recreational project purposes such as this, should at least be held in abeyance until the return of normal times.[249]

Segura ended his letter with "Mr. Greene, further, asked me to express to you his regrets at our Company's inability, for the reasons embodied in the above-transcribed resolution, to dispense with the use of any part of our ranch land." To that, Sparkes scribbled a note on the top right hand margin for Tolson's eyes. It read: "This letter disgusts me after our efforts & their supposedly desire to co-operate."

Undeterred, Sparkes wrote to Hayden informing him of a possible meeting between the Governor Pyle with the President of Mexico. She asked him to write a letter to Interior Secretary Oscar L. Chapman to "assign Mr. Tolson to the all important task of accompanying Governor Pyle's representative to Mexico City this month, for the conference on this Project with President [Miguel] Aleman Valdis."[250] Unable to resist a parting shot at Wiswall, Sparkes wrote, "I am disappointed, as many others, in the attitude taken by the Greene [sic] family and particularly Mr. Wiswall, for I feel he could have given the 'go' signal. After what this country has done for Mexico and the Greene interests there…."[251] A few days later, Hayden requested Tolson's participation in the meeting.[252] Soon after, Dale E. Doty, acting Secretary of the Interior responded saying that Tolson may participate "if and when the Mexico City meeting is to be held."[253]

In preparation for the meeting, Governor Pyle sent President Aleman a letter in August briefing him of the already long history in the establishment of the Coronado International Memorial. He explained the objectives, and the ardent desire, on the part of the Arizona Coronado Memorial Commission to have Mexico's reciprocity in the matter. In Pyle's view, two issues needed to be ironed out. The first was to ascertain the terms under which the Cananea Cattle Company would donate land in Sonora for the government sponsored Mexican memorial. The second involved the issuance of a decree by the Mexican Government to establish its portion of the International Memorial in Sonora. In order to facilitate the "reopening" of negotiations, Pyle asked President Aleman to grant Halseth and Tolson an audience at the earliest convenient date.[254] Hayden endorsed the letter by writing President Aleman for his support in calling the requested meeting.[255] By November 20, after a three-month wait, Pyle expressed his discouragement. He wrote to Sparkes saying, "Our efforts…have…bogged down again. President Aleman has failed to answer my letter which would seem to indicate that the Mexican Government prefers to ignore the whole matter."[256]

Suddenly hope revived, especially when Manuel Pello, Secretario de Relaciones Exteriores in Mexico City, wrote Pyle a short, polite letter acknowledging receipt of his letter by the President. All Pello said was "In accordance with the instructions of the President, I have taken the necessary steps with the other governmental agencies who have an interest in this subject in order to obtain mutual consideration of the same."[257] There was no commitment nor embellishment on Pello's part. In an exchange of letters, Pyle and Sparkes, however, chose to read between the lines of Pello's translated letter. The only real thing about the letter was that President Aleman acknowledged Pyle's request for an audience. Pyle assumed that Pello was expressing his interest in the Coronado International Memorial. Pyle wistfully responded, "We hope with all our hearts that your association with this project will guarantee its fulfillment."[258] Sparkes and Pyle felt it was great news, and passed on a copy to Tolson, who eagerly awaited its arrival as proof that the Mexican Government was interested. Quietly, they braced themselves for another disappointment. Months later, at the end of January 1952, Tolson interpreted Pello's letter correctly. He wrote to Sparkes saying that Paul Eaton, Hayden's administrative assistant, feels "as I do, that the letter indicates that no definite action will be taken as a result of Governor Pyle's request for a meeting in Mexico City."[259]

Meanwhile, Dr. Neasham, now Regional Historian in San Francisco, contacted Don Perry, whose sister had married into the Greene family. Perry, referred him to Frank Greene who was then living in Sausalito, California. It turned out that Greene was the "step-son of President Wiswall of the

Cananea Cattle Company." For some reason, that surprised the National Park Service and likely added perspective to the power wielded by Wiswall, now in his 70s. Wiswall's life was no secret. He began working for Colonel Greene in 1901 and helped establish the Cananea Cattle Company in 1907. Aside from being General Manager of the Cananea Cattle Company, he was president of the Banco de Cananea. In 1918, he married Colonel Greene's widow.[260] Hence, he was Frank Greene's step-father. Nonetheless, Neasham and Greene agreed to meet during the last week in October, depending on "the outcome of Mr. Wiswall's illness," for he was "seriously ill and...expected to live only a short time."[261] Apparently Neasham hoped to persuade Greene on finalizing the donation of land for the Mexican memorial on the border. Consequently, Neasham vowed to keep contact with Greene.

Six weeks later, Neasham reported that Wiswall had survived his scrape with death and had "resumed his duties, in Cananea, as General Manager of the Cananea Cattle Company." In his discussions with Neasham, Greene admitted the reasons for the Cananea Cattle Company's vacillations in regard to the donation of land to Mexico. He said,

> ...the Board of Directors of the Cananea Cattle Company is afraid, if land is given to the Mexican Government for international memorial purposes, the Mexican authorities might take steps to confiscate additional lands in line with their agrarian policy; also, that the land proposed for incorporation within the boundaries of the Coronado International Memorial area on the Mexican side contains valuable spring and water resources which the Cananea Cattle Company claims are needed for its cattle.

Suddenly Greene proposed to Neasham that if the Cananea Cattle company received an equal amount of land from the Mexican Government elsewhere, then "some arrangement might be made to turn over the Memorial land to that Government."[262] Greene suggested that Wiswall be contacted as he had complete control over the matter and full support of the Board of Directors. Looking to take the next step, Tolson noted that President Aleman had not yet responded to the request for a meeting. Perhaps, thought Tolson, Greene's proposal could be brought up at that meeting.[263]

December 1951 ended with no action from the Mexican Government. On January 2, 1952, Hayden wrote Sparkes agreeing with Tolson's suggestion to "ignore the Mexican angle and see if our Congress can be persuaded to set aside the generally agreed upon public lands located in the United States as a National Monument to the Coronado Expedition."[264] As Pyle had not received a response from President Aleman regarding his proposed meeting, Sparkes also agreed.[265]

On January 28, 1952, Tolson again tried reasoning with Wiswall. The object of his letter was to present Wiswall with Greene's idea of an exchange of land in Mexico equal to that needed to establish the Memorial on the Mexican side. Tolson also suggested that the Cananea Cattle Company could negotiate future uses of water and grazing resources within the proposed Mexican memorial. To that end, Tolson offered Wiswall any assistance the National Park Service or the Commission chaired by Tillotson could render toward this cause.[266] Hoping for a quick reply, Tolson sent his letter via air mail.

The abeyance, caused by the constant change in the memberships of the Mexican commissions, left the National Park Service with no one to contact in Mexico City. That, coupled with the seeming lack of cooperation on the part of the Cananea Cattle Company, which had not, as of February 21, responded to Tolson's January 28 letter to Wiswall, moved the National Park Service to work toward amending the Act of August 18, 1941. That remedy had become abundantly clear. Acknowledging the effort made with Mexico and the Cananea Cattle Company for nearly twelve years, Tolson informed Sparkes that Hayden "is seriously considering the possibility of proceeding with the plan to amend the Act of August 18, 1941," establishing Coronado National Memorial.[267]

Two weeks later, Hayden sent Sparkes a copy of his proposed bill to amend the Act of August 18, 1941. "Before I introduce the bill," he wrote, " I shall be glad to have you advise me of the present thinking along this line of you as Chairman of The Coronado International Monument Commission of Arizona."[268] Despite the stern move under consideration, hope sprang eternal. Tolson remarked to Sparkes, "If this action is taken, the Mexican Government will probably take steps eventually to set aside a companion area in Sonora so that an International Memorial to Coronado can be created."[269] In response, Sparkes agreed saying, "I definitely feel we should not lose more valuable time and that by going national through the introduction of your bill we may later accomplish the international angle, when Mexico and the Greene interests iron out their problems. Time has a way of fleating (sic) and our Project has hung fire too long."[270] Blaming Wiswall, she wrote: "Many feel as I do, that Mr. Wiswall could give the *nod* and the job there would be complete."[271] In the meantime, Sparkes, Halseth, Pyle, and others endorsed Hayden's proposed bill. At the February 25, Chamber of Commerce meeting at the Copper Queen Hotel headquarters in Bisbee, the membership unanimously pledged its approval and support of Hayden's bill.[272]

Charles Wiswall died on February 29, 1952 at age 74.[273] In her letter to Hayden dated March 6, 1952, Sparkes wrote of the possibilities of reopening negotiations with Mexico and the Cananea Cattle Company. She wrote:

"With Mr. Wiswall's death, I am wondering if the Ranchos de Cananea and the Mexican Government might be disposed to follow suggestions of Mr. Frank Greene to Dr. Neasham re: exchange of land—outlined in Hillory Tolson's letter to Mr. Wiswall, Jan. 28, 1952."[274] Surprised that "Mr. Charles E. Wiswall has passed on," Hayden informed Sparkes that "I shall take no action regarding amendatory legislation until I have received further information from the Coronado International Monument Commission of Arizona." Accordingly, Governor Pyle convened the Commission to determine their druthers on the matter,[275] and Hayden was disposed to await their response to the situation.

March 18, 1952, proved pivotal in deciding whether to proceed with Hayden's bill. Upon hearing of Wiswall's death, Tolson expressed his sympathies to Sparkes, but added "This might change the attitude of the Cananea Cattle Company toward the Memorial project."[276] Simultaneously, Tolson informed Sparkes that he would instruct Neasham to contact Frank Greene in Sausalito to "ascertain, if possible, as to whether there is a possibility of such a change." Although Neasham had reported that Greene was favorable toward the Coronado International Memorial project, the response from the Cananea Cattle Company was chilling.

On March 18, Tolson received Wiswall's posthumous response to his letter of January 28. In a letter dated March 11, Emile Segura, Secretary, Ranchos de Cananea, representing Wiswall's wishes, informed Tolson that Neasham had "misquoted" Frank Greene. Segura stated, "the Companys [sic] stockholders continue to be unalterably opposed to proposed segregation of any part of grazing land constituting its cattle ranch for Coronado Memorial or any other purposes."[277] Segura reasserted that "Mr. Frank T. Greene, with whom we had taken the matter up, has directed us to advise you that he has been misquoted, as he never made any of the statements attributed to him according to the second paragraph on page 2 of your letter under reply."[278]

On that same day, Sparkes telegramed Hayden advising him that the International Monument Commission had met and unanimously approved that he proceed with his bill amending the Act of August 18, 1941.[279] The next day, Tolson communicated to Sparkes, that the NPS had no alternative than to "follow the suggestion I made several years ago, and in which Senator Hayden concurs, that a Coronado National Memorial be established in Arizona."[280] Adding a postscript, Tolson, having seen Sparkes' telegram of March 18 to Hayden, remarked "I understand that he proposes to introduce the necessary bill to do this very soon."[281]

On March 24, Hayden introduced Senate Bill 2909 requesting that "the words 'Coronado National Memorial' be hereby substituted in lieu of the words 'Coronado International Memorial' wherever such words occur in the Act of August 18, 1941." Section 1 of the Act of August 18, 1941 "is hereby amended by striking out" the portion requiring Mexican participation in the establishment of the Coronado International Memorial. A month later, on April 23, H.R. 7553, a companion bill in the House of Representatives, was introduced. The language was the same.[282]

The long wait was almost over. Hayden and the Arizona Coronado International Memorial Commission were now committed to a course that would establish the Coronado National Memorial. Sensing an end to the long struggle to establish the Memorial, Sparkes asked Hayden "if you would have your file on our Coronado Project bound and sent to us—or present it to the U.S. Park Service." She also asked Tolson, Rockwell, Halseth, and others to do the same saying that they would be kept in the "museum" at Bisbee.[283]

By the end of June 1952, S.2909 had passed the Senate and the House bill was pending on the Calendar of the House.[284] On July 2, 1952, Hayden wired Sparkes the following message "HOUSE TODAY PASSED S. 2909 CLEARING IT FOR THE PRESIDENT."[285] The next, time-consuming, step toward creating the Coronado National Memorial would be the preparation of a Presidential Proclamation.[286] The proclamation worked its way slowly to President Harry Truman, but first it had to clear the Bureau of Budget then the Attorney General.

On October 24,[287] George A. Brubaker, Hayden's aide, advised him that Tolson had announced that the "Proclamation" for the Coronado National Memorial had cleared the attorney general's office and had been sent to the White House over the weekend.[288] Closely watching the situation, Hayden had impressed on Brubaker the need to report immediately on any news related to the "Proclamation." Others, including Tolson, were in communication with Hayden's constituents. Writing to Sparkes, Tolson remarked "This refers to your letter of September 11 acknowledging a copy of my memorandum of August 20 to Tillie [Tillotson] concerning the proclamation to establish the Coronado National Memorial. I know that you and the other members of your Commission are anxious to learn about its status."

Opportunistically, Sparkes asked Hayden for the pen and holder used by the President of the United States to sign the bill. "Remember," she wrote, "we want this for the Museum—the finale to your wonderful effort for this great historical project."[289] On July 10, Hayden received a charming letter from Charles S. Murphy, Special Counsel to the President saying that "I have the pleasure in sending you, herewith, the pen used by the President today in approving S. 2909."[290] Sparkes must have also requested the pen to be used in signing the Proclamation as well.

Reading a Western Union telegram from Brubaker in Washington D.C., Hayden, now in his Phoenix office, must have allowed himself a smile as he uttered the words: "Just been advised President Truman on November 5, signed Coronado National Memorial Proclamation, Executive Order 2995."[291] Regarding the second pen, Hayden, on November 14, told Sparkes that "it is not possible to produce the pen used in signing the Proclamation due to the lapse of time between the date of signing and receipt of your request here. It has not been possible to locate the particular pen used."[292]

The Proclamation punctuated an historical moment. Earlier, when Sparkes led a tour to the site on July 25, 1952, she knew the place, the historical moment, and the panoramic view were right. In that tour were Conrad L. Wirth, Director of the National Park Service, R.L. Lee, Assistant Director, and M.R. Tillotson, Regional Director. As they wound their way down from Coronado Peak, Sparkes recollected later, "it was way beyond my expectations, for it goes beyond the thought of a place for an historical marker—there lies the route before you of Coronado—you actually feel it and see it."[293] Still, in her heart, she wished that one day Mexico would come around to make Coronado National Memorial an international area.

Chapter IV

A Memorial to Mr. Coronado?
A Monument to Misunderstanding:
The View from Cananea

> *...bringing good will and understanding between the two nations -- Mexico and the United States...* –Grace Sparkes, *Bisbee Daily Review*, 1951.

> *The Agrarian Reform represents raising to their ultimate culmination the principles of social justice...set forth in the supreme law of the republic.* –- Mexican President Adolfo López Mateos.

> *Polley denounced the drive to break up the huge Greene holdings as communist-inspired.* —Attorney for the Greene family, *Bisbee Daily Review*, 1952.

After the Coronado Commission decided to place a monument at the point where Coronado's expedition crossed into what would become the United States, they had to determine exactly where to put it. First, a commission concluded that Coronado traveled through the border area going north along the San Pedro River. Then, the Huachuca Mountain site, which was not on the projected Coronado route but which did possess an impressive view of it and the surrounding countryside, was selected. The

Huachucas had already been promoted as the site for an international monument for at least four years by local boosters.[294]

According to Senator Hayden, the decision on the placement of the monument was made in consultation with officials of the Mexican government and the Cananea Cattle Company, which owned the land directly south of the border. Twelve thousand acres, half in each country, was designated for inclusion in the projected monument.[295] On April 11, 1940, Anderson assured Hayden that no land within the United States would be taken from private hands. It would only be transferred from the Forest Service to the Park Service, from one federal agency to another.[296] Even this, however, did not satisfy Hayden. He noted that the specified land contained "patented mining claims and patented private grazing holdings" must be protected. He "objected to its size suggesting that there was no necessity of including this much land in the American part of an international monument."[297]

True to Hayden's word, the 1941 legislation authorizing Coronado International Memorial contained language specifically protecting the rights of ranchers and miners to pursue their vocations within the park. Of the two pages that made up the statute, one focused almost exclusively on the topic. Rights to water used for stock were protected along with grazing privileges. Future road and fence construction would have to include access routes for cattle in order to ensure that development of the park did not threaten existing grazing and water rights.[298]

The cattle operation known as Ranchos de Cananea had its origins in the controversial operations of William C. Greene around the turn of the twentieth century. Greene, who had bestowed upon himself the title of "Colonel," was once toasted as "the Cecil Rhodes of America."[299] Rhodes was both admired and vilified for expanding the British Empire, and his own, in Africa through his own ambition and the exploitation of native labor. In like manner, Greene carved his own empire out of the mountains and desert of northern Sonora and southern Arizona. The copper mining complex in Cananea, Sonora, which profited from a labor system that discriminated against Mexican workers, was his greatest undertaking.

"Colonel" Greene's accomplishments in Cananea have been viewed in conflicting manners. His biographer called Greene "a frontiersman to the end--a man looking for new country and new challenges, a lone fighter pitting his strength against nature and hostile human beings," the soul of "honesty, responsibility, independence, labor, and dedication."[300] In Mexico, the "new" country in which Greene made his fortune, his legacy is less positive. It stems from the events of 1906, when the Cananea miners struck in protest of company policies toward them. They demanded higher pay and shorter hours. They were, moreover, angered by the control that Greene had over the region and their lives. His companies owned their houses and land, controlled roads and regulated transportation, and held the local water concession. They also ran the slaughterhouse and the company store that monopolized the retail market.[301]

Inequality, the word most often written about and shouted from the barricades was the most galling affront to Mexican workers. Anglo-American miners were paid more for the same work and provided better housing than their Mexican counterparts. They also filled all supervisory positions in the mines. The strike quickly turned into a violent confrontation. Greene viewed the events as an attack on his authority and a threat to his operation. At his call, seventy-five armed "volunteers" crossed the border from Bisbee and hurried to Cananea. Governor Rafael Izábal of Sonora saw the strike as a rebellion and allowed the vigilantes to cross. Taking further action, he sent for two thousand troops to quell the disturbances. According to a conservative estimate, between thirty and one hundred Mexicans and four United States citizens were killed during the Cananea strike.[302]

The United States Ambassador to Mexico was later told that the Mexican government viewed the 1906 events as an attempted revolution.[303] That opinion would prove prescient. Although doubtful that many of the miners in Cananea expected their actions to lead to the downfall of the autocratic, thirty-year old regime of Porfirio Díaz, a later historian concluded that:

> Cananea is famous in Mexican history because of a strike in 1906 that was one of the direct antecedents of the Mexican Revolution. The central issue in the strike was pay scales that gave Mexican workers less than comparable American employees. Because the Sonoran state governor allowed Greene to bring armed irregulars from Bisbee into Mexico, the strike focused nationalistic discontent against the United States on Mexico's own subservient regime.[304]

In 1906, Cananea symbolized the fight against the collaborative domination of the economy by foreigners and the Díaz government in impovershing the Mexican people. When Díaz was forced to flee Mexico in 1911, Cananea was seen as one of the opening salvos of the revolution.

Before the revolution began in 1910, Greene had lost control of the Cananea mines. By his death in 1911, he owned an enormous amount of grazing land in both Mexico and the United States. In Mexico, his holdings were described as an irregularly shaped area extending forty-two miles from north and south; sixty-eight miles east to west; and two hundred miles in circumference. Some of the land, fully integrated into his ranching operation, was leased from two Mexican families. Still more was leased long-term from the Cananea Consolidated Copper Company for a nominal fee, a deal consummated by Greene before he lost control of the mining company.

Eventually, in 1929, that land was sold to the cattle company.[305]

Along the border, the Greene ranch extended from east of Naco, Sonora, to west of the Huachuca Mountains. It fronted all of the land considered in the United States for designation as the Coronado Memorial. Upon his death, his wife and children inherited all of his holdings. Ranch manager Charles E. Wiswall, who married Greene's widow, continued to run the operation for the family until his death in 1953.[306] The Mexican property was officially separate from the Greene holdings in the United States and was broken up on paper into seven units in order to evade national laws that limited property size.[307] It was said that Greene and his heirs never allowed Mexican nationals to work on the small part of the vast ranch dedicated to agriculture in order to avoid the establishment of a community that had the right to request its own common land.[308]

Land was guaranteed to farmers by the post-revolutionary constitution of Mexico. Land reform was a centerpiece of the presidency of Lázaro Cárdenas, 1934-1940. The Cárdenas administration distributed some eighteen to twenty million hectares (nearly fifty million acres) of land, benefiting around 800,000 recipients.[309] Regardless of interpretation, most historians agree that his controversial presidency was decisive in the development of modern Mexico.[310] The events in Cananea in the 1930s, and after, must be seen in the context of these contemporary political upheavals throughout the state of Sonora and the nation of Mexico. Wiswall watched these events with keen and personal interest.

Sonora was affected by national influences during the Cárdenas era more profoundly than it had previously been. Although Sonora had produced many preeminent leaders of the Mexican Revolution, it was "largely untouched by revolutionary change."[311] Entrenched and independent in its power, the Sonoran elite was connected to the ruling clique in Mexico City by factional and familial ties. At the sufferance of the Sonora faction presided over by Plutarco Elías Calles, Cárdenas ascended to the presidency and quickly established his own independence. Having forced Calles into exile, Cárdenas projected his own modernizing program into all regions of Mexico. His actions triggered multiple conflicts in Sonora.

Mexico is a country known for its regionalism and loyalty to *patria chica* above the nation-state. Sonora in the 1930s was no exception and its people, not unlike many regions, were jealous of their local autonomy. Elites controlled the state through a combination of patronage and repression and did not appreciate any meddling by outsiders. Popular organizations followed their lead in resisting interference by the central government. "But regionalist discourse was often less a defense of state autonomy against the center than veiled manipulation of chauvinism in defense of (upper) class interests."[312] The career of Román Yocupicio Valenzuela, governor of Sonora from 1936 to 1939, illustrates the Byzantine character of Sonoran politics at the time.

As a partisan of President Alvaro Obregón, Yocupicio felt marginalized by the Calles regime. He was supported by the remnants of Obregón's clique as well as by a large network of friends and cronies cultivated during years of fighting and politicking in the Obregón cause. Yet, as Cárdenas was defeating Calles, Yocupicio appealed to interests opposed to Cárdenas and to important aspects of the revolution itself. His defense of the Catholic Church, which had been at war with the Calles regime, won him support, including that of the majority of women in the first election in which they were allowed to vote. As a Mayo Indian and friend of a well-known Yaqui leader, Yocupicio gained access to indigenous groups which had only recently fought against the government.

Wielding the threat of a regional revolt and representing local power over centralization, Yocupicio agreed to join the national party of Cárdenas, the National Revolutionary Party (Partido Nacional Revolucionario, PNR) and participate in its primary selection process. By cobbling together a diverse coalition of seemingly incompatible interests, Yocupicio was able to construct a base strong enough to defy the central government. Although he openly championed the interests of merchants and landowners over peasants and workers, for example, he garnered most of the miners' votes. From within the party, Yocupicio became "one of Cárdenas's most stubborn opponents."[313] Despite the open antagonism between them, neither Cárdenas nor Yocupicio was willing to risk any action that might precipitate open violence. Through his term in office, Yocupicio exploited multiple conflicts to gain political power and maintain it. Coincidentally, he set himself up in a lucrative business to enjoy in his retirement.[314]

Aside from U.S. interests in Mexico, the same pervasive antagonisms contributed to controversies surrounding the Greene land near Cananea. The Cárdenas reforms faced opposition from north of the border because of the massive amount of investment and land ownership in Mexico by U.S. citizens. In particular, Mexican expropriation of land, railroads, and oil from U.S. (and British in the latter case) companies threatened binational relations.[315]

In 1935, the government moved against another bastion of foreign capital when it announced that it would place stringent limits on the size of cattle ranches in the north of Mexico. The Cananea Cattle Company took a leading role when the ranchers went to Mexico City to negotiate. Eventually, the government retreated from its original plan and multiplied the limit, setting it at 40,000 hectares (almost 100,000 acres). The Cananea Cattle

Company lost some land in the settlement, most of which was returned two years later as part of decree that protected the cattle industry.[316] It would not be the company's last brush with expropriation.

Aside from the Cárdenas administration's land reform, another threat to the Greene empire appeared closer to home. Cananea had long been a stronghold of the miners' unions. In the wake of the global crisis of 1929, unemployment rose and new organizations emerged in the area. These included organized woodcutters, prospectors, and veterans of the revolution. Accusing management of deliberately dismissing workers who were owed compensation for contracting silicosis in the mines, these unions became increasingly militant. Their efforts to gain access to firewood and gold placers brought them into conflict with the Cananea Cattle Company, which controlled virtually all the land around Cananea.[317]

The Cananea unions drew support from fragments of a factionalized labor and peasant sector. Labor faced the same multiplicity of frictions as the rest of society. It, too, became embroiled in the Sonora-Mexico City power struggle. In 1937, PNR organizers traveled to Sonora's capital at Hermosillo to unify peasants of that state under the Cardenista banner. Much to the dismay of Governor Yocupicio, they promised to distribute land in the fertile Yaqui Valley. Shaken, the United States Vice-Consul on the scene complained about the anti-imperialist rhetoric of the "outsiders" from Mexico City.[318]

Out of the process of regional organization, the National Peasant Confederation (Confederación Nacional Campesina, CNC), was founded in 1938 as an affiliate of the ruling party.[319] Perhaps more interested in channeling peasants into the ruling party than in representing them, the CNC, in Sonora, came to be considered as too conservative and bureaucratic. More Sonoran peasants turned instead, to the Confederation of Mexican Workers (Confederación de Trabajadores de México, CTM), the workers union meant by the national government to complement rather than compete with the CNC. The CNC, in turn, became the champion of the more conservative peasants backed by anti-Cardenista forces at both the state and national levels.[320]

Even before the end of his term, Cardenas had retreated from his more radical programs in what has been characterized as a counter-reformation.[321] Pressured to endorse the party line, official labor and peasant organizations, for example, supported national development and private ownership over agrarian reform, and national unity over class struggle.[322] By the late 1940s the CTM was purged of its more radical elements, especially those promoting the formation of an independent and popular party of workers and peasants.[323] A new organization, the General Union of Mexican Workers and Peasants (Unión General de Obreros y Campesinos Méxicanos,

UGOCM), emerged to represent the interests of workers and peasants outside the ruling party.[324]

In the meantime, agitation for, and opposition to, land reform continued. In 1945, the Secretary General of the CNC spoke of "white terror" and a "silent and bloody civil war" surrounding the ejidos.[325] In January 1948, the Federation of Workers of the State of Sonora (Federación de Trabajadores del Estado de Sonora) launched a movement for expropriation and distribution of the lands of the Cananea Cattle Company. The movement was spearheaded by the Committee of Veterans of the Revolution, peasants, and prospectors of Cananea (Comité de Veteranos de la Revolución, campesinos y gambusinos de Cananea). Soon, a popular organization in Naco and a miners union local in Cananea added their voices to the demand for expropriation.

They presented a petition to the Attorney General (Procuradía General de Justicia) and an investigation ensued, led by Abel Ortiz Noriega, of the Federal Office of the Treasury (Oficina Federal de Hacienda) and Public Ministry (Ministerio Público). It concluded that ranches were illegal under Mexican law.[326] Not only was the land holding too large, the Mexican Constitution of 1917 specified that no foreigners could own land within one hundred kilometers of the border.[327] Nonetheless, the Secretary of Agriculture declared that the lands were immune to seizure due to their being completely and necessarily exploited. For his part in the controversy, Abel Ortiz Noriega was immediately relieved of his federal duties. The Cananea Cattle Company denounced the movement and its supporters as tools of the Communist Party.[328]

The government reportedly entered into negotiations with the land owners but nothing of note was accomplished. Through the middle of the 1950s, groups of prospectors, many of them former employees of the Cananea mines, were violently expelled from Cananea Cattle Company lands by company guards and the police. Their encarceration led to demonstrations by the miners local and confrontations with officials in Cananea. In early 1957, the president announced that the land would be expropriated, but as the year ended nothing more of the plan had been revealed.[329]

Neither government opposition nor company redbaiting slowed land activism in Sonora. In fact, going into the late 1950s petitions for distribution of land and peasant invasions of disputed estates followed one another at an accelerating pace. "As important as these conflicts were to the survival of agrarismo in Sonora during the counter-reform, the outstanding invasion of the period took place in Cananea."[330] In February 1958, one year after the presidential decree, a group that included Jacinto López, an old radical representing the UGOCM,[331] and Ramón Danzós Palomino, a local Communist Party leader, seized the radio station in Cananea. They declared their intention to invade the Cananea Cattle Company lands, announced they had trucks to transport participants, and invited local peasants to join them. Estimates of the number of families that accepted the invitation vary widely, but rancho Cuitaca, of the Ranchos de Cananea, was invaded and construction of a settlement, including a school, began.

In a response redolent of the events of 1906, the army was called out, the new settlement destroyed, and its residents loaded onto military trucks. They were taken into Cananea and, initially, thrown out in the streets in weather remembered as cold, rainy, and snowy. Later, the families were allowed to use the dubious shelter of the local baseball stadium. A witness to a contemporary land invasion elsewhere in Sonora described the army using tear gas against families in order to disperse and eject them. Despite such repression, agitation against the Greene *latifundio* continued. Another invasion was discussed but never carried out after the leadership was jailed, first in Cananea and later in Hermosillo. Jacinto López served a six month term on a charge of "social dissolution."[332]

Pressure was growing for the government to bring social peace to the region. In addition, the character of events were a direct assault on the explicit ideology, or mythology, of the PRI. After the Revolution of 1910, the winners, under the banner of a succession of official parties, wore the mantle of the guardian of the Mexican nation, and especially of its peasants and workers. Yet, in Cananea, the army had attacked those very groups in defense of the foreign owners of a constitutionally illegal property. As if to symbolize the conflict between the myth and the reality of the PRI, peasants in Ciudad Obregón, Sonora, wrapped themselves in flags as the police approached to evict them from land that they had occupied.[333]

As the conflict over land escalated in Cananea, and across Sonora, it became evident that expropriation was inevitable. At least since the Cárdenas era, the government policy alternated between radical reform meant to satisfy the ruling party's social base and a conservative program that promised stability to business owners and investors, domestic and foreign.

Distribution of the Ranchos de Cananea lands would transform a large, vocal, and active population into clients, completely dependent upon the government for their homes and livelihoods.[334] The expropriation of Ranchos de Cananea was announced before the end of 1958. In February 1959 the president of Mexico, Adolfo López Mateos, came to Cananea to distribute the land in collective ejidos. In his speech he evoked the honor of the Revolution and referred to the *opprobrious latifundio*.[335] In typical style, the list of beneficiaries compiled by the UGOCM over a six year span was scrapped in favor of one submitted by the government's own CNC. That increased the membership of the CNC and the PRI while ensuring a tractable *ejido* population. "Once again, the CNC 'carpetbagged' at the expense of the UGOCM."336

The Cananea Cattle Company land, when seen in the context of the agrarian reform program of Mexico and of the politics of Sonora and Mexico, suddenly appears as more than an empty piece of desert. Charles E. Wiswall, writing to a Phoenix attorney about the international memorial, stated "there is nothing in that flat country which is of any interest except to the people who are running cattle on it."337 He was wrong, and knew so. Elsewhere, Wiswall qualified his assessment somewhat, stating more than once that the land specified for the Memorial on the Mexican side contained springs that were critical to the company's cattle operation.338

Wiswall pointed out that it was unlikely, at best, that Coronado or any member of his company ever went on the property delineated in plans for the Memorial. He added that he believed that historical places should be marked but went on to specify that a roadside plaque near the San Pedro River would be sufficient.339 When either Wiswall, or Frank Greene, son of the Colonel and part owner of the Cananea Cattle Company, expressed any specific opinion regarding the Memorial it was consistently negative, though the reasoning changed somewhat from time to time.

Besides the springs mentioned by Wiswall, the company argued it could not afford to lose any grazing land. In a resolution by the owners of the Cananea Cattle Company that was forwarded to the Bisbee Chamber of Commerce on June 18, 1951, the company expanded on its opposition to using any of its land for an international park. Although existing herds had already overtaxed the land and water base, the current company policy aimed to increase beef production for markets in Mexico and the United States. The resolution added that they considered their efforts as "a material contribution to the [Korean] war effort." Additionally, given the scarcity and high cost of fencing, it was difficult to obtain enough to satisfy simple maintenance and repair needs. The planned international park would require more fencing at great cost. Finally, the resolution concluded, "in the present situation of international emergency, the proposed spending of money and use of scarce materials, for recreational project purposes such as this, should at least be held in abeyance until the return of normal times."340

Along with the cattle company's concern for the interests of the United States came a perceptible antipathy toward the citizens of Mexico. Also during 1951, Wiswall told Tolson, that the company was opposed to anything, such as a park on the border, that would encourage Mexican nationals to cross company land. He expressed concern that they would engage in illegal woodcutting, hunting, and cattle rustling.341 Undoubtedly, he was also thinking about prospectors and squatters, but he did not mention them to Tolson.

Of course, the company's greatest anxiety was over the prospect that the government might, as they eventually would, expropriate the land. Wiswall and Frank Greene said that if they agreed to release any property for the park it could lead the government to seize more. Perhaps they feared that by volunteering to relinquish land they would show that they didn't need it all and undermine their claim, and the government ruling, that the land was being fully utilized.

If the company was unwilling to risk weakening its position for the sake of the Memorial, however, it was happy to use the Memorial to solidify its hold on Mexican land. Greene suggested to NPS officials that the company might be willing to negotiate an exchange of the land for a similar parcel elsewhere. Of course, if the Mexican government made such a deal they would be compelled to give the company a guarantee of ownership of the land that it would receive. In addition, by negotiating as equals with the company, the Mexican government would grant a renewed legitimacy to its claim to its other lands as well. Tolson suggested that U.S. officials might present Greene's exchange proposal to their Mexican counterparts if talks took place.[342]

Such a willingness by U.S. officials to negotiate on behalf of the Cananea Cattle Company or between it and the Mexican government raises an important issue. The Cananea Cattle Company operated in Mexican territory and under Mexican laws. The status of its land was a matter to be settled with the Mexican government, just as it was up to the United States government to deal with landowners on the north side of the border. It is doubtful whether U.S. officials would have looked kindly upon Mexican suggestions regarding property in their country. Yet, from the Bisbee Chamber of Commerce to the U.S. Senate, suggestions of what Mexico should do regarding the Cananea Cattle Company flowed freely.

One factor that explains this proclivity for prescription is undoubtedly national chauvinism toward Mexico. Another is that as fellow U.S. citizens, politicians, and bureaucrats felt far more in common with Greene and Wiswall than they did with Mexican officials or citizens. Colonel Greene, the founder of the Cananea Cattle is, after all, considered a pioneer and hero of Arizona history, though his image is much different in Mexico. The original location of the park was determined, at least in part, by the existence of a large tract of National Forest Service land near Coronado's route. Protection of the private property and grazing rights of cattle ranchers was an integral component in drawing its boundaries.

As it happened, the land across the international border belonged to icons of Arizona society and history. Officials and boosters in the U.S. simply assumed that the primary goals of the Mexican government in the area would be protection of the cattle company's rights and founding of the park, in that order. The fact was that the citizens and government of Mexico, as well as the Cananea Cattle Company, were far more concerned with the expropriation issue than with the construction of a memorial to Coronado. Thus, statements by Greene, Wiswall, and the company as a whole regarding the Memorial, must be considered in the context of the expropriation struggle in Mexico.

Early in the process, the Coronado Cuarto Centennial Commission of Arizona used the certainty that the Cananea Cattle Company would donate land south of the border to assure the Arizona Cattle Growers' Association that grazing rights would be protected in the Memorial's design.[343] Later, boosters on the U.S. side recalled that the "Greene cattle people" had initially agreed to donate land for the park "with the understanding that their stock interests should be protected. Through correspondence from various officials, the Mexican government did not wish to comply with those terms and we have been stymied."[344] Onus for the failure to create a park, in the view from the north, fell squarely on the Mexican government.

Those involved believed the Mexican government could easily solve the problem by agreeing to the demands of the Cananea Cattle Company. At a 1950 meeting of the Bisbee, Arizona, Chamber of Commerce attended by Wiswall, M.R. Tillotson, summarized the NPS position: "We would be agreeable to leaving the land unfenced except for a small area around the improvements that we would propose to build, the balance could be used for grazing land so far as we are concerned." Grace Sparkes spoke for the Chamber of Commerce. Alluding to her conversation with Hayden, she reiterated the Senator's position:

> …he would like to see the Greene people's water and grazing rights protected and if they do give this land in the event it should never be used for this purpose it would revert to the original ownership. We hope through Senator Hayden in his high standing and the things he has done for Mexico that he could bring this about, legislation with Mexico, comparable to our own.

Tillotson and Wiswall discussed potential compromises and agreed to visit the area together and "see what kind of deal they could make."[345]

Tillotson wasn't the only U.S. official to consider negotiating with, and on behalf of, the Cananea Cattle Company about its land in Mexico. In a meeting of the "reactivated Coronado International Monument Commission of Arizona," Chairperson Grace Sparkes appointed herself to handle negotiations with the "Green [sic] Cattle Company."[346] Tolson suggested a meeting of officials from his agency, the Arizona Commission, the Mexican government, and the Cananea Cattle Company to work out the details of the park.[347]

In the same letter, Tolson wrote that he and the Park Service supported the conditions under which the Cananea Cattle Company had first agreed to contribute land on the Mexican side of the border. He also disclosed that he had received information that Wiswall has protested creation of the Memorial to the U.S. State Department and the Mexican government. The State Department believed that because the financial interests of U.S. citizens were involved the Mexican government should not be pressed on the issue.[348]

Elsewhere, Tolson noted that the State Department was unwilling to involve itself "in view of the delicate situation which has developed along the border with respect to American interests in Mexico," probably a reference to the expropriation issue.[349] The U.S. Consul in Agua Prieta, Sonora, weighed in with his opposition to the Coronado project as well, giving the State Department, in Tolson's words, "Wiswall's point of view."[350] Even earlier, Tolson had been told by the State Department that it would not support either the Coronado International Memorial or a similar project planned at Big Bend because of the involvement of financial interests in the United States.[351]

Eventually, it became clear that the Cananea Cattle Company was not interested in cooperating in the creation of the Coronado Memorial. While Wiswall and Greene were discussing the project in reasonable terms with the National Park Service and Bisbee Chamber of Commerce, they were channeling their opposition to the highest levels of government in Mexico City and Washington, D.C. For almost a decade, Arizona boosters had taken the side of the Cattle Company and blamed the Mexican government for not acceding to its demands in order to expedite the development of the International Memorial.

Wiswall told Tillotson in late 1950: "I don't want you to think that we are obstructionists. I am sure that we can find some way to work this out."[352] Memorial promoters were only too willing to believe him. By the middle of 1951, Grace Sparkes recognized the truth of the matter. She concluded that Wiswall "could have given the 'go' signal" on the Memorial had he so desired.[353]

In early 1952, Senator Hayden, too, realized the futility of the effort, recognizing that "so long as [Wiswall] has anything to say about it, there will be no Cananea Cattle Company land made available for a Mexican area as a part of a Coronado National Monument."[354] Hayden was correct, but he did not go far enough. Upon Wiswall's death, both Greene and Emilio Segura, representing the Cananea Cattle Company, went out of their way to confirm that they were "unalterably opposed" to the International Memorial.[355] It became obvious that the earlier appearance of cooperation was only constructed in the service of the company's interests, not a manifestation of public spirit.

Undoubtedly, Wiswall and Greene would have been willing to donate a small parcel of their massive holdings in return for other land guaranteed by the Mexican government or for assurances that they could keep the remainder of the *latifundio*. Failing that, however, they were perceived as a roadblock to development of the Memorial. For its part, the Mexican government had much larger concerns in the area. The Ranchos de Cananea were illegal, contrary in both the letter and spirit to the national constitution as well as to the legitimating mythology of the ruling party. Expropriation was coming, whether or not the government wanted it, and taking land from foreign citizens only to dedicate it to a joint project with a foreign government was not politically feasible.

In the middle 1960s, another serious attempt at an international memorial seemed to make more headway. This time, the *ejidos* and their residents were taken into account. Several factors could have contributed to the failure, among them the complex organization of the administration of Mexican *ejidos*. Each *ejido* had its own General Assembly as well as an Executive Committee. In the case of Cananea, the seven *ejidos* operated as one unit in some areas, such as ranching, but separately in others. In addition, two federal agencies were also involved in running the *ejidos*. The Department of Agrarian Affairs and Colonization (Departamento de Asuntos Agrarias y Colonización) was responsible for protecting the rights of *ejidatarios*. The Ejidal Bank (Banco Nacional de Crédito Ejidal), part of the federal Department of Agriculture and Ranching (Secretaría de Agricultura y Ganadería) administered credit and offers technical advice. That may sound unobtrusive, but the Cananea branch had fifty employees who were deeply involved in the *ejidos*, in planning, finance, purchasing and sales, and more. Moreover, their yearly plan had to be approved at the national level.[356]

With so many national, state-level, and local interests to be satisfied, a change to the *ejidos* of the magnitude of the International Memorial was difficult to effect. The opening of Mexico's democracy has created more opportunity for conflict by adding party politics to the mix. Finally, the neo-liberal assault on the collective *ejidos* during then last two PRI administrations (1988-2000) throws in yet another dynamic. It adds pressure for privatization, but not necessarily for nationalization, of the land. It may also place the *ejidatarios* in somewhat the same position that the owners of los Ranchos used to be–loath to give up control of anything lest they lose it all.

Although few of those in the United States who were involved in the creation of the Memorial seem to have bothered to learn about events south of the border, many of them were more than willing to involve themselves in affairs there more than was appropriate. One who noticed that unfortunate proclivity was Odd S. Halseth of the Arizona Coronado Commission. In July 1951, Halseth commented to Grace Sparkes, "From the beginning I have had the feeling that we neither had any business to negotiate with a Mexican company, nor that our good intentions necessarily would be considered so by the Mexican government. Reverse the situation and consider the possible reaction by our State Department." He did not think that their actions had done real harm, but added that he could "only trust it has not been considered undue meddling in their own affairs."[357]

When Hayden referred, above, to a "Mexican area" of a "National Monument," he was probably thinking of the upcoming founding of the Coronado National, rather than international, Memorial. In the way that the Memorial was conceptualized and promoted it was always a sort of United States "National Memorial" with a "Mexican area" instead of an equal partnership between Mexico and the United States. Local and national boosters focused narrowly on extending the Memorial, as designed to please private interests in Arizona, into Mexico.

When the important events being played out in northern Sonora were noticed in the United States they were usually misunderstood because few cared to look closely enough to see them in their own context. One Arizona newspaper, for example, misinterpreted the expropriation of Greene land holdings as a hostile communist act. It described "a Moscow-trained Mexican labor leader" in threatening tones and quoted a Greene family lawyer who "denounced the drive to break up the huge Greene holdings as communist-inspired."[358] In the United States of the 1950s such activities could only be seen as a communist offensive in the Cold War. In Mexico, the expropriation signified a fulfillment of the highest "principles of social justice...set forth in the supreme law of the republic."[359]

At a higher level, the same conflict in interpretation plagued the concept of the Memorial itself. In 1980, Cuauhtémoc Cárdenas, the son of Mexican President Lázaro Cárdenas, and then a government official in his own right, visited Coronado National Memorial. He told officials of the National Park Service and the Coronado International Memorial Commission that Mexico was not interested in building a monument to Coronado or to any other Spanish conquistador.[360] Mexico's independence originated in a peasant and Indian revolt against Spain. Through its history as an independent nation, Mexico has suffered interventions and invasions by Spain, France, England, and the United States. Modern Mexico celebrates, at least symbolically, its Indian heritage rather than the arrival of European colonizers. The arrival of the Spanish Christian civilization is seen as having begun a process of pillage, plunder, and slavery.

As if to deliberately illuminate the difference between their view of history and that held by most citizens of Mexico, Memorial boosters in the United States added another facet to the purposed project in 1950. Grace Sparkes, of the Bisbee Chamber of Commerce, raised the notion of "a monument established for Mr. Greene and Mr. Wiswall and the company they represent as they pioneered that country." She added that the whole park project would be "a living memorial to the work of Mr. Wiswall and the man who established their company, Mr. Greene."[361] This idea was meant to win the support of Wiswall and his associates, and may have originated with Wiswall himself.[362] Two years later, Historian Aubrey Neasham was still pushing "a memorial room to the original Mr. Greene" as part of the International Memorial.[363]

This, finally, may be the most potent symbol of why the International Memorial never took root. Intended to commemorate the shared history and common experiences of Mexico and the United States, it instead highlighted the divide between them. In its conception, the Memorial to Coronado takes a positive step to include a Spaniard among the pantheon of mostly Anglo-American explorers and pioneers celebrated by the United States. However, Mexico has too often suffered from European expansion to celebrate the conquest in any form.

A proposal to honor Coronado and Greene in the same monument is an unwitting confirmation that the European conquest of Mexico continued from the arrival of Cortéz in 1519 through the U.S. invasion of 1846 to foreign ownership of the lands and mines of Sonora in the twentieth century. At the same time that the United States was building a monument to the men who "pioneered" the region, the Mexican public was demanding their exclusion from their history books. An invitation to celebrate the imposition of foreign domination appeared to have little interest to a society engaged in resistance to it. Despite that sentiment, the United States continued to pursue the development of Coronado National Memorial.

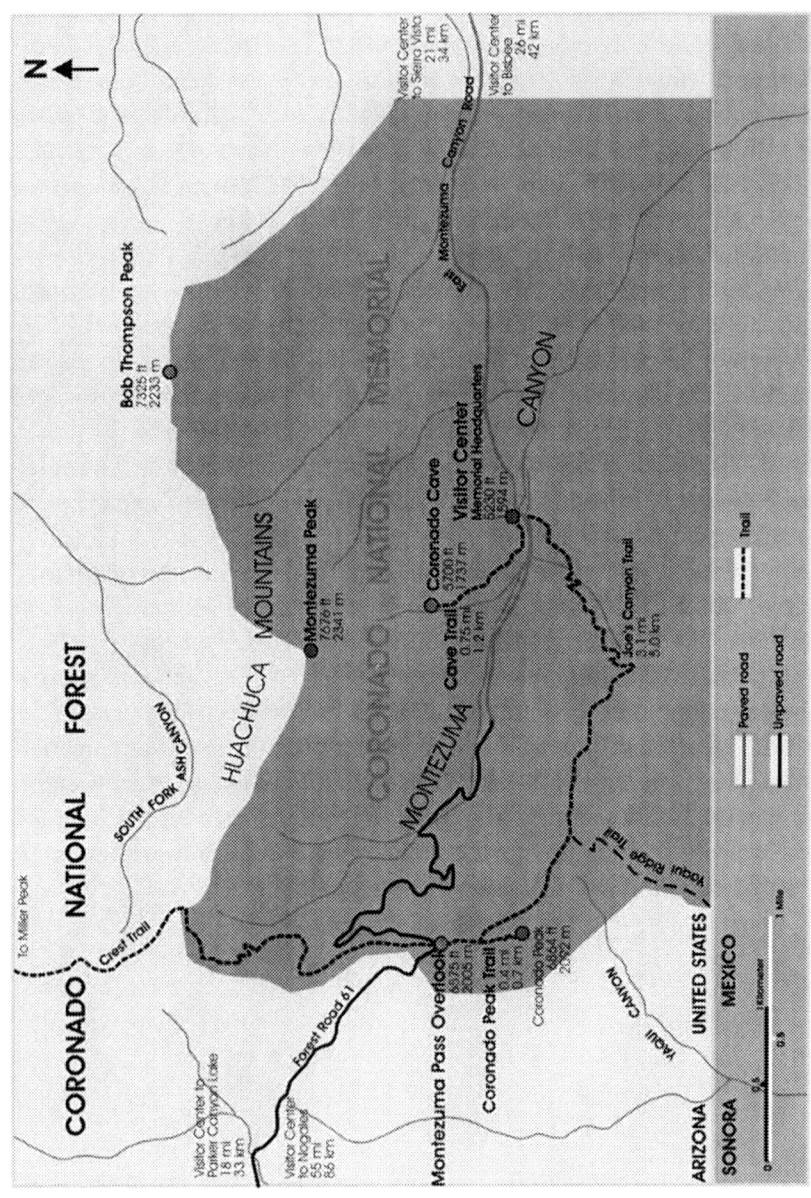

Coronado National Memorial and the surrounding area. (Map by Mario Millones, 2006)

Chapter V
From Master Plan to Mission 66 Accomplishments: Early Development of Coronado National Memorial, 1952-1966

It would appear that Coronado National Memorial is in business at last. As you can imagine, we are exited [sic] about it and anxious to get started—Carroll A. Burroughs, Acting Superintendent to Grace Sparkes, November 5, 1955

The outcome was the intention. And this was just at the end of an era of daydreaming for the National Park Service. Mission 66 was a time of great daydreaming and a time of great accomplishment—John Cook, former Intermountain Regional Director, National Park Service, interviewed on his recollections of his role in Coronado National Memorial's past, February 6, 2002

For nearly fourteen years the land selected for the Coronado National Memorial lay fallow while the National Park Service and the Arizona Coronado International Memorial Commission attempted to meet the terms of the Act of August 18, 1941. During that time no development took place on the site. Following the amendment of the Act of August 18, 1941, the National Park Service moved forward with plans to develop Coronado National Memorial. Beginning in 1952, the National Park Service assessed ways to develop the area and make it accessible to visitors. The process by which Coronado National Memorial attained its identity had already developed a history of its own. In 1952, the sun shown brightly on the Memorial as it changed from an abstract idea to an actual physical place.

On May 9, 1952, Tolson wrote to Governor Pyle advising him that the time had come to discuss, in earnest, the development of Coronado National Memorial—once legislation for its establishment had been completed. On April 14, the month prior, Sparkes, Rockwell, and Halseth of the Coronado International Monument Commission of Arizona met with Regional Director Tillotson in Phoenix to discuss the proposed legislation to create Coronado National Memorial. Among the matters reviewed was the "very general development plan" that had been discussed in the 1940s for the area. It involved the construction of an enclosed observation station on 'Coronado Peak', a parking area, and a trail from there to the contact station. The plan called for an administration-exhibit building, a utility area, a superintendent's residence, and a road leading from the main highway into the developed area.[364] As much time had elapsed since any initial planning had been discussed, and as the plan for an international memorial had been dropped, Tolson felt it was time for a formal, official plan to be drawn for implementation purposes.

Without a budget, a Master Plan for Coronado National Memorial, however, was still off in the future. Urging Hayden to assure proper funding, Sparkes on August 20, 1952, wrote to him saying "we must look to you for action to get some of the important things moving—the trail to the Peak, the observation tower—the road and parking space and utility facilities."[365]

Two years later on June 3, 1954, Hayden submitted one of the first requests for funding for the Memorial. In the Committee report on the Interior Department appropriation bill for the next fiscal year, Hayden marked $65,000 for Coronado National Memorial.[366] The appropriation broke down as follows: $9,000 for management and protection services and 56,000 for construction of minimum roads and trails to accommodate visitors to the Memorial.[367]

Meanwhile, Sparkes explored avenues for other developments in the area of the Memorial. Reporting to Hayden, she wrote that

> The County is paving a few miles of the road from the entrance at 92 highway....I sincerely hope you will be able to induce the Forest Service to improve their section of the road. It is down to rocks. With Fort Huachuca declared 'permanent'—the great industrial work at Bisbee (an outstanding tourist attraction) and now some definite action on our Memorial, there is every reason why more attention should be paid to the Montezuma Canyon road linking Bisbee and Nogales....certainly, the travel

merits improvement—ranchers, miners, cattle people use it in numbers, as do discriminating tourists."³⁶⁸ Sparkes had identified outside-the-park influences that could futuristically be helpful.

Counting his votes, Hayden remarked that he already had secured Senate approval for funding, and was confident that the House of Representatives would follow suit. "Once work is started," he wrote, "it is not likely that the Congress will fail to appropriate additional funds as needed."³⁶⁹ On June 29, 1954, Hayden announced that funding for Coronado National Memorial had been approved by Congress.³⁷⁰ This action was the first Congressional appropriation made specifically for Coronado National Memorial.

As soon as funding was secured in 1954, Luis Gastellum, Assistant General Superintendent, Southwestern National Monuments (SWNM), in Globe, Arizona, able, knowledgeable and experienced, was assigned to oversee the initial development planning of Coronado National Memorial. On October 15, 1954, he wrote Sparkes informing her of the progress made on the Memorial planning. That summer, three separate groups had been at Coronado to study the area in preparation for a General Master Plan for the eventual development of the area. "One of the principal things we require," he wrote, "before we proceed with the development of a road and trail at the pass…is a formal boundary survey." To that end, the Bureau of Land Management had been contacted to make the boundary survey after January 1. "As soon as the boundary survey is completed," wrote Gastellum, "we expect to make certain improvements on the road within the area at …at the top of the pass." After that, he explained, "we expect to develop a footpath to the overlook, where we hope to construct an exhibit as indicated in the next paragraph."³⁷¹ Additionally, Gastellum reported that orientation devices would be placed at the edge of the parking area, at the trailhead, and at the overlook for visitors to acquire information about the Memorial. Numbered stakes would be set along the trail to identify plants of interest and correspond to a self-guiding pamphlet. In his letter, Gastellum indicated that the program would, "barring unforeseen obstacles", be up and running by April 1954.³⁷² In all, Gastellum had provided a thumbnail sketch of the Master Plan to Sparkes. The plan so far was simple. Except for the Wayside Exhibit plan described, and possibly a temporary shelter for contacting visitors near the parking area, Gastellum informed Sparkes that "no funds have been provided during the current year for the erection of any buildings."³⁷³

Meanwhile, Carroll A. Burroughs, acting Superintendent at Wupatki National Monument, had been selected as acting Superintendent of Coronado National Memorial. Gastellum shared some personal biographical information about Burroughs with Sparkes. Married, without children,

Burroughs and his wife were expected to move to Coronado sometime in late November or early December 1954. Of the talented Burroughs, Gastellum wrote:

> You may be interested to know that Mr. Burroughs specialized, in his post-graduate study, in early Spanish contact with the aboriginal inhabitants of the Southwest. He possesses an unusually fine personality and has a strong interest in administration. He will have a very keen interest in the early Spanish history, and we feel indeed fortunate to be able to appoint this very outstanding man as Acting Superintendent of Coronado.[374]

Gastellum proudly revealed that during World War II Burroughs had served with the U.S. Navy as a Lieutenant-Commander. Afterwards he had received a degree in anthropology and nearly a Ph.D. (he lacked writing a dissertation) at the University of New Mexico. Shortly thereafter, he had been an instructor of Anthropology at the University of Washington. Undoubtedly, Sparks was pleased with Gastellum's glowing report about Burroughs.

From his office in Flagstaff, Burroughs wasted little time in responding to an earlier letter from Sparks. On November 5, he enthusiastically announced to Sparks, "It would appear that Coronado National Memorial is in business at last." As for his move to the Memorial, Burroughs outlined his plans to move there. Momentarily residing in Globe, Arizona, he had planned to visit the Memorial in mid-December to plan details for its development. "Most of the research and fabrication of exhibits must be done in Globe," he wrote. Before any construction commenced, Burroughs informed Sparks that "it will be necessary for the Bureau of Land Management to run a boundary survey…probably…in January." After the New Year, he planned to "move down and go to work on the ground."[375] Bureaucratically, those plans would be altered before the week was out.

On November 9, Gastellum informed Burroughs about changes to his assignment to Coronado. Modifying Burroughs plans, Gastellum instructed him of the necessity to spend two days in Globe before proceeding to Coronado where, beginning December 1, he would spend three to four weeks supervising the construction of the trail. During that time, he could better acquaint himself with the local people. After winter set in between January and February, Burroughs would report to Globe to participate on exhibit and trail planning with "the headquarters personnel." His entrance on duty date was backdated to November 7, although he would still be at Wupatki.

Meanwhile, Gastellum told him that a trailer house would be set up for him at Coronado. "Incidentally," wrote Gastellum ever conscious of cost effective management, "as you will recall, the couch in the trailer is not in too good shape and would require a major overhaul, perhaps even replacement, if you plan to use it while at Coronado. If you do not have a couch that you plan to move into the trailer, please let us know and we will see what we can do about repairing the one there now. If you plan to use your own furniture there would be no point in spending money on this unit."[376]

Sparkes took a liking to the amiable Burroughs and immediately made plans to introduce him to supporters of the Memorial—including the influential Margaret Rockwell, owner of the Adams Hotel in Phoenix.[377] Apparently, Burroughs had been to Bisbee during the first week in November to survey the work ahead of him. Writing to Tolson, Sparkes stated that "Considerable publicity has been given to Mr. Burroughs appointment but I shall issue the releases where I feel they will do the most good."[378] Banking on the good relations between Sparkes and Burroughs, Tolson informed her that when Burroughs returned in the springtime that NPS would take up her offer adding, "We will want to rent one of your cabins for use as an office."[379]

Tolson also noted a setback due to restrictions in the disbursement of next fiscal year monies. "We had hoped," he began, "to be able to construct a trail and parking area at Montezuma Pass during this winter but because half of the funds allotted to Southwestern National Monuments for such work cannot be disbursed until next fiscal year, it will not be possible to carry out this plan." Tolson had hoped that engineering plans for the trail and contract for construction would have been awarded soon, but were postponed to June as they could not be used until after July 1. The good news, he wrote, would be that a "low standard trail to Coronado Peak" would serve in the interim until the better one could be constructed.[380]

The Master Plan for Coronado National Memorial provided a schemata for future development of the 2,745 acres[381] set aside for that purpose. Aside from trails, roads, interpretive and exhibit facilities, the plan projected a futuristic view of the goals to make the area accessible to visitors. Prepared by Al Schroeder, Luis Gastellum, and Harold A. Marsh, Landscape Architect, in consultation with others, the Master Plan of 1954, although subject to later revisions, formed the basic interpretation and development plan for the Memorial. Two features stood out under "Special Problems." Far reaching in its concept, the planners for the Coronado Memorial were mindful of making the area accessible on a linguistic basis. True to their concern to encourage good relations with Mexico, the planners provided the following statement: "No special problems exist at present, though future use by Mexican nationals will necessitate a bilingual interpretive program, and possibly…personnel who can speak Spanish as well as English."[382] Another important feature of the Master Plan was the recognition that continuous research would be needed to "determine whether the San Pedro or Santa Cruz Valley side of the Memorial was the most probable one…taken by Coronado. Data on later Spanish and Indian trails in this vicinity…must be examined in this context." Research pertinent to flora and fauna of the region was highly recommended. Specifically, they recommended research to "determine the location of San Heronimo, the site founded for the main portion of Coronado's army, believed to have been located close to or on the San Pedro River near the International Border." The writers of the Master Plan believed that the location and identification of that site would "have a direct bearing on the location of Coronado's route across the present international border."[383]

The interpretive program, a prerequisite for a successful memorial, would be developed. At that point, no reception facilities existed. The plan proposed a contact station at the projected parking area or nearby on a small flat above the parking area. The building would also serve as an administrative center for the superintendent and a ranger. Its exhibits would be placed either in the lobby or along the walls of the assembly room. Their primary focus would be expeditions that passed across the International Border in the vicinity of the Memorial with emphasis given the Coronado Expedition of 1540-42. Another function of the building would be to host periodic lecturers who would present on "various phases of Spanish expansion or events regarding the exploration of the Southwest." Such lectures would round out the significance of Coronado National Memorial.[384] In anticipation that Mexico would one day commit to an "international" memorial, the Master Plan stated "it will be necessary to correlate exhibits and lectures accordingly and perhaps handle the bilingual aspects of the interpretative program in a different fashion."[385]

In 1954, the location of the Memorial had drawbacks. Electrical power, for example "ended one mile east at the Sparkes' ranch," and delayed development of contact-comfort-administrative structures at the Memorial. Still, the writers of the Master Plan maintained "This proposed location has been selected because the Mexican government may yet set aside land immediately to the south, and assist in making this an international memorial."[386] The Master Plan warned that, "Any future action by the Mexican government concerning an addition to the…south side may affect the location and operation of the proposed headquarters area."[387] The location of the parking area and its facilities was pivotal because from there "all traffic to the proposed overlook and interpretive devices will be controlled."[388] To facilitate the visitor experience two-fold leaflets and self-guiding pamphlets would be provided to visitors at that point.

Near the parking lot, the Master Plan called for a small structure with limited office space to be used as a visitor contact and comfort station.

Temporarily, the office would be used for operations purposes whilst the headquarters area was developed. Although contemplated, the plan did not include workrooms, study facilities, collections, library, darkroom, or storage rooms. In time, the proposed headquarters area and contact building would become "the primary interpretive center." Graphic exhibits, a large assembly room for orientation talks, meetings, and film projection as well as an information booth, library, comfort station, and administrative offices would be a part of that structure.[389]

Development of Coronado National Memorial featured the parking area with a contact station; the overlook; the residential-utility area; and, the headquarters area. At that point, no facilities existed even though a "previous Master Plan proposed a short road to be constructed up the backbone of the ridge from the present forest service road for a distance of approximately 1000 feet terminating in a parking area where a contact comfort station was proposed." From there, two trails would continue to the proposed Coronado Peak Overlook and interpretive exhibit.[390] This proposal was eliminated because the 12% grade was too steep to reduce. Construction of it would leave "a very noticeable scar on the ridge visible for many miles;" and, its developmen would destroy or cause the removal of certain "species of nature, shrubs, and flora" which could be used on the self-guiding nature trail.[391] Nonetheless, a trail to the Coronado Peak overlook would start at the parking lot.[392]

Meanwhile, Leslie P. Arnberger, an NPS Naturalist; worked to identify local plants; and, Al Shroeder, an NPS Archeologist, had begun historical research regarding the Coronado Expedition.[393] In the midst of the writing of the Master Plan, Gastellum's boss, John M. Davis, General Superintendent, inspected the Memorial site. He concluded, "Any master plan prepared for Coronado National Memorial can at best be only guesswork until such time as a boundary survey of this new area has been made. A boundary survey was scheduled as of the spring of 1953, but apparently it has not been possible to have this work done."[394] Accompanied by Howard Marsh, a certain O'Neil from the Washington Office, and a certain Allman, from the Western Office, Davis visited the site and matched the draft master plan to the terrain. They all agreed that "it would be practicable to build a road to the proposed residential and utility area as now shown."[395] The residential and utility area was chosen "primarily because this is the only portion of the area where the ground is relatively sloping or flat and where there is an assurance of obtaining a sufficient water supply."[396] In later correspondence, reviewers of the draft Master Plan said they could not envision sufficient space for the residential and administrative areas. Once convinced that space existed within the boundary, all disagreements on that issue disappeared.

According to the plan, the Overlook would be reached through a self-guiding foot trail from the picnic area above the parking lot.[397] It would include trailside exhibits and/or a small building to facilitate interpretation. Generally, the structure would remain unattended and interpretive devices would explain the significance of the area. Small "pertinent" exhibits could be added to the orientation structure "to round out the story presented." Meanwhile, publications and library facilities would be housed in the contact station below. The Overlook, the highest point on the Memorial from where the Coronado Expedition story could be told and the topographic features of the land in all directions could be explained, tied the area together internationally.

Burroughs had his work cut out for him. His job, as soon as fiscal year monies became available, would be to implement the Master Plan. By late April, General Superintendent Davis learned that within 30 days, electrical power would be available to the Memorial.[398]

In the midst of establishing the Memorial, the National Park Service contended with an old wound that everyone thought had disappeared over the years. Sometime in late spring and early summer of 1955, Senators Carl Hayden and Barry Goldwater received separate petitions with very similar letters.[399] Subsequently, Hayden sent a copy to Tolson writing, attached is "a letter addressed to me on May 24, by several residents of Nogales protesting appropriations of funds for the Coronado National Memorial."[400] Hayden asked him to write a reply to it. The old wound stemmed from the rejection of Nogales as a place for the Memorial; but historians could not conclude that the Coronado Expedition entered Arizona through there. The Nogales protestors resented that the Memorial was placed in an out-of-the-way site near Bisbee. The Nogales letter read:

> We feel that the expenditure of these funds for improvements to the 'Coronado National Memorial' is extremely wasteful. The doubtful benefits…derived from this in no way justify the expense involved in the improvements. First, there is nothing of historical value that would attract the public. Second, it is… doubtful whether Coronado chose a mountain to cross over when there were valleys on either side. Third, there is nothing of natural beauty, no trees with exception of scrub brush. Fourth, even though used for camp sites or picnic grounds, the cost of establishing such and the developing of water would be far too excessive…this particular spot is hot in summer and cold in winter. There is just nothing there to warrant such expenditure.[401]

The Nogales protestors wondered why a "monument" could not be established on the border instead of a "memorial" at the chosen site.

In his response, Tolson rebutted the Nogales claim explaining the decision for a memorial on the site chosen for the Coronado National Memorial versus a monument anywhere along the border. He wrote:

> When the plan to commemorate the Coronado expedition was first discussed in 1939 and 1940, the idea of constructing a monument on the international boundary, where the expedition entered what is now the United States, was considered and abandoned in favor of setting aside the above-mentioned land area. It was hoped that Mexico would set aside a companion area in Sonora, to constitute an international memorial, which would, it was believed, assist in maintaining good relationships between Mexico and United States. The Mexican Government, however, after many years of consideration, failed to establish its portion of the international memorial....[402]

For the moment, his response appeared adequate.

Doubtless, Tolson must have wondered why the people of Nogales had not responded for nearly twenty years. Yet, in 1939 when the question was raised about how to commemorate the 400th anniversary of the Coronado *entrada*, the people of Nogales felt that the $10,000 appropriation would be suitable for the erection of a monument in their city. In his support of the Nogales proposal, Clinton P. Anderson, then the managing director of the Coronado Exposition Commission, defied historical correctness when he, in 1939 wrote that he was "inclined to agree" with the people of Nogales in their agrument. Anderson added that they had hoped for a monument and a museum. There, he said, tourists "passing to and from Mexico" could see them, "not off in a ravine which Coronado may have followed, and hence is bound to become inaccessible, unproductive, and, therefore, a temptation to those people who did want to pass into disuse and eventually into abandonment.[403]

The Nogales proposal was not new, and their protest was based on the resurrection of an old idea. The idea of a monument to commemorate the event had been, as Congressman Morgan had told Anderson, replaced by the proposed international memorial and a museum.[404] One would have thought, especially after the passage of the Act of August 18, 1941, that the issue had long been settled.

Hoping to soothe the Nogales protestors, Hayden reminded them that the 1949 commission appointed by Governor Garvey included James V. Robins, Mayor of Nogales.[405] If the Nogales taxpayers hoped to make money an issue, Hayden pointed out that the Memorial "does not anticipate the expenditures of a 'vast sum of money' either in the immediate future or at a later date."[406]

On the heels of the Nogales protest, came another, which did make taxpayer money an issue. Twenty-eight residents from Tucson, Elgin, Tumacacori, Wilcox, Amado, Hereford, Patagonia, Douglas, Santa Cruz River, inclusive of two from Los Angeles and Rivera, California, wrote Senator Goldwater protesting the appropriation of taxpayers' money for Coronado National Memorial. One of the signers was Fred d'Albini. They wrote:

> One newspaper article states 'that the creation of the 'Coronado National Memorial' symbolizes the importance of the Spanish background of the history and culture of the entire Southwest… and the close relationship still existing today between Arizona… the Union and the neighboring states of the Republico [sic] of Mexico….' We cannot see that justification….we do not see the necessity of setting aside a piece of ground miles away from any bordering state to symbolize a unity that is a natural one….when this project first originated, it was with the idea of Mexico also contributing an adjacent piece of ground, which they have evidently declined to do, we therefore do not see that it symbolizes the close relationship between Arizona and the Republico [sic] of Mexico…[407]

The strongly worded protest seemed aimed at the people of Bisbee. "We feel," they added, "that there are undoubtedly some selfish individual interests connected with the pushing of this project, and any historical value is very questionable. We, as taxpayers, do object to throwing money into the improvement of a project like this without some real reason for it."[408] The reply was the same penned by Tolson to the people of Nogales.

Halseth, of course, quipped, in a letter to Hayden, "I was as much surprised as you were at this late objection to the 'Coronado National Memorial' by the Nogales group; but a recent talk with Margaret Rockwell confirmed my suspicion that the action was motivated by a self-interest in grazing permits."[409] His comment may well have been aimed at other protestors.

Meanwhile, Sparkes, while visiting in Prescott, smelt a rat. She contacted Folsom Moore and Mrs. James Allison to "investigate and take what action they might feel would be necessary."[410] She also asked them to speak with Burroughs at his temporary headquarters[411] to inform him of the protest. A month later, Moore reported his conclusions to Hayden. After spending an afternoon in Nogales investigating the names on the petition, Moore concluded that they were of little consequence. But, he hoped to find out who circulated the petition in the first place. "My guess," he wrote,

> is that a Chochise [sic] county cow man named d'Albini is the gentleman, but must reserve judgment until I am certain. I

know that d'Albini had such a petition in Cochise county asking signatures, but evidently failed to receive proper cooperation, so has let the matter rest.[412]

The matter seems to have been dropped. The allegations against d'Albini were never substantiated beyond Moore's and Sparkes' suspicions.

Meanwhile, Burroughs expressed his confusion at that news. He knew that local ranchers were generally opposed to the Memorial. He believed, nonetheless, that "cordial" relations with D'Albini and the other local cattlemen existed. In addition, he had consulted with D'Albini "provided for cattle guards, trails, driveways and fencing which will, in fact, make his operation there easier than at present." When he had last spoken with him, D'Albini "was quite in agreement with the whole thing."[413]

Burroughs speculated on other possible factors, including general opposition to any improvement of roads that would bring additional visitors to the area. He thought it probable that there was some sort of alliance between ranchers on the U.S. side and the Cananea Cattle Company in Mexico. He pointed out that the planned development reintroduced the international concept with a visitor center on the border, which could exert new pressure on the Greenes to give up land for the Memorial. If the proposal was defeated within the United States it would lessen the likelihood that it would again be brought up in Mexico. Finally, Burroughs summarized the "personal antagonisms" and "long-standing feuds" that may have contributed to the petitions. Evidently D'Albini was antagonistic toward the Memorial because of his dislike for Sparkes, who was deeply involved in the Memorial as a promoter, landlord, and part-time employee. He also had a grudge against his neighbor, and fellow rancher, Joe Zaleski, whose land NPS was negotiating to buy as part of the planned development.[414]

The following year, the Bisbee Chamber of Commerce, still under Sparkes, reported that "Preliminary plans and studies of the entire area are being made; also, a boundary survey of the area, made by the Bureau of Land management, and a topographic survey of the area. Need for improvement of the road is stressed. An ever increasing number of tourists, interested students and scientists from many states visit the Memorial."[415]

On February 11, 1957, Sparkes wrote Hayden saying "Something must be done on the Montezuma Canyon road—travel has increased since the park improvements at the pass, Coronado Peak Trail, etc., the use by the Ft. Huachuca Military, and general travel between Santa Cruz and Cochise counties to such an extent that the road merits widening, surfacing and sudt palative of some kind laid….Surely between the Forest, the Park, the Army something should be done. So far it has been a 'ring around the rosy."[416] To that, NPS Director Wirth stated that the "road is, I believe, a part of the State or Federal Aid Highway system and its reconstruction would, therefore, be handled by the State Highway Commission."[417]

The Memorial's development moved quietly in the late 1950s. Then, on February 27, 1957, Superintendent Philip Welles, reported on a surprise visit to his office by several gentlemen. The visitors were "Mr. Galvn [sic] Wilkins, Division Engineer, Bureau of Public Roads, Phoenix, Mr. Jacob Erickson, District Engineer, Bureau of Public Roads, Mr. William E. Willey, State Highway Engineer, Phoenix and Mr. Folsom Moore of Cochise County." Welles said they told him that they were there to inspect the Montezuma Canyon Road, look at visitation numbers to the Memorial, and examine the need for "getting an improved road to the pass and beyond." Welles explained that NPS policy "was as much as possible to avoid responsibility for the maintenance of this or other through roads."

Regarding a survey, all agreed, however, that one was needed to make cost estimates for road improvements. Additionally, it was suggested that an "air survey showing contours and at a fairly large scale would be invaluable." That discussion raised questions regarding the extension of the survey to include the road as far as the pass. To that Welles commented, "Since the bids will be opened on March 17, I felt there was hardly time to re-write them even if the Service should wish to extend the survey but I did think that perhaps the company winning the contract should be open for a dicker." In the course of the discussion, Welles told them of plans to acquire lands at the "east end of the memorial."[418] The visit, though pleasant, caused Welles to pause. Warily, he documented the meeting in case repercussions would result.

The visitors had a slightly different view of the same meeting. As a result of the visit with Welles, nonetheless, Moore requested that the Park Service extend the aerial survey to cover the canyon from the Forest Boundary to the western end of the Memorial limits on the west slope of Huachuca Mountains. Welles appeared uncomfortable with the request explaining that he doubted that the Park Service would want to spend more money for the survey of the ground where the construction would take place. To that, Moore asked Welles to write the Regional Director "at Albuquerque" (meaning Santa Fe) about the matter, and to send him a copy of his letter. Moore felt that as the Park Service was going to bring in an aerial survey party for the small survey outlined in the call for bids, it seemed to him that they could make the survey of the road—at least to the Pass—for but little more cost. In his letter to Hayden in which he discussed his meeting with Welles, he asked him to encourage the NPS to choose a bidder at the March 17 opening. "It will speed the possibility of road construction at least five years," he wrote, "And it should be of material benefit in the laying out of trails, a labor which is now being done by Memorial personnel on foot."[419]

Moore suggested that a better survey could be made with a combination aerial-and-on-the-ground effort.

After the "Coronado International Memorial" proposal was made, the first order of business called for the creation of its boundaries. The enabling legislation provided that the President of the United States would declare, by proclamation, any lands within the dedicated area for the Memorial's use. Although the Memorial was restricted from causing any recreational or other development within a sixty-foot strip north of the international boundary between the United States and Mexico, a basic description of the Memorial's holdings were presented in the legislation. Based on the Gila and Salt River meridian, the original boundaries totaled 2,880 acres.[420] The basic grant of land that would establish "Coronado International Memorial" would be the start of a land acquisitions history filled with turns and twists.

Writing in *Arizona Highways* in 1957, Richard E. Klinck noted that Coronado National Memorial was established without fanfare. "The memorial itself," he wrote,

> has but a short history. The establishment of Coronado National Memorial was done quietly and there were few who were aware of the addition of this newest of Arizona's many and varied national park units, which include a park, 16 monuments and a recreational area. It entered the national park registry just four years ago, approved by an Act of Congress on July 9, 1952, and officially signed into being by presidential proclamation on November 9 of that year. Previous to this the lands contained within the memorial had all been a part of Coronado National Forest. Units of this forest are spread across southern Arizona and edge over into New Mexico. One unit of the forest still surrounds the memorial.[421]

Klinck noted that C.A. Burroughs was the Memorial's first and only permanent ranger. Anecdotally, Klinck commented that when Burroughs reached Coronado National Memorial, "he found he was thus superintendent of no one other than himself, and he had arrived just in time to really go to work"[422] –undoubtedly an oft-quoted remark by Burroughs, himself. As an observer, Klinck wrote that Burroughs "found himself with his hands full of a variety of major tasks, plus the initiation of the fulfullment of a grand and glorious ideal."[423]

Burroughs's administration paved the way for future developments that were already underway. Klinck told readers of the Mission 66 planning, the widening of the road through Montezuma Pass for additional parking at the summit, and a newly built half-mile Coronado Mountain Trail. The trail would take visitors to the crest of the Huachucas to a view shed of the wide valley below where Coronado presumably passed. "This peak" wrote Klinck, " is about to be christened Coronado Peak."[424] Additionally, Superintendent Burroughs hoped to get Coronado National Memorial's first publication. Of it Klinck wrote, "A Southwestern National Monuments booklet will soon be available in printed form which will provide a silent, though well-versed, guide for those who follow this fascinating trail."[425]

A boon for the National Park Service, Mission 66 was intended to develop and staff National Park Service areas for the wisest possible use, the maximum enjoyment of visitors, and the greatest protection of the cultural and natural resources within the system. Construction, therefore, formed an important element of the program. Calling for modern roads, well-planned trails, utilities, camp and picnic grounds, and the structures needed to support administrative and public uses, Congress, in the mid-1950s, instituted the Mission 66 program in the National Park Service to meet the requirements of an expected 80 million visitors in 1966. As a long-range program, the plan recognized that it would take ten years to accomplish the goal in time for the National Park Service's 50th year anniversary. The plan was timely for the needs of Coronado National Memorial.

The 1961 "Master Plan for the Conservation and Use of Coronado National Memorial: Mission 66 Edition" presented a clear statement that reflected the direction planning documents would assume regarding the role of key park personnel in implementing the approved programs. By all means, the superintendent would bear sole responsibility in directing all operations in the Memorial to accomplish the Park Mission and to assure efficient operation of the entire park organization. Under his direction, interpretation, ranger services, and maintenance and operation of the physical facilities would be delegated to appropriate members of his staff. The declarative statements for each one was as follows:

> *Interpretation*: Acquire, assemble and present knowledge about the Memorial for the protection of park resources and the enriching of visitor.
> *Ranger Services*: Protect park resources and facilities and the welfare of Memorial visitors.
> *Maintenance & Operation of Physical Facilities*: Operate and maintain the physical plant in the manner contributing to the efficient functioning of the Memorial staff, to the welfare of visitors and to preservation of park resources.[426]

The pattern for the accomplishment of park objectives that had evolved in previous planning documents during the 1950s, was, by 1961 solidly, entrenched.

In the mid-1950s, the Memorial, despite its long history dating to 1940, was basically only three years old! Its development had been sparse, its staff skeletal, its funding minimal, and its identity incipient. The Memorial lacked administrative and visitor facilities. Full interpretation services could not be carried out without an interpretive center. The limited recreational facilities, such as picnic areas, needed to be raised to a level of compatibility of other parks. On the eve of Mission 66 development at Cornado National Memorial, the superintendent was still living in a trailer house and his office was a small shed, both on rented ground. Mission 66 responded to park requirements for administrative and interpretive facilities, and housing for staff at Coronado National Memorial.

A contact station at Montezuma Pass was among the priorities. The plan called for exhibits there to complement those in the visitor center and the trailside exhibits on Coronado Peak. The purpose of the combined exhibits would be to stress the importance of the Memorial in commemorating "the Coronado expedition and the effect of Spanish explorations and colonization upon the history and development of this section of the United States."[427] Beyond enhancing the visitor experience, the Mission 66 planners hoped that the NPS visitor center would encourage the Mexican Government "in the establishment of the international aspect of the Memorial which was the original plan."[428]

Aside from the exhibits, picnic and recreational sites had been on the discussion table since the 1940s. Mission 66 would provide picnic areas for daytime use. Such areas would encourage visitors and local residents to use them. The controlled environment would enchance educational purposes as "the area abounds in plant and animal life."[429] Safety-wise, the regulated picnic areas at the Memorial would encourage people to use them instead of other uncontrolled sites, thus preventing "the possibility of fires spreading from undeveloped sites."[430]

The cost of the Mission 66 at Coronado National Memorial in 1957 was calculated to be $603,200. Roads and trails would cost $98,000; and, buildings and utilities would run $505,200.[431] Given the lack of facilities at the Memorial, the planners stressed the necessity of administrative facilities for protection and maintenance of the area. They hoped to make the Memorial an attraction for visitor enjoyment. Aware of the deficiencies, the planners realized that the project would not be completed for several years. Field surveys and detailed construction plans had yet to be developed; they would take time. In the end, the planners were confident that "the area will remain a day-use area, but will provide picnic or lunch areas for those who enjoy a few hours in the open and appreciate the beauties of the woodland in which the area is located."[432]

By October 1, 1957, the Prospectus for Coronado National Memorial was approved.[433] The Prospectus would clarify the direction of Mission 66 developments and bring the Master Plan and its development outline in line with it. Upon reviewing the Prospectus, Director Wirth wrote the Regional Director in Santa Fe saying portentously, "numerous suggestions and opinions were advanced, many of them on matters that we believe will automatically resolve themselves in the normal course of events."[434]

Wirth's transmittal included a "Notice of Approval: Coronado National Memorial Prospectus." The approval included additions to the Prospectus inclusive of needed basic scientific data aimed at assisting park management in the protection and interpretation of park resources. Specifically, the recommendation was made for archeological data that would identify the prehistory of the area.

Other recommendations concerned grazing privileges and the related fencing issue. The reviewers wrote "The proposals for the purchase of grazing permits are not feasible as appropriations for such purchase are not obtainable. The statements concerning such elimination by purchase… should be revised to indicate elimination or reduction by negotiation."[435] As regards fencing, it was recommended that "the fencing along the summit of Montezuma Peak, which bisects the trail from the parking area to the peak, be relocated to exclude all of the public use area."[436]

The reviewers postponed their comments on the section on Park Organization pending further review and over-all evaluation of all planning documents for Coronado National Memorial to better determine the progress and requirements necessary. Staffing and operating costs, for example, were established only as a guide for future planning. The recurring costs for operations called for nine employees—five permanent and four seasonal employees totaling $53,790 per year. Four permanent employees, aided by three seasonals, were slotted for Management and Protection. The total cost for the seven employees would be $36,390 per year. In Maintenance and Rehabilitation, one permanent and one seasonal would be hired at the annual cost of $17,400. Wirth agreed with reviewers that the program staffing needs must be "more definitely defined."[437]

The two areas of development were reviewed: public use facilities and service facilities. In the area of public use facilities, Wirth prioritized construction of the visitor center, contact station, administration building, improvement of roads and trails, comfort station, picnic area, and partial fencing.[438] The need was clear; the subject Mission 66 Prospectus stated that the day-use area by visitors would average from 2 to 4 hours per visit.[439] The service facilities priorities included the extension of utility systems, employee housing, utility building, and partial area fencing. The cost for both categories, as stipulated earlier, totaled $603,200.

The review comments and recommendations were aimed at controlling the development of the Memorial. Regarding cost estimates, Wirth warned that "Acceptance of the development schedule is not to be construed as a final approval of each specific item or a firm estimate of cost as such is dependent on further refinement of the proposals, to be accomplished through established planning and estimating procedures."[440] Wirth, however, went further, stating, "Any deviations from the intent of the principles and proposals set forth in the approved prospectus shall constitute a revision of the prospectus and will require the clearance of the Regional and Design and construction Offices, and approval by the Washington Office."[441]

In the months preceding the approved Prospectus, much discussion and planning had occurred in which many ideas and concepts as well as wishes evolved regarding the development of Coronado National Memorial. Everyone recognized that the Memorial would commemorate the pioneering efforts of the Coronado Expedition as well as celebrate the positive relationships and the common history experienced by the United States and Mexico. Hope remained that Mexico would eventually join in commemorating the ideals for which the Memorial stood.

By March 1957, planning documents were simultaneously being developed to provide data for the Prospectus. The Land Status report indicated that the Federal acreage for the Memorial totaled 2,745.33 acres. Additionally, the boundary status report proposed that "in order to provide a desirable area for the development of a headquarters site, and picnic area," it would be necessary to "include approximately 75.33 acres of Forest Service land and 100 acres of privately owned land belonging to Mr. Joe Zaleski."[442] Although Zaleski's land would have to be purchased at the cost of $100 to $200 per acre, Forest Service land could be transferred from the Coronado National Forest. The cost of land had risen because vacation homesites in the area were being subdivided and sold at that competitive cost.[443] Moreover, the reactivation of "Fort Huachuca and Atomic Energy" accounted for the increased land activity in the general area.[444]

The "Buildings" section of the Master Plan Development Outline for the Memorial drawn in May 1957, contained information related to climate, temperature, prevailing winds, altitude, latitude, topography, vegetation, soil data, snake and insect considerations such as scorpions, cone-nose bugs, "numerous flies," and rattlesnakes. The Plan offered recommendations for construction plans and their attendant architectural influences.

At the time, it was felt that the architectural design would be based, not on Spanish Colonial influences, but on the fact that the architectural styles of the area were "non-descript." So, it was decided to adopt "a simple, functional, contemporary design best suited to the landscape [rather] than to emphasize the historical aspect."[445] In time, that sentiment changed and a style would be adopted "reminiscent of the early Spanish-Mexican ranch type buildings, still to be seen in modern buildings along the route taken by Coronado through the Mexican west coast states. The burnt adobe walls, red tiled roofs and general architectural theme used in the present administration building and contact station," completed in 1960, is carried on in the public buildings of the Memorial.[446] Indeed, the Construction Data report of 1963 stated that "Residences should conform to the general pattern of the recently constructed residences with burnt adobe wall, low pitched roofs, wide overhangs on porches and adjacent terraces."[447]

In 1957, building materials dominated discussions regarding construction plans. A long list of building stones and sources were identified in Naco, Douglas, including an entity, that sold coarse rock, called "Paul Spur" between Bisbee and Douglas. Sand and concrete could be found in Douglas; Western Yellow Pine logs in Bisbee; lumber in Tucson and Bisbee; concrete blocks in Tucson and Bisbee; brick and tile, mixed concrete, and plaster in Tucson and Bisbee; reinforcing steel in Bisbee; and adobe bricks in Naco. Later, in 2002, John Cook, former Intermountain Regional Director, commented on the origins of the adobe bricks used in some of the structures at Coronado National Memorial. The bricks, he said were the "burnt bricks that Phil Welles got out of Mexico,"[448] meaning in the Cananea vicinity. Although the full range of materials could be found in Tucson, about 100 miles away, many of the items could be acquired in Bisbee.[449] Therefore, the list demonstrated the availability of construction matierials. Work at the Memorial commenced as soon as contracts were released for that purpose.

The report included a study on soils for conservation purposes. The Soil and Moisture Conservation segment of the Master Plan Development Outline compiled in July 1955 specified that the soils of the Memorial were largely clay loam. On ridges and rock, the soil was thin and close to the surface. Given the mountainous topography with steep slopes with some cliffs of conglomerate and limestone, the planners figured that runoff from rainfall during the late summer could cause a drainage problem in the area. Even though soil erosion was classified as slight on 90% of the Memorial and "moderate in the remainder," grazing had caused much of the erosion. The planners agreed that fencing to exclude livestock would help restore vegetation, particularly, brush, grass, and woodland, and ultimately return the area to its natural state. As the Memorial area fell within the Hereford Soil Conservation District, the park's efforts would certainly benefit the watershed of the San Pedro Valley.[450]

Years later, in the 1960s, after the Memorial had been firmly established and construction programs were underway, did Park personnel begin to realize the park's identity and place within the National Park Service. The Master Plan revisions in 1962 and 1963, the Design Analysis and Construction Data reports for the Master Plan for the Preservation and Use of Coronado National Memorial ("rev. March 1964") demonstrated that progress had been made.

The Memorial's experience since 1952 showed that visitation was relatively light without marked seasonal peaks. The anticipated construction of a reservoir to the "westward in Parker Canyon" raised hope that it would cause "an increase in visitation and through traffic via Montezuma Pass."[451] Park staff hoped that the hazardous and unimproved Nogales-Bisbee Road would be improved "in the immediate future" so that access from the East Entrance to Montezuma Pass would be facilitated.[452] Meanwhile, the Memorial could be accessed from Nogales, Tucson, and Bisbee via State Highways 82 and 92.

On the Memorial, a Residential-Utility Spur Road led to the administration, residential, and maintenance areas. From there, a primitive Maintenance Road ran from the Residential-Utility Spur Road by way of a 25 foot easement through Coronado National Forest land for some 300 feet to the NPS water storage tank on the slope above the headquarters area.[453]

Near the administrative building, constructed in 1959, which also housed the main visitor contact station and public restrooms, a visitor parking area had been constructed. Another contact station, the Montezuma Pass Contact Station would eventually serve as the beginning point of the proposed "nature trail."[454] The existing pit toilets would eventually be replaced by a comfort station served by a septic tank.[455]

Near there, a Lunch Area Spur Road provided access to a 21-site lunch area for those who would bring their lunches. Another proposed spur road mentioned in the Design Analysis report would lead to an unmanned interpretive shelter at the International Border.[456]

Mission 66 provided for water-use projects. In 1964, a drilled well immediately southwest of the Residential area provided water. Water was pumped to a 50,000-gallon storage tank on the mountainside north of the headquarters. A gravity-flow system from the tank to the entire headquarters development supplied water for park needs. Water problems plagued the Montezuma Pass development. There, the planners, hoped that water would be collected in a catchment from the parking area run-off, or, at very least, be hauled up from the headquarters area.[457] Similarly, a gravity-collection system, septic tank, and the drain field in the administrative area disposed sewage. The lunch area was serviced by a comfort station with a separate septic system.[458]

Regarding other utilities, the Memorial fared comparably to other rural areas. An REA power line, for example, delivered electric power to the Park, although Montezuma Pass still lacked power. Electricity provided fuel for heating and cooking. Fireplaces augmented heat in residential areas. Commercial telephone service, moreover, sprang from the electrical power system, but the Globe network by radio facilitated contact with the General Superintendent's Office in Globe.[459] By 1964, the Memorial was serviced by a 12-party line telephone system,[460] a common practice of the day.

Fencing continued to be an issue for park planners at the Memorial. Although by 1964 the residential-administrative-maintenance complex had been fenced thwarting further trespass by cattle, it was felt that additional fencing could be required in the future.[461] The Memorial's policy regarding grazing, however, had been clearly stated. Principally, "there should be no objection to moderate grazing so long as other biological factors are not upset." Although park planners had correctly noted that the range livestock industry was a significant "aspect of Spanish culture,"[462] others argued myopically that grazing was incompatible with the park theme because Coronado "did not actually introduce livestock grazing as an industry in the southwest."[463] Nonetheless, it was recognized that he was, in fact, the first European to introduce horses, cattle, goats, and sheep into the region. Still, through Spanish-Mexican settlers, the cattle industry, of great importance to the west, had been firmly established. At that time, Mission 66 planners felt that it was logical to interpret the cattle industry from its earliest Iberian times to the present.[464]

Meantime, the Memorial went ahead with its plans to implement fencing and construction programs that had an effect on park administration and visitor use. During those years, all plans came to fruition and Coronado National Memorial came into being with an evolving identity as a National Park Service unit. Nothwithstanding the National Park Service's planning processes, public support was vital to the effort, particularly in the early days of the Memorial's founding.

Chapter VI

The "keen interest of...the people of Cochise County and elsewhere:" Grassroots Support for the Memorial

> *I have done a good deal of work also to protect the claims against the Coronado Exposition idea...This has meant work with the Arizona Commission, The Forestry, U.S., Park and other officials.* –- Grace M. Sparkes to Burdett Moody, 1940.

> *This area is truly a wonderland and I am most anxious to see it given the recognition it deserves by both Mexico and the United States.* –- Grace M. Sparkes to Senator Carl Hayden, 1947

Official planning for the Memorial was longstanding and involved a number of individuals who gave of their time toward this worthy effort.[465] On March 10, 1936, Frank "Boss" Pinkley of the National Park Service wrote to Gus R. Michaels of Bisbee, Arizona regarding a proposed International Park to be located at the south end of the Huachuca Mountains. Michaels replied that he had spoken with several people, all of whom were enthused with the idea but were not entirely certain what the idea entailed from the government's side. Michaels added that "the area we had in mind on the American side of the line, is at present all within the National Forest, and can possibly be made as extensive as desired, extending over through Santa Cruz County and north as far as Fort Huachuca."[466]

Pinkley's letter was a response to one sent by Michaels after he and his colleagues had seen newspaper articles about the possibility of a park on both sides of the international boundary where it runs through the Huachucas. The movement for commemoration of the 400th anniversary of Coronado's expedition was already underway in New Mexico, when it spread to Arizona through the efforts of local and state boosters.[467] After discussing it, Michaels and friends contacted Pinkley, even at this early date. As the longtime Executive Secretary of the Bisbee Chamber of Commerce, Michaels's name appeared early in the story of Coronado Memorial. He, and the Bisbee Chamber of Commerce, would remain involved with planning and promoting the Memorial for some time.

Michaels and the Bisbee Chamber of Commerce were involved in another, contemporary, project commemorating the early Spanish colonial heritage in southeastern Arizona. In early 1938, they made plans to celebrate the four-hundredth anniversary of the 1539 arrival of Coronado's predecessor, Fray Marcos de Niza, into present Arizona. To mark where the friar entered the state, the Bisbee Chamber of Commerce formed a committee to commemorate the event.[468] F.C. Bledsoe, President of the Chamber, contacted many of the same people who would become involved in the Coronado Memorial. Among them were M.J. Cunningham, Chair of the Committee; John Wood, Vice-President of the Chamber of Commerce, Vice-Chair; S.S. Shattuck, also a Vice-President of the Chamber of Commerce; Reverend James P. Davis; Folsom Moore; and John Ball. Mrs. J.H. Macia, of Tombstone, was also written in on the first list.[469] Shortly, she was replaced by Harlie Cox.[470]

The Fray Marcos de Niza Association of the Bisbee Chamber of Commerce met in early April. Their plan became evident when Gus Michaels wrote to Arizona state officials to ask their help in the planning of a one hundred foot high pyramid topped by a larger than life statue to be placed in the vicinity of Palominas.[471] In August 1938, the "Four Hundredth Anniversary Committee" met again. They now had a plan to build their monument in a roadside park to be located two and one-half miles west of Palominas. The plan indicated that the land would be owned by the state Highway Department and the monument would be constructed by the Works Progress Administration.[472] In November, sketches were considered and a design in the shape of a cross was approved by the Bisbee Committee.[473]

The monument to Fray Marcos was never built at Palominas. Instead, a monument was erected at Lochiel, some twenty miles, as the crow flies, west of the eventual site of Coronado National Memorial, and further from the San Pedro River Valley. It is not entirely clear from available evidence why the Lochiel site was selected, but the choice may have been the result of a struggle between Bisbee and Nogales. Father Bonaventure Oblasser, O.F.M., a leading booster of the Fray Marcos Monument, later wrote that he did not blame Bisbee or Nogales for the isolated location of the Monument, implying that their efforts had something to do with the decision. Instead, he criticized "those who took me from Arizona, in the midst of my efforts for this cause."[474] He was, evidently, referring to his reassignment by his superiors in the Franciscan order.

Although Bisbee and Nogales competed for which should be honored as the site of the entrada of Coronado, they, along with Lochiel, seem to have clashed over the route of Fray Marcos as well. Fr. Oblasser recalled later that only after he had been informed that the Bisbee plan could not be carried out did he support the Lochiel site. In the end, his Niza project received financial support from Nogales and probably some help in locating the monument as well.

In 1941, Oblasser hoped to combine the Niza Monument at Lochiel with the Coronado Memorial project. Given that the Niza Monument was a thousand dollars in debt after its construction, he hoped the Coronado Memorial would absorb the debt.[475] Oblasser did not like that the Niza Monument was located on a little used dirt road in an out-of-the-way small town. Lochiel was then in terminal decline from its heyday as a border crossing for both legal and illegal products.[476] Connecting it to the larger, better funded, and more accessible proposed Coronado International Memorial would certainly increase its visibility.

Oblasser offered to approach prominent friends in Mexico, who held a higher opinion of Niza than of Coronado, to urge them to cooperate in the Coronado International Memorial.[477] Gus Michaels responded to Oblasser that it was impossible to change the Coronado legislation. He held out the hope that the establishment of the Coronado Memorial would lead to the construction of a highway from Montezuma Canyon to Nogales via Lochiel. That highway would connect the Niza Monument to the Coronado Memorial in both concrete and conceptual terms.[478] Michaels avoided mentioning the outstanding debt of the Niza Monument promoters. Although the Coronado Memorial was developed, the highway was not, and the Niza Monument languished in the obscurity of Lochiel, now a ghost town.

The Coronodo Memorial supporters worked incessantly toward their goal. Michaels participated in the Coronado Memorial site selection process delegation to the Huachucas in 1939-1940. Sparkes was a member of the Arizona's Coronado Cuarto Centennial Commission that visited the Huachucas in 1939 with Park Service Officials and historian Herbert Bolton, whose study decided on Coronado's route through the area. Among them were Bisbee representatives Michaels, John Wood, W.E. Clark, and R.E. Souers.[479] As the Clerk of the Cochise County Board of Supervisors, Clark was deeply involved in the effort to get the Memorial established.[480]

The first Arizona Coronado Cuarto Centennial Commission was named in July 1939 by a proclamation of Governor R.T. "Bob" Jones. Its chair was Stuart M. Bailey. Other members were Charles M. Morgan, Executive Secretary; Odd S. Halseth, Treasurer; Mrs. Foster Rockwell, Vice-Chair; Frank Sufea; Julius Becker; and Rev. Emmett McLoughlin.[481] Halseth was identified a few years later as the Superintendent of Parks and Recreation for the city of Phoenix.[482] Morgan and Bailey's new roles paralleled their positions in the Arizona Historic Memorials Association. That is, they were to press forward with the work of the Cuarto Centennial Commission.[483] Morgan, however, claimed credit for the founding of both the Historic Memorials Association and the Cuarto Centennial Commission.[484] He later called himself "the person responsible for the very existence of the Coronado Memorial."[485]

Morgan may have exaggerated his role a bit, but he was certainly in the middle of Memorial efforts for many years. Like most members of the Arizona Commission, Morgan was not from Cochise County.[486] The Cuarto Centennial Commission members were all from Phoenix except Frank Sufea and Julius Becker, of Flagstaff and Springerville, respectively.[487]

In 1939, a State Advisory Board, complementing the National Committee, was named comprising of one member from each county plus several At-Large and Ex-Officio members. Similarly, most of the At-Large and Ex-Officio Members were from Phoenix, none from Cochise County.[488] By late 1940, turnover on the Commission brought some new members. Among them were Leo Weaver of Flagstaff; Mrs. T.C. O'Connell, identified as a special representative;[489] Nick Hall, Tucson; Peter Riley, Clifton; Andy Matson, Flagstaff; Walter R. Bimson, Phoenix; Miss Georgia Thomas of Ray.[490] The sole member from Cochise County was Mrs. J.H. Macia.[491]

Although listed under her husband's name, customary for the period, Ethel M. Macia operated the Rose Tree Inn in Tombstone.[492] She was part of the first delegation to the Huachuca site in 1939.[493] In February 1940, she wrote to Michaels saying how pleased she was with the conclusion that Coronado had followed the San Pedro River north across the modern international boundary. Because of obligations related to her business, she felt she would not be able to contribute much to choosing a site for the Memorial.[494] Three weeks later, however, Macia was in the Huachucas with the second official delegation.[495] Most of the people in the first 1939 group, returned to visit the proposed site with Ethel Macia, John Ball, R.E. Souers, and a representative of the 'Bisbee Review.'"[496]

After choosing the San Pedro route, Gus Michaels wrote to NPS historian Aubrey Neasham asking when the decision would be made on the site of the Memorial, within or adjacent to the San Pedro Valley.[497] That day, February 29, 1940, a letter went out from the Arizona Commission to the Chambers of Commerce of Bisbee, Douglas, Nogales, Tombstone, and Tucson. Each Chamber would send a representative to meet with state and federal officials in Bisbee on the morning of March 5. From there, the delegation would inspect an unnamed memorial site.[498]

Members of the Coronado Monument Committee of the Bisbee Chamber of Commerce greeted their guests in Bisbee on the appointed day. Among them were Michaels, M.J. Cunningham (Chair), John Wood, Rev. James P. Davis, Folsom Moore, John Ball, Mrs. J.H. Macia,[499] and S.S. Shattuck, President of the Chamber of Commerce.[500] This group joined the second party to the Montezuma Canyon site, on March 5, 1940.[501] Although deeply committed to the Memorial, W.K. Caley, the Mayor of Bisbee, could not make the trip that day.[502]

On March 6, Gus Michaels wrote to Fred Guirey of the Arizona Highway Department notifying him that "the site of the Coronado National Monument and Museum has received the approval of Coronado Commission both National and State and the Park Service. The official announcement of course will have to come from Washington, and should be received within the next week or 10 days." He asked that at least one sign commemorating the actual anniversary of Coronado's passage be ready for display by its date, April 14. He also suggested several places where signs could be placed.[503]

There was obviously much going on behind the scenes that does not show up in these documents. Correspondence dating back to 1936 confirms that the Montezuma Canyon site was considered long before it was visited by delegations, and even before the San Pedro route was confirmed by Bolton and his committee. Local boosters, like Gus Michaels, involved themselves with state and national efforts to promote their region, and directed them to the Huachuca Mountains.

Michaels was involved in other projects connected with the Coronado Memorial as well. In the spring of 1940, right after the decision on the Huachuca site became official, Morgan approached Michaels with an idea to commemorate the Mormon Battalion's travels through the San Pedro Valley in 1846 with an event and a marker. Morgan concluded that "the result will be – besides publicity and a good stunt, another permanent attraction, spang alongside the road to the Fort and the Coronado Museum."[504] Michaels agreed to work for the cooperation of Fort Huachuca in the plan.[505]

Michaels also communicated with local and state interests that were opposed to the Coronado Memorial. In a 1940 exchange with the Arizona

Cattle Growers' Association, he defended the project as positive for tourism, which would expand the tax base of the state and reduce the burden on ranchers and miners. One of its members, Henry D. Lee, who grazed cattle on some of the National Forest land proposed for the Memorial, was against the memorial despite the founding legislation specifically guaranteeing his grazing rights. According to Michaels, Lee "made a ride to every ranch house in southern Arizona and has conveyed the impression to everyone he has met that he is being robbed and put out of business." An editorial that reflected Lee's opinion in the *Arizona Daily Star* demonstrated that he had lobbied its editor as well.[506]

Michaels added that he had consulted "Long established conservative cattlemen who make up your Association," who could not see how Lee could possibly be hurt. Michaels ended his letter by noting that the Bisbee Chamber of Commerce had always consulted the cattlemen on any matter that concerned them. "We would appreciate if the cattlemen would sit down with us and go over this situation in its entirety before sending a barrage of telegrams to our Senators in Washington on a matter which has only been brought to their attention by one individual."[507] Clearly, Michaels was willing to go toe to toe, even with the most powerful interest groups, in defense of the Coronado National Memorial.

Mrs. J.M. Keith's name is also prominent in the documents, but on the other side of the issue from Michaels, the Bisbee Chamber of Commerce, and the Cuarto Centennial Commission. As secretary and spokesperson for the Arizona Cattle Growers' Association, Keith wrote letters defending the rights of ranchers from both real and imagined threats posed by the Coronado Memorial. Keith and the Association pressured Senator Hayden to push for a smaller memorial, and he responded that he had raised its concerns and those of two of its members, Henry Lee and Alex D'Albini, in talks with the Park Service.[508]

Keith asserted that the Cattle Growers' Association was not, "(c)ontrary to the belief which has gotten about," opposed to the memorial idea.[509] However, its first concern was the cattle industry and its success. She thought that parks were "desirable when and where there is any particular person or thing to commemorate." However, she did "not believe the National Monuments and parks would be so attractive if it were not for the stock industry surrounding them." Ranchers, then, were of equal tourism value to historical or natural resources. Keith also disputed the argument that tourism would help to ease the tax burden felt by ranchers.[510]

Thus, Keith defended the cattle growers from memorial plans from the standpoint of tourism as well as economics. She was also willing to adopt a historical tone if the need should arise, as when she suggested that the memorial be restricted to the top of the Huachuca Range, steep terrain less suited to grazing. As if daring anyone to disagree with her, she began her argument with the words, "We know, of course, that Coronado climbed the highest peak...nothing lower than the highest vantage point would have satisfied him." She ended by saying that the memorial should be built at the point that was "actually hallowed by his footsteps."[511]

As has already been discussed above, there is little primary data on Coronado's trip through the San Pedro Valley and no evidence that he approached the Huachuca Mountains or climbed a particular peak. Mrs. Keith and the Arizona Cattle Growers' Association, however, were willing to use any argument available to them to defend their interests; and they saw their interests threatened by the Coronado Memorial.

Local interests, lined up on both sides of the Coronado Memorial issues, waited to hear from Washington as the haggling continued at home. In late June 1940, Senator Hayden's Secretary, Paul Roca, wrote to Folsom Moore, of the Bisbee Chamber of Commerce and its Coronado Monument Committee, to tell him that Hayden had changed the founding legislation to satisfy all the concerns of rancher Henry Lee.[512] During the same week, W.E. Clark, sounding quite exasperated, wrote to Hayden, "Your bill to establish Coronado Monument should meet all objections valid or otherwise...We trust same will be enacted shortly."[513] On July 31, 1940, Hayden's office wrote to Caley, Cunningham, and Shattuck as it became clear that the legislation would not be passed in 1940.[514]

In August 1941, the legislation was passed by Congress. Shortly thereafter, sketches of the proposed memorial were circulated to supporters. Gus Michaels wrote to Margaret Rockwell of the Arizona Cuarto Centennial Commission. He told her that he had looked at the sketches, as had M.J. Cunningham, Folsom Moore, S.S. Shattuck, J.T. Gentry, John Wood, Reverend James Davis, and John Ball, among others.[515] All of these men are mentioned above as Bisbee boosters and longtime supporters of the Coronado Memorial. Little was accomplished toward establishing the Memorial on the ground during World War II. However, the Bisbee contingent continued to correspond with Park Service officials. In 1944, a delegation from the Park Service took a tour of southern Arizona that included a visit to Bisbee and a discussion of the Coronado Memorial. In Bisbee, the group was hosted by Michaels, Shattuck, Wood, and Ball.[516] Shortly after the war, Michaels disappeared from the Bisbee scene and from the historical record concerning the Coronado National Memorial.[517]

It was during World War II that the name of Grace Sparks first surfaced in connection with the Memorial in a big way, though she had shown interest at an earlier date. Sparks first became involved as part-owner of the State of Texas mining properties, in Montezuma Canyon. Upon her father's death, Grace Sparkes became the partner of Burdett Moody of Los Angeles,

California. When she wrote to Moody early in 1939 to inform him of her father's death, Sparkes told Moody that she had not visited the property in two years.[518] From her home in Prescott, Arizona, she attempted to reopen the mine while Moody was only interested in divesting of his share of the State of Texas properties.[519]

As Sparkes tried to convince Moody to invest in the State of Texas, she told him how she was defending their property. "I have done a good deal of work," Sparkes wrote in April 1940, "to protect the claims against the Coronado Exposition idea." She continued that this "has meant work with the Arizona Commission, The Forestry, U.S., Park and other officials."[520] During the same month, Sparkes wrote to Margaret Rockwell of the Arizona Cuarto Centennial Commission. While she assured Mrs. Rockwell of her support for the Memorial, her primary concern was that it not threaten her mine holdings.[521] Sparkes thought she had good reason to fear federal projects on her land. She later informed Moody that the "entire camp was stolen when the CCC [Civilian Conservation Corps] constructed the road through the canyon."[522]

Grace Sparkes had long been involved in tourism and community service in Prescott, serving, for example, as secretary of the Prescott Frontier Days Rodeo from 1915 until 1945.[523] In her book *Our Southwest*, published in 1940, New Mexico author Erna Fergusson described a Prescott Chamber of Commerce representative as a quintessential booster.[524] Sparkes's biographer, Mona Lange McCroskey, identifies this character as Sparkes. Unhappy with the portrayal, Sparkes complained to Clinton P. Anderson of New Mexico. According to McCroskey, Anderson was a friend and co-worker on the Coronado Commission.[525] Sparkes was not listed as a member of the Coronado Commission at the time; nor did she seem to be a very solid supporter. However, as an Arizona booster, Sparkes probably was connected to the Coronado effort.

In May 1944, Sparkes wrote to Senator Hayden, as President of the Arizona Chamber of Commerce Secretaries Association, to inquire about the status of the Coronado project.[526] Hayden addressed letters about the Memorial to Sparkes at Yavapai Associates in Prescott in 1944 and 1945.[527] Yavapai Associates was a non-profit tourist promotion group established by Sparkes and her associates that included civic groups around Yavapai County.[528] Before the end of 1945, Yavapai Associates lost its funding to political infighting and Grace found herself unemployed as of August 1.[529] Shortly thereafter, she left Prescott and moved to the State of Texas mine in Montezuma Canyon.[530] The end of World War II in the same year led to the cessation of mineral production at the mine in 1946.[531] With the help of her brother-in-law, Perry Bones, Sparkes tried to turn the mine into a tourist attraction, "Montezuma Canyon Mineral Village."[532]

Once she lived in Montezuma Canyon, Sparkes became more involved in the Coronado Memorial project as a supporter, soon making contact with both Senator Hayden and the Park Service.[533] In late 1947, Sparkes wrote to Hayden, urging him to take action to make the Memorial a reality. She told Hayden that

> Frankly, this section of Arizona needs your earnest action. The loss of Ft. Huachuca has been a big loss; small mines are hopeful that you will still convince the President of his error in vetoing the premium price plan and that they will be given a chance to live; ranchers and resorts look to this Park for the stimulant they need to induce travel; Bisbee has organized a Sunshine Club to advertise its marvelous climate...[534]

It is interesting to note that Sparkes assumed, at least in her letter, that everyone in the area supported the Memorial. She even invoked the ranchers, whose interest can, at best, be described as tepid.[535]

It is also noteworthy that Sparkes focused on the economic benefits that the Memorial would provide for all of southeastern Arizona, except the miners, among whom Sparkes counted herself. She made a different request, that did not involve the Memorial, to make on their behalf. Sparkes concluded, "I am greatly interested and enthusiastic to see something accomplished."[536] In another 1947 letter to Hayden, Sparkes wrote enthusiastically about the beauty and resources of Montezuma Canyon. She also mentioned that she hoped to get some benefits, such as utilities and a good road, out of the project.[537]

In 1949, with the International Memorial still pending, Governor Dan E. Garvey of Arizona reactivated the state's Coronado Commission. Odd Halseth returned along with new members Ray Busey, former mayor of Phoenix; John Howard Pyle, radio commentator and soon-to-be governor; William R. Mathews, Tucson newspaper publisher; and Nogales mayor James V. Robins.[538] Halseth, whose involvement in the Memorial had continued during the Commission's interregnum, was still in Phoenix, now occupying the post of "City Archaeologist" and an office at the Pueblo Grande Museum.[539]

By the end of 1950, Sparkes was the Chair of the Bisbee Chamber of Commerce National Parks and Monuments Committee. On behalf of the Committee, she wrote to the governor of Arizona urging him to name Margaret Rockwell to the state Coronado Commission.[540] She was supported by M.R. Tillotson of the National Park Service. Tillotson also hoped that someone from the Bisbee Committee would soon join the Arizona Commission. Sparkes suggested members James Brophy and John Wood as likely candidates. Brophy, a former President of the Bisbee Chamber of Commerce, responded by nominating Sparkes.[541]

In December 1950, just before he left office, Governor Garvey named Ben Arnold, the mayor of Coolidge, to the Commission. A month later, in January 1951, Margaret Rockwell was again named to the Commission, along with Grace Sparkes, by the new governor, John Howard Pyle.[542] The appointment of Sparkes marked the first time that a person from the area of the Memorial was chosen for the Arizona Commission. Sparkes was soon elected Chair of the Commission.[543]

In 1952, the other members of the Bisbee Chamber of Commerce National Parks and Monuments Committee were listed as Reverend Father John Howard, M.J. Cunningham, George B. Smith, Arthur Blunt, Nancy Nelms, James Allison, Robert Hargis, Joe Zaleski, Fred McKinney, David Ruth, R.O. Owens, and Charles A. Smith. The Committee had been appointed by Brophy when he was the president of the Chamber of Commerce and was then resolutely supported by his successor, John Caldwell. John Wood and Spencer S. Shattuck were also past presidents of the Chamber who continued to contribute to the Memorial effort.[544]

With Sparkes on the Bisbee Committee were two others who resided closer to the Memorial than to Bisbee. Nancy Carter Nelms bought the Montezuma Ranch in 1949 and, along with manager Don Brooks, ran it as a dude ranch and summer camp for young girls until 1955.[545] Joe Zaleski and his son, Frank, at one time owned most of the land at the mouth of Montezuma Canyon. In 1952, they had sold the Montezuma Ranch but still owned considerable land there.[546] Zaleski soon offered to sell a small tract to the Memorial to be used for a proposed road construction project.

That sale, and other planned development, sparked a new round of opposition from other locals. Contributing to the dissension, according to Carroll Burroughs, the Memorial's first superintendent, were "personal antagonisms" between neighbors. Alex D'Albini, who had opposed the Memorial from the beginning, was said to have "long-standing feuds" with Joe Zaleski as well as with Grace Sparkes.[547] Their support may have spurred him to again stir up protests. Thus, even those local landowners who supported the Memorial could unwittingly contribute to controversy and friction.

The Arizona Commission continued during the 1950s, with some turnover. John McCarroll of Wickenburg was appointed in 1954 and reappointed in 1957. Odd Halseth and Margaret Rockwell remained on the Commission, both were reappointed in 1954. Harry Saxon of Willcox was named to the commission in 1955. Grace Sparkes remained as chair to round out the commission as constituted in 1957. The Bisbee Chamber of Commerce National Parks and Monuments Committee of 1957 was still chaired by Grace Sparkes as well. It also included James Allison, Arthur

Blunt, James C. McPhee, Folsom Moore, Reverend John Howard, Austin Jay, and Fred McKinney, of Bisbee; Carl W. Morris and James E. Brophy, of Lowell; and Sparkes, Zaleski, Colonel E.N. Hardy, and W. Foy Herschede, of Hereford.[548]

Once Coronado National Memorial was established, in 1952, Sparkes became deeply involved in its development and operation. The 1952 bill that created the Memorial appropriated no money and its Congressional supporters assured their colleagues that no funds were then needed.[549] Funding was, in fact, not approved until July of 1954.[550] In the interim, periodic patrols were carried out from other parks in the region.[551] Even after the Memorial was funded, it still lacked a Master Plan, structures, and personnel.[552] As soon as she heard of the 1954 appropriation, Sparkes came to the rescue with an offer of shelter. She wrote to NPS, "I want to cooperate and would like to have your Park official quartered at our camp," meaning the State of Texas mine.[553]

The National Park Service soon responded positively to the idea of renting her cabin for use as an office.[554] A house trailer, with the necessary electric and plumbing hook-ups, was also placed on the property.[555] Before the end of 1954, a temporary agreement was worked out and a series of more permanent leases commenced at the beginning of 1955.[556] They covered an expanded area as the Memorial's needs increased.[557] The State of Texas Mine remained the home of Coronado Memorial facilities and personnel until early in 1960.[558] The last lease ran until June of that year.[559]

During this same period, Sparkes was also hired by NPS as a seasonal caretaker, beginning in September 1955.[560] She was later promoted to the full time position of Ranger/Historian.[561] McCroskey's biography of Sparkes notes that she worked at the Memorial until January 1963, when she reached the mandatory retirement age of seventy. She died in October of the same year.[562] Memorial records, however, indicate that Sparkes was furloughed early in September 1963 and expected to return to work on October 26.[563] Her death on October 22 came as a shock to her fellow employees, who still identified her as "Ranger/Historian Grace Sparkes."[564]

Over the last two decades of her life, Grace Sparkes was closely associated with Coronado National Memorial. She served on, and chaired, both state and local promotional bodies. She was the only member of the state Commission from southeastern Arizona and the first member of the Bisbee Committee from the Hereford area. As a local landowner, she battled with the Memorial over its boundaries and road construction; but she also was, in the early years, the Memorial's landlord, and later attempted to sell her property to the park. She hoped, it seemed, to profit from the development of the Memorial by gaining utilities and a better road. When Sparkes was hired as caretaker, and later Ranger/Historian, she finally attained the same position which she had enjoyed in Prescott: being paid to promote the Memorial and her home, both of which she loved.

When Sparkes died, the Memorial lost one of its most energetic supporters; and, the state Commission, it seems, went dormant. In 1965, both the state Commission and the international memorial idea got another boost when Philip Welles was named to the Coronado International Monument Commission of Arizona.[565] Welles had served as the Superintendent at the Memorial for seven years before his retirement. His enthusiasm for Coronado was amply demonstrated during his tenure when he vacationed to Compostela, Nayarit, Mexico, the starting point for the Coronado expedition.[566] He visited the State Historian to discuss Coronado, then traced his route back to Arizona, taking photographs along the way.[567]

Welles was eager to reinvigorate the movement toward extending Coronado Memorial south of the border. He had been acquainted with some Mexican officials who had sounded positive about the notion and also had contacts in the *ejidos* that occupied the land formerly owned by the Cananea Cattle Company. Throughout his tenure, Welles used letterhead that listed Grace Sparkes as the Commission Chair. At some point Bassett T. Wright of Mesa had replaced Odd Halseth. Old stationery being used in 1967, four years after Grace's death, served as a reminder of that Commission.[568]

Welles thought that "if the commission is to be anything but a somewhat vague 'honor,'" it needed to formulate a plan to present to the governor of Arizona and Mexican officials. He quickly found that the other members of the Commission did not share his enthusiasm. He wrote to another member that "I am a bit discouraged by the general apathy; maybe it would be just as well to say 'the hell with it' and let it go at that."[569] His blunt approach soon got most of the members to a meeting, at which Welles was elected the Chair of the Commission. At that point the Arizona Commission consisted of Welles; longtime member Margaret Rockwell; D. Tenny Lamoreaux of Chandler; Thomas H. Peterson of Tucson; and John H. McCarroll, editor and publisher of the *Wickenburg Sun*.[570]

Welles, in the name of the Arizona Commission, promoted the international memorial concept on both sides of the border. Shortly after his appointment, Welles wrote that "most of the San Pedro [*ejido*] people are in favor of an international monument and many were frequent visitors at our memorial."[571] He immediately invited representatives of the Mexican government and the *ejidos* to begin discussions.[572] Since the expropriation of the Ranchos de Cananea, he wrote, the proposed memorial site was on "federal land assigned to the Ejido Jose Maria Morelos." It would not require the participation of private owners or the withdrawal of grazing land. The *ejido* could benefit from running "small concessions such as a cafe, curio shop, and riding stables."⁵⁷³

Welles succeeded in building consensus in Arizona, at least from his own Commission and the governor. He received supportive correspondence from officials in Mexico, including the Governor and Director of Tourism for the State of Sonora. Meetings were scheduled with leaders of the affected *ejido* and the Ejidal Bank, which handles much of the administration of the collectives.⁵⁷⁴ Despite these positive steps, the international memorial effort soon disappeared from the radar again. Changes in administration on both sides of the border may have contributed to the decline in interest. Welles later explained that a meeting and barbecue had been scheduled for state and federal officials and other interested parties from both sides of the border in 1967. According to his recollection, when tear gas bombs given by the Arizona police to their counterparts in Sonora were used against University of Sonora students, international cooperation ground to a halt.⁵⁷⁵ Undoubtedly, the resignation of Philip Welles in 1969 was a major factor in the advent of another period of dormancy for both the Arizona Commission and the idea of an international memorial.⁵⁷⁶ The energy level of the State Commission tended to follow that of its most active members and, usually, of its Chair. In any case, the Commission disappeared, to be reactivated several years later.⁵⁷⁷

In late 1975, the Arizona Commission again began to round into action. During the first days of 1976, Coronado Memorial Superintendent Laurel Dale responded to a request by Ben Avery for recommendations for members of a new Commission. Avery was a former outdoor writer for the *Arizona Republic* of Phoenix and a member of the NPS Western Region Advisory Board. He was also the first name on Dale's list of potential members.⁵⁷⁸ Two months later, a new "Revived Coronado Memorial Commission" was named by Governor Raul H. Castro of Arizona. The first four members were Ben Avery, again the first name on the list; Gilbert Ronstadt of Tucson; Bernard Fontana, of the Arizona Museum on the University of Arizona campus in Tucson; and James Officer of the University of Arizona.⁵⁷⁹ An editorial in the *Bisbee Review* noted that none of the members of the new Commission were from Cochise, or even Santa Cruz, County in southeastern Arizona. The slight was especially galling given that Governor Castro was born in Cananea and grew up in Cochise County.⁵⁸⁰

Considering his early activity and prominent place on the listings of potential and then appointed Commission members, Ben Avery may be seen as a driving force behind the new Commission. At its founding and in its earliest days, Charles Morgan had provided much of the impetus for the Arizona Commission. Later Grace Sparkes kept the dream of an international memorial alive through her leadership of the state Commission as well as the

Bisbee Committee. Philip Welles restarted effort in the 1960s and operated under the auspices of the Arizona Commission until he was forced to resign for health reasons. In 1975 and 1976, Ben Avery's name was prominent in the unfolding of the newest Arizona Commission.

This Arizona Commission found counterparts in Mexico who shared their vision and commitment to the cause of the international memorial. Sergio Bribiesca, the State Director of Tourism for Sonora, worked with the National Park Service staff on special events at the Memorial. At the September 1976 Borderlands Symposium, at Coronado National Memorial, Bribiesca announced that the government of Sonora was about to set aside three areas for international parks on its border with Arizona. An international Coronado Memorial would be joined by a new binational cultural center near Nogales and a cooperative effort at Organ Pipe and Pinacate.[581] That initiative never took place. Those involved blamed officials higher up in both national governments for their lack of support.

Within the National Park Service, Chief of the International Park Affairs Division Robert C. Milne encouraged his colleagues to drop the Coronado issue in talks with Mexico lest they torpedo other plans. Milne wrote that Mexican officials had "strongly and emotionally" expressed their opposition to commemoration of Spanish conquistadores in binational talks. Other projected cooperative plans, such as Organ Pipe and Big Bend, were much more promising, especially if the controversial topic of Coronado was taken off the agenda.[582] Arizona Commission Chair, Bernard Fontana suggested that Coronado's name be dropped from the Memorial in favor of "Pimería Alta," the Spanish colonial name for the region, if that would improve the prospects of the international project.[583] After almost four decades, such a change of name and theme was most unlikely. Several months later, Fontana resigned from the Commission, saying that he felt that the international memorial could only be accomplished at the federal level. Despite "tremendous cooperation and support" from Sonorans, nothing had been done by the national governments of either country. He added that Ben Avery favored abolishing the Commission until such time as it had more likelihood of success.[584]

During the same time, state commission members took another approach to gaining federal backing for the international memorial. In 1977, they seized on a statement by the first lady, Rosalynn Carter, that she would be interested in working with her counterpart in Mexico to establish international cultural centers in the border area.[585] The Commission invited Mrs. Carter to attend the next year's annual Historical Pageant.[586] The letterhead of a follow-up to this invitation shows that the Commission in 1978 was made up of Bernard Fontana, of the Arizona State Museum in Tucson, Chair; along with Avery as Secretary, Officer, Ronstadt, and Dr.

Alfred R. French of Phoenix.[587] Mrs. Carter did not attend, or at least there was no mention of it in descriptions of the 1978 event.

Thus, another period of state activity failed to bear fruit in the form of an international memorial. In October 1982, James Officer reported that the governor "has reappointed me to the Commission, but I can't imagine we will begin to function until after Mexico installs the new president."[588] He could have gone further, as Fontana and Avery had, and recognized that no state commissions, in either Sonora or Arizona, was likely to succeed without the energetic cooperation of both national governments. According to Charles Morgan, the Commission was at some point "legitimized by a legislative act," as a permanent entity.[589] It had long been more a front organization for particular energetic promoters than an enduring structure. As the story of the land acquisition of 1978 demonstrates, Coronado National Memorial had, by that time, garnered support, as well as opposition, from a number of groups and individuals. With its future existence much more certain, the energy of its allies could be expended on site rather than in the political arena.

NEWS RELEASE
u.s. department of the interior
national park service

For Immediate Release   Date (602) 366-5515

CORONADO GENERAL MANAGEMENT PLAN COMPLETED

The final General Management Plan for Coronado National Memorial and its Environmental Review are available for public review and comment, Superintendent Laurel W. Dale announced today.

The General Management Plan will guide management and development of the Park's historic and natural resources over the next several years.

Major actions proposed in the Plan include boundary revision and land acquisition; providing for interpretive facilities, and improving the Montezuma Pass Road and the Visitor Center Museum.

In compliance with the National Environmental Policy Act of 1969, the National Park Service made a study of the plan that determined there would be no significant adverse environmental impacts from the proposed actions. Consequently, an Environmental Statement will not be required for the Plan and a negative declaration will be filed.

The Plan and Environmental Review are available for public inspection at Coronado National Memorial, Rural Route #1, Box 126, Hereford, Arizona 85615; the National Park Service's Southern Arizona Group Office, 1115 N. 1st Street, Phoenix, Arizona 85004; and the National Park Service Western Regional Office, 450 Golden Gate Ave., San Francisco, California 94102.

The public is encouraged to review and comment upon the planning documents. Written comments should be submitted to the Superintendent, Coronado National Memorial, at the above address by December 9, 1976. Proposals in the Plan will not be undertaken until after the 30-day public review period.

- NPS -

Prepared November 5, 1976

Coronado National Memorial   Rural Route 1, Box 126   Hereford, AZ 85615

News release announcing the completion of the General Management Plan for Coronado National Memorial (1976) and its availability for public review and comment. (Coronado National Memorial Archives, National Park Service)

Ryan - Int. 3439

DEPARTMENT OF THE INTERIOR
INFORMATION SERVICE

NATIONAL PARK SERVICE

For Release Upon Receipt   NOV 13 1952

File in Dev Outline
original files. R.

CORONADO NATIONAL MEMORIAL ESTABLISHED

Secretary of the Interior Oscar L. Chapman today announced the establishment, by proclamation of President Truman, of the Coronado National Memorial in southern Arizona on the United States-Mexico boundary.

Located entirely within the Coronado National Forest, this 2,745-acre scenic area includes Coronado Peak from which may be obtained a sweeping view of the region traversed by the Spanish explorer, Francisco Vasquez de Coronado, and his men on their journey in 1540 from Mexico into what is now the United States.

Legislation enacted by Congress in 1941 authorized the establishment by the United States Government of a memorial to Coronado in Arizona, provided arrangements for establishing a similar area in Sonora, Mexico, containing the starting point of the Coronado expedition, were made by the Mexican Government, the two units to form an international memorial, with each Government in charge of its own particular section.

Necessary arrangements for establishing the United States section of the proposed international memorial were completed some time ago, but land problems and other complications have made it impossible for the Mexican Government to set aside an adjoining companion area in Sonora. Last July, legislation amending the 1941 Act of Congress was enacted which authorized the establishment, by Presidential proclamation, of a "national" instead of an "international" memorial.

Secretary of the Interior Chapman expressed the hope that the way will soon be cleared for the Mexican Government to set aside lands for a companion memorial so that the long-cherished idea of an international memorial commemorating the Coronado expedition, one of the significant events in early North American history, may be realized. Such an international memorial, the Secretary added, would not only further cement goodwill between the peoples of both countries, but would be of inestimable value in furthering cultural relations.

All of the land in the newly established memorial, which is under the jurisdiction of the National Park Service, is in Federal ownership.

x x x

P.N. 30832

Department of the Interior Information Release for November, 1952 in which Oscar L.Chapman, Secretary of the Interior announces the establishment of Coronado National Memorial by proclamation of President Truman. (Coronado National Memorial Archives, National Park Service)

Clinton P. Anderson, congressman and senator from New Mexico, was the managing director of the United States Coronado Exposition Commission (1939-1940), and an early supporter of the Coronado International Monument idea. (Clinton P. Anderson Photo Collection, Center for Southwest Research, University Libraries, University of New Mexico)

Miner R. Tillotson, Regional Director, National Park Service, Santa Fe, New Mexico, 1940-1955. (Coronado National Memorial archives, National Park Service)

In A. Grove Day's book, Coronado's Quest: The Discovery of the American West, *published in 1940, he proposes the area of Naco as an entry point for Francisco Vázquez de Coronado. (Courtesy of the* Honolulu Star-Bulletin*)*

Luis Gastellum, Assistant General Superintendent, Southwestern National Monuments in Globe, Arizona, was assigned to oversee initial development planning of Coronado National Memorial in 1954. (Courtesy of Agatha Gastellum)

Archaeologist Albert H. Shroeder was among the persons involved in the preparation of the Master Plan of 1954 for Coronado National Memorial. (Courtesy of Agatha Gastellum)

Grace M. Sparks (nearest the car), was an early advocate of the proposed Coronado International Memorial and later Coronado National Memorial. (Courtesy Fred Wilson Photographs, Arizona Collection, Arizona State University Libraries)

Members of the band El Mariachi Juvenil San Xavier at a Borderlands Festival at Coronado National Memorial, 1981. (Coronado National Memorial Archives, National Park Service)

121

National Park Service employees, among them Tom Carroll (bottom right) in a reenactment of Coronado entering in what is today the Southwestern United States. (Coronado National Memorial Archives, National Park Service)

Guide to the National Monuments in the Southwest which also included Coronado National Memorial. Issued in 1956 by Southwestern National Monuments Headquarters. (Coronado National Memorial Archives, National Park Service)

Part II—Land Acquisition

Chapter VII

Early Peoples, Settlers, and Speculators: The Land before the Memorial

> *Nothing Ever Happens in Cochise County*—Al Arrowhood, local historian

> *…there is nothing in that flat country which is of any interest except to the people who are running cattle on it.* — Charles Wiswall, Cananea Cattle Company, 1950

> *Romance, history, buried treasure, gold mines, camping, and picnic areas and soul-restoring scenery are offered by our beautiful Huachuca Mountains.* -- Grace McCool, Tombstone Epitaph, 1967.

Coronado National Memorial commemorates the arrival of the first Europeans in southeastern Arizona. Human habitation in the area dates to a far earlier period. Long before the Spanish imagined golden cities to the north of Mexico, hunter gatherer groups had developed into agricultural communities along the river basins of southern Arizona. Later, invaders and settlers raised crops and livestock, cut timber, mined ores, built forts, homesteads, and, eventually, retirement villages. In the twentieth century, recreation and tourism drew more people to the Southwest than tales of gold and silver or grants of public land. Parks like the Coronado National Memorial are a recent but important part of the story of land use.

In the early 1950s, as the Coronado Memorial dream finally became reality, archeologists unearthed intermingled bones from humans and mammoths in the San Pedro and Sulphur Springs valleys just to the east. When tested, those artifacts proved to be some 11,000 years old.[590] The prehistoric culture that developed in the area was given the name "Cochise" by archeologists for the county in which they found many of the sites that defined it. Stages within the Cochise culture, which lasted from about 10,000 to 2,500 years ago, were taken from local geography as well. The ultimate stage of Cochise Culture is named "San Pedro" in honor of archeological finds in the valley adjacent to the Coronado Memorial.[591] Several Cochise Culture sites, primarily from the Chiricahua Stage (8,000 to 3,000 B.C.), have been found in Montezuma Canyon.[592]

Over time, through the movement of people and ideas, various regional cultures developed, among them the Mogollon, Hohokam, and Salado. The San Pedro River lay at the margins of these cultures. Ruins within the valley and its tributaries exhibit mixtures of characteristics and influences, and scholars disagree as to the exact relationship between the groups in the area or cultural affiliations of each site.[593] The exact relationship between the prehistoric cultures studied by archeologists and the groups first met by the Spanish in the fifteenth and sixteenth centuries is also less than certain.

It appears that several sites in the San Pedro Valley were settled during the few centuries preceding the arrival of the Spanish. Evidence of human occupation during that period has been found within the boundaries of Coronado National Memorial.[594] According to scholar Harold Sterling Gladwin, the San Pedro Valley was one of only a few centers of the great sedentary cultures to survive in the Southwest as late as 1400.[595] At that time there were pueblos on the San Pedro and Babocomari rivers and at the mouths of the major canyons along the eastern edge of the Huachuca Mountains.[596] Despite the existence of apparent archeological gaps, Charles DiPeso concludes that the residents of the San Pedro Valley had a continuous heritage from the mammoth hunters of the distant past to the residents of the *rancherías* found by the first Spaniards to enter Arizona.[597]

The journals of Coronado and his immediate predecessor, Fray Marcos de Niza, only add confusion to the task of describing the San Pedro River valley of their time. Fray Marcos evidently described places that he never saw and was not universally believed by his own peers. In addition, his account is so sketchy as to be nearly impossible to match to specific locales. The San Pedro Valley in the vicinity of the Memorial is one of the more controversial areas in the debates concerning Coronado's route. The historiographical debate surrounding that topic was covered in Chapter 2, above. One disputed issue involved the description of the native population in areas thought to be the San Pedro Valley.

It seems, following DiPeso, that sixteenth-century Spanish expeditions should have encountered settled farming communities if or when they passed through the San Pedro River Valley. Certainly, that was the character of the archeological sites from a century before Coronado. More than another century would pass after Coronado before another Spanish chronicle described the area's natives. However, during that time, Spanish settlers and settlements drew ever closer.

In the middle of the seventeenth century, the hacienda, later town, of Bacanuchi was founded south of Cananea by José Romo de Vivar. At various times, Romo de Vivar had several native *rancherías* under his jurisdiction, including some in the San Pedro Valley north of the later international border. One village under his administration was San Joachín de Huachuca, on the Babocomari River north of the Huachuca Mountains.[598] Father Eusebio Francisco Kino described a trail from Quiburi, a few miles north of Fairbank, going west to Huachuca.[599] According to James Officer, Romo de Vivar "had property in Cananea and at the south end of the Huachuca Mountains as early as 1680."[600] Officer's citations do not bear him out on that particular point, but certainly Romo de Vivar was no stranger to the Huachuca Mountains.

Before the Spanish became established on the San Pedro, they already had conflicts with the resident Sobaipuri Pima Indians and knew them as fierce fighters. The Sobaipuri were long suspected of stealing horses from the Spanish. According to Spanish Captain Juan Mateo Manje, that suspicion was tempered by the results of a battle in which the Pima, evidently those known as Sobaipuri, killed sixty Apaches and captured seventy horses.[601] A military expedition was mounted against the Indians of the San Pedro in 1692. Rather than bloodshed, however, it led to the beginning of a long and friendly relationship. Soon thereafter, the famous Jesuit priest, Father Kino, visited the Sobaipuri on the San Pedro River for the first time. He referred to the river as the Río de San Joseph de Terrenate, or de Quiburi.[602]

A few years later, in late 1697, Captain Manje accompanied Kino to the San Pedro and described the country and its people. At Santa Cruz de Gaybanipitea, on the west side of the river near Fairbank, Manje saw a hilltop town surrounded by irrigated farmland. He counted about one hundred people living in twenty five houses. The Spaniards were put up in a flat roofed adobe house that, recounted Manje, had been built for a missionary that the Indians had requested. The village had one hundred cows, which had earlier been brought by Father Kino.

The next morning, Kino and Manje traveled one league north, downstream along the San Pedro River, to the village of Quiburi, where they stayed in another adobe house. Manje described pasturelands and irrigated fields of corn, beans, and cotton. He counted one hundred dwellings and five hundred residents. The Indians wore cotton clothing. Quiburi was the home of a celebrated Sobaipuri chief the Spanish called Captain Coro. Coro and his people displayed trophies from their battles with the Apaches, including scalps.[603] DiPeso notes that Quiburi had only been settled in the few years prior to Manje's visit though Indians had lived on the site, at least intermittently, for centuries.[604] From, Quiburi, Kino and Manje continued downstream, passing other villages along the way, some of which were deserted.[605]

Manje's description is of, perhaps, the golden age of the Sobaipuri of the San Pedro River. The Spanish desired to use the Sobaipuri as a bulwark against the Apache and their allies to the east. They purposely forced a break in relations between the groups and isolated the San Pedro villages from their neighbors, then proved unable to provide the support essential for carrying on the incessant warfare that they had provoked. Within a year of Manje's visit, in 1698, a large battle on the San Pedro, though won by the Sobaipuri, proved that the area had become too dangerous, and Quiburi was abandoned. It was later resettled, but the Sobaipuri finally deserted the San Pedro for good during the 1760s.[606] Father Kino often expressed the hope that missions would be established along the San Pedro River, but his dream never came to fruition. The area was to be the site of Spain's imperial wars but not peaceful settlement.

A presidio occupied the site of Quiburi for a short time after the departure of the Sobaipuri but its existence, too, was brief and contingent. The Presidio San Phelipe de Guevavi, or Terrenate, was located west of the San Pedro River and south of the present international border from 1742-1775. In 1774, work began on a new site only a few leagues to the east, on the Arroyo de las Nutrias. Within a year, both the old presidio and the las Nutrias site were abandoned and the company moved to Quiburi in 1775. The presidio was called Santa Cruz, Kino's name for the village where the 1698 battle had taken place. The "presidio of Santa Cruz, formerly of Terrenate," lasted only five years. It was abandoned after much of its company, including two captains, had died at the hands of the Chiricahua Apaches. In 1780, the company was moved back to las Nutrias, but only stayed there until 1787, when it moved again, this time to Soamca, south of Lochiel, Arizona. That presidio site survived well into the Mexican period.[607]

In December 1766, an official expedition stopped at the Paraje de las Nutrias, then a well-known but undeveloped camping stop. Engineer Nicolás de Lafora described a *laguna* (small lake), into which ran a creek that came from a mountain three leagues, somewhat less than eight miles, to the north. He called the mountain "Guachuca," or Huachuca, and wrote that it contained an abundance of silver. He added that it was yielding ore despite the lack of men to work it due to danger from Indians.[608] Lafora's commander, the Marqués de Rubí, however, specified that only in more peaceful times was the "Sierra de Guachuca" a rich source of ores.[609] Unfortunately, that is the only known reference to Spanish mining in the Huachuca Mountains. Obviously, they faced the same problem with hostile natives that later miners of the Southwest would. Also like later miners, rich strikes yielding "consistent large operations" eluded the Spanish miners.[610]

A new era in the history of settlement in the San Pedro Valley began during the early nineteenth century when land was granted by the Mexican government to private landowners. The legal process of making the first grant in the vicinity of the Memorial was under way as Mexico's struggle for independence neared its end in 1821. José Jesus Pérez, a soldier from Arizspe, Sonora, requested four leagues of land in the vicinity of the abandoned town of Las Nutrias on which to graze livestock. Local officials negotiated with Pérez and another citizen who was already grazing stock along the river and a tract was surveyed. At issue was a *ciénaga*, or marsh, which both considered the most significant source of water in the area. The *ciénaga* described in the documents may have been in the same place where Lafora earlier described a *laguna*, only during a drier time.

The San Pedro Grant was measured northward from a house known as San Pedro, evidently within the town of the same name, about seven miles south of the present international border. The line passed "the foot of Huachuca Mountain" just north of the mid-point of the grant. The granting process continued with Pérez paying stipulated fees for the land and papers being forwarded to the proper authorities to be approved. At that point Mexico gained its independence and the procedure was, as far as can be told, never completed. In 1832, the land was transferred to Rafael Elías and a legal title was issued. However, subsequent to the United States-Mexican War of 1846-1848 and the Gadsden Purchase of 1853 much of the San Pedro Valley belonged to the United States and all land titles had to be confirmed by the new rulers. The San Pedro Grant was rejected by the United States, mainly on the basis of government evidence that supported a contention that the grant was wholly within the new boundaries of Mexico.[611]

The disputed boundary of the San Pedro Grant, in turn, affected the eventual disposition of two grants directly to its north along the San Pedro River. In 1827, the San Rafael del Valle Grant was measured from the north line of the San Pedro Grant and the San Juan de las Boquillas y Nogales Grant north from it. During its confirmation, the case of the San Rafael del Valle Grant had the distinction of being appealed to the United States

Supreme Court twice, for different issues, once by the government and once by the petitioners. In the end, both grants were confirmed, though neither ended up being nearly as large as the petitioners thought. Though they were all originally surveyed, as noted, with common boundaries, the resulting grants did not come near touching one another.[612]

Members of the same family, named Elías, were involved in both the San Pedro and the San Juan de las Boquillas y Nogales grants but the family had transferred its interests before the confirmation process. The Elías clan had other interests in the area as well, being the original claimants to the massive San Ignacio del Babocomari Grant, north of the Huachuca Mountains on Babocomari Creek.[613] The San Rafael del Valle grant had been sold to members of the Camou family of Hermosillo, Sonora, before it was confirmed.[614] In 1905, copper and cattle baron William Cornell Greene added it to his transnational empire. Greene already owned the San Rafael de la Zanja Grant, directly west of the Huachuca Mountains, at that time. In 1912, after Greene's death, his family sold San Rafael del Valle to the Boquillas Land and Cattle Company along with over fifty smaller ranches in Arizona and Sonora.[615]

The Boquillas Land and Cattle Company owed its name to the San Juan de las Boquillas y Nogales Grant, which it had purchased in 1901 from the famous Hearst newspaper family of California. Senator George Hearst, the father of William Randolph Hearst, had been a partner of George Hill Howard, who had bought up the grant from the original heirs. The Boquillas Company eventually became a subsidiary of the Kern County Land and Cattle Company, one of the largest landowners in the United States through its ranching and farming interests all over the west. In 1967, the Kern Company merged with Tenneco, Inc., which has developed some of its land in the San Pedro Valley.[616]

The tale of the San Pedro Valley grants, with featured roles played by such large-scale landowners, and prominent families, as the Elíases, Greenes, and Hearsts, illustrates one aspect of the region in the nineteenth century. Mixed in among the giants, however, were many small operations run by poor families just trying to survive the arid climate on the bounty of their land. When settlement increased in southeastern Arizona after the Gadsden Treaty, the newcomers, like their predecessors, sought the water necessary to survival in the desert. Much of the land along the San Pedro River was controlled by the Mexican grants and then by their successors. The earliest homesteads in the valley were founded in the early 1880s along the river's tributaries and at nearby springs. Among the existing water courses that drew early settlers to the area was Montezuma Creek.

William Ratliff, originally of the Big Bend country of Texas, was the first Anglo-American settler in Montezuma Canyon. He moved his family from the Gila River Valley in New Mexico to the Huachucas by covered wagon in the 1880s or 1890s.[617] Ratliff chose Montezuma Canyon because it had a permanent stream at that time and he planned to do some farming. To provide immediate income, the Ratliff family began to log in the Huachuca Mountains, delivering the wood to Naco.[618] They brought some horses and a small herd of cattle to the area at the same time.[619] The Ratliff family is thought to have begun building a residence on Montezuma Creek in 1902.[620] At the very least, the residence, later known to locals as Baumkirchner's adobe house, was built prior to 1916.[621]

According to documents filed by the Surveyor General's office in 1917, William Ratliff officially applied for his 160 acre claim on October 22, 1911. The survey was executed March 12-13, 1914, and approved August 8, 1917 for 158.23 acres. Ratliff's Homestead Entry Survey 311 consisted of the south half of the northwest quarter and north half of the southwest quarter of Section 17, Township 24 South, Range 21 East, Gila and Salt River Meridian. Montezuma Wash ran through the southwest corner of the property from northwest to southeast.[622]

Ed Ratliff, William's oldest son, made a homestead claim directly west of William's place. Papers filed in 1917 show that Ed Ratliff applied for his 160 acre claim on February 3, 1911. The survey was executed March 11-12, 1915, and approved August 8, 1917, with 157.72 acres. Ed Ratliff's homestead consisted of the south half of the northeast quarter and north half of the southeast quarter of Section 18, Township 24 South, Range 21 East. Montezuma Wash ran through it from northwest to southeast as well.[623]

Another son, named William, came to own claims to the east and southeast of his father's land.[624] The younger William's property was, according to a later family member, sold to George Brown.[625] In addition, an adopted daughter named Inez, but called "Tiny," married John Pyeatt, who owned the claim directly east of the original Ratliff homestead. Pyeatt's claim, later known as the Montezuma Ranch, is discussed below. By the middle of the second decade of the twentieth century, then, the Ratliff family was settled all around the base of the Huachuca Mountains along Montezuma Creek.

William Ratliff died in 1917, leaving the land to be split among his heirs. At the time he was also grazing cattle on National Forest land. Ed Ratliff was the executor of his father's will and representative of the heirs. In 1932, nine Ratliffs by name or marriage transmitted their claims to George Ratliff, another son of the elder William. Ed and his wife, Ira, quit claimed an unspecified tract, evidently Homestead Entry Survey 310, to George in a separate transaction. On 30 September 1933, George and Annie Ratliff conveyed both Homestead Entry Surveys, 310 and 311, to Marko Vucinich.

On 21 November 1933, Vucinich, in turn, transferred both homesteads to Joe Zaleski.[626]

Zaleski came to own at least four homestead entry surveys at the mouth of Montezuma Canyon. Another was the Homestead of John Pyeatt. Pyeatt first took up a claim in Cochise County under the Homestead Act in 1909. His first claim was on the east side of the San Pedro River, northeast of Coronado National Memorial. He built a small house and repaired an already existing structure, strung fence, and put in a crop on five or six acres. Later in the same year a flood destroyed or damaged all of the improvements that he had made on the land. Deciding that he could not afford to start over again, Pyeatt abandoned the entry. He was able to sell the vestiges of his improvements on the land to Rufus M. Thompson for $250.00 before the end of 1909.[627]

In November 1915, Pyeatt settled on the Montezuma Ranch site. He applied for a homestead claim in June 1917.[628] That tract had also been claimed and relinquished previously. Cornelius N. Driscoll had first claimed the Montezuma Ranch land in July 1913.[629] By the middle of 1914, as Pyeatt was migrating west, Driscoll moved east across the San Pedro River and made a new claim under the Homestead Act. Driscoll explained that he had relinquished his first claim because the road to it had washed out. In addition, he had learned from neighbors that water was a problem as the creek was then dry and wells needed to be drilled to a depth of 200 feet.[630]

Pyeatt's claim to the Montezuma Ranch property was approved and a deed was granted in July 1921. Pyeatt's patent was recorded, having "been established and duly consummated, in conformity to law," on December 4, 1925. The 160 acre property was described as the south half of northeast quarter and north half of the southeast quarter of Section 17, Township 24 South, Range 21 East of the Gila and Salt River Base and Meridian, Arizona.[631] John Pyeatt, as already mentioned, married Inez "Tiny" Ratliff, the adopted daughter of the family that owned the two claims west of his new homestead and probably more. According to local lore, Inez's parents worked for the Ratliffs. They suddenly left one night, leaving their daughter behind with the Ratliffs, who adopted her.[632]

As John and Tiny were filing their homestead claim, around 1917, they built a small house on the property. It was remodeled and added to over the years, but remains as the center of a ranch house that exists today. That house is the furthest west of the two large buildings still standing on the Montezuma Ranch.[633] John Pyeatt was dead within four years of his receiving final approval for his second homestead. His widow moved to Paso Robles, California, and in March 1929 she sold the lot to Joseph Zaleski.[634] Joe Zaleski's granddaughter, Betty Peterson-Stowe, added that Zaleski was approached by the president of the Miners and Merchants Bank which, evidently, held a loan on the property, about buying it from Tiny Pyeatt. The Zaleski family then lived on a homestead in the Hereford area.[635] According to one source, they owned other land in Cochise County as well, some of it located within what would eventually become the town of Sierra Vista.[636]

A few years after he bought the Pyeatt homestead, Zaleski also bought the Ratliff properties, to the west, as described above. Filling out Zaleski's small empire was the Kudzmi claim to the south. The Kudzmi Homestead was made up of the South half of the Southeast quarter of Section 17 and Lots 1 and 2 of Section 20, Township 24 South, Range 21 East, Gila and Salt River Base and Meridian. It was first claimed within the 160 acre homestead claim of Elmer L. Hertel, as reflected in field notes dated March 3, 1915.[637] Simon Kudzmi, a naturalized immigrant from Russia and veteran of World War I, settled on the same land in October 1928 and built a house in February 1929. Joe Zaleski was one of the witnesses for Kudzmi when he filed the final proofs for his homestead, which was approved at 133.67 acre.[638] Eventually, Zaleski bought the claim from Kudzmi.

About 1935 or 1936, Zaleski, with a partner named Rudy Becker, converted his property into a dude, or guest, ranch. They called it the Border Ranch and later Montezuma Ranch. When they opened Border Ranch, Zaleski and Becker built another house, originally one story with a basement, to the east of the original cabin. The house contained common rooms as well as guest rooms. Guests also stayed in small cabins. The Border Ranch was run as a family business and was frequented by locals as well. A 1937 feature article named Rudy Becker's son Wes as one of the "top wranglers" and Frank Zaleski, Joe's son, as a "top cowhand." Neighbor George Brown was described as "one of the most interesting and up-to-date ranchers in the state."[639]

Guests at the ranch enjoyed many activities, including participation in seasonal round-ups, watching rodeos in which local cowboys competed, and western dances in Hereford. Most of the pastimes, according to descriptions, centered on horseback riding. Among the destinations were local landmarks such as Smuggler's Pass and "the Caves." One could also ride into the mountains to fish for trout, pan for gold, visit nearby gold mine shafts, and take in the now famous views. Across the plains, guests were encouraged to visit neighboring ranches and cross the border into Mexico.

Naco, Arizona, offered golf, while the Sonora side featured shopping for souvenirs and the "thrill in visiting a foreign country." Also across the border was the possibility of "a fiesta in one of the neighboring Mexican villages where you can enjoy watching the people from another land." At the border crossing were "dashing, colorful Mexican vaqueros herding the cattle through the disinfectant vats." Dude ranches were marketed to an urban audience as relaxation in a rustic setting, and the Montezuma Ranch was no exception. As an added attraction, the Montezuma Ranch also offered the exotica of ready access to a romanticized vision of Mexico.[640] World War II cut into the tourist business but occasioned the expansion of Fort Huachuca. For a time, the Army used the guest ranch to house officers.[641]

The Zaleski and Becker names both remained associated with the ranch for more than a decade. Neighbor George Brown thought that Becker bought Zaleski out. Becker was sometimes listed as the manager of the dude ranch, as was Frank Zaleski. Frank Zaleski came to own the property and he kept it until the end of 1949. After World War II, around 1946 or 1947, Harry H. and Ruth Ethlyn Petersen began to manage the Montezuma Ranch.[642] Citing a source from the Cochise County Assessor's office, one author asserts that the Petersens purchased the ranch from Frank Zaleski on December 13, 1949.[643] However, in a June 1947 letter, Mr. Petersen described his wife and himself as the owners of the Montezuma Ranch.[644] Very likely, the Petersens bought the property earlier, but paid off the property in 1949 when they sold it. On the same day that the Petersens completed their purchase in 1949, they transferred title to the property to Nancy Carter Nelms.[645] In October 1950, Joe Zaleski transferred ownership of the rest of his property to his son Frank by way of a Gift Deed.[646]

Nancy Nelms, along with managers Don Brooks, Jean Faye, and Rex Watts ran Montezuma as a dude ranch and a summer camp for young girls for a few years. The summer camp taught horseback riding among other things. During that time a concrete swimming pool was installed near the original ranch house. A 1950 newspaper article described the 80,000 gallon, 30 foot by 60 foot, pool as a Christmas gift from Nelms's mother. Guests at Montezuma Ranch continued to go on cattle round ups on the adjacent Zaleski ranch. Frank Zaleski still owned over 400 acres around the mouth of Montezuma Canyon as Coronado National Memorial prepared to open in 1952.[647]

Aside from the 1766 remarks by Spanish observers Rubí and Lafora noted above, nothing is known of early mining in the area. In virtually every place where the Spanish trod in the Southwest there are stories of lost mines and hidden riches; the Huachucas are no different. Substantial mining came to the San Pedro Valley and surrounding mountains in the late 1870s.[648] The original papers of the Lena Claim, the "oldest historic mine claim in Montezuma Canyon," located it next to evidence of older mines. The origins of the older workings are unknown, but they are assumed to date from the Spanish or Mexican periods and are often thought to represent workings from Lafora's day or even earlier.[649] In his study, *Islands in the Desert*, John Wilson, parenthetically, declared that Lafora was describing workings in Cave Creek Canyon, on the south side of the Huachuca Mountains.[650]

The last mine in the canyon to produce in a big way, the State of Texas, occupied the same site as the Lena. The Lena was located in May 1878 by George J. Rasking and John L. Harris and recorded the next month by D.B. Ren. An 1880 newspaper article noted that there were then nine mines working in Montezuma Canyon. The Lena was renamed the Chicago Mine in 1885 under the ownership of Peter Connor and A.W. Emanuel.[651] Connor (sometimes spelled Conner) and his partners filed several claims in Montezuma Canyon in 1879, among which was the Lookout, also thought to be on land later occupied by the State of Texas and its companion claims.[652]

The State of Texas Mine itself was founded in the same location in 1889. Writers disagree as to the exact ownership of the State of Texas during its first few years of operation. Geoffrey T. Bohrer cites an 1889 claim by August Baron that reported a find of "mineral bearing quartz."[653] However, Peter M. Van Cleve, using Deeds of Mines in the Cochise County Recorders Office in Bisbee, Arizona, writes that Richard C. Van Dorn made the first State of Texas claim in 1889. According to Van Cleve, Van Dorn soon sold a one-third share of the mine to Peter Connor, who, in turn, sold it and other local mine interests to William Graf in 1892. In the meantime, in 1891, August Baron, exercising power of attorney for Van Dorn, sold the remaining two-thirds share of the State of Texas Mine and another mine to Graf. Then, in 1893, Baron purchased all of Graf's interests, including the State of Texas.[654]

In any case, by the middle of the 1890s, the State of Texas Mine belonged to August Baron, a banker and miner from Tombstone. Baron had the claim surveyed in 1897 and the plat was approved in 1898.[655] Some time later, Charles Gerdes, then of Gleeson, Arizona, stated that he had been Baron's partner and "did the greater part of the development work on the claim" at that time.[656] According to reports, twenty-five tons of high grade lead-silver-zinc ores were shipped to Canon City, Colorado, in 1897. Forty-two tons were shipped in 1898-1899.[657]

In 1902, over forty mines in Montezuma and Copper canyons, including the State of Texas, were leased by the Mitchell Mining Company of Ishpeming, Michigan. The Mitchell Company mined copper at the site for a few years before relinquishing the leases to their former owners in 1906.[658] Almost immediately, the Gray Metals Company began to operate the State of Texas, which was still owned by Baron. By 1914, the State of Texas No. Two, Extension, Bonita, Josephine, and New York mines had been added to the operation.[659] A new 350-foot vertical shaft was dug near the main workings around the same time. Records indicate that ore was cut at varying depths, but do not indicate the quality of ore. That shaft has now been caved in for many years. The *Arizona Mining Journal* of 1920 reported that ore containing silver, lead, and zinc was shipped by Gray Metals Company.[660]

August Baron died in 1913 and his mine properties were passed on to his wife, Christine. She promptly sold them to Douglas Gray of Tombstone, the owner of Gray Metals Company. In 1920, Gray took on two partners, Maurice Clark, of Douglas, and William H. Stilwell, of Phoenix, and incorporated a new incarnation of the Gray Metals Company as a publicly owned corporation. Gray sold his mines to the new corporation in 1920 for $20,000. Only two years later, the State of Texas, Texas No. Two, Extension, Bonita, Josephine, and New York mines were sold at public auction as part of a court judgement against Gray. Nathan L. Amster bought them in August 1922 for $9,370.90.[661]

In September 1926, T.J. Sparkes of Prescott, Arizona, and Burdett Moody of Los Angeles, California, purchased several mining claims in the Hartford Mining District from Nathan L. and Estelle D. Amster for $5,000. The purchase included the State of Texas, State of Texas No. Two, Extension, Bonita, Josephine, and New York mines.[662] The partners did little or no mining over the next fifteen years.[663] In a January 1939 letter, Grace Sparkes told Burdett Moody that her father, T.J. Sparkes, had recently died and discussed her family's efforts to reopen the State of Texas Mine. She added that she had not visited the property in two years.[664]

Moody replied that he and T.J. Sparkes had been hoping to sell the property and that he still wished to do so. He estimated that he had $8,000 to $9,000 invested in the mine property. A few months later he wrote that he was "in around $5000 to $6000 altogether."[665] Given that the property had only cost $5,000 and had not been operated since its purchase, it can be surmised that Moody had put up the vast majority of the partners' investment. T.J. Sparkes, a mining engineer, supplied expertise for the moribund enterprise.[666]

Over the next few years, Grace Sparkes continued to pursue loans to reopen the mine and encouraged Moody to support her. She shared ownership of a half interest in the State of Texas property with her siblings as joint heirs to their father, T.J. However, she seemed to be the most active partner. Meanwhile, Moody persisted in his desire to divest of the State of Texas properties.[667] Grace Sparkes was not alone in seeing the potential for turning a profit from the State of Texas. She and Moody received many offers from miners wishing to lease the property. None were accepted, as Sparkes was determined to keep the property and make it pay off for her rather than have others make money off her claim.[668]

Sparkes saw threats to the property from other sources as well, including the then new idea of the Coronado National Memorial. In April 1940, Sparkes wrote to Moody, "I have done a good deal of work also to protect the claims against the Coronado Exposition idea," meaning the Memorial. She continued that this "has meant work with the Arizona Commission, The

Forestry, U.S., Park and other officials."[669] During the same month, Sparkes wrote to Margaret Rockwell of the Arizona Commission, Coronado Cuarto Centennial Exposition. While she assured Mrs. Rockwell of her support for the Memorial, her primary concern was that it not threaten her mine holdings.[670] Two years later, she informed Moody that the "entire camp was stolen when the CCC [Civilian Conservation Corps] constructed the road through the canyon."[671]

In 1942, Grace Sparkes was given total control of the State of Texas mine property. In June, Moody quit-claimed his share with the stipulation that he would receive half of future net profits or half of the net proceeds of any future sale.[672] In September, the other Sparkes heirs quit-claimed their shares to Grace as well.[673] She finally obtained a loan from the federal government in connection with the World War II effort, also in 1942, and the mine produced zinc from 1943-1946.[674] Burdett Moody died in 1946. It is unclear what the relationship between he and Sparkes was at the time and whether his widow retained an interest in the property.[675] As the 1950s began, Grace Sparkes controlled the State of Texas property and was also active in promoting the Memorial.

The Huachuca Mountains and Montezuma Canyon were full of mining claims during the early decades of the twentieth century. A complete description of them could fill a book by itself. By 1978, when the Memorial expanded to the north side of Montezuma Canyon, thirteen claims had come to be owned by the Victorio Company. They became an issue for the Memorial and the National Park Service. Most of the claims eventually controlled by the Victorio Company had once been owned by Bruce Doredor. Doredor is thought to have immigrated from Italy.[676] The claims were in two groups separated by the State of Texas mine properties. To the east were Doredor, Paring No. One, Paring No. Two, Paring No. Three, and Paring No. Four. To the west were Z.T. Parker, Chief, Fraction, Rubio, Tunnelsite, Miss Stake, Grub Stake No. Two, and Grub Stake No. Three.

According to a summary of mine claims compiled at Coronado National Memorial, the Miss Stake, Grub Stake No. Two, and Grub Stake No. Three mine claims, along with three others in their immediate vicinity, were claimed by Felix Livericio in March 1899. The Doredor, Paring No. One, Paring No. Two, Paring No. Three, Paring No. Four, Z.T. Parker, Chief, Fraction, Rubio, and Tunnelsite were claimed by Bruce Doredor. The four Paring mines were claimed in 1901 and the Doredor claim in 1920. The western group are said to have been claimed in 1909.[677] All thirteen claims were patented by Bruce Doredor on April 10, 1920.[678] One source placed Doredor in the canyon and on those claims much earlier, probably before 1900.[679]

The same summary of mine claims cited above lists purchase of Z.T. Parker, Chief, Fraction, Rubio, Tunnelsite, Grub Stake No. Two, and Miss Stake by "Clark/Smith" in 1938.[680] Bill Clark was on the Board of Supervisors and was said to have purchased the property for back taxes.[681] Clark and Smith owned the claims through the 1950s but did little or nothing to exploit them.

As Coronado National Memorial was being designed during the 1940s, mining property within its eventual boundaries was largely limited to two owners. The State of Texas claims were owned, or at least managed, by Grace Sparkes, while two groups of claims surrounding the Sparkes lands were owned by Clark and Smith. The same was true of the lands formerly contained in four homesteads at the mouth of Montezuma Canyon on the east side of the Huachuca Mountains. The Zaleski family still owned three and had just sold the forth. The Montezuma Ranch was still being run as a camp and tourist ranch.

The physical design of the Memorial was explicitly shaped by a desire to avoid mineral deposits and protect the grazing rights of a few local ranchers within the area. The outcome was the Memorial that was proclaimed by the President on November 5, 1952, its specifications were based upon "section 1 of the act of August 18, 1941, 55 Stat. 630 (16 U.S.C. 450 y) as amended by Public Law 478, 82nd Congress, approved July 9, 1952."

The Memorial was originally located in Township 24 South, Range 20 East: Section 10, Section 11, Section 13, Section 14, Section 15, Section 22, Section 23, and Section 24; and Township 24 South, Range 21 East: Section 17, Section 18, Section 19, and Section 20.[682] Those sections are along the international boundary, in the south end of the Huachuca Mountains, both east and west of Montezuma Pass, and generally south of an unpaved road that became the main road through the Memorial.

The seemingly neverending story of the Memorial's land took on a history of its own. In the next decades, as the Memorial expanded its protective boundary, other adjacent lands came into play.

Chapter VIII

Private Development and "Boundary Adjustment - a Radical Proposal," 1952-1978

> *Although CORO has been set aside as a historical area, its primary use is by those interested in the wildlife and scenery.*
> -- Coronado Superintendent Hugo Huntzinger, 1970.

Coronado National Memorial was founded in 1952[683] through a land transfer from the National Forest Service to the National Park Service. The Memorial's configuration was shaped through a process that focused more on domestic political concerns, mostly the protection of private property and mining and grazing rights, than on natural resources or historical commemoration. The Park Service and Memorial staff would soon find that the land they had been given charge of was not conducive to preservation or development as either a historical or environmental entity, let alone as both. That realization, recognized in stages, led to two major boundary adjustments, in 1960 and 1978. The second change would bring sizable private inholdings within the Memorial. That private land went through changes in ownership and status over the decades before it was brought into the Memorial that would create problems for the future acquisition program.

Nancy Nelms owned the Montezuma Ranch in the late 1940s and early 1950s, as the Memorial was opening, and ran it as a summer camp and dude ranch. By 1951, Nelms cut back operations, in line with the general decline of the market for such operations. In 1955, she listed the Montezuma Ranch for sale with realtor George Howe of Tucson. Howe went for a visit, reportedly so that he could better describe it in sales materials, and was impressed with the property. Howe was so impressed that, on November 21, 1955, he and his wife, Martha, purchased Montezuma Ranch themselves. With the departure of Nancy Nelms, the dude ranch period came to an end. The Howes earned some income on the ranch by renting apartments to people from Fort Huachuca but could not make it profitable. Nonetheless, they held onto it for nearly two decades.[684]

At that time, much of the rest of the property at the mouth of Montezuma Canyon belonged to the Zaleski family. The Zaleskis owned the former Ratliff Homestead Entry Surveys, numbered 310 and 311, west of Montezuma Ranch. Both contained just less than 160 acres. They also owned the 133.67 acre Kudzmi homestead, south of Montezuma Ranch. Joe Zaleski had ceded the three homesteads to his son, Frank, by way of a Gift Deed in October 1950. In 1956, Frank quit-claimed it all back to Joe.[685] The next year, in April 1957, Joe Zaleski sold the same property to John A. and Inez Z. Jones. Included in the sale were over one hundred head of cattle, a few horses, "miscellaneous tools, equipment, and furniture," and a stock brand.[686]

After Coronado National Memorial was founded, in 1952, the National Park Service plotted its development. However, the 1952 bill specified that no money would be appropriated for the Memorial.[687] It was not until July of 1954 that funding was finally approved for the Memorial.[688] Shortly thereafter, the Memorial still had no money, no Master Plan, and no permanently assigned personnel. Nor was it known where personnel would stay once they were assigned to the Memorial.[689] Upon hearing that funds had been appropriated, Grace Sparkes, owner and resident of the State of Texas mine, immediately contacted NPS. She wrote: "I want to cooperate and would like to have your Park official quartered at our camp."[690] Sparkes, a member of the Coronado Commission, had already proven herself a supporter when she signed a right of way agreement in June 1951, before the Memorial was actually established.[691]

In the fall of 1954, Sparkes received a response from NPS, saying that they would, indeed, like to rent her cabin for use as an office.[692] They asked how much rent she would charge on the cabin and added that they would also like to put a house trailer on the property and hook it up to water and electricity. The trailer would require installation of a septic tank as well.[693] Within a couple weeks, a purchase order was sent to Sparkes to cover rent for twenty-six days in December 1954. Meanwhile, a more permanent lease agreement was worked out to start at the beginning of 1955.[694] In January 1955, the first of a series of leases took effect, covering a cabin, space for a trailer, and electricity and water. The cabin rented for thirty dollars per month, trailer space for five dollars per month, and water and electricity for another five dollars.[695] An annual lease commenced in July of 1955 which specified that eight dollars a month would be charged for electricity and two dollars for water, while the cost of the cabin and the trailer space remained the same.[696] During this same period, Sparkes was also hired by NPS as a seasonal caretaker, beginning in September 1955.[697] The July 1956 lease raised the price of the trailer space to ten dollars per month.[698] In 1957, a 1500 square foot storage lot and space for another trailer were added to the lease. The charge for each trailer space was fifteen dollars per month; each month's electricity was ten dollars per trailer; water was four dollars per trailer; and the storage lot was six dollars a month.[699] The annual leases of 1958 and 1959 retained the same prices, for total yearly prices of $1128.[700]

In the meantime, immediate plans were formulated for two residences for Memorial staff and a building containing a visitor center and administrative facilities. In February 1960, the Memorial took possession of the two residences and the new administration and visitor center.[701] Memorial staff moved into the new, permanent, facilities during the same month.[702] The last lease agreement between Grace Sparkes and NPS ran out in June 1960.[703] That ended the use of the State of Texas land for Memorial administration and housing. The land on which these new buildings were placed did not yet belong to the Memorial. However, NPS had already reached an agreement with the Forest Service to make an exchange that would bring it into the Memorial.[704] Further, legislation was in the works to make the agreement a reality.

The plan for the International Memorial, to the extent that it was developed, had called for a museum and visitor center to be located on the south flank of the Huachuca Mountains. Such a location was more accessible from the Mexican side of the international border than from the north. A 1940 study indicated that a proposed "borderline parkway" connecting Douglas and Nogales, Arizona, which would traverse an international memorial south of the border, would offer the best access. The same document recognized that "heavy road construction" would be required to create an approach to a high elevation lookout.[705]

Before long, it was realized that the land that had been set aside for the Memorial within the United States did not contain suitable sites for visitor facilities. In 1954, several boundary adjustments were suggested by the first officials to consider the development prospects of the Memorial.[706] One acquisition was explained by the need "to develop a desirable headquarters and residential area" within the park. Another addition was "required for picnic area development and a construction of a road to the proposed public use area at the International Boundary."[707] Note that, at the time, a visitor center was still planned for a site on the international boundary, on the south flank of the Huachuca Mountains, on the southwest side of Montezuma Canyon. Such a center would, of course, require the participation of the Mexican government and dedication to the Memorial of the land south of the border.

It was during this time that the Nogales protest took place. Upon the first published rumors that the Park Service intended to develop Coronado Memorial, the same opposition excited by the Memorial's founding immediately resurfaced. The issue, however, slowly dissipated.

Meanwhile, the National Park Service continued its efforts to acquire a portion of Homestead Entry Survey 310 for road right of way. It then belonged to Frank Zaleski, but soon passed to his father, Joe Zaleski, and then to John A. Jones. Jones indicated that he was willing to sell the land for inclusion in Coronado Memorial. However, he insisted that he would transfer only the amount absolutely necessary, after which the acquisition proposal was scaled down from about one hundred acres to around fifty.[708] The National Park Service could not acquire the land until after legislation had been passed and funding specifically targeted for the purchase. In the interim, officials were concerned over Jones's physical and mental health. He had suffered two heart attacks and, in late 1958, was being treated for "for a mental illness." Superintendent Welles at Coronado worried that if Jones died or became permanently incapacitated the land could be held up in probate or other legal complications. Finally, though he was sure that one of Jones's sons would carry out the sale of the property, he had doubts about the other.[709]

The Park Service had two options for securing the land before the money was allocated for its purchase. It could have attempted to negotiate a long-term option that would have been contingent on enactment of the legislation. The other alternative, which was pursued, was to approach the Southwestern Monuments Association, a non-governmental entity, to purchase the property for eventual resale to the Memorial once the legislation was passed.[710] In May 1959, a 49.856 acre portion of Homestead Entry Survey 310 was purchased by Southwest Monuments Association (SMA)—the predecessor to Southwest Parks and Monuments Association (SPMA)—from the Jones family for a total cost of $3,000. The property was a roughly triangular tract of land, most of which was in the south half H.E.S. 310; a small portion extended into the southwest corner of the north half 310. It was in the North Half of the Southeast Quarter of Section 18, Township 24 South, Range 21 East, Gila and Salt River Base and Meridian.[711]

The Southwestern Monuments Association purchase paved the way for a boundary adjustment that was approved on September 2, 1960. It altered the Memorial boundary in four ways, adding three tracts and withdrawing one. The 49.856 acre triangular tract bought by S.M.A. from the Jones's was purchased by the Park Service for the Memorial. Just to the northwest of the triangle, 75.33 acres were transferred from Coronado National Forest, a unit of the National Forest Service, to the Memorial. It comprised lots 2 and 7 of Section 18, Township 24 South, Range 21 East. This was where the visitor center, staff housing, and picnic area had already been located.

Some mining land was excluded from the Memorial by the 1960 legislation, including the Billy Boy claim in the State of Texas group of claims and the Z.T. Parker claim, later of the Victorio Company properties. The land reverted from the Memorial to Coronado National Forest, National Forest Service. The mining claims remained with their owners. This property was described as the north half of the southwest quarter of the northwest corner of Section 13, and the north half of the southeast quarter of the northeast quarter of Section 14, Township 24 South, Range 20 East. Each section contained twenty acres, for a total deletion of forty acres.[712]

Another small segment was also added by the 1960 legislation. It was a sixty foot wide strip along the border in the southeast corner of the Memorial, lots 5 and 6 of Section 20, Township 24 South, Range 21 East, comprising 3.6 acres. In correspondence preparatory to the adjustment, it was depicted as an inadvertent exclusion from the original Memorial boundaries.[713] Considerable confusion surrounded the status of this strip. For one thing, it did not appear to exist, according to most maps. Sections 19 through 24 of Township 24 South, Range 21 East, and the same sections to the east and west, began just north of the border. As they were abbreviated by their proximity to the border, they were shown on some maps as including only four lots, numbered 1 through 4, each comprising 27 acres.

Bureau of Land Management plats depicted lots 1 through 4 as extending only from the north boundary of the section to the north side of a sixty foot strip along the international border. The sixty foot strip itself was split into four more, very small, lots. Lots 5 and 6 of Section 20 should have been within the boundaries of the Memorial.[714] It was noted that the rest of the strip had been included within the original boundaries of the Memorial.[715] Interestingly, later descriptions of the strip did not refer to any lot numbers above the number four.[716]

There was also doubt as to what agency administered the sixty foot strip. The 1941 legislation that created the Memorial specified that the National Park Service would be restricted in its activities within sixty feet of the border. As that strip had been "withdrawn" in 1907 by Presidential proclamation, the Secretary of State had to be consulted prior to "any recreational or other development" within it.[717] The legislation which revised the Memorial in 1960 was written to transfer the boundary strip from the National

Forest Service. During consultation, the question was raised whether the Department of State actually controlled the land.[718]

The issue of the sixty foot strip on the border would be revisited in just a few years. In the early 1960s, the United States Section of the International Boundary and Water Commission in El Paso, Texas, acted to divest itself of land within a 60 foot wide strip running along the border. The National Park Service moved to obtain those portions within the Coronado National Memorial and Organ Pipe Cactus National Monument, both in Arizona. Evidently, after a considerable amount of paper was shuffled, the land did change from one federal agency to another, though with little effect since it was already considered part of the Memorial.

The description of the border strip within Coronado National Memorial is interesting in the wake of the 1960 transfer:

> the southerly 60 feet of the following subdivisions:
> Township 24 South, Range 20 East (Gila and Salt River Meridian)
> Section 22, Lots 1, 2, 3, and 4;
> Section 23, Lots 1, 2, 3, and 4;
> Section 24, Lots 1, 2, 3, and 4;
> Township 24 South, Range 21 East (Gila and Salt River Meridian)
> Section 19, Lots 1, 2, 3, and 4;
> Section 20, Lots 3 and 4;
> Totaling 32.504 acres more or less.[719]

That includes land which was already defined as within the Memorial in 1941 as well that added in 1960. The 1960 addition is here shown as being within lots 3 and 4 of Section 20. In none of these sections is there a hint of lots 5 through 8. That, taken with the correspondence leading up to the 1960 addition, might suggest that the "sections 5 and 6" did not actually exist, and were, in fact, added unnecessarily in 1960. The point was moot. No matter how the maps were marked, or when the land was acquired, it all belonged to the Memorial.

As the Park Service worked to rectify problems of development and control of the Memorial through small boundary adjustments, private lands that would one day belong to the Memorial were also in flux. The mining claims on the north side of Montezuma Canyon had just gained security from the 1960 adjustment. It had transferred forty acres from the Memorial to Coronado National Forest in order to keep the mining claims and potential development out of the Memorial and in the National Forest.

Part of that land belonged to the State of Texas mining properties belonging to Grace Sparkes. During the 1950s, Sparkes had become interested in selling the State of Texas property. She improved the property and upped her asking price from thirty thousand dollars to $32,500, though it was said that she had not formally listed it. Supposedly, potential buyers had approached her about the property in 1957. Superintendent Philip Welles opined that Sparkes was asking more than the land was worth. However, he also recognized that the land had value to NPS over and above its monetary worth. It had a water source that was estimated as sufficient for the Memorial's future development needs and contained structures that could be, and were at the time, used by the Memorial. Its location, right on the main road through the Memorial, probably increased its market value; it certainly made it more consequential to the Memorial as well. Welles recognized a "nuisance" factor in the event that "persons unfriendly to the area or to the service" should buy the land.[720]

Sparkes preferred the idea of selling the land to the Park Service for inclusion in Coronado Memorial. In 1958, she wrote that NPS had earlier expressed interest in some of the land, but she had then thought that she might return to mining. Her circumstances, as well as mineral prices, had changed, and Sparkes was determined to sell, preferably to NPS.[721] She mentioned its water resource and hoped that the buildings, still being remodeled, could become a ranger station. Sparkes hoped that in an upcoming "expansion" of the Memorial, NPS could "take over" her land.[722] By then, the land and buildings that were added in 1960 had already been planned. During her lifetime, Grace Sparkes never did sell to NPS or anyone else. She died in 1963, leaving the State of Texas mine property to her four nephews. [723]

In July 1970, Ruth M. Clark, a widow, and Charles A. and Paquita C. Smith, sold several mining properties, including the thirteen Doredor claims in the Hartford Mining District of the Huachuca Mountains that fell within the eventual boundaries of Coronado National Memorial. Evidently, the sellers were Bill Clark's widow and his partner. The buyers were Coronado Investment Company, a partnership comprised of Peter G. Wray and H. Wayne Pruett.[724] In 1973, the properties were transferred to Pruett-Wray Cattle Company, made up of the same partners.[725] By 1979, Pruett-Wray had changed its name to "Victorio Land and Cattle Company" and then to "The Victorio Company."[726]

Back at the mouth of Montezuma Canyon, land was changing hands and developments occurring, some of which would one day be problematical for the Memorial. The remainder of Homestead Entry Survey 310, all of Homestead Entry Survey 311, and the Kudzmi Homestead, were given by John A. and Inez Z. Jones to John Z. and Lawrence D. Jones "for and in consideration of the love and affection" of parents for their children in 1962.[727] The Jones brothers sold the total amount to Everett and Fred Baumkirchner and their respective wives, Margaret E. and Mary Ann, in

1965. The purchase price was not recorded, but John and Lawrence Jones carried a $45,000 mortgage on the property.[728]

The Baumkirchner brothers grew up in Miller and Hunter canyons of the Huachuca Mountains, the sons of a university educated German immigrant who mined in the area. Over the years they owned several local businesses and built up a substantial ranching operation stretched along the east side of the Huachuca Mountains.[729] The Baumkirchners evidently obtained the Jones property for the purpose of speculation. They soon subdivided it and put portions on the market. The first tract was sold in September 1966. The Baumkirchners sold one acre, that was later labeled Tract 101-15, to Calvin R. and Esther Teague.[730] The Teagues sold it to William L. Cashman and Ramona E. Cashman in April 1971.[731] By 2001, William and Jean Cashman continued to reside in this house and property, an inholding of Coronado National Memorial.

On July 21, 1967, two more small parcels were sold by the Baumkirchners. On that date, the Baumkirchners sold the one acre portion of H.E.S. 311 later known as Tract 101-13 to William and Eloise Archie.[732] The Archies held the land until November 1972 and then sold it to Robert G. and Betty J. Chavez.[733] They, in turn, sold the property to Eileen Owens in April 1978.[734]

Also on July 21, 1967, the Baumkirchners sold two acres to Lawrence Edward Ray.[735] Ray borrowed $14,400 from the Farmers Home Administration of the United States Department of Agriculture for the purchase. F.H.A. held the deed to the property as collateral.[736] Next, Ray sold the property to James M. and Billie Jean Tyra in August 1971.[737] After NPS acquired the surrounding property, this parcel became known as Tract 101-11, Parcel 1. A month after the Tyras purchased Parcel 1 from Ray, the Baumkirchners sold two acres, a tract that came to be known as Parcel 2 of Tract 101-11, to the Tyras.[738] The Tyras seem to have borrowed money for both purchases from the Baumkirchners which they repaid when they sold Tract 101-11 to NPS in 1980.[739] Those two purchases placed the Tyras in possession of four acres, which came to be labeled Tract 101-11.

In 1971, there were two more sales of land within H.E.S. 311. In August, the Baumkirchner brothers and their wives sold two one-acre lots to Dewitt and Doretta Ruth Green.[740] These two parcels became Tracts 101-12 and 101-14. The Baumkirchners also sold a six-acre tract to a son of one of the brothers, Everett M. Baumkirchner, Jr. In October 1971 the property was transferred pending payments totaling $6,000.[741] In 1980, when the younger Everett sold the land to the Park Service, another Warranty Deed for Tract 101-16 was transferred from the elder Baumkirchners to him. It was probably given after the last money owed on the property was paid to the sellers and cleared the title for ownership by NPS and inclusion into Coronado National Memorial.[742]

In 1973, the Baumkirchners traded 541.43 acres to the National Forest Service "for and in consideration of...certain national forest land, which does not exceed in value the land herein conveyed." Included in the land exchange was most of their land in the area of the Memorial. The National Forest Service acquired the entire Kudzmi Homestead, the remainder of H.E.S. 310 not already within the Memorial, and a 50 acre portion of the southwest corner of H.E.S. 311.[743] After the Baumkirchners sold fifty acres of H.E.S. 311 and subdivided they rest, they kept the biggest piece, later called tract 101-10. That property was sometimes listed as two separate parcels although they were transferred together. A 1979 appraisal described 94.23 acres. The described property contained several building improvements, including rental units, residences, barns, and sheds. Access was by paved highway. The property was generally located in Section 17, Township 24 South, Range 21 East, Gila and Salt River Meridian.[744]

The old Pyeatt homestead also changed hands around the same time. In April 1973, according to a Joint Tenancy Deed filed at the time, the Montezuma Ranch was sold to George F. and Elsie R. Weick of Illinois.[745] The Weicks would sell the property within a few years. After Richard Richards bought it in 1979, Elsie Weick would again become involved, as Richards's mother and creditor and, again, as a landowner. Weick's interest and involvement in the Montezuma Ranch would continue for the next few decades, at least.

All of the privately owned land discussed above was within the original homesteads at the mouth of Montezuma Canyon and on the north side of the canyon further up into the Huachuca Mountains. The issue over its status came to a head at Coronado National Memorial in 1978. An anonymous, undated, memo entitled "Boundary Adjustment–a Radical Proposal" discussed reasons for making significant adjustments to the boundaries of the Memorial. It discussed reasons for additions to and withdrawals from the Memorial. The portion of the Memorial west of Montezuma Pass, according to the memo, was not really enjoyed by the visiting public except as a scenic backdrop in any case. In addition, it represented seventy percent of the grazing land within the Memorial. Both land and water resources had been damaged by overgrazing. Withdrawal of that land would relieve NPS personnel of the headache of patrolling and administering the overgrazing of the unused land.

All of Montezuma Canyon was, said the memo, already thought of by the public as part of the Memorial.[746] It could be managed efficiently only if all of it was brought within the Memorial. These concerns can be seen as addressing a changing vision of the Memorial. First promoted as an overlook of the valley through which Coronado entered the United States, the pristine character of the view needed to be maintained if the Memorial was to be worthwhile. Set aside to be enjoyed by the public for its natural beauty and resources, it would become a multiple use area.

In a 1970 memorandum, Coronado Superintendent Huntzinger of was more explicit regarding the purpose and needs of the Memorial. He wrote "Although CORO has been set aside as a historical area, its primary use is by those interested in the wildlife and scenery." He went on to point out that the Memorial did "not at present exist as an ecological entity." He specified that most of Montezuma Canyon, the heart of the Memorial, was not within the Memorial. In addition, a "rather shoddy county estate subdivision is developing immediately to the east of the Memorial."[747] Such a development would destroy the view and the visitor experience.

A letter from a planning team member summarized its feelings about the importance of maintaining the viewshed of the Memorial. "Certainly the entire historic scene of the San Pedro Valley cannot all be protected but this segment of 270 acres pointing at the heart of the Memorial must be acquired to prevent obnoxious developments which would detract from the visitors park experience."[748] Thus, a plan to adjust the Memorial began to emerge. The proposal spelled out the problem:

> "Because the Memorial lacks visible remains and is not the site of any dramatic occurrence, its historical value lies in the fact that it is able to set a reflective mood suitable for contemplation of the Coronado Entrada. Retention of the pastoral grassland scene of the distant San Pedro Valley is important if this area is to fulfill its purpose and effectively Memorialize and interpret history. This historic scene lies largely outside the current park boundaries and therefore is subject to adverse use and esthetic deterioration that will seriously compromise the park's efforts to provide a quality visitor experience."[749]

According to the idea under consideration, land additions would bring all of the Montezuma Canyon watershed into the Memorial. The Park Service staff already had responsibility for maintaining the road through the canyon. Control of the entire canyon would enable the Memorial to open more trails, expand opportunities for environmental study programs, provide a better water source, and aid in environmental protection. It would also allow the Memorial to control existing and potential development in areas then immediately adjacent to the Memorial. All of the land west of Montezuma Pass was to be removed from the Memorial and reclaimed by Coronado National Forest. It was unlikely that sufficient development would occur in that area, so far from pavement and services, to seriously affect the viewshed from Montezuma Pass.

The new Memorial lands would also include National Forest Service lands that had been part of the Kudzmi Homestead and Homestead Entry

Surveys 310 and 311. In the extreme southeast corner of the Memorial, and making up the southeast corner of the land transferred in 1978, was a square tract labeled 101-19, 137.31 acres in size. It included the 133.67 acre Kudzmi Homestead plus 3.64 acres. That 3.64 acres was very likely a strip directly along the international border, much like the 3.6 acre border strip in the 1960 land transfer. That land was relinquished by the United States Section of the International Boundary and Water Commission [see above]. Also added to the Memorial was a 1.03 acre strip running the length of the boundary between Homestead Entry Survey No. 311 and the Pyeatt Homestead. These small additions filled in between lands claimed earlier in the century.[750]

Another element that was central to discussions of a potential boundary adjustment to the Memorial in the late 1970s was the siting and construction of an outdoor amphitheatre north of the road. It would require an access road and parking lot and would include another scenic overlook. The size and location of the amphitheatre, meant to hold at least two thousand people, varied through different plans and alternatives. It was thought necessary because an annual historical pageant, begun a few years earlier, had outgrown the picnic area and required a permanent home.[751] The amphitheatre was never constructed and the pageant itself was soon discontinued, but the remainder of the adjustment process continued.[752]

Public comments on the adjustment proposal were solicited, eliciting both support and opposition. Opposition centered around several themes.[753] The Arizona Game and Fish Department, for example, represented the interests of hunters who utilized the land slated for acquisition and opposed a change in status. The Department's major concern was that the land slated for addition to the Memorial was "preferred by deer, quail, and javelina hunters." According to their letter: "The actual exchange would not benefit range or wildlife management since cattle grazing allotments would remain as they are."[754] Evidently, the hunters, and the state agency that undertook to represent them, would have preferred that land be withdrawn from grazing rather than hunting.

Given the historic identification of the Huachuca Mountains and Montezuma Canyon with mining, it is not surprising that there was concerted opposition to adding land to the park from mining interests. Some groups and individuals were against any action that would might remove mineral lands from potential exploitation. The Southwestern Minerals Exploration Association opposed any change, stressing that "under *no* circumstances should any additional potentially mineral bearing lands be withdrawn. Withdrawals to date have already diminished our resource base to the point that the United States will be unable to maintain current living standards."[755]

One citizen of Tucson, John Kinnison, opposed the withdrawal of any land until a thorough study of its mineral potential could be undertaken; and he also opposed spending the money to conduct such a study. In fact, he was generally averse to any enlargement of the Park Service or the expansion of its personnel base.[756] Similarly, D.A. Heatwole, a geologist for the Anaconda mining company, weighed in, on company letterhead, with the certainty that it was only a matter of time before large lodes, probably of copper, would be found in the area under consideration.[757] Charles Morgan, who had been deeply involved in the creation of the Memorial commented more specifically on the mineral issue. Identifying himself as "the person responsible for the very existence of the Coronado Memorial," Morgan expressed the opinion that the State of Texas mine had the potential to be developed into "another big copper mine." He thought that possibility should not be "foreclosed by its inclusion in the Memorial."[758] The National Parks and Conservation Association (NPCA) disagreed, specifying that such a possibility, anyplace within view of Coronado Peak, should be averted through legislation.[759]

The issue of including more mining lands within the Memorial took on additonal importance, and dissension, with an act passed by Congress late in 1976, while the adjustment process was being debated. One section of this act applied directly and solely to Coronado National Memorial. It repealed the section of the original act of 1941 that permitted mining within the Memorial. More generally, the 1976 act gave the Secretary of the Interior the right to regulate mining within the National Park System "In order to preserve for the benefit of present and future generations the pristine beauty of" the parks.[760] By the 1976 act, the protection previously guaranteed to miners took a back seat to protection of the Memorial's resources.

The only other patented claims besides the State of Texas known to be directly affected were those owned by the Victorio Company. At the time the land adjustment was under consideration, the Victorio Company was negotiating a land swap, which would never be consummated, with the Forest Service.[761] In 1978, although as yet unable to actually purchase the land, the Park Service entered into discussions with the landowners regarding the Victorio property. The two parties disagreed over the value of the land and it was listed with several local brokers.[762] Before the end of 1979, NPS was informed that the Victorio property had been divided and the sale of a portion of it was imminent. A.W. Gray, of the NPS Division of Land Acquisition, requested that the sale be delayed to allow the Park Service, which by then had the necessary funds appropriated, to approve an appraisal and bid on the land.[763] However, the sale was consummated, leaving NPS to negotiate with other owners as well as the Victorio Company.

Some opposed any expansion of Park Service lands even if it only came at the expense of the Forest Service. Their concerns were with big government in general. Others generally shared the same feelings, but phrased their opposition in terms of concern for property rights, sometimes mentioning the loss of tax base that would occur if the private inholdings were later acquired by the Memorial. One representative comment was "We need private property;"[764] another: "We do not have the right to impose anything on private property owners...This is a free(?) country yet."[765]

Others supported the adjustment, including environmental groups and assorted citizens and scientists who had visited the Memorial and enjoyed its resources. The Baumkirchner brothers, who had owned a lot of land in the Montezuma Canyon area and still retained a sizeable tract, were in favor of the swap. They pointed out that land in the area was being bought up quickly. If public entities did not act quickly it would be too late to set aside much needed space for recreation, public use, and sanctuary for wildlife.[766] The transfer was approved in 1978. The land acquired by the Memorial encompassed private land within Homestead Entry Surveys 310 and 311 along with the State of Texas and the Victorio mining properties. They would have to be added through purchase, which would excite more opposition to the Memorial as it grew to its present size and shape.

Coronado Borderlands Festival, April 28, 1987. (Coronado National Memorial Archives, National Park Service)

Chapter IX
Resources Made Available for the Enjoyment of the Public: 1978 to the Present

> *The beauty, purpose and setting of the park should not be destroyed by an urban development within the very scenic heart of this Park.* -- Coronado supporter Gordon Douglas to Secretary of Interior James Watt, 1981.

> *We feel you have abundant land to serve your purpose and that this is just another land grab.* -- Coronado opponent William P. Ullrich, 1980.

The 1978 adjustment brought Coronado National Memorial into line with a workable version of the original vision behind its founding.[767] It was now contained within, and confined to, the watershed of Montezuma Canyon. The expanse of land that spread out through the Huachuca Mountains west of the Montezuma Pass, used more by cattle than Memorial visitors, was gone. Montezuma Canyon was entirely under the control of the National Park Service. And it had all been accomplished by a simple exchange with the National Forest Service, a deal between two federal agencies. On paper, the swap seemed to solve many problems for the Park Service and Coronado National Memorial. However, on the ground were several tracts that were still in private hands. In order to fulfill the goal of the 1978 adjustment, these lands needed to be acquired. That action would open a new can of worms.

Land acquisition policy regarding inholdings at Coronado was confusing within the Park Service and controversial without. In 1978, as the swap was heading toward completion, General Superintendent John Clay of the Southern Arizona Group of the Park Service wrote to the Regional Director of the Western Region. He recalled that, as he was preparing to hold public meetings regarding potential acquisition of inholdings at Coronado, he had asked the appropriate official for a clarification of policy. He was told that "the policy was the Service acquired land on a willing buyer/willing seller basis and not by condemnation. Therefore, this is what Supt. Dale and I told members of the public at the several meetings held relative to the Coronado plan, and what appeared in the master plan approved by" the Regional Director.[768]

Subsequent communications had established that, while negotiated sales were the preferred alternative, "it may be necessary to resort to eminent domain proceedings in some instances to establish the fair market value." Further, "What was purportedly stated at public meetings was done so [sic] without full knowledge of the normal acquisition processes and at best was an erroneous statement."[769] Clay wondered if the policy had changed since that time, if the changes would be retroactive, and if they would reverse commitments already made to the public. If so, Clay continued, it placed "an agent or officer of the Service in the untenable position of having his statements or committments [sic], that were made in honesty and candor, nullified by subsequent administrative policies. On a personal level, it abrogates the integrity of the manager."[770] At issue was the need for policies to be consistent and officials to be able to keep promises to a suspicious public in a tense situation.

Some of the public was already hostile to the Park Service and the Memorial's plans. The State of Texas Mine had been a specific concern of the "Radical Proposal," discussed in the last chapter, that became the new Memorial.[771] It became the immediate target of the same forces opposed to the 1978 boundary adjustment. In September 1979, well after the Park Service had entered into negotiations with William Sparkes, Grace's nephew, an article appeared in a Tucson newspaper, entitled "His aunt helped build park that could dispossess him." It reported Sparkes's determination to retain ownership of the land and his rejection of a compromise that would have allowed him to stay on the land after acquisition by the Memorial. Sparkes recounted the promise made a few years earlier, probably by Clay and Dale, that private landowners would not be forced to sell and threatened to launch a petition campaign.[772]

Several months later, in the spring of 1980, a petition against acquisition of the State of Texas Mine arrived bearing 448 signatures.[773] It was accompanied by a letter from William P. Ullrich, of Hereford, that summarized the feelings of the signers: "We feel you have abundant land to serve your purpose and that this is just another land grab."[774] Just a few weeks earlier, the Huachuca Conservation Council had forwarded a resolution urging acquisition. It singled out the State of Texas Mine as "an unattractive inholding," and the only exception to the "exquisite scenic setting" of the Memorial.[775] A letter from the same organization also favored "quick acquisition of all other inholdings."[776]

The superintendent of the Memorial at that time, Laurel W. Dale, agreed that the Sparkes property presented "a cluttered appearance." He explained that the owner was a general contractor who, lacking other storage facilities, kept his equipment parked along the main road through the Memorial. However, Dale also recalled the key role of Sparkes's aunt, Grace, in the establishment of the Memorial. He concluded by urging "that the Service refrain from any actions that would seriously undermine the very good relationship that we now have with the Sparkes family."[777] There was also a professional relationship between William Sparkes and the Memorial. Sparkes and his contracting company, Payne & Sparkes, used the equipment to provide maintenance services for the Montezuma Pass Road under contract with Coronado National Memorial.[778]

Sparkes was a supportive neighbor in emergency situations as well. In December 1974, the Memorial thanked him for his help in a recent rescue effort.[779] Superintendent Dale also supported Sparkes when Sparkes planned to remodel his house on the State of Texas mine. He thought that the remodeling might improve the appearance of the property. He added that "They have been really good neighbors and have always lent a helping hand when needed. If we do all that can be done legally and in the process help our neighbors and keep their friendship, then we have half the battle won already."[780] Apparently, the relationship between Sparkes and the Memorial was more cordial in person than it was in local politics and newspapers.

The State of Texas properties were designated as three separate tracts, numbered 101-06, 101-07, and 101-08. Tract 101-06, 20.59 acres, consisted of one patented mining claim, the State of Texas No. Two, and was vacant of building improvements. It was located in the Southwest quarter of the Southwest quarter of Section 12, Township 24 South, Range 20 East.[781] Tract 101-07 was the State of Texas Lode Mining Claim.[782] This property was 20.66 acres, generally bisected by the section line between Sections 12 and 13, Township 24 South, Range 20 East. It contained a small unoccupied wood cabin.[783] Tract 101-08 was the ten acres patented mining claim, "State of Texas No. Two Millsite," in the South half of the Northwest quarter of the Northwest quarter of Section 13. It was improved with several residential cabins, utility buildings, and other miscellaneous improvements and was bisected by the paved Coronado Memorial Highway. All three were described in National Park Service records as in mountainous terrain.[784]

The State of Texas Lode Mining Claim, Tract 101-07, was shared by four heirs of Grace Sparkes until spring 1980. Charles J. Sparkes, Jack M. Sparkes, Thomas Frederick Sparkes, and William J. Sparkes each held a quarter interest.[785] They transferred it to William J. Sparkes in April 1980. Thomas F. Sparkes acknowledged the quit claim before a notary on the same day, Charles and Jack did so in 1986.[786] Ownership of Tracts 101-06 and 101-08 was described in 1979 as belonging to William J. Sparkes, with a part being shared by Patricia Sparkes, as William's spouse on July 18, 1974. "Spouse failed to disclaim at time of acquisition of an interest in the property by instrument recorded in Docket 948, page 457 to 460."[787] Parenthetically, the September 1979 *Arizona Daily Star* article identified Sparkes's wife at that time as "Dean."[788] It was later recalled that Will Sparkes had vowed that NPS would never get the land while he was alive. However, after he suffered a stroke and had some financial problems in early 1986, he contacted the National Park Service and a deal was eventually consummated.[789]

Tracts 101-06 and 101-07 were appraised for mineral value together. "Appraiser Robert F. Temple included within the Sparkes appraisals (Tracts 101-06 and 101-07) a mineral value of $119,540 as furnished by the Division of Mining and Minerals." He mentioned a very unstable silver market and added that, with the exceptions of lead and zinc, the precious metal market was expected to remain volatile.[790] On December 29, 1986, William J. and Patricia M. Sparkes sold 51.25 acres to NPS for $540,000 plus relocation expenses. The sale included all three tracts, 101-06, 101-07, and 101-08, and brought all of the State of Texas land into the Memorial."[791]

When the boundary adjustment of 1978 occurred, lands on both sides of the State of Texas mine properties were also in private hands. The Victorio properties were considered as two separate tracts, above and below the State of Texas. The westernmost parcel, identified as Tract 101-05, consisted of the Z.T. Parker, Chief, Fraction, Rubio, Tunnelsite, Miss Stake, Grub Stake No. Two, and Grub Stake No. Three claims. It held a total area of 154.54 acres.[792] It was improved with three structures, an approximately 756 square foot frame building, a rock house about 590 feet square, and a corrugated metal shed estimated to be 280 square feet in area. All were believed to be unoccupied. Access to the property was difficult.[793]

The eastern properties, the Doredor, Paring No. One, Paring No. Two, Paring No. Three, and Paring No. Four claims, made up Tract 101-09, 84.31 acres in size. Tract 101-09 was further divided by sale in 1979. The western half of that property was sold to James J. and Jacqueline S. Wardle and became known as Tract 101-22.[794] The eastern half of Tract 101-09, which continued to be owned by the Victorio company, was designated Tract 101-21. Tract 101-21 was 42.16 acres and made up of portions of the Doredor, Paring No. One, Paring No. Two, Paring No. Three, and Paring No. Four lode mining claims. On March 26, 1980, The Victorio Company sold 196.73 acres to NPS for $340,000. That sale comprised Tracts 101-05 and 101-21."[795]

After the Wardles, and their Wardle Realty business of Sierra Vista, obtained Tract 101-22, they quickly moved to develop and market it. Evidently, negotiations with the National Park Service began almost immediately. Near the end of December 1979, an appraisal of $101,200 was approved as a base for negotiations by the government. The owners countered with a figure of $160,000. In March, the Wardles lowered their asking price to $125,000, "provided the transaction could be promptly consummated." Unfortunately, it could not be consummated for quite some time due to budgetary constraints. So, the Wardles set about dividing and developing the property.[796]

Already, in January 1980, Jacques and Audrey C. O'Keefe bought the western portion of Tract 101-22 in a deal financed By the Wardles under an All-Inclusive Agreement that scheduled payments from the O'Keefes. This property, including just over twelve acres, was split into three tracts, numbered 101-34, 101-35, and 101-36.[797] The Memorial petitioned for condemnation to head off further development of the Wardle property and continued to do so for the next few years. In May 1980, the major concern of the Superintendent was that one or more roads would be built into the lands owned by Wardle and O'Keefe.[798]

Going into 1981, it was reported that Wardle was cutting trees to clear access for a road into a portion of the property that he had recently sold. Wardle told an NPS official, Bob Cousins, that the new owner intended to build a single family residence. Cousins reported that, due to the site's high visibility from the main road, "Superintendent Dale feels it is of highest priority to acquire this parcel by a Declaration of Taking." Therefore, Cousins continued, it would be monitored closely for evidence of building activity so that such action could be taken.[799] In April, a road was bulldozed into the Wardle property.[800]

As the National Park Service continued to worry about development of the Wardle and O'Keefe properties, Wardle was expressing equal concern about the actions of the Memorial staff. An exchange of letters in 1982 resulted from Wardle's complaint to his political representatives that federal officials had interfered with his attempts to sell his land. Wardle asserted that potential buyers had been told that "The Forest Service [sic] is in the process of buying up (taking over) all of that property," and "There isn't any water up there."[801] National Park Service officials, the actual targets of Wardle's complaint, replied that their only mention of water was a statement that there was no surface water on the land. They admitted that "Superintendent Dale mistakenly informed one individual that a Declaration of Taking had been filed against the Wardle property." In the future, promised NPS Acting Director Ira Hutchison, interested parties would be referred directly to the owner.[802]

In March 1983, rock was blasted on the road that had been bulldozed in 1981. Wardle Realty said that more roadwork was planned, and the Memorial staff braced for residential development.[803] In 1983, the O'Keefe's subdivided and sold their land. With the Wardles also selling some of their holdings in the same year, most of the property bought from the Victorio Company by Wardle was transferred during that year. The first parcel to go was Tract 101-35, the southwest section of Tract 101-22, which included portions of the Paring No. Two and Paring No. Three mining claims.[804] It was sold by the O'Keefes to Paul E. and Laurel A. Froelich in April 1983. A Joint Tenancy Deed was signed naming the Froelichs as tenants and the O'Keefes as "Grantor, Mortgagor or Trustor."[805] On the same day, a Warranty Deed transferring the property from the Wardles to the O'Keefes was also signed, showing that the O'Keefes still owed money to the Wardles as part of the 1980 All-Inclusive Agreement.[806]

On August 29, 1983, the O'Keefes sold Tract 101-36, the western section of Tract 101-22, and made up of portions of the Doredor, Paring No. Two, and Paring No. Three mining claims.[807] It was purchased by Valentin Castro III and Deborah Castro in August 1983.[808] On the same day, the Wardles sold Tract 101-33 to Richard D. and Judy L. Compton.[809] Tract 101-33 was made up of the southeast section of Tract 101-22, portions of the Paring No. Two and Paring No. Three mining claims.[810] The Comptons also bought a tract, called Tract 101-34, from the O'Keefes.[811] Tract 101-34 was made up of a portion of the Doredor claim, in the northwest section of Tract 101-22.[812]

As the year 1983 came toward an end, Superintendent Dale summarized what was occurring to the land that had formerly made up Tract 101-22:

> Instead of having one owner as we did in early 1980, we now have five owners and potential private homes – a small subdivision in the heart of the Memorial. This parcel of land is highly visible and any building of private homes and roads would be very noticeable and obtrusive – especially from the Montezuma Pass area. The beauty, purpose, and setting of the Memorial should not be destroyed by an urban development within the scenic heart of this Park.[813]

Dale closed with yet another plea for acquisition: "In view of the high visibility of this land, the imminent threat of construction and the adverse impact this construction would have on the natural features of the Park, the acquisition of this parcel should be given immediate emergency attention."[814]

Soon thereafter, in early 1984, the Huachuca Audubon Society weighed in on the side of NPS acquisition of the Wardle property. A letter from its president to Senator Barry Goldwater, however, criticized NPS inaction on the issue, suggesting that the slow moving Park Service did not fully grasp "the true ecological and historical significance of this unique bit of real estate." In fact, it went on, "key personnel...may not be well acquainted with the fact that Coronado National Memorial was established as both a natural and historical site."[815] A February 1984 summary of inholdings in the Memorial concluded by making one exception to its opposition to acquisition by condemnation. The property still identified with Wardle, despite the fact that it had multiple owners, was deemed a "new and blatant intrusion and disregard of the natural resources of the area," which should be condemned before further damage could be done.[816]

Thus, the battle lines seemed to be drawn and interests lined up for and against acquisition. The Wardles had been willing to sell the property that then made up Tract 101-22 to the Memorial and, in early 1980, had compromised on price, offering it for $125,000. Aware that the money for purchase was unlikely to be made available any time soon, they had moved to subdivide and develop the property. NPS officials, at the Memorial and elsewhere, continued to petition for acquisition, by sale or by condemnation. As the process dragged on, state and federal representatives responded to Wardle's concerns that his private property rights were being infringed upon, while environmentalists and park supporters sought to expedite the acquisition. At one point in 1981, it was explained that acquisition funds were limited "to assist President Reagan in his efforts to reduce the Federal budget."[817]

Eventually, funding was made available. In 1985, the Memorial finally acquired the remainder of the lands that had once made up the Doredor/Victorio mining claims. On February 6, 1985, James J. and Jacqueline S. Wardle sold Tract 101-37, 16.75 acres, to NPS for $120,600.[818] On February 12, the Comptons sold Tract 101-33, 13.05 acres, in three parcels, to the Park Service for $118,750. On the same day, the Comptons also sold the 4.02 acre Tract 101-34 to NPS for $33,400.[819] On February 25, Valentin Castro III and his wife, Deborah, sold Tract 101-36, 4.04 acres, to NPS for $33,400.[820] To complete the series of sales, on July 5, Paul E. and Laurel A. Froelich sold the 4.03 acre Tract 101-35 to NPS for $32,250.[821] In the four years that elapsed between 1980, when the Wardles offered Tract 101-22 for $125,000 and 1985, when the sales were completed, the price of the property had jumped to $338,400.

As a result of the 1978 boundary adjustment and the 1976 "Act to Provide for the Regulation of Mining Activity," one other set of properties came into dispute, though they were not purchased or condemned by the Park Service. The dispute itself is somewhat confused, but concerned several unpatented claims worked by W.P. Witkopp of Sierra Vista and his partner, John T. Porter. Witkopp was involved in thirty-two claims north of Montezuma Pass, in Coronado National Forest, with his company, Tako Mining.[822] Porter was a partner in some of his operations, including five claims, all or part of which were brought within the boundaries of the Memorial as a result of the 1978 adjustment.[823]

Exactly what happened to Witkopp's claims is unclear from the various accounts of his story to be found in extant documents. In February 1982, the Bureau of Land Management ruled that a total of nine claims, including those that extended into the Memorial, were abandoned and void due to failure to file appropriate paperwork before a deadline in late 1980. Samuel Riley, who leased the claims and acted as Witkopp's agent at the time of the missed filing, appealed the ruling unsuccessfully in April 1982. He offered, according to the decision, no new evidence, but stated that he was still working the claims.[824] Witkopp, himself, appealed in October 1983. He testified that Riley had been dealing with family illness at the time of the original problem and had only missed the deadline by days, that they had since lost contact , and that he, Witkopp, had not been informed of subsequent decisions.[825]

In a letter which he wrote to President Reagan in 1984, Witkopp added that Riley "had taken the liberty to assume authorization to file the affidavits" that had not been filed. This time he also added that, even before the deadline for filing, the disputed claims had been confiscated by the Park Service. He recalled that he had heard rumors of the land exchange in 1978 and approached Memorial staff. They responded, according to Witkopp, "that as far as NPS was concerned that I had no mineral rights within the area whatsoever and that the NPS and USFS were Federal agencies, and as such could do whatever they wished at any time they wished."[826] Elsewhere, he wrote that he first heard about the exchange from a Park Service employee in July 1979. He was, according to this telling, told that as soon as the legislation was read into the Federal Register the claims would become NPS property and he could no longer work on them.[827]

Immediately after the exchange, the Park Service agreed that Witkopp would be owed compensation for his claims provided that they proved valid and after their value was appraised.[828] A preliminary examination of the claims was conducted and Witkopp was notified that a survey would follow. However, he was soon told that there would be no survey or settlement because the claims were void, based upon the BLM ruling.[829] The Park

Service informed Mr. Witkopp that it had no basis for acquiring his claims unless they were properly filed. Since he had failed to file in a timely fashion in 1980, the claims were null and void as ruled by BLM and on subsequent appeals. In addition, it was pointed out that BLM was responsible for making the ruling regardless of what federal agency actually controlled the land on which the claims were located.[830]

While the whole tale of W.P. Witkopp's claims is not entirely comprehensible from the documents, it seems that he may have been caught in a confusing tangle of agency overlaps and bureaucratic rulings as well as by his own undoing. Through it all, though, he continued to profit from his claims, and his bad experience, up to the last possible minute. Well after the 1978 or 1979 date when he later said that he understood that he had been dispossessed of his claims by the Park Service, he continued to lease them, first to Samuel Riley and later to Wayne Jeppson. In 1983, he asserted that he was facing fraud charges for the latter lease because BLM had ruled against him but failed to notify him that he no longer owned, or could lease, the claims.[831] However, as noted, he later claimed that his responsibility for the claims ended four to five years earlier. Most probably, Witkopp, like most people would in his position, changed tactics and stories based on what seemed most likely to work. It also seems that NPS officials were not totally clear about what was occurring on every front while they were trying to sort out the extent of Witkopp's rights and their responsibilities. In that, the Witkopp case was far from unique in the annals of Coronado National Memorial.

The 1978 boundary adjustment also brought several inholdings at the mouth of Montezuma Canyon into Coronado National Memorial. The bulk of both Ratliff homesteads, Homestead Entry Surveys (H.E.S.) 310 and 311, as well as the Kudzmi homestead, had been acquired by the National Forest Service before 1978. That land became part of the Memorial as part of the exchange. Part of Homestead Entry Survey 311 was still in private hands as was all of the Pyeatt homestead, known as Montezuma Ranch.

The Baumkirchner brothers, as mentioned in the last chapter, had subdivided the portion of H.E.S. 311 that they had not traded to the Forest Service and begun to sell it in small lots. These were fairly quickly acquired by the Memorial. On March 19, 1980, Everett M. Baumkirchner Jr. sold 101-16, six acres, to NPS for $36,000.[832] On the same day, another Warranty Deed for Tract 101-16 was transferred from the Baumkirchner brothers and their wives to Everett Jr. The second Warranty Deed was probably given after the last money owed on the property was paid to the sellers, which cleared the title for ownership by NPS and inclusion into Coronado National Memorial.[833] At about the same time, on March 20, 1980, the Baumkirchner brothers and their wives sold the remainder of their holdings, 94.23 acres, to NPS for $471,200. The deed listed and described the two separate parcels that made up Tract 101-10.[834]

By the end of 1971, James M. Tyra and Billie Jean Tyra owned four acres of H.E.S. 311. They had purchased half of it from the Baumkirchners and the other half from Lawrence Edward Ray, but seem to have borrowed the money for all of it from the Baumkirchners. They held the land in Joint Tenancy Deeds until they sold it to NPS on March 25, 1980. The Tyras received $62,000 for the two parcels, which totaled four acres, called Tract 101-11.[835] On the same day, a Warranty Deed for both parcels of Tract 101-11 was transferred from the Baumkirchners to the Tyras, signifying that the mortgage on the property had been paid and the title cleared.[836]

On April 3, 1980, Dewitt and Doretta Ruth Green sold two acres to NPS for $19,000. That sale included Tracts 101-12 and 101-14.[837] Tract 101-13 had been bought by Eileen Owens in April 1978.[838] In January 1985, Owens sold it to Allan and Leona Cerkowniak.[839] As of the summer of 2000, the Allan Cerkowniak still resides in this house and property. William and Jean Cashman also remained as a private holding in the summer of 2000.

The other private inholding at the mouth of Montezuma Canyon, the Montezuma Ranch, was to cause considerably more problems for the Coronado National Memorial. To reprise the recent ownership of the Montezuma Ranch, George F. and Elsie R. Weick of Illinois had purchased the property from George and Martha Howe in April 1973. They sold the ranch to Patricia H. Hughes in 1975 and she sold it to Richard B. Richards and his wife, Cheryl in March 1979.[840] However, Weick's interest and involvement in the Montezuma Ranch would continue for the next two decades, at least.

A 1979 appraisal described Montezuma Ranch as Tract 101-18, 160 acres. The appraisal specified that the tract was improved with several buildings, including residences, barns, sheds, a swimming pool, and miscellaneous outbuildings. There was excellent access to the property. Its location was described as the west half of Section 17, Township 24 South, Range 21 East, Gila and Salt River Meridian, Arizona.[841]

The subdivision of the Montezuma Ranch began in late 1979. The first hint that Memorial staff had came with a phone call on September 24, 1979. Bob Gibbons, of the Western Regional office, was told by Leland Auslender, of Los Angeles, that he had bought twenty-five acres of Tract 101-18 from Richard Richards. Auslender hinted that he would be interested in selling the land. An appraiser should contact Richards, who would continue to be Auslender's agent, for an appointment.[842]

At this point Tract 101-18 was divided into two tracts. At first, they were labeled Tracts 101-23, 165 acres, and 101-24, twenty-five acres.[843] There was some confusion on everyone's part regarding the actual size of the property which Auslender bought from Richards. In May 1980, Tracts 101-23 and 101-24 were deleted because they had been "listed with erroneous acreages." In their place were Tract 101-25, ninety-five acres, belonging to Richards, and Tract 101-26, sixty-five acres, owned by Auslender.[844] By that time, on April 21, 1980, Auslender had sold his land, sixty-five acres, to the NPS for $325,000.[845]

Tract 101-25 was subsequently subdivided into Tracts 101-27, 101-28, 101-29, and 101-30, all of which remained in the possession of Richard Richards and his wife, Cheryl. Tract 101-27 was formerly the northeast corner of 101-25; Tract 101-28 was the southeast corner; and Tract 101-30 was made up of land on the north side of Tract 101-25.[846] Before long, the Richards's sold all three tracts to the National Park Service for inclusion in Coronado National Memorial. On December 15, 1981, they sold ten acres to NPS for $50,000. That sale comprised Tracts 101-27 and 101-28, each containing five acres.[847] On August 3, 1982, the Richards's sold Tract 101-30, 2.5 acres, to NPS for $12,500.[848]

When the ninety-five acre Tract 101-25 was divided, 82.5 acre Tract 101-29 retained most of its land.[849] Tract 101-29 was christened Sunrise Farms and operated by Richards as an organic farm. Among other things, Sunrise Farms produced fruit, broccoli, garlic, and carrots. Richards also made and marketed carrot juice from the crop. Montezuma Ranch was also host to other enterprises, at least one of which, it would turn out, was illegal. Richards raised turkeys, horses, and ostriches, and sold satellite television dishes. At one time, he sold foam roof covering, with which he coated an entire house, "(f)rom the foundation up to the peak."[850]

On 4 February 1985 Richard Richards and Cheryl Richards, husband and wife, sold a scenic easement to NPS for $549,000. The conditions were spelled out in attachments. They were aimed at "preserving and protecting the scenic value of the said lands" by limiting construction, landscaping, and land use. Some Arizona Cypress trees were to be planted to screen the property and park personnel were to be permitted limited access.[851]

Despite the restrictions contained in the scenic easement agreement signed by NPS and Mr. and Ms. Richards, the landowners soon floated several development schemes for Tract 101-29. They included fee sale of twenty-five acres, including all structures; contracting with the state to run a half-way house for paroled felons; operating a nursing home; developing a mini-RV park; and sub-dividing the property into five new building sites. Richards also proposed selling the property to NPS with the stipulation that he be allowed to remain.[852]

Another issue involving the scenic easement on Tract 101-29 and relations between Richards and the Memorial was waste disposal on the property. In May 1990, new superintendent Edward Lopez conducted a hazardous waste survey of the Richards property and submitted a report expressing concern about the dump sites and recommending that a more thorough inspection be performed.[853] On the request of NPS, the Arizona Department of Environmental Quality inspected Richards's 82.5 acre property on June 19, 1990. They issued a report in August identifying "Several Solid Waste issues" including "three unapproved refuse landfills, diesel fuel leaks, fiberglass resin discharges, and various waste containers of oil and paint, and waste batteries."[854] While some dump sites, litter, and abandoned vehicles were present before the easement agreement, it was clear that the property had deteriorated since it was signed.[855]

Subsequent to the easement agreement, Richards began attempting to sell Tract 101-29. He claimed financial hardship, partly due to the restrictions in the easement, adding in 1990 that he was by then divorced and otherwise in debt as well. In 1988, Richards first suggested that NPS purchase the property, stipulating that he wanted to continue living there and using the land for agriculture. Given his ongoing circumvention of the scenic easement and degeneration of Tract 101-29, some NPS officials supported the idea. Superintendent Joseph L. Sewell recommended fee acquisition by NPS and renewable one-year special use permits that allowed Richards to stay on the land.[856]

It was, belatedly, recognized by NPS officials that the scenic easement was ineffective as written. There seemed to be no enforcement mechanisms which specified consequences for violations. In addition, NPS had no pictures or descriptions of the property to document the appearance of the property at the time of the agreement in order to prove that violations had occurred. Obvious violations of specific items in the easement agreement had already taken place without retribution. One example was the granting of right-of-way to the Sulfur Springs Valley Electrical Cooperative. Now, Richards was prepared to pursue further development, unconcerned about the seemingly unenforceable easement. In addition, stipulated screening efforts had been ineffective and would likely continue to be so. Finally, Richards was determined to sell the property, and probably subdivide it. If NPS did not acquire it, the same problems were likely to continue with the new owners.[857]

Requests to Washington, D.C., for acquisition funding raised concerns. The Director's office noted that the landowner was claiming a hardship based upon an easement for which he had already been paid. Fee acquisition would then be used as a remedy for repeated violations of the easement. Even after acquisition, the violator would remain on the property under a special use permit. In effect, NPS would pay for the land twice and it would still be under the control of a private landowner who had proven uncooperative in the past. Such a course would be inconsistent with existing policy and set a dangerous precedent for future acquisitions.[858] When hardship funds were requested to allow immediate acquisition, a Congressional Subcommittee also expressed concern that purchase was proposed as a means of preventing development that was specifically prohibited by the already purchased easement.[859]

When Edward Lopez met him in December 1989, Richards introduced himself as "the person that 'had taken the NPS for over $500,000 and was in the process of taking another one half million from them again.'"[860] Thereafter, Richards continued his attempts to subdivide and sell Tract 101-29, promising prospective buyers that they could build as long as they were replacing one of the many buildings already on the property. He also continued to plead hardship to NPS On October 16, 1990, Acting Western Regional Director, Lewis S. Albert explained that the Richards family was losing all their equity through possible bankruptcy and had not marketed the property because they were counting on NPS to buy it. He went on to discuss the insufficient regulation that allowed Richards to the violate easement and the mess that he had already created and would likely exacerbate.[861] By early 1991, NPS was negotiating purchase with a Chapter 13 Trustee, suggesting that the property had been foreclosed. However, funding was not then available and was not thought likely to be until after October 1, 1992.[862]

On the evening of July 25, 1991, the status and fate of the Richards property was suddenly changed. As Superintendent Lopez was leaving the Memorial he was flagged down by Linda Sorenson, who lived with Richards on the property. At her request, Lopez contacted the Cochise County Sheriff's Department. Sorenson had been assaulted by Richards and said that she wanted to retaliate by turning him in for marijuana cultivation. However, she had, evidently, already been in contact with the Sheriff's Department regarding the matter. Together, Sheriff's deputies and Park Rangers searched the Richards property and the adjacent area of the Memorial. They found marijuana growing within the house as well as thirty-eight marijuana plants on NPS land.[863]

According to Superintendent Lopez, the Department of Justice, United States Attorney's Office, and Drug Enforcement Agency approached him shortly after the drug bust to assess NPS interest in obtaining the property through the seizure process. NPS officials discussed the offer and responded that they would indeed be interested in acquisition.[864] In August 1991, the U.S. Attorney's Office filed for seizure of Tract 101-29 in its entirety.[865] Subsequently, Richards pled guilty to domestic violence. As part of his plea bargain, Richards agreed not to contest the seizure. As part of the forfeiture he also agreed not to have any later interest in the land. Richards continued to live on the property until April 1993, paying rent to the U.S. Marshal Service.[866]

Lopez recalled that the property came under the custodial ownership of the Department of Justice, U.S. Marshal Service, some six weeks after the arrest.[867] In May 1992, NPS was informed by the U.S. Attorney's office that the land had been seized as part of the plea bargain with Richards. The U.S. Attorney offered the National Park Service the opportunity to acquire it for the price of all existing liens plus interest, taxes, and expenses incurred by the Marshal's Service. Agreeing to a stipulated total, projected for August 5, 1992, of $227,016.34, the National Park Service wanted a guarantee that Richards and certain property, including trees and a carrot harvest but not fencing, would be off the property before the Memorial took possession.[868]

However, between his arrest and seizure of his land by the Department of Justice, Richards's mother, Elsie Weick, the former owner of the Montezuma Ranch, had filed a lien on a portion of the property for money owed to her. The Department of Justice contested the Weick lien. According to NPS employees, the general feeling was that Ms. Weick filed the lien so that her son would come out of the process without losing everything. An eventual settlement provided for Ms. Weick and the Department of Justice to split the proceeds from the sale of the parcel determined to be covered by the lien.[869] Because of uncertainty about the outcome of the Weick lien and its value, NPS could not guarantee payment of outstanding claims and expenses previously agreed upon. Therefore, the Asset Forfeiture Office of the Department of Justice could not continue its efforts to transfer Tract 101-29 to NPS.[870]

There were two other outstanding liens on Tract 101-29 as well, belonging to Western Farm Credit Bank and Citibank. There was some confusion regarding exactly what land secured what loan. That confusion stemmed from the legal descriptions defining the land base of the collateral.[871] One property, 56.91 acres in size, which became known as Tract 101-39, was eventually connected to a lien held by Western Farm Credit Bank. The remaining 25.59 acres of the original 82.5 were eventually assigned to lien-holders as well. Elsie Weick and the Department of Justice were to split the proceeds from the sale of 20.47 acres, while Citibank was assigned 5.12 acres; both contained residential structures.

From that point on, the 82.5 acre Tract 101-29 was usually considered as three separate tracts numbered 101-39 (56.91 acres), 101-40 (5.12 acres), and 101-41 (20.47 acres). For the next few years, however, it was still, sometimes, discussed and dealt with as one large lot, particularly when the issue was hazardous waste. During 1996, NPS conducted a "Level I Survey: Contaminant Survey Checklist of Proposed Real Estate Acquisition" inspection on all of the 82.5 acres which formerly made up tract 101-29.[872]

Subsequently, in 1997, Coronado National Memorial took bids for clean-up of the properties that had made up Tract 101-29 as part of the process of acquiring all of them.[873]

The origin of Tract 101-39 was in a $120,000 loan to Richards from Western Farm Credit Bank on December 9, 1988. According to Bob Cousins, there was some confusion regarding the land base used as collateral for this and another loan from United Bank of Arizona. After that conundrum was sorted out, Western Farm Credit Bank was able to foreclose on 56.91 acres, which became Tract 101-39. In September 1992, it was the subject of a notice of impending Trustee's Sale.[874]

In November 1994, NPS was contacted by an agent for Western Farm Credit Bank regarding the sale of Tract 101-39. In December, Sondra S. Humphries, Chief, Division of Land Resources for the Western Region, responded with an offer for $24,000. Her letter detailed some intermediate steps which would have to precede.[875] It took until April 1996 for the property to be cleared by a hazardous waste inspection and in May an official "Offer to Sell" was transmitted to the bank.[876] On June 17, 1996, Superintendent Lopez made final inspection and took possession of Tract 101-39.[877] The sale was recorded the next day.[878] Finally, Tract 101-39 had been purchased, 56.91 acres for $24,000.[879] That left two tracts of Montezuma Ranch in private hands.

Tract 101-40 was collateral for a $26,500 loan to Richard Richards by United Bank of Arizona in July 1988, which came due June 7, 1989. Like the loan by Western Farm Credit Bank, this one did not have a well-defined piece of property assigned as collateral. Eventually, as the lien morass was sorted out, Citibank, as successor to the United Bank of Arizona, was able to foreclose on 5.12 acres, which became Tract 101-40. In April 1994, Citibank made notice of a Trustee's Sale to be held the following July.[880]

On March 26, 1997, Elsie Weick bought Tract 101-40 from Citibank for an undisclosed price. Weick thus became at least part owner of two of the three lien-encumbered tracts formerly owned by her son. Tract 101-40 was held under a deed of trust.[881] Within a few months, Richards was acting as an agent for Weick in marketing Tract 101-40, which NPS opposed, considering it a violation of the plea agreement in which Richards was prohibited from acquiring interest in the property.[882] Late in 1997, NPS was still working to acquire the remainder of the Montezuma Ranch properties and was accepting bids for clean-up as part of the appraisal process.[883]

On February 5, 1998, Tract 101-40 was transferred from Elsie Weick to "Sunrise, A Trust," which shared Weick's Wood Dale, Illinois, address, for the sum of ten dollars. Weick was the only "co-trustee" listed on the document.[884] The title company did not show a change in the ownership of the property and Weick and her representatives continued to act as they had before the transfer.⁸⁸⁵ Negotiations dragged on through 1998 and 1999. Weick's representatives tried to drive the price up and NPS countered by promising condemnation.⁸⁸⁶

In 1999, NPS continued to address other issues, like clean-up, that arose from violations of the scenic easement agreement. In February, an administrative waiver was signed by Memorial Superintendent Jim Bellamy which would allow NPS acquisition in spite of the existence of an easement for power lines.⁸⁸⁷ In May, Bellamy filed a complaint with the Cochise County Planning Department, Building & Zoning Division. It reported extensive renovation to the two story house without a permit.⁸⁸⁸ Bellamy was concerned that such improvements would increase the price which NPS would eventually pay for the property, after which the buildings would likely be demolished.⁸⁸⁹ The Cochise County Planning Department investigated and agreed that the work was in violation of Zoning Regulations.⁸⁹⁰

As 1999 came to an end, Tract 101-40 was still for sale, as was demonstrated when a potential buyer contacted Coronado National Memorial for information about NPS acquisition plans and existing easements. Meanwhile, condemnation proceedings were instituted against the property by NPS after they were unable agree with the owners on a fair price. NPS offered $41,000 and Weick made no counter-offer. The final price was to be decided by an administrative court.⁸⁹¹ In July 2001, Superintendent Bellamy was able to report that "a settlement has been reached on the remaining 5.12 acres of the old Montezuma Ranch property, and it looks like we will receive title very soon."⁸⁹²

Negotiations over the sale of Tract 101-41 also dragged on through the late 1990s. April 1996 found Richards's attorney, Ethan Steele, trying to list the property for sale by the Marshal's Service. Steele described three appraisals of $80,000, $220,000, and $60,000 and expressed his opinion that the last was the most accurate. He also mentioned the scenic easement, deteriorated structures, and approximately $20,000 in back taxes as liabilities to the tract. Finally, Steele stated that the U.S. Forest Service was then offering $60,000 for the property.⁸⁹³

Finally, in January 1998, the acquisition of Tract 101-41 moved forward when Superintendent Lopez signed a Department of the Interior Certificate of Inspection and Possession.⁸⁹⁴ On January 23, 1998, Alfred W. Madrid, United States Marshall for the District of Arizona, sold 20.47 acres of described land to NPS for $56,500. According to the deed, the land was forfeited by Richards on December 21, 1992. On January 8, 1996, "a Forfeiture Judgement was entered pursuant to written stipulation by the parties as to claimant Elsie Weick, declaring the interest of Weick, in the above described real estate, was forfeited to the United States of America." The United States Marshall was then charged with the duty to dispose of the property."[895] On February 2, 1998, the title was officially passed to the National Park Service.[896]

As the new century began, all but three of the inholdings within Coronado National Memorial, as defined in 1978, had been acquired by the Park Service. The unobtrusive single-family dwellings of the Cerkowniaks and Cashmans, near the east entrance, caused no worries. The residents remained good neighbors who created no problems for the Memorial or its staff. Their land could eventually be acquired.

If the process of creating the Memorial had taught anything it was not to assume that any acquisition would ever be completely trouble free. The last tract of the Montezuma Ranch was still owned by Elsie Weick. Her son, Richard, no longer lived there but still came regularly to work on the large house.[897] After sometimes acrimonious negotiations, it seemed likely that the property would be condemned and its value judged by an arbitrator. In a May 1999 request for condemnation, Memorial Superintendent Jim Bellamy noted that, since the structure would be demolished after acquisition, the only point of Richards's renovation work was to drive up the value of the land. Richards told Bellamy that money was the only issue, and the parties were far apart in their estimates of the land's value. NPS had offered $41,000 for the property, while Richards informed Bellamy that his mother wanted $150,000.[898]

The overly long, drawn-out, process of acquisition of the Montezuma Ranch, as well as of the other inholdings in Coronado National Memorial, seems from a distance to be a matter of poor planning. More accurately, it is a consequence of an evolving vision of the Memorial. In its original form, the entire Memorial was, by design, made up of land already owned by the federal government. Little consideration was given to the resource itself, or to its viability as an ecological entity. It was, in addition, envisioned as an international park with its visitor facilities located on the border, and more accessible from the Mexican side than from the north.

In 1960, the boundary was adjusted to bring in suitable land for a road to a visitor center, still projected for construction on the border, and also to construct facilities adjacent to the road through the Memorial within the United States. As far as private interests were concerned, the only effect of the 1960 legislation was to transfer two small pieces of mining land from the Memorial back to the Forest Service. The mining claims remained with their owners.

The 1960 boundary change made the existing land base more manageable, but it did not make of the Memorial a coherent and cohesive unit. Coronado National Memorial was originally dedicated to the commemoration of a historic event that did not occur on its property. Its value was as a viewpoint, a place to reflect on the Coronado entrada, which required a vista that looked much as it did when the event took place centuries earlier. The ecosystem of the southeastern Huachuca Mountains, itself, was the resource, a seemingly obvious fact that was not explicitly recognized in the founding of the Memorial. With the recognition that the Memorial's value lay at least as much in its natural as its historical resources came the need to again change the boundary.

The boundary adjustment of 1978 had brought all of Montezuma Canyon into the Memorial and excluded all other land. The Park Service would now be able to concentrate on a manageable unit and to develop it in an appropriate manner. To do so would require, by necessity, acquisition of several private inholdings that the adjustment brought within the Memorial. Given that the Memorial was expressly designed forty years earlier to avoid conflict with private property, the new direction represented an about face.

Moreover, circumstances had changed over the course of the Memorial's existence, for the worse as far as acquisition was concerned. Subdivision of grazing and mining land multiplied the number of landowners in the area, and the total was increasing by the year. The local population was expanding rapidly, driving up land prices and bringing developers into the picture. Finally, as the 1970s wound to a close, the country was moving to the social and political right, producing a climate hostile to "big government" and a Republican administration intent upon slashing domestic spending. All these circumstances conspired to make the acquisition prolonged, arduous, and expensive.

In the end, as the final result comes into clearer focus, Coronado National Memorial is emerging as a valuable resource for recreation as well as for environmental study and preservation. The vaunted views of the San Pedro Valley remain relatively pristine, even as urban development approaches from the northeast. They still evoke reflection on the rich history of the region, a history interpreted by the Memorial staff and facilities. Coronado National Memorial, however, has become more. Through the course of boundary adjustments and land acquisitions on a domestic level, the Memorial has fulfilled the dreams of its creators and has far surpassed them.

Part III—Contemporary Issues

Chapter X
The Border: Mexican and American Issues, 1940—present

> *A binational, bicultural, bilingual, regional complex or entity is emerging in the borderlands. Nothing quite like this zone of interlocking economic, social, and cultural interests can be found along any other border of comparable length in the world.*—Carey McWilliams in Joel Garreau's *The Nine Nations of North America*, 1981

The establishment and development of Coronado National Memorial occurred against an international backdrop that continues to influence the Memorial's planning. To understand the salient border issues revolving around the administration of Coronado, the recent past must be constantly revisited.

The early 30's brought the economic disruption of the Great Depression, which greatly affected the border cities of Ciudad Juarez, Agua Prieta, Nogales, and Tijuana. These and other border cities expressed concern over economic losses during this period because they depended heavily on tourism from the United States. From 1933 to 1939, these cities were able to convince the Mexican central government that free trade zones were needed to avoid population and capital decreases in the area brought about by immigration. The free trade zones would allow them to import tariff-free products from the United States, stimulating the economy along the border regions.

Tourism has always been important to the economy of the border regions. It is estimated that U.S. tourists driving across the border in the 40's reached as many as eight million.[899] This was made possible by the interconnecting system of roads toward the interior of Mexico. In the post-Korean War period, Mexican visitors along the border increased; but in the 70's, 80's, and 90's, with the devaluation of the Mexican peso, their spending power decreased. On the other hand, between 1935 and 1970 more Americans traveled to Mexico for entertainment and to visit places like the mercados where they could bargain for lower prices on goods they purchased.

In 1961, Mexico established Programa Nacional Fronterizo (PRONAF) or "National Border Program." Its goals were to boost tourism, raise the standard of living along the border, replace Mexican manufactured goods with imported ones, and promote the sale of Mexican manufactured items to foreigners. By the late 1960's, large numbers of Mexicans along the border shopped in border cities like El Paso. PRONAF recognized this difficiency among Mexican border cities and supported the construction of shopping complexes on the Mexican side that would supply the same goods. That effort resulted in shopping centers like, for example, Rio Grande Mall in Ciudad Juárez.

Federal spending in the border regions during World War II transformed the economy of these areas. By the end of the 20th cntury, federal expenditures in the western states had reached approximately 40 billion dollars, much of which was military in nature. Similarly, companies like Lockheed, Rockwell International, Motorola, Sperry Corporation, and General Dynamics invested in the borderland region to become large technological leaders, often with the help of federal dollars. Federal projects such as Hoover Dam in 1936 aided in attracting post-World War II industries to the border states by providing low cost electricity to growing cities and military production projects.

Meanwhile, Mexico invested in its northern states resulting in large areas under cultivation influencing industrial expansion and growth of cities in the 40's and 50's. By 1940, irrigation projects in Mexico had created 370,000 acres of irrigated land in much of the arid regions of the north. Sonora, for example, received one fourth of the funds spent on irrigation from the late 40's to the early 60's. Mexican agriculture grew to cover large areas of farmlands. By the 1970's, the majority of Sonoran ejidos rented their land to larger private agricultural businesses.

Some of the border states declined while others boomed in the post-1950s. When the production in copper mining fell, Arizona and Sonora, important suppliers of copper, were affected. Meanwhile, in the Gulf States, Tamaulipas experienced new wealth resulting from new discoveries of natural gas. In the oil industry, Tamaulipas and Texas exploited the wealth from the same oil reserves.

Since World War II, the large demand for workers in the United States, especially in agriculture, has been an impetus for the large migration of Mexican workers to the United States. Agricultural employers wanted low-wage imported Mexican laborers, which resulted in the Bracero program that began in 1942.

During the period 1942-1964, large numbers of Mexican workers under government supervision entered the United States on temporary contracts. The program, lasting beyond World War II, was formally instituted in 1951 as Public Law 78 reflecting the labor shortage during the Korean War. The majority of workers were in the border states of Texas, New Mexico, Arizona, and California. The number of braceros fluctuated from 4,203 in 1942 to a peak 450,422 in 1957. In 1964, the last year of the program, the number of braceros reached 181,738.[900] At least half of the Mexican laborers worked as farm laborers in California. The border states have been profoundly changed by Mexican worker immigrants.

The Bracero program ended in 1964 and displaced many of the Mexican workers on the program. This coincided with another large migration which began about 1965.[901] Mexican illegal immigrants apprehended in 1965 rose to 55,000 and to 265, 000 in 1970. As businesses in the United States lost workers that had been earlier provided by the Bracero program, they began to rely on illegal immigrants to fill their labor shortages.

In 1965, Mexico established the Border Industrialization Program (BIP) to resolve problems dealing with the displacement of Mexican workers and to support the manufacturing industry of the northern border-states. An important feature of BIP, the maquiladoras were Mexican assembly plants that imported U.S. parts, assembled them, then shipped the finished products back to the United States. The maquiladora was an outgrowth of a relationship between Mexican and U.S. businesses along the border. Restrictions placed on these enterprises limited the sale of the individual components and the machinery used in the assembly. Additionally, the final manufacturing of products and the sale of the final product were banned in Mexico. The goods were destined for reexport and final sale in the U.S. and other countries. Mexican manufacturers only paid tariffs on the added value of the finished product. Unlike other businesses in Mexico, the maquiladoras did not require majority Mexican ownership.

Despite slow investments, maquiladoras became more widespread between 1965 and 1970 along the border in cities like Nogales, Ciudad Juarez, Tijuana, and Matamoros.

A twin plant operating system quickly developed in these areas. Much of the labor-intensive work was accomplished on the Mexican side while the U.S. side supplied the capital and worked on development. In 1972 the maquiladoras were allowed to move away from the border area, though the great majority remained there. Later, in the 80's a plan evolved, but not fully executed, to locate some of these plants further from the border as in the case of Cananea where several maquiladoras were built.

The maquiladoras had become an important source of Mexico's manufactured products for export. In 1965 there were approximately 12 of these plants in Mexico. By 1996, the number had grown to 2200. By the year 2000, the projected number of workers had surpassed one million.

As product lines changed so did the restrictions. Items most often manufactured by the maquiladoras were clothing, furniture, toys, electronic equipment, processed food, tools and other equipment. By the 1980's, most of the television sets, refrigerators, and computer keyboards sold in the U.S. were assembled at or near the border.[902] By the early 1980's these plants were allowed to sell a portion of their goods within the country. The number of products allowed for sale in Mexico grew from 20% in 1983 to 50% in 1989.

The maquiladoras were successful because of the basic economic disparities between Mexico and the United States. Although the maquiladoras were physically located in Mexico, U.S. and other foreign companies owned them. The wages paid to Mexican workers in these plants were generally much higher than in other areas of Mexico yet much lower than any wage earner in the United States. In the mid- to late 1980's, workers were receiving approximately three dollars a day.

Although no one denied the economic benefit of these plants for both countries, the inherent disparities were cause for concern. The success of the maquiladoras was contingent on low wages paid to workers. This meant that the owners of these concerns discouraged labor unions. Consequently, women were favored over men because it was thought that they were less likely to be union organized. It was also argued that manual dexterity was higher in women than in men for certain jobs. Thus women were in the majority in the maquiladora work force.

Mexicans criticized the maquiladoras for operating as if they were within the United States and not subject to Mexican intervention. Moreover, the low wages paid at these sites was seen as exploitation of Mexican labor for the benefit of the U.S. consumer. A major concern in Mexico was that there was little sharing of technology with Mexican industries. Another important consideration was the effect of these maquiladoras on the health of Mexican workers and on the environment. Almost undeniably, the revenues generated by the maquiladoras were destined for the U.S., very little of which filtered back into Mexico.

Affecting the economies of the border-states, the slow decline of the U.S. economy beginning in 1969 was accelerated by the collapse of the Soviet Union in 1989. Since the 1940's, western states, including those along the border, benefited greatly from federal funds related to defense spending. Needless to say, the demise of the Soviet Union also meant a decline in federal spending for military purposes. Unemployment took its toll in the four U.S. border states. Arizona unemployment rate, for example, rose to 7.7%. Not until the late 90's did the trend reverse itself. California, as expected, was the quickest to recover.

Observers noted that the economies of the two countries at the border were now more closely linked than at any other time in history. Yet, the North American Free Trade Agreement (NAFTA), passed by Congress at the end of 1993, caused intense debate. In fact, the agreement did little to change or add to what was already in place. Trade, for example, had been relatively free before NAFTA which did little to change the economic disparity between both nations. NAFTA did, however, create a framework to facilitate and regulate future trade and commerce in North America. As a result of the economic crisis of the 1980s, recent Mexican presidents have made free trade a part of their economic policies. Meanwhile, Mexico has reduced tariffs through constitutional changes meant to spark foreign investment. Committed to a freer world trade environment, Mexico joined the General Agreement on Tariffs and Trade (GATT). Mexican free trade initiatives were driven by their domestic economic policy.

Although unfounded, U.S. companies feared that through NAFTA jobs would be lost and manufacturing companies would relocate south of the border. Most of NAFTA's efferects were felt in the service sector, a new area of U.S. capital investment, which had little influence on jobs lost in the United States. Areas such as retailing, banking, communications, transportation, insurance, publishing, tourism, film distribution, educational civil engineering, software design, natural gas, and electric-power distribution were of prime importance during the first years of NAFTA.[903]

A free exchange of goods at the industry level took place in the early period of the agreement. Companies from both countries traded items such as electrical machinery, telecommunication equipment, automatic data processing equipment, office machinery parts, and furniture.

The new NAFTA regulations caused disagreements along the border. In 1995, a chain of stores in Tijuana imported milk from producers in Yuma, Arizona. Local producers in Baja California complained that they had enough milk to supply the regional demand. They explained that this action would hurt the milk industry in Mexico as well as put people out of work. Consequently, the Ministry of Agriculture banned imported milk from the United States. Complaints from U.S. officials that these actions violated NAFTA, caused the Mexican government to review NAFTA requirements. Within a short time milk produced in Yuma was again being sold to Mexican clients. Similar disagreements involved products like corn, tomatoes, avocados, green peppers, oranges, strawberries, and grapes.

Other disagreements over NAFTA demonstrated the economic disparities between the two countries. NAFTA did little to change this. In some cases, each nation sometimes blocked the implementation of certain NAFTA provisions. In 1995, the Clinton Administration delayed the implementation of NAFTA by stopping the free movement of Mexican trucks across the border, citing safety and other issues. Another impediment to the agreement was the halting of 800 million dollars worth of tomatoes from Mexico to appease Florida growers. Mexico also chose methods to impede the progress of the free trade agreement standards that obstructed the importation of such products as cherries, peaches, and grains. Like the United States, Mexico imposed standards that obstructed the importation of such products as cherries, peaches, and grains. In certain industries it implemented non-tariff barriers to limit imports and protect domestic business interests.

Despite difficulties in the implementation of the North American Free Trade Agreement, the border area continues in the forefront of an active exchange of materials and products. On the threshold of the new millennium, Mexico remains one of the United State's most important trading partners. There are, however, other issues that continually heighten the apprehension of both countries.

Mexica immigration is a recurring issue that troubles the United States. For many Americans, especially those living along the border, these issues are topics of constant discussion. Researchers agree that despite the fundamental importance of immigration in the development of the United States, there is a constant demand for its control. Immigration policy, in many ways, touches many component of American life ranging from national identity, public policy, family reunification, agricultural policy, national security and racial policy. [904] For the immigrants, however, they seek only the right to better their living conditions and that of their families.

Much of the critical debate in the U.S. has focused on setting and enforcing immigration limits. Borders are set by a number of factors, such as geographical features and treaties that presuppose an historical evolution to ownership of territory. Most often, as in the case of Mexico and the United States, these borders are a result of negotiation or the exercise of military power. Often, the immediate and continued effect is the alienation between groups of people. Along the Mexico-U.S. border, immigration is a constant concern.

Recent immigration research reveals its beneficial effect on both Mexico and the United States.[905] Many immigrants receive benefits through various public services in the U.S., such as primary and secondary education. To employers and consumers, those benefits are a trade off for low employee wages and low food prices. As long as the situation is beneficial to both, it seems unlikely that the United States will be able to stop Mexican migration north.

With such benefits are liabilities associated with immigration. In its January 17, 2000 issue, *The Arizona Republic* carried the headline "State is pipeline for illegal drugs." No part of the state is unaffected by the "pot, methamphetamine, and heroin [that] roll across the southern border," the paper suggests. The affects of the darkside of clandestine activities are, unfortunately, associated with immigration.

Southern Arizona faces a continuous challenge to rid itself of drug trafficking. In Nogales, storm drains provide a smuggling superhighway, with traffickers parking over sewer grates to load cars through holes in the floorboards. A barrio on Nogales's east side faced abandonment because of the violence wrought by a narco-gang whose leader lives just across the fence in Sonora on a hill overlooking town.[906] Other cities such as Tucson and Phoenix have emerged as important in their drug trafficking connections. The newspaper cites that, "according to the Office of National Drug Control Policy, 11 major drug trafficking organizations are based in Arizona working directly with Mexican cartels." As a result, U.S. and Mexican relations have been strained.

Both countries blame the other for the situation. Mexico cites the high demand for drugs by U.S. drug users as the problem. The U.S., on the other hand, complains that Mexico is a source country and blames Mexican officials for their inability to stop the drug trafficking. In the 1980's, Mexico replaced Colombia as the leader in the drug trade that distributes and markets in the United States. Regarding cocaine, for example, the Andean countries controlled the production of the drug while Colombia was responsible for its refinement. In response, Mexican officials demonstrate that they have been extremely concerned and very active in an extensive drug interdiction program. Too, Mexican officials are quick to charge that they cannot stop the high demand in the U.S. for such drugs. One estimate reveals that more that 50 billion dollars a year are spent on illegal drugs in the United States.

It is clear that the problem is broad and many will deal with solutions as they see fit, be it legally or illegally. The popular mind, however, can justify all sides of the story; but, those affected by the drug trafficking are quick to choose sides. The result is sometimes deadly. With impunity, southeastern Arizona ranchers have taken the law into their own hands by forming vigilante groups who take up arms against the smugglers and illegal immigrants.[907]

Despite the influx of agents and other law enforcement personnel to the area, no one envisions a foreseeable end to the dilemma. Some dangerous attitudes may make things worse as another headline declares, "U.S. Customs official lives for the thrill of the chase." The content of the article underscores the atmosphere of antagonism and confrontation:

> On the wall of his office are images of John Wayne, a rattlesnake skin and 'trophy pictures' of [Lee] Morgan at a big drug bust. Morgan was an Army sniper in Vietnam for 11 months, working mostly with spooks on secret operations. Then he came home and got a job fighting America's other war. He started with the Border Patrol in Douglas and Naco a quarter of a century ago, then joined Customs in 1987. After 25 years on the job, his eyes still brighten at the memory –the legal high—of his first drug bust… 'I think everybody loves the chase,' Morgan says with a slight Texas drawl. 'The day you don't get that feeling when you're got a load of dope, you need to go look for another job. You lose your edge'… From a bluff he looks down on the San Bernardino Valley. Only a barbed-wire fence marks the border. It is a barren place of prickly pear and rocks. Radios and cell phones are beyond range in the badlands. 'You're on your own," Morgan says. 'Out here, you're all the law there is.'[908]

When custom officials live for the thrill of the chase and display 'trophy' pictures on the wall next to those of John Wayne, the portrayal communicates a sense of fulfillment mixed with hostile attitudes and behavior that can pervade this broad expanse of land between Mexico and the United States.

Like nearby towns such as Douglas, Naco, and Sierra Vista in Cochise County, Coronado National Memorial has become one of the major thoroughfares for illegal border crossings and drug trafficking. In an environment filled with a heightened sense of awareness and frustration, it is never quite clear how to solve some of these problems. The *Sierra Vista Herald/Bisbee Daily Review* headline story read, "Flow of illegal immigrants wearing down park land."[909] The article tells of the problems faced by the National Park Service's Coronado National Memorial. As a border park at the southern end of the Huachuca Mountains, the continuous flow of immigrants through the area has had a profound effect on the Memorial. The trampled high grass pointing northward forms a broad path through the park and testifies to the many who have crossed. Clothes, blankets, water jugs, children's toys, a piggy bank, diapers, feces, and toilet paper are among the items left behind. Fred Moosman, Chief Ranger at Coronado National Memorial has encountered many of these items in various places in a spiderweb of trails across the Memorial.

The park has nearly 90,000 visitors a year, most of them unaware of the illegal immigrant presence in the area. In the *Sierra Vista Herald/Bisbee Daily Review* story, Chief Ranger Fred Moosman and Superintendent Jim Bellamy relate some of the difficulties faced by the illegal migration through the park:

> "These people do not realize they are destroying the environment..." While Moosman said he understands most are trying to seek a better life they are doing it "at nature's expense in the United States." What bothers him most is that illegal immigrants are victims of unscrupulous people on both sides of the border. "They are preyed upon, they are attacked" Moosman said. But still "wave after wave" continues coming north, which is evident by the huge amount of grassland crushed by the footprints of the illegal immigrants… Jim Bellamy, the memorial's superintendent, said the goal of his staff is to ensure the natural resources are protected and the visitors' security and safety are ensured.[910]

In this tense and dangerous atmosphere, the staff at Coronado National Memorial continues to struggle with issues of safety and protection of resources in one of the primary immigrant crossing points along the Arizona-Mexico border.

One of area's heaviest crossing points is through Cochise County which means that immigrants must travel through properties in the care of the National Park Service, the Bureau of Land Management, and the U.S. Forest Service. To the east about five miles away is the San Pedro River. Today that corridor is a pathway for many immigrants moving northward to other areas of the United States.

The realities of the border area today are only indicators of the future. It will be difficult to fathom or predict what the intricate framework of the complex region will be. Certainly though, the area will present significant transboundry challenges. Still, the founders of the Memorial hoped that Coronado National Memorial would be a place where people of two great nations would come together to share in the valued natural resources of the region and join together in appreciation of their mutual cultural heritage.

Hispanic Heritage was the theme of the International Historic Pageant on April 28, 1974. (Coronado National Memorial Archives, National Park Service)

Chapter XI
The Memorial's New Direction: Ecology and Biodiversity along the U.S. and Mexican Border

> *Along the border, our two countries share ecosystems that do not recognize political boundaries. Thus it is necessary to recognize that the tasks completed by the governments for conservation, preservation and maintenance of the biodiversity found in their respective territories can be developed in a coordinated and harmonious manner in accordance with the policies of each country in order to use human and economic resources in the accomplishment of that common objective.* — Proposal for the Establishment of Protected Natural Areas of Bi-national Ecosystems, Mexico-United States Protected Area for Flora and Fauna Maderas del Carmen/Santa Elena Canyon-Big Bend National Park, February 1997.

Coronado National Memorial shares many ecological concerns with neighboring Sonora. Consequently, Coronado is an integral part of a vast region with numerous transboundry ecosystems. The region is seen as inhospitable, challenging anything living. Of it, John Steinbeck wrote, "In the war of sun and dryness against living things, life has its secrets of survival. Life, no matter on what level, must be moist or it will disappear."[911] Its physical environment is dominated by varying degrees of aridity reflected in the vegetation and topography.

From the Gulf of Mexico to Baja California the borderlands progress from semiaridity to extreme aridity common in desertscapes. Mountain forests in the United States and Mexico provide transitions from steppe to desert. The southern Rocky Mountains in the U.S. and the Sierra Madre Occidental and the Sierra Madre Oriental in Mexico demonstrate this characteristic. Regarding historical settlement patterns in the region, Alvar W. Carlson remarks "Aridity is a fact in the Borderlands, and man's perception of how to cope with it has largely determined his settlement locations and land use patterns."[912]

Water and its management loom important on both sides of the border. Despite difficulties, the two countries have addressed use and conservation and continue to develop ways to deal with water issues. Beyond that, both governments have signed multilateral agreements dealing with preservation, conservation, and use of the natural resources of the region.

Important milestones mark cooperative efforts between the two countries. In 1936, both signed the Convention for the Protection of Migratory Birds and Mammals which, in 1972, was supplemented with a new agreement. Both agreements dealt with migratory bird species and mammals used for game that crossed the border. Aside from establishing refuges, the policies provided for regulatory measures in the transport of various species. In 1940, both countries agreed on the Convention on Nature Protection and Wildlife Preservation in the Western Hemisphere in which similar concepts were established regarding parks, reserves, national monuments, and migratory species. Only migratory species were considered genuine transboundry resources. Both countries agreed to adopt the necessary measures to protect them.

Other agreements followed: The International Plant Protection Convention (1951), the Convention on Wetlands of International Importance Especially as Waterfowl Habitat (1971) and the La Paz Agreement on Cooperation for the Protection and Improvement of the Environment in the Border Area (1983). In 1975, the Mexico-U.S. Joint Committee on Wildlife and Plant Conservation was created. The committee aimed to facilitate cooperation between the current Dirección General de Conservación y Aprovechamiento Ecológico de México, (formerly within SEDUE and SEDESOL) and the U.S. Fish and Wildlife Service. On December 5, 1984, the Clairmont, California, meeting began a new era of cooperation between Mexico and the United States. Both agreed to revise and expand the Mexico-U.S. Joint Committee on Wildlife and Plant Conservation. The joint committee brought together the Mexican Flora and Fauna Division of the Secretariat of Urban Development and Ecology (Secretaría de Desarrollo Urbano y Ecología) and the U.S. Department of the Interior's Fish and Wildlife Service.

In 1987, the Joint Committee met in Albuquerque and adopted two new cooperative agreements: Research, Studies and Scientific Collection of Territorial and Aquatic Species of Wild Flora and Fauna, and the Control of Traffic in Wild Species of Flora and Fauna. These agreements broadened the dialogue on conservation issues between both countries. In 1988, the Joint Committee identified and classified four categories of cooperative projects in this field which involved protected areas, endangered species, migratory bird management and administration and law enforcement.[913]

On March 16, 1988, Mexico, the United States and Canada adopted a Memorandum of Understanding to analyze existing agreements between the U.S. and Mexico, and between the U.S. and Canada. "This examination," wrote Alberto Szekely in 1989, "could create the prospect of establishing trilateral cooperation for the conservation of natural resources, resources for which the three countries may have ecological responsibility."[914]

On November 30, 1988, the U.S. National Park Service and the Secretaría de Desarrollo Urbano y Ecología met in Mexico City and signed a Memorandum of Understanding on "Cooperation in the Management and Protection of National Parks and Other Protected Natural and Cultural Heritage Sites." The memorandum established a framework for binational cooperation for the conservation of protected natural areas and their biodiversity and the preservation of cultural heritage and natural resources. Significantly, the agreement sought to recognize the sustainable development alternatives for rural Mexican communities.[915]

Binational environmental cooperation provides the means for the two nations to express their concerns. For example, the United States-Mexico Integrated Border Environmental Plan, (1992-1994) provided incentive to develop an environmental infrastructure to deal with pollution. And, the North American Free Trade Agreement (NAFTA) of 1993 provided funding for toxic waste clean up, the enforcement of pollution standards, and the construction of sewage treatment plants in Mexican twin cities.

Despite signed agreements between the United States and Mexico, there are differences that complicate their implementation. For example, with respect to conservation and nature-protected areas, Harold Eidsvik reported in 1989 that the U.S. had more than 250 protected areas, which covered about ten percent of its territory.[916] In contrast, Mexico's protected areas fluctuated between 0.8 and 1.6 percent of its territory.

Land use along the border has grown tremendously through the years. Prehistorically, indigenous people exerted their influence over the land through use of grasslands, forests, native flora and fauna, and the use of fire. Europeans later introduced grazing livestock that has profoundly changed the grasslands. Aside from agricultural demands, the growth of modern population centers has influenced and changed both sides of the border area. Within the last forty years Mexico's ecosystems along the border have deteriorated greatly due to regional activities that have linked the border regions closely to comestibles in the United States such as meat, dairy, and agricultural products.

Across Mexico's northern border, land use is generally divided into four categories. They are irrigation-based agricultural lands and related topographical constraints; high-risk seasonal agricultural lands and precipitation amounts; land for raising livestock for export; and, land used in the exploitation of economically beneficial species of plants. The last category includes new and traditional uses.

Traditionally, Native Americans have used plants for both medicinal and dietary purposes. The Seris in Sonora, for example, have used at least 70 species of plants as nutritive food items. Throughout the Sonoran desert ecosystem, 40 plant species are identified for their potential use as food, forage, medicine and industry. Representative plants are candelilla, lechugilla, guayule and jojoba. Although some plants demonstrate great economic potential, they are endangered because of overexploitation, ignorance, and illegal trafficking.

Historically, the livestock industry has had the most widespread impact on the land. Cattle, formerly owned by the Cananea Cattle Company and the Greene Cattle Company, grazed on thousands of acres on both sides of the border near present Coronado National Memorial.

Another impact involves the introduction of U.S. single-crop agricultural techniques into northern Mexico. As a single type of exotic pasture replaced the native flora of the region, much of the original ground cover was lost. These new plants were dependent on fertilizers, herbicides and pesticides, many with high toxicity. Similarly, over-grazing on many northern Mexican areas eliminated ground cover by stunting its regeneration. The area south of the Memorial and lands surrounding Cananea exemplifies this process.[917]

Efficient practices in agriculture, stockraising, urban and industrial development balanced with high productivity and sensitive environmental policies has increased conservation in the United States. Still, the U.S. has suffered losses and transformations of ecosystems. In some areas, the native habitat is completely changed with new exotic species.

Although there are important differences that may be considered, both countries share similar resources along the border. Both, for example, share ecosystems with a tremendously rich ecological diversity. Both possess a great number of endemic plants and animals, some of which hold a great economic potential, that need to be protected.

Binationally, the environmental impact on ecosystems is inextricably linked to the flora and fauna and should be considered together in conservation and preservation efforts. As early agreements demonstrate, both countries have approached problems of conservation from generally two perspectives: environmental pollution and protection of migratory birds and mammals. To be effectively considered, they must be placed within the context of the ecosystem of which they are a part. Both must recognize that the loss of habitat precipitates the loss of endemic flora and fauna.

It is a truism that the detrimental impacts on shared ecosystems are influenced by what occurs in the areas surrounding them. That principle is reflected in State of the Environment: An Assessment at Mid-Decade which explains:

> Protected land, whether in private or public ownership, is subject to pressures from the development of nearby areas.... Seven of the 14 most frequently reported management problems related...to land-use practices outside the refuges themselves. Similarly, the National Park Service found that a majority of the pressures on natural resources inside the National Parks come from activities on lands outside them.[918]

The seven referenced problems are soil erosion/sediment, wildlife disturbance, flow decrease, wildfires, land development, flow increase/floods, and fertilizer runoff. A 1984 National Park Service publication recognized similar external threats to protected areas citing them as: "Industrial and commercial development projects on adjacent lands: air pollutant emissions, often associated with facilities located considerable distances from the affected parks; urban encroachment; and roads and railroads."[919]

On the Mexican side of the shared ecosystems, the adverse external effects are quite high. In recent years, detrimental impacts have been caused by farm and livestock businesses and new industries along the border together with increases in population in border cities. In the municipios (Mexico) and counties (United States) that surround areas like Coronado National Memorial, population increases on both sides demonstrate the potential impact these populations pose:

Population of Mexico and U.S. Border Municipios and Counties[920]

(Population in the thousands)

Municipios/ Counties	1960	1990
San Luis R.C. (Sonora)	42.1	111.5
Puerto Peñasco (Sonora)	5.7	35.9
Caborca (Sonora)	12.4	58.5
Altar (Sonora)	3.0	6.4
Sáric (Sonora)	1.8	2.1
Nogales (Sonora)	39.8	107.1
Santa Cruz (Sonora)	1.3	1.5
Cananea (Sonora)	21.0	27.0
Naco (Sonora)	3.6	4.6
Agua Prieta (Sonora)	17.2	39.0
Yuma (Arizona)	46.2	106.9
Pima (Arizona)	265.7	666.9
Santa Cruz (Arizona)	10.8	29.7
Cochise (Arizona)	55.0	97.6

Undoubtedly, unregulated growth in these areas will impact protected areas on both sides.

Historically, binational cooperation has driven the conservation of ecosystems with the broadest diversity possible. Consequently, adverse effects generated by areas outside protected zones can be regulated. Within the protected zone, the selection of protected areas is based on biological and geographic criteria that shows continuity between regions without breaks between them. To overcome breaks where they occur, both nations work to establish corridors that link protected areas on both sides. Another way is to establish shared binational reserves, which could result in the improved preservation of diverse flora and fauna across both nations.

Border parks and protected areas experience special problems. Protection and enforcement actions are often easier in the United States than in Mexico. At Organ Pipe Cactus National Monument, for example, enforcement of protection laws often drives offenders across the border to the Sierra del Pinacate where undermanned Mexican personnel are unable to control their areas effectively. Illegal fires, trespassing, and the extraction of wild species is often the result. Shared resources and frequent communication might be a partial solution.

Although U.S. goals may be the same or similar, the Mexican point of view is often different. Influenced by history and political tradition, U.S. laws concerning protection and conservation do not always address problems faced in Mexicans protected areas. The Wilderness Act of 1962 is a case in point. In the Act, the word "wilderness" means "the preservation of an area in its natural condition." In Mexico, the inhabitants of an area are often considered part of the "wilderness" and as such are an integral part of its resources development, consumption, and management.

The UNESCO Man and the Biosphere Programme (1974) attempts to integrate local populations, use and conservation of natural resources:

> The biosphere reserve network....is a key component in MAB's objective of achieving a sustainable balance between the sometimes-conflicting goals of conserving biological diversity, promoting economic development, and maintaining associated cultural values. Biosphere reserves are sites where this objective is tested, refined, demonstrated and implemented.[921]

In short, the Man in the Biosphere Programme attempts to balance preservation issues with cultural values of a region and the sustainable use of the area resources.

Biosphere reserve programs have also been developed in Mexico. Despite their ecological benefits, local involvement has been minimal owing to poor communication between local residents and government offices, ecologists, scientific institutions, and universities. By accentuating the needs of management, residents, and users, a more viable relationship in the protection of resources is forged. Dialogue on sustainable development, between official planners and residents, is essential in developing proposals for conservation areas.

The Biosphere Reserve Concept divides types of conservation areas into three primary functions: conservation, development, and logistic support. Conservation means preserving resources, ecosystems and the landscapes. The developmental function serves to incorporate sustainable economic principles with development. The logistical support function involves environmental education, training, and research. Concerning broader issues of conservation and sustainable development, logistical support is essential.[922] Theories and ideas found in the Biosphere Reserve Concept are included in conservation efforts by federal, state and private entities interested in preserving the resources of this border region.

On May 27, 1997, José María Guerra Limón, director of the Mexican National Forest Reserve, Sierras Los Ajos, Buenos Aires, y La Púrica, wrote Regional Director John Cook, National Park Service, Denver, proposing a closer relationship between Coronado National Memorial and Chiricahua National Monument and his unit. Given the involvement of the Secretariat of Environmental Natural Resources and Fisheries (Secretaría de México, Ambiente, Recursos, Naturales y Pesca, SEMARNAP), he wrote,

The reserve is interested in promoting a cordial relationship in the collaboration and exchange of technical and operational support through the following:
1. Exchange of training programs
2. Develop a collaborative educational program on the environment.
3. Develop a collaborative program on ecological tourist attractions.

Lastly we would like to thank your courtesy and interest in promoting an exchange program of scientific and technical support, by allowing your personnel to visit.[923]

Cook was delighted with the proposal and wholeheartedly encouraged the formation of binational conservation partnerships between the two countries. A flurry of correspondence followed paving the way for future collaboration.[924]

On February 3, 1998, a Letter of Agreement formalized the collaboration between Coronado National Memorial, Chiricahua National Monument, and the Mexican National Forest Reserve of Sierra Los Ajos, Buenas Aires and La Púrica.[925] All agreed, "the primary goal between all three areas is the conservation of natural and cultural resources across borders."

The relationship satisfied a need to share information about natural wildfires in "sky island" ecosystems. Sky islands are like islands in the sea. They form unique ecosystems that contain a variety of plants and animals. Metaphorically, the mountain forests that rise up from Sonoran Desert valleys of Arizona and Mexico comprise of some of the most ecologically diverse areas in the region.

The relatively short 100-year-plus record of wildfire suppression in the U.S., makes it difficult to understand how areas appeared in their natural state. Given its pristine character, the Mexican Sierra de los Ajos National Forest Reserve provides the perfect opportunity to study what the flora and fauna might be like in regions with regular wildfires. Coincidentally, the Huachuca and Chiricahua mountains share many characteristics with the Ajos, Buenos Aires, and la Púrica.

In October 1997, managers from the Sierra de los Ajos National Forest Reserve visited Coronado National Memorial and Chiricahua National Monument and agreed to work together to benefit public lands on both sides of the border.[926] One of Director Guerra Limón's goals for the Sierra los Ajos, Buenas Aires, la Púrica, National Forest Reserve was to prepare a Management Plan in consultation with his U.S. partners. By October 1997, staff from the three conservation areas met to devise long-term plans that would include outside participating interests. National Park Service units mentioned in the document included Organ Pipe Cactus National

Monument, and Tumacacori National Historical Park. The planners recommended a contact station at Los Ajos with semi-permanent housing, and an administration trailer. And, they discussed management-training plans for all three conservation areas, development of volunteer programs at Los Ajos, library resource development at Los Ajos, and workshops on Mexican conservation law.[927]

In a second draft Letter of Agreement objectives of the first Letter were expanded upon. Although not signed, the draft included new ideas among them, the temporary transfer of equipment and supplies to Los Ajos-Bavispe for operational support. Apart from environmental education and training programs for all areas, the draft Letter stressed the inclusion of local communities in order "to promote public awareness, understanding and participation in conservation and the sustainable use of border resources."[928]

The agreements and letters promoted collaboration, thus broadening interest and involvement by stakeholders in the area. They included a large number of public and private organizations across southern Arizona and northern Mexico. These common interests form a corridor of interconnected ecosystems at binational, federal, state and local levels.

The San Pedro River contains ecosystems that interest Coronado National Memorial. Nearly five miles separates the Memorial and the river. Nearby, the river enters Arizona from Sonora. Flowing north between the Huachuca and Mule Mountains, it joins the Gila River about 100 miles downstream. Coronado lies within the Upper San Pedro River Basin. The area contains a series of ecosystems that includes the Sierra los Ajos, Buenas Aires, la Púrica, National Forest Reserve and the Forest Reserve and Wildlife Refuge Ajos-Bavispe, as well as the sierras La Elenita, La Mariquita and the San José.

Within the larger ecosystem extending north-south from the border is the smaller San Pedro Riparian National Conservation Area (NCA). Designated in 1988, it covers 40 miles of the upper San Pedro River, and contains about 58,000 acres of public land in Cochise County. The San Pedro Riparian NCA abounds in flora and fauna. In this riparian corridor are a variety of plantlife including the Fremont cottonwood, the Goodding willow, the Arizona ash and walnut, netleaf hackberry, and soapberry. Throughout the corridor, Chihuahuan desert type tarbush, creosote and acacia as well as mesquite and sacaton grass can be found.

An extensive wildlife population lives alongside the vegetation in this NCA providing sustenance for a variety of species of birds. Of the over 350 species there, 100 are breeding birds, while 250 are migrant and wintering species. The majority of thirty-six species of raptors found there are the gray hawk, the Mississippi kite and the crested caracara. The green kingfisher, the northern beardless-tyrannulet and the yellow-billed cuckoo nest there too.

Over 80 species of mammals are identified in this area. White-tailed deer, mule deer, javelina or peccary, desert cottontail, and black-tailed jackrabbits coexist with mountain lions, bobcats and several species of bats. Among the 40 species of amphibians and reptiles are the Mexican garter snake, the Mojave green rattlesnake, the Gila monster, the western diamondback rattlesnake, the desert grassland whiptail lizard, the Sonoran box turtle, and Couch's spadefoot toad. Only two endemic species (the longfin dace and the desert sucker) of the 14 original species of fish that once inhabited the waters of the San Pedro remain. Some of the more common non-native species of fish are the carp, the yellow bullhead and the mosquitofish.[929] Aside from these species, Coronado National Memorial possesses other types of flora and fauna.

Coronado's natural environment is typical of the transition zone between Upper Sonoran Zone and high Chihuahuan Desert throughout the mountains of southeastern Arizona. At 6,575 feet above sea level, the view from Montezuma Pass sweeps across the San Pedro Valley to the east and the San Rafael Valley to the west. In the Memorial's lower elevations the desert grasses and shrubs include honey mesquite and desert willow. In the upper canyons, oak, Mexican piñón pine, and alligator juniper abound. Along drainages, sycamore and walnut can be found. Other plants found in the Memorial are manzanita, agave or century plant, Schott's yucca, sacahuista or beargrass, and sotol or desert spoon. A variety of cacti range from pincushion and rainbow cacti to prickly pear and cane cholla.

Common mammals seen at Coronado are the white-tailed deer, javelina, coyote, coatimundi, gray fox and a variety of bats, including the endangered lesser long-nosed bat which resides in abandoned mines at the Memorial.[930] The more elusive mammals found at Coronado are the bobcat, the black bear and the mountain lion.

Migrant birds, which can be seen at different times of the year, inhabit the Memorial. More than 140 species of birds (50 are residents) have been recorded at Coronado, among them, acorn woodpeckers, gray-breasted jays, Gambel's quails, rufous-crowned sparrows, painted redstarts, white-winged doves, Montezuma quails and various hummingbirds.[931]

Coronado National Memorial and San Pedro Riparian NCA are integral parts of the Upper San Pedro River Basin. Together, they provide important habitats for flora and fauna in the region. The Upper San Pedro River Basin is particularly susceptible to human influences on its fragile environment. In the last few years the detrimental effects have been a concern to both countries.

In *La Crónica de Hoy*, a Mexican on-line newspaper, Rigoberto Aranda writes about his 1999 teleconference interview with Secretary of the Interior

Bruce Babbitt. The article features environmental dangers to the Upper San Pedro River and Basin.[932] Quoting Babbit, Aranda writes that the San Pedro River runs the risk of drying up because the United States over-uses its waters for human consumption, agriculture, and livestock. Babbitt also spoke about an agreement the Department of the Interior signed with the Mexico, specifically the Secretariat of Environment, Natural Resources and Fisheries (SEMARNAP).[933] According to Aranda's article, the binational agreement recognizes the degradation of the San Pedro due to human water consumption, agriculture, mining and contaminants poured into the riverbed from the United States.

Aranda describes a section of the San Pedro River Basin located in northeastern Sonora in the municipalities of Cananea, Naco and Santa Cruz with a surface area of 107,000 hectares (approximately 264,397 acres). The environs contain a rich mountainous region of oak and pine forest that house, among other species, the tiger salamander, the prairie dog, the black bear, and the spotted owl.

In the article, SEMARNAP Secretary Julia Carabias explains that Mexico was redefining its guidelines to their Natural Protected Area program to include parts that are of interest to both nations. To that end, 1.5 million dollars was earmarked for a binational nature conservation agency concerned with environmental stewardship. Carabias stated that Mexican areas of the San Pedro River Basin were in good condition and well conserved. Praising the accord, she said:

> This agreement is special because, for the first time, conservation actions are being considered that take the entire ecosystem into account. There is not a single resource, such as water, that is the central focus, as is the case for the Río Bravo.[934]

The basin's ecosystem has become the focus of binational efforts in which the flora and the fauna are as important as the ecological system that surrounds them. For example, the Los Ajos area is encompassed by *ejido*[935] lands with a population of approximately 32,000 inhabitants. The *ejidos* are Emiliano Zapata, Mututicachi and Cuquiarichi. In this area of the San Pedro River Basin, the wildlife is made up of 72 species of mammals, 102 species of birds, 51 reptiles, 15 amphibians, and two endemic species of fish.

In the agreement, both nations committed to "strengthen cooperative actions with a goal of establishing joint mechanisms to improve and conserve the natural and cultural resources of the Upper San Pedro River Basin, including the river and riparian zone."[936] Significantly, the agreement recognized "the need to develop strategies that are balanced and respectful of national sovereignty and the particular economic and social characteristics of the inhabitants of the watershed." Additionally, the agreement provided for research plans to study the physical and hydrological conditions of the region and the coordination of policy related to the conservation of natural resources for the Upper San Pedro River Basin. To strengthen the goals of the agreement, SEMARNAP promised "to develop legal instruments that give the Upper San Pedro River Basin…within Mexico…some category of protection," suggesting that it be included in the Sierra los Ajos-Bavispe Natural Protected Area and management plan.[937]

The large binational Upper San Pedro River Basin contains private lands, state lands, military reservations, lands managed by the National Park Service, the Bureau of Land Management, the National Forest Service and various agencies of the Mexican government. Within these jurisdictions are important sub-sections, among them, the Arizona Trail that begins at the U.S.-Mexican border in Coronado National Memorial.

Regarding funding issues, the Department of the Interior stated it would establish partnerships with private and public institutions for economic support of conservation activities in the U.S. portion of the Upper San Pedro River Basin. Accordingly, the Interior Department promised to seek funds for land acquisition, and conservation easements in the Basin. Portions of the basin overlap with parts of the Sonoran Desert.

The Sonoran Desert covers approximately 120,000 square miles. In Mexico it stretches from the western side of Sonora to Baja California Norte. In the U.S., the desert covers portions of southeastern California and southwestern Arizona. The Sonoran Desert encompasses the Yuma and Colorado deserts in the U.S. and El Gran Desierto de Altar in Mexico.

The topography of the Sonoran Desert ranges from semi-arid to arid desert, the hottest, driest and largest part being the Lower Colorado Valley Region. The Arizona Upland, in contrast, has the largest concentration of mountains in this desert. For centuries many indigenous groups including the Tohono O'odham, the Seri, and the Pima survived by exploiting its resources.

In May 1997, Babbitt and Carabias signed a letter of intent to protect the natural resources along the border. Because of their continuous involvement in binational, national, and public inclusion in their conservation efforts, the letter of intent involved Coronado National Memorial and Organ Pipe Cactus National Monument. In Arizona, they are important stakeholders in the transboundry, inter-agency and cross-sector collaboration in the management of these important areas.

Coronado National Memorial, particularly, lies between two ecological systems, the Chihuahuan Desert and the Sonoran Desert. Its active participation in conservation and preservation efforts in these binationally distinct regions can reinforce and emphasize the need for partnerships.

Chapter XII

Epilogue: The Development of Coronado Memorial and its Interpretive Program

> *...at the present time it is simply a block of land lying along the border set aside from our public domain* -- Congressional debate on 1952 bill.
>
> *We want to assure you that the step-child attitude of the past toward Coronado has changed...* – NPS Acting Regional Director E.W. Watkins, 1966.
>
> *I believe that Coronado, properly developed and interpreted, could become an unforgettable experience for visitors* –- NPS Historian Bill Brown, 1967.

When, on August 18, 1941, legislation was passed that would eventually lead to the creation of Coronado National Memorial, its framers clarified that it would be "for the purpose of permanently commemorating the explorations of Francisco Vázquez de Coronado."[938] In its nascent stages, the Memorial idea was, in the words of E.K. Burlew, acting Secretary of the Department of the Interior in 1940, conceived as "of value in advancing the relationship of the United States and Mexico upon a friendly basis of cultural understanding." He went on: "Such a monument would stress the history and problems of the two countries and would encourage cooperation for the advancement of their common interests."[939] This aspect of the Coronado project was reflected in the original plan for an international memorial.

Also on the minds of promoters of the Memorial was the unique natural resource found in the southern Huachuca Mountains. In 1950, local resident and tourism booster Grace Sparkes wrote that it was important to move quickly to secure protection for the flora and fauna of the area. She went on to say that "(t)here isn't a week that we do not meet interested people and scientists" doing research. Sparkes illustrated by describing researchers from the University of Arizona and from Mexico who had recently visited, both looking for specific plants said to be nearly unique to the area.[940]

The legislation and Presidential Proclamation that actually established the Memorial in 1952 did more than change the language of the 1941 bill. The 1941 bill was amended, dropping the word "International" and revoking the necessity of waiting for action on the part of Mexico. Thus, it established a national memorial in place of the original international concept. Groups opposed to the Memorial seized on the change to argue that the Memorial could not very well commemorate relations between Mexico and the United States if the two countries could not cooperate on the project itself.[941]

The 1952 Presidential Proclamation established the Coronado Memorial and its boundaries that set aside the designated property, but it did not immediately lead to the appropriation of funds. In fact, during a short Congressional debate on the matter, two members asked specifically how a park could be created without any funding. They were assured that, while in the future, funding would be requested for construction at Coronado, "at the present time it is simply a block of land lying along the border set aside from our public domain."[942] Finally, in July 1954, money was appropriated for Coronado Memorial.[943] Shortly thereafter, a superintendent, Carroll Burroughs, was hired.[944] But, as 1954 drew to a close, the Memorial still lacked a Master Plan, structures, and a staff.[945] For five years, Coronado National Memorial was based in rented quarters at Grace Sparkes's State of Texas Mine. Meanwhile, the NPS had to figure out how to develop the resource.

As a backdrop to the process, the region was undergoing a development process of its own. Grace Sparkes mused about the possible reactivation of Fort Huachuca in 1950 and its effect on the Memorial area.[946] Fort Huachuca was long the locus of great population change in the San Pedro Valley. Tombstone was a boom town that quickly declined along with its silver lodes. It lived on, and continues to exist, as a tourist attraction. The mines of Bisbee, across the San Pedro Valley in the Mule Mountains, grew and ebbed with the market for copper, and for tourism as well. In the immediate neighborhood of Coronado, increase and decrease in the population of the

San Pedro Valley reflected the changing fortunes of Fort Huachuca.

Fort Huachuca was founded in 1877, but has since gone through a few apparent deaths and subsequent rebirths.[947] Since the founding of Coronado National Memorial, its major turning points have, coincidentally, been concurrent with some of Fort Huachuca's growth spurts. In 1941, as boosters and legislators were acting to make the Memorial a reality, on paper at least, Huachuca was changing from border outpost to modern military base. In that year, its population grew larger than it had ever previously been. As the United States entered World War II, it continued to grow.[948] In 1947, as the Memorial languished in the limbo of legislative existence, Fort Huachuca was deactivated.[949]

In the early 1950s the fort and Memorial seemed to stumble together through an obstacle course of attempts at regeneration. In 1951, Fort Huachuca was reactivated as part of the Korean War effort, and, in 1952, legislation was passed to establish Coronado National Memorial in reality as well as on paper.[950] Fort Huachuca closed briefly in 1953 but again opened in 1954, just as Coronado Memorial received its first funding, named its first superintendent, and prepared to move into Montezuma Canyon.[951] As the first Master Plan was being created, the Fort was undergoing considerable expansion.[952] In the late 1960s and 1970s, Fort Huachuca expanded exponentially as it became the army's main center for electronic warfare.[953]

As the base grew so did its surrounding community. Sierra Vista grew as home to the military personnel and civilian employees at the fort. To that number were added, in ever increasing numbers, military retirees who came to the area for the climate and for services that the base could provide. Finally, Arizona has become home to large number of retirees from all walks of life, many of whom settled in the San Pedro Valley. The ongoing influx of residents provided both a challenge and an opportunity to the staff of Coronado National Memorial as they worked to create a worthwhile and manageable park from their Congressional mandate.

While the headquarters of the Memorial was based at the State of Texas Mine, NPS worked to create a manageable unit and an interpretive theme. An early planning document from that period asked "What are the significant values of Coronado National Memorial?"[954] It answered:

> The establishment of Coronado National Memorial on the high ridges overlooking the San Pedro Valley, through which the Coronado expedition passed en route north from what is now Mexico, gives the visitor the opportunity to view the vast plains and mountains for a great distance into Mexico on one hand and the United States on the other. It also provides an opportunity to review the historic events following the Spanish occupation of the region, and the similar backgrounds of the

two countries; and to remind the people of the United States and of Mexico of their mutual struggles and their continuing friendships. More important than the actual specific biological and scenic values of the area is this symbolic importance.[955]

It appears that almost the entire focus of interpretive planning was on the Coronado expedition and its legacy. The importance of the natural resource base was specifically denied, for it was considered less significant than the Coronado Expedition theme.

By 1961, a similar document still highlighted the Coronado expedition and the ongoing Hispanic legacy of the southwest but did not mention Mexico–U.S. relations, perhaps a result of the failure of the international memorial idea. However, more significance was placed on the natural resource, both as evocative of the historic scene and in its own right. The views were said to "offer solace and beauty to the civilization-harassed town and city dweller; the biology of the area, with its many forms of plant and animal life ordinarily not occurring in other portions of the nation, is of almost equal significance with the story."[956] The balance between the historical theme and natural resource would continue to trouble planners while it shaped the evolution of Coronado National Memorial.

While the importance of the natural environment grew in the minds of interpreters, it was, by necessity, central to park planning concerns from the beginning. The first NPS groups to survey the Memorial for planned development, in 1954, quickly saw that the area set aside by Congress was unsuited for visitor facilities or road improvement. Already, before any staff was in place, they suggested boundary adjustments to add land.[957] One acquisition would "develop a desirable headquarters and residential area" within the park. Another was "required for picnic area development and a construction of a road to the proposed public use area at the International Boundary."[958] This was the binational museum and visitor center planned for the border, on the south flank of the Huachuca Mountains. It would never be built because of the failure of the Mexican government to dedicate land south of the border to the project.

The first development plan for Coronado Memorial included the museum on the international border along with interpretive facilities in the area of Montezuma Pass and Coronado Peak. Both were envisioned in terms of interpreting the Coronado story:

> The development of a contact station at Montezuma Pass parking area and the supplementing of the exhibits in the building with trailside exhibits on Coronado Peak will give the visitors an insight into the historical significance of the area. These will provide a more effective realization of the importance of the Memorial in commemorating the Coronado expedition

and the effect of Spanish explorations and colonization upon the history and development of this section of the United States.⁹⁵⁹

Coronado Peak and Montezuma Pass were chosen as accessible viewpoints of Coronado's route through the San Pedro Valley. The natural beauty of the area itself was, in the beginning, secondary at best.

Given the almost exclusive focus on the Coronado expedition in early planning and the possibility that Coronado passed near, but not through, the Memorial site, the view of the San Pedro Valley was of primary importance. Its command of the valley and convenience to the Montezuma Pass Road made Coronado Peak the logical place for viewing the Coronado route. An observation shelter on the peak was one of the first structures to be planned for the Memorial.⁹⁶⁰ It was, at one time, conceived as an enclosed building with a road extending from Montezuma Pass closer to Coronado Peak.⁹⁶¹ Over time, there were a few different conceptions of exactly what would be built on Coronado Peak. By the summer of 1956, a sixty-five space parking lot was preparing to open adjacent to the road atop Montezuma Pass.⁹⁶² The building that was placed there held little more than rest rooms. Trails to Coronado Peak were developed and supplied with interpretive materials and benches by the Memorial staff through the late 1950s.⁹⁶³

The focus on the Montezuma Pass area necessitated an increase in traffic on the Montezuma Pass road. That road had only been built in the early 1930s. Before then, trips to the west side of the Huachuca Mountains had to be routed around the southern flank, through Mexican territory.⁹⁶⁴ Before, the Memorial was even established on paper it was recognized that "heavy road construction" would be required to create an approach to any high elevation lookout.⁹⁶⁵ As plans for developing the Memorial took shape, well before it existed on the ground, road improvement was on the minds of some planners and promoters. Grace Sparkes hoped to benefit personally from an improved road even as it brought visitors to the Memorial.⁹⁶⁶ However, the National Forest Service then administered the road. Its officials determined that the amount of work needed "to put the Montezuma Pass Road in good condition" was beyond its budgetary means. Like other roads in the region, it had been "built to a low standard" because of prevailing drainage patterns.⁹⁶⁷

Grace Sparkes signed a right of way agreement in June 1951, before the Memorial was actually established.⁹⁶⁸ A decade later, she was negotiating a new agreement to expand the width of the right of way for the improvement of the road. In 1960, Congress passed legislation that appropriated funding for improvement of the road.⁹⁶⁹ Sparkes disagreed with the planned road improvement. She supported paving the existing road all the way to the facilities at the top of Montezuma Pass and adding some scenic turnouts along the way. What was projected, instead, was a widened road that was only paved about as far as her home. The result would be, according to Sparkes and her allies, unnecessary destruction of vegetation and faster traffic without the benefit of an improved road all the way to the pass.[970] Eventually, Sparkes came to an agreement with the Park Service and the road was improved, as planned.[971]

The same 1960 legislation that allocated money for improvement of the Montezuma Pass Road also appropriated funding for land acquisition and authorized a boundary adjustment. This land acquisition had been envisioned, as described above, from the time that the Memorial became a reality. It made possible the construction of a building to house the visitor center and administrative offices as well as staff housing. It addition, it brought in land to be used for a picnic area and for the road to the ill-fated center at the border.

After 1960, Coronado Memorial began to look like a National Park Service unit, with its own visitor facilities and staff housing and an improved road. However, from the standpoint of protecting or interpreting the natural resource base of the Memorial, it was still unwieldly. In terms of the other themes present, the historical connection to the Coronado expedition and international relations, there were no tangible resources and limited opportunities for interpretation. The subsequent evolution of the Memorial would consist of efforts to improve interpretation and protection of both the natural resources and historical themes.

The natural resource of the southern Huachuca Mountains was originally conceptualized simply as a place from which to view the route of the Coronado expedition and the surrounding country. That resource was difficult to administer as it was created. The land west of Montezuma Pass was not, effectively, part of the Memorial. It was part of the viewshed, but, from the standpoint of interpreting the Coronado expedition, the focus of the view was the San Pedro Valley, to the east. The western side of the Memorial was seldom visited by the public and there was no NPS development planned that would draw people to it.[972]

On the other hand, there was little immediate expectation that real estate development would threaten the view westward if NPS protection was withdrawn. Meanwhile, seventy percent of the grazing land within the Memorial was west of the pass and both the land and water resources were threatened by overgrazing. If that land were to be withdrawn, it would relieve NPS personnel of the headache of patrolling and administering the overgrazing of the unused land. Montezuma Canyon, meanwhile, was a much more likely site for detrimental development and was not fully protected. Moreover, there were no distinct features marking NPS boundaries within Montezuma Canyon; it all seemed to the public to be inside the Memorial.

The core area of the Memorial was Montezuma Canyon and it could be managed efficiently only if NPS acquired the entire watershed.[973]

Even without taking resource protection as a primary mission of the Memorial, the issue was forced to the forefront by the grazing issue and potential development. It came to be acknowledged that the pristine character of the view must be maintained if the Memorial was to be worthwhile. From that point, it was a smaller step to conceptualizing the land as a resource in itself. As noted above, in 1970 Superintendent Hugo Huntzinger acknowledged that the Memorial's "primary use is by those interested in the wildlife and scenery." He also observed that the Memorial did "not at present exist as an ecological entity. e.g., most of the Montezuma Canyon bottom (where the road is located), drainage, and scenery, is located outside of the Memorial boundaries (USFS land)." Moreover, a "rather shoddy county estate subdivision is developing immediately to the east of the Memorial" in Montezuma Canyon.[974] That development made resource protection a necessity, even if only to protect the view.

A few years later, as boundary adjustments were being discussed, development and maintaining the view were considered together. Acquisition of more land was planned to "prevent obnoxious developments which would detract from the visitors park experience."[975] The importance of the environment to the mission of historical interpretation was detailed:

> Because the Memorial lacks visible remains and is not the site of any dramatic occurrence, its historical value lies in the fact that it is able to set a reflective mood suitable for contemplation of the Coronado Entrada. Retention of the pastoral grassland scene of the distant San Pedro Valley is important if this area is to fulfill its purpose and effectively Memorialize and interpret history. This historic scene lies largely outside the current park boundaries and therefore is subject to adverse use and esthetic deterioration that will seriously compromise the park's efforts to provide a quality visitor experience.[976]

Thus, the natural resource was central to the Memorial's ability to interpret the historic theme. Throughout the 1970s, disparate boundary modification and development proposals were suggested and discussed, leading eventually to a significant adjustment legislated in 1978.

At the same time that the future of the Memorial was being discussed in terms of its optimum shape and size, the interpretive program was also getting a close look. In late 1965, Southwest Regional Historian Bill Brown visited Coronado Memorial to begin work on a new Interpretive Prospectus. Some months later, the Regional office wrote that, as a result of that visit, "we have done much thinking about the interpretive program at Coronado. In the past, no systematic approach to interpretation has been taken. As a result, a central interpretive theme, to which all interpretive efforts and media are directly related, has not been pressed." The new Interpretive Prospectus, it was believed, would "be a beginning in changing present interpretive diffusion into a main-line interpretive experience of real significance for visitors."[977]

In closing, Acting Regional Director E.W. Watkins wrote: "We want to assure you that the step-child attitude of the past toward Coronado has changed. And, using the draft Prospectus as a start, we look forward to a creative dialogue with you on a revised and strengthened interpretive program for Coronado."[978] The confusion that was perceived as surrounding interpretation was, evidently, reflected in a lack of institutional support and, it turned out, ambivalence about its very existence. The 1967 Prospectus, written by Brown, began where Watkins left off, with previous neglect of the Memorial. It continued that "Coronado has been considered an area whose resources could not sustain the mission and the values for which the area was established."[979]

Brown wrote: "I disagree with this judgement, and I believe that Coronado, properly developed and interpreted, could become an unforgettable experience for visitors." As a result, he submitted "more than a prospectus. It is an essay and a plea...designed to arouse interest in this area." Brown hoped that ensuing discussions would "result in a basic decision that Coronado National Memorial is worth the expenditure of time and money and imagination necessary to give it a systematic and inspiring interpretive program."[980] Brown's Prospective, then, as he and his superior described it, would clarify the interpretive program by giving it one organizing theme.

Brown again noted the problem facing him and his colleagues. "By legislative fiat, Coronado National Memorial, an area whose physical *resources* are natural and scenic, has been assigned the role of conveying historical *values*." The natural resource had often "overwhelmed" the historic theme in past interpretation. Brown specified that the Huachuca Mountains themselves, "provide a *viewing platform*, which, through various interpretive approaches and media, can and must stir the visitor to a deep, essentially emotional realization of the import of the Coronado theme." The natural resource would be interpreted independently on a separate return trail from Coronado Peak, "after the climax of the historical interpretation at the peak."[981]

The 1967 Interpretive Prospectus was far from the last word on the subject. When, after the passage of a few years, Huntzinger wrote that Coronado's "primary use is by those interested in the wildlife and scenery,"[982] the seeming contradiction was less between two visions of the Memorial than between Brown's "legislative fiat" and the reality of visitor priorities. In 1974, another version of the Interpretive Prospectus was released. It, too, was written by Brown, but Memorial staff seem to have participated in its creation as well. That may have been, at least in part, because the staff was more stable and capable in 1974 than in 1967. The 1974 Prospectus was much like the 1967 edition but it envisioned more interpretation of the natural resources of the Memorial. It pointed out that "the scenic resources and values of the Memorial are so intimately related to its historical purpose and values, there is no conflict between the scenery and the main historical interpretive theme." The natural resources could be used to further interpretation of the historical theme. "But natural history interpretation for its own sake, as a sequel to added benefit beyond the main historical themes, is highly valid."[983]

The interpretive program was still geared toward preparing the visitor for taking the right historical impression from the views from Coronado Peak:

> The culminating experience is at the Coronado Peak Overlook. All orientation and interpretation is designed to prepare the visitor for this experience. So that he may not only *look* but also *see* the historical and geographical panorama revealed to the *perceptive viewer* from this point. In the main, this viewer will be a product of the Memorial's orientation and interpretive program. If the reasonably intelligent and interested viewer is not perceptive when he gets to this point, our interpretive program will have failed.[984]

Thus, it was the task of the staff and interpretation to take visitors, most of whom came to see the scenery of the Huachuca Mountains and surrounding area, and to convince them to think about the historical importance of the views as well.

Visitation was then steadily increasing, according to reports filed by Coronado Memorial. In 1958, 12,982 visitors were reported; that number grew year by year, reaching 39,964 in 1964.[985] During the early 1970s, the population of southwestern Cochise County was growing rapidly. Expansion of Fort Huachuca sparked a boom in Sierra Vista, and the population was expected to quadruple over the next twenty-five years. "Yet," reads a 1974 Master Plan, "in spite of the large number of people living within an easy drive of the area visitation is relatively light, 61,000 in 1972. This is attributable to the area being located away from the main routes of travel (52 miles south of Interstate 10/US80), lack of general knowledge of the area, and lack of eye catching programs."[986]

Interpretive programs would be expected to draw more visitors to the Memorial and then to put them in the mood to perceive the historical significance of the Coronado expedition and the Memorial's connection to it. In the spring of 1972, a series of annual programs at the Memorial began with "a modest Art Festival in which local communities in Mexico and Arizona were involved."[987] The 1972 Festival had its roots in the recommendations of a January 1971 Management Appraisal that contacts be made with academic, political, and civic leaders in Mexico; an annual commemorative celebration be inaugurated; and a Living History presentations begun.[988]

The International Art Festival was held May 13-14 at the Memorial Headquarters. It drew about eight hundred visitors, somewhat less than expected, and 325 entries into the art competitions, plus others artists whose work was displayed but not judged. The Art Festival enjoyed significant participation from Mexicans, including art entrants, entertainers, and a keynote speaker, Dr. Sergio Bribiesca of Agua Prieta, Sonora. In addition, nearby Arizona communities such as Sierra Vista and Bisbee, and many arts and civic organizations took part in the festivities.[989]

Coronado Memorial staff's in-house evaluation of the 1972 event concluded:

> CORO's combined Centennial Art Festival and Living History program was a successful experience that will not soon be forgotten. They involved many people, both in-Service and from the local communities of Arizona and Mexico. They represent a new beginning – a new direction for the Memorial which will serve as a springboard to an annual historical event for Southern Cochise County.[990]

The Art Festival also inaugurated the Memorial's Living History program, in which employees dressed as members of the Coronado Expedition. That program was planned to continue on weekends and holidays and for special events.[991] Two years later it was handled by seasonal personnel and was undergoing "review and change as area staff attempt to interpret history in a more direct and vital manner."[992] Later discussions of the Living History program focused on the need for sensitivity and delicacy, as well as for the accuracy and authenticity of the costumes.[993]

In April 1973, the Art Festival of the year before was replaced by the International Historical Pageant. This one day event was conceived as a counterpart to such local annual celebrations as Tombstone's "Helldorado Days," the "Little Britches Rodeo" in Sierra Vista, and Bisbee's "Brewery Gulch Days." It featured Spanish and Mexican themed melodrama, music, and dance from both sides of the border as well as Papago and Apache Indian dancers.[994] The 1973 Historical Pageant drew 4,300 people to the Memorial, a success that ensured that it would become an annual April event.[995]

Over the next two years, attendance at the Historical Pageant increased substantially. The 1974 event drew 7,600, leading Superintendent Laurel Dale to forecast that it would have a bright future.[996] Dale was not alone in his optimism for the future of the Pageant. The Southwest Mission Research

Center Newsletter (SMRC) predicted that it "will surely become one of the most appreciated annual bi-cultural events along the entire United States and Mexican border."[997] In addition, Dale thought that, with the success of the Historical Pageant, other annual celebrations were likely to follow.[998]

After the 1975 International Historical Pageant attracted 13,000 visitors, Dale proclaimed it "one of the finest bi-cultural events along the entire...border." The SMRC declared that it had "become Arizona's annual outstanding international cultural and historical event."[999] The 1975 event represented the high water mark for attendance at the Historical Pageant. Dale's prophecy about additional events, self-fulfilling though it may have been, proved true the next year.

In 1976, a more academically oriented Borderlands Symposium was scheduled along with the Historical Pageant. In addition, two Bicentennial programs visited Coronado Memorial. One, a touring play called "We've Come Back for a Little Look Around," performed two shows for audiences of 250 and five hundred in May 1976. It had also visited in August 1975, playing two shows for a total of 550 spectators as part of a "pilot" tour.[1000] The other, in August 1976, was a tour of Mexican folk musicians sponsored by the Smithsonian Institution and called "On Tour: Mexico." "On Tour: Mexico" played a Concert performance at the Memorial for an audience estimated at 550. Coronado Memorial cooperated with other regional groups in coordinating the southern Arizona appearance segment of the Smithsonian tour. The group also appeared at Tumacacori National Monument and at Bisbee and Tucson.[1001]

The Borderlands Symposium, in September 1976, featured four speakers from Mexico and three from the United States who addressed regional historical issues. In addition to the formal presentations, there was a "campfire round table" discussion with the participants, a barbecue, and a performance of Mexican folk dances. A summary of the event concluded "This is the first major symposium to be held at the Memorial, but with the enthusiasm which the event has already aroused it is very possible that this could become an annual event."[1002] In the long run that would not necessarily be the case.

The Historical Pageant in April 1976 drew a respectable crowd, 8,150 people, despite some evident problems with publicity.[1003] In 1977 the attendance went down to five thousand.[1004] Superintendent Dale felt that the size of the crowd "'just right' though less than for previous pageants."[1005] He suspected that the food vendors, whose businesses did poorly, might disagree. The timing and circumstances of the event may have been responsible for the decline in both attendance and appetites. The Pageant was held on Mother's Day and the temperature climbed to over ninety degrees.[1006]

Beginning at roughly the same time period in the early 1970s, the Coronado staff began to frame and implement an Environmental Living, or "Live In," program at the Memorial. It was described in 1974 as:

> an expanded role-playing situation which simulates historical reality. This has exciting potential for bringing the Park and the local classroom together in a learning situation where young people, living as closely as possible to the reality of the time and culture represented by the historic site, become more acutely aware of their heritage as well as of their present environment.[1007]

Environmental Living Programs began in National Park and State Parks as well as private sites in Arizona and California in 1969.[1008] Teachers from both states helped to implement the program at Coronado Memorial in early 1974.[1009] Before that time, Coronado National Memorial had initiated an "Environmental Study Areas-Workshop" program in conjunction with area schools. It was "designed to assist teachers develop environmental education activities for the classroom as well as for outside the classroom." In addition, an "Environmental Study Area" was "planned for the Memorial where teachers can take students for nature field study experience."[1010]

Coronado's Environmental Living Program began with a teacher workshop involving participants from southeastern Arizona as well as northeastern Sonora. The first group of students followed a few weeks later.[1011] The program consisted of classroom preparation led, ideally, by teachers who had attended a workshop with Memorial staff and program coordinators; an introductory visit by students and teachers; classroom research and preparation; an overnight stay in various camps in the Memorial; and later follow-up and evaluation in the classroom.[1012] Over time, local educators were recruited to implement and administer Environmental Living.

Environmental Living programs throughout the country featured diverse experience depending upon the region and character of the site. From a desert cabin in Utah to a ship moored in San Francisco Bay, the program tailored the educational curriculum to the material resources where it took place.[1013] At Coronado National Memorial, theme camps interpreted the Coronado expedition; Mexican miners; the Papago; and Apache Indians. Participants camped, cooked, and participated in games and crafts reflecting the chosen culture and its environment. In addition, role-playing and problem solving exercises attempted to place the students within the history of the people whose lives they studied.[1014]

Despite its promising start, Environmental Living at Coronado never seemed able to turn into a vital ongoing program. In March 1976, the Environmental Living Coordinator for the Western Region of NPS wrote to Coronado Memorial. He outlined four reasons for the "lack of activity" in the Environmental Living programs at Coronado and in southern Arizona in general. He named the "malaise" of local school systems due to economic recession and, for some reason, "the rural nature of the communities." In addition, the park was remote from potential partner schools and the campground lacked structures. Finally, the letter blamed "the lack of a concerted 'sales program.'"[1015]

In April, Superintendent Dale wrote to local school principals about the Environmental Living Program. Dale wrote that, because of "logistical difficulties related to school funding and the distances involved," the Memorial "decided to make the program itself, not the specific site, the primary focus of the presentation."[1016] If the students could not go to the Memorial, the staff could go to the schools. That idea addressed the concern that schools' unwillingness or inability to make one or more trips to the Memorial was at least partially to blame for their failure to participate in the program. Another problem faced by the Memorial in this as well as other programs was a constant lack of sufficient staff.

The decision was made to add a consultant to coordinate the program and make teacher contacts. Laura Barry, of Willcox, had previous experience with the same program at Fort Bowie National Historic Site.[1017] She had participated at Fort Bowie as a teacher and it was thought that her connections as a teacher in Cochise County together with her enthusiasm for the Environmental Living Program would enable her to revitalize the program at Coronado for the 1976-1977 school year.[1018] Mary Lou Baldi was contracted to write a handbook.[1019] A Doctoral student at the University of Arizona and Reading Specialist in the Sahuarita School District, south of Tucson, she had been involved in the first teacher workshop in 1974.[1020]

In May 1977, Dale looked back on the school year as a success, writing to teacher Cecilia Gross of Sierra Vista, that it "has finally gotten off the ground."[1021] That same month, a newspaper article in the *Fort Huachuca Scout* followed Mrs. Gross and sixty Fort Huachuca through the program. According to the article, they were "among the first in southern Arizona to take advantage of a unique National Park Service program."[1022] During the 1976-1977 school year, the Environmental Living Program at Coronado National Memorial was, according to these sources a success, and seemed to presage a bright future. However, after that period, it disappears from the record.

In the 1980s, other outreach programs continued to connect the Memorial to schools on both sides of the international boundary. In March 1988, for example, a pilot School Outreach Program was presented at Palominas Elementary School. Its purpose was to familiarize students at all grade levels with the Memorial and its significance. The "location of the Memorial, the Coronado expedition, the Spanish influence on the origin of southwestern

Hispanic-American culture, and the role of Coronado National Memorial in preserving and protecting the natural resources of the region" were all discussed.[1023] It seemed as if, as Dale had written in 1976, school outreach programs had outlasted the "Live-In" aspects of environmental and cultural education at the Memorial.

The Environmental Living Program was more explicitly connected to an international Cultural Exchange Program involving schools in Palominas, Arizona, and Arizpe, Sonora. An undated budget for the program is labeled "Environmental Living Program."[1024] The program was also referred to as, among other things, the "Arizpe/Palominas Environmental Cultural Exchange Program."[1025] The Memorial staff continued to conceive of this project as an Environmental Living Program. Superintendent Dale described the May 1983 event as "An international/intercultural bi-lingual [sic], Environmental Living Program." The Memorial's major role that year was as the site of a campout for about eighty fifth graders from Palominas and Arizpe.[1026] However, NPS staff from Coronado and all over southern Arizona also provided translation, interpretive skills, and consultation on the program.[1027] By 1985, the Memorial was no longer involved with the exchange program, possibly because of time constraints for a reduced staff.[1028]

In the 1970s, a variety of interpretive programs, including the annual Historical Pageant and ongoing Environmental Living Program, began. They would continue for some time in various forms. In part, the expansion of programs reflected NPS determination to create better interpretation. That was certainly reflected in the 1967 Interpretive Prospectus and its successors. Also a factor was the coincidental arrival of the Bicentennial with its touring programs and special funding. According to one participant, though, a major reason for the development of the early 1970s was the presence of one man, Hugo Huntzinger. Huntzinger served as Superintendent during the period and was, according to Historian and Interpretive Specialist Tom Carroll, responsible for the Historical Pageant. "The new programs...in Interpretation," said Carroll, "are complementary and illustrate the direction that the Memorial is going."[1029]

The direction that the Memorial was going was a topic very much in doubt in the 1970s. Coronado Memorial was a small park on a dirt road that had little and seemingly needed more in developed facilities. Its resource was, by design, an almost pristine environment from which the visitor could appreciate the historical landscape experienced over four centuries earlier by Coronado and his contemporaries. Interpretation, as defined in 1967, was aimed toward preparing the visitor for the view from Coronado Peak. As the interpretive program turned toward large events, however, access to the Memorial became an issue as well.

In the 1950s a proposal to build a road from Montezuma Pass toward the viewpoint on Coronado Peak had been discussed but not constructed because of the difficulty of the terrain. In the 1967 Interpretive Prospectus, the idea of an alternative "viewing platform" at the east end of the Memorial was raised. It would serve the elderly, the infirm, and those uncomfortable with the mountain driving required by a visit to Montezuma Pass.[1030] By 1974, that idea was combined with a proposal for a four thousand capacity amphitheater which would be used for the annual Historical Pageant and other events.[1031] The amphitheater — viewpoint complex, including a large parking area, would be located "in the southeast benchlands" and would be accessible via a new access road.[1032]

Other, even more grandiose, plans were also floated in advance of the 1978 boundary adjustment. One, with two alternatives, involved construction of a tram, an idea that had been around since, at least, 1965.[1033] It would run either to Montezuma Peak, northeast of Montezuma Pass, or to Ash Peak, also on the north rim of Montezuma Canyon. The Ash Peak tram would begin from Ash Canyon, necessitating a large exchange or addition of lands. These ideas carried radically contrasting alternatives, such as closure of the Memorial; turning it over to the Forest Service; or moving to another site in Arizona, New Mexico, or Kansas.[1034] When it is remembered that all of these plans were contemporary with both the expansion of interpretive programs at Coronado and other proposals that led to the 1978 land swap it becomes obvious that the Memorial was suffering from an identity crisis. The Park Service was still uncertain as to the direction that Coronado Memorial should take in its development and, indeed, whether it should exist at all.

It is not clear how seriously the Park Service considered plans to close Coronado Memorial, but in the end it did not seem to be one of the alternatives presented to the public. Among the options that were circulated for comment, the aggregate of public opinion agreed with the fiscal concerns of NPS officials. The exchange with the Forest Service of the land west of Montezuma Pass for that within Montezuma Canyon was approved by a majority of respondents. However, the amphitheater complex met with general disapproval.[1035] A reading of responses of Memorial supporters again confirms that Coronado was at a turning point. Various people pointed to the excessive cost and intrusiveness of an amphitheater. Some thought that more events should be scheduled to justify the cost of the amphitheater while others worried about the adverse affect on the natural resource of construction and doubted the wisdom of encouraging large crowds. NPS officials, who had already expressed concerns with capital intensive projects, may have been happy to be able to take the proposal off the table.[1036]

The fact was that in its first few years of existence, the Historical Pageant was already outgrowing the Memorial. If it continued to grow, as seemed likely at the time, a new site would have to be found. Laurel Dale felt strongly that a gravel pit just east of the Memorial, which belonged to the state of Arizona, had the potential to be the best site for it and other future events. Its location in the flats to the east made it less prone to high winds and extreme temperature fluctuations. Moreover, it was closer to the highway and already had sufficient parking.[1037] Dale faced opposition from others in the Park Service and uncertainty as to the reaction of the state.[1038]

The gravel pit was never acquired or dedicated to Memorial events, but the state did cooperate in the staging of the pageant by allowing it to be used for parking.[1039] The Historical Pageants continued through the 1980s. They continued to feature cultural acts from southeastern Arizona and northeastern Sonora. Food concessions were handled by local non-profit groups such as the Boy Scouts, Veterans of Foreign Wars, and a high school marching band from Sierra Vista. The event drew well, with attendance ranging from 3,000 to 7,000 depending upon the weather and competition from other local community events.[1040]

There were ongoing problems with the pageant, which became the Coronado Borderlands Festival with the 1985 production.[1041] Of course, the weather for the event changed from year to year, which affected the turnout and the experience for visitors. In 1985, approximately 4,000 people turned out on a rainy, windy day.[1042] About 3,000 braved a chill wind in 1988. That year, the staff also had to deal with a rabies scare and confusion over the date of the event in the local papers.[1043] Ongoing difficulties with staffing and funding plagued the annual festival in a variety of ways. A look through the collections of festival materials shows that the each year, the staff scrambled to cover all the tasks necessary to producing a successful event. Even with help from other parks in the region and volunteers, it is clear that there was seldom as many workers as jobs needing to be done. Further staff cutbacks in 1983 raised the specter of a cutback in services, including possible cancellation of the Pageant.[1044]

One particular staff-related issue seemed to raise a problem every year. That was the lack of a bilingual staffer to work on organizing and staging the Festival. Spanish language services had always been handled on an ad hoc basis. In 1982, James Officer of the University of Arizona Anthropology Department, who acted as Master of Ceremonies every year, was thanked for making announcements in Spanish as well as English. He also offered to translate Festival related correspondence that year.[1045] The next year, the Buena High School, Sierra Vista, Spanish Club helped with translating letters and was asked to help at the event. The staff organizer, Theda Adcock, wrote that the Memorial "had requisitioned a language translator" but did not expect to get one soon, especially given that the staff had recently been cut.[1046]

The language problem came to a head in the wake of the 1984 Festival. Master of Ceremonies James Officer submitted a list of criticisms of the show, which included the need for a bilingual staff person to make contact with Mexican communities and performers both personally and in writing. He also listed the need for a stage manager, preferable bilingual so that he or she could communicate with and coordinate acts from both sides of the border.[1047] Officer's comments were seconded, in a considerably more vitriolic tone, by Jim Griffith, Director of the Southwest Folklore Center in Tucson. Griffith accused the Coronado staff of treating "perceptive Hispanics and others" with "indifference and contempt." He specified that there were "repeated refusals to take the same kind of pains with the linguistic and cultural aspects that are taken with, for instance, details of parking and sanitation."[1048]

Griffith did not regularly attend the Festival, but was connected to its organization. In 1983, he booked a band for the event, but regretted having to miss it "once more."[1049] Griffith, like Officer, criticized other aspects of the Festival, particularly the seeming unfocused approach to booking and sloppy production. However, both seemed most concerned that the language problem caused the Memorial, and the National Park Service, needlessly to project an image of cultural insensitivity. NPS acted quickly to address all of the problems raised by Officer and Griffith. Cesar Flores, Equal Employment Opportunity Hispanic Coordinator for the Western Region, was assigned to help with translations and contacts and to act as stage manager for the event. Physical improvements to the stage area were also proposed along with ideas to tighten the focus and improve the production of the event.[1050]

Unfortunately, the fine tuning of 1984 did not solve all the Borderlands Festival's problems. In 1986, a supportive critique pointed to a lack of clear focus to the program and, again, shoddy production.[1051] Also in 1986, an angry note pointed out fourteen errors in the Spanish version of the poster. It went on to blast the audience attracted by the Festival – as if the intended publicity was focused on a single group. The note read:

> As a dog and pony show for the rednecks of the area (no others need apply) this is a fine endeavor on the part of the US gummint. As an "entercultural" experience [referring to one of the errors] done with taste and empathy, forget it. If I were Jim Officer I'd boycott the bastards. Hell with 'em.[1052]

Sadly, the best intentions, when faced with a lack of budget and qualified staff, were not enough to succeed in pulling off the kind of event that the Memorial was aiming for.

Preparations for the 1987 Festival began with an attempt to go outside of NPS for help and ended, evidently, in a disaster. In the summer of 1986, the Memorial negotiated with Carlos Nagel of the Cultural Exchange Service of

Tucson. Nagel offered to produce the show, translate all relevant materials, and stage manage for $4080, broken down into several individual tasks and charges.[1053] Coronado proposed costs for the same list of tasks; they added up to $3580, but the Memorial rounded down to a total of three thousand dollars.[1054] At around the same time, performers were already being told that the budget for 1987 was expected to be cut, necessitating lower payments than in the past.[1055]

It appears that the Memorial and Nagel came to some sort of agreement, until early in 1987, just a few months before the April event. In January, Nagel was said to have agreed to a more limited menu of work for $950. The arrangement seems to have been tentative and involved a third party actually performing some of the services.[1056] It fell completely apart over the next few weeks. On February 2, Nagel told Superintendent Joe Sewell and others that "he simply doesn't have the time to do the legwork in No. Sonora."[1057] Two days later, James Officer was asked if he would emcee as in years past. Officer had made other plans after he had been told that "Nagel would be organizing the Festival," but agreed to try to rearrange his schedule.[1058]

On February 6, Nagel pulled out altogether and the Memorial staff began looking for a new translator.[1059] The next day he wrote a letter to the Acting General Superintendent of the Southern Arizona Group, NPS. He wrote:

> It is apparent to me that there needs to be an administrative decision and the political will to permit this Festival to develop its potential. Unless that decision is made and the necessary resources provided this cannot happen. The Festival should have the resources that are necessary or it should be discontinued.

Nagel went on to describe his past involvement in events and activities meant to improve cross-border relations. He said their success depended upon the "a long-term personal relationship between individuals who would work on a given activity...The Festival must develop these relationships if it is to justify the effort and investment that is currently involved." He concluded "Should the committment [sic] be made to transform the Festival into a meaningful borderlands activity I will be pleased to assist."[1060] Evidently, Nagel wanted to take over the production, and be paid a fair price for his services.

Nagel's "quick about face" was discussed at the Memorial along with the question "could we have inadvertently hurt some feelings there?"[1061] Whatever else may have been involved in the abortive attempt to involve Nagel, one of the issues was certainly the low budget available for the Festival. Theda Adcock, who was the main staff organizer before and after Nagel's brief involvement, wrote later that "procurement regulations and other obstacles" were to blame for the decision to again handle the Festival in-house.[1062] It is certain that Nagel did not think that there was enough money available to do what he thought was necessary to do the job right. Nor was there sufficient money in 1987 to pay the acts what they had previously received for performances. Finally, by the time Nagel abandoned the effort altogether, there was less than three months to go before the event, and planning continued to fall apart. In the middle of March, the stage manager expressed his regrets that he had a scheduling conflict and could not be there.[1063]

The day of the 1987 Borderlands Festival went no better than did the preparation. Adcock apologized to Officer after the event because, as had happened in years past, he was left alone on the stage. She was "so dismayed by all the behind-the-scenes foul-ups." In addition, she had been told not to find extra Spanish speaking help for the stage area because of the planned presence of Nagel.[1064] The only bilingual employee spent much of the day at the international border trying to solve a problem with crossings; and such difficulties were becoming more common.[1065]

One of the acts that would have been trying to cross from Mexico cancelled without warning because some of the dance group had chickenpox.[1066] Things were grim at the parking area as well. "Because of liability insurance requirements with the Sierra Vista School District, we had to go another route this year."[1067] That route did work. Although a crowd of some 6,000 attended, "We lost a good portion of our audience because of a breakdown in the shuttle service."[1068] One of the three rented busses, driven by a driver from Tucson, got lost and then had a flat tire. A second spent most of the day waiting at the border for the act that never arrived; that left one working shuttle. Those who did arrive at the border were held up more than ever before filling out paperwork, added because more people were crossing illegally than in the past.[1069] In short, just about everything that could go wrong with a Borderlands Festival did go wrong in 1987. The attempt to get outside help had, as it worked out, made things worse.

The 1987 experience left the Memorial staff in doubt for the future of the event. Theda Adcock concluded that "there are many things that have to be resolved before we start to organize another Festival if there is to be one."[1070] Superintendent Sewell inventoried the ongoing problems, such as shortage of personnel, parking and shuttle difficulties, increased troubles at the border, and the language barrier. In frustration, he wrote: "Though the Borderlands Festival is the main interpretive program of the year for Coronado National Memorial, each year it becomes more difficult to justify the expense and effort."[1071]

In 1988, cold, windy, weather, a rabies scare, and confusion over the date of the event in the local papers kept the crowd down to about 3,000, probably a mixed blessing for the staff.[1072] That was only the calm before the final storm. The first problem addressed by NPS was parking. Before the end of 1988, Sewell proposed parking within the east boundary of the Memorial. The site had been trampled by a firefighter's camp the previous summer and was overgrown with an invasive exotic grass. In addition, it would not truly begin to recover until the rainy season later in the summer.[1073] Sewell's proposal was turned down because of concern for damage to vegetation.[1074]

That left two parking possibilities for the Festival. One was the state owned gravel pit just outside of the east boundary; the other was the nearby Palominas School.[1075] In January, NPS wrote to the Arizona State Land Department to ask "permission to once again" use the gravel pit. The letter also asked that the site be improved by filling and leveling, at state expense. It also suggested an alternative site on state land, in the same area; it needed work as well, though less than the gravel pit did.[1076] The state replied that fees in the amount of $375 would be required; a survey was needed, also to be paid by the permittee, NPS; and that they could not do improvements of any kind on the land.[1077]

Faced with these roadblocks, in March the Festival was postponed until a tentative date in September. The reason given for the rescheduling was that roads and trails as well as picnic and parking areas needed repair after damage from the previous year's fire and subsequent unusually heavy rains. The new date was contingent on those repairs being completed and propitious weather during the interim months. The public service announcement that revealed the postponement did not mention the parking dilemma.[1078] In the meantime, efforts continued toward an eventual event.

The second parking option was Palominas School. However, the Superintendent was unable to convince the local school board to waive an insurance requirement in the amount of one million dollars. The nongovernmental support group, Southwest Parks and Monuments Association (SPMA), agreed to approach their insurer for a rider. They were not optimistic because the use was outside park boundaries and the insurance would need to cover the general public, performers, vendors, and crafts people as well as NPS employees.[1079] Eventually, the SPMA's lawyers advised the group "not to get involved."[1080] Finally, the state of Arizona informed the Memorial at this point that parking would no longer be permitted on state road right of way, as it had been in the past.[1081]

Insurance came up in another important way in 1989. Once the issue reared its head, the Southern Arizona Group office decided to investigate more thoroughly how all insurance needs should be handled for festivals at Tumacacori, Fort Bowie, and Coronado. Officials from other units of NPS who regularly handled such matters were contacted and a meeting was convened. The outcome was not positive for the future of the Borderlands

Festival. The participants insisted, unanimously, that all outside groups who operated with NPS property must be insured. Because the small, informal, vendors, craftspeople, and performers who participated in the Festival were unlikely to conform to that requirement, "umbrella" coverage with the help of support groups was suggested. Unfortunately, SPMA had already explored that option and decided against it. In addition, the consultants strongly recommended that foreign nationals not be invited to participate, as in the event of a claim against them NPS was almost certain to end up holding the proverbial bag. For Tumacacori and Coronado such a policy would negate the very reason for their events.[1082]

It was finally suggested that an outside entity, such as a "friends" group or nearby town should be asked to sponsor the Festivals. On that subject, Interpretive Specialist Frank Sumrak wrote, "Of course, by doing so, the NPS might possibly lose its current control and the festival risks the possibility of taking on a frivolous, carnival atmosphere."[1083] A report on this meeting summarized its results thusly:

> It appears that seeking outside support is one way for our festivals to continue. We certainly cannot continue as we have in the past, with little or no thought given to the liability coverage our festival participants should "legally" be carrying. It's only a matter of time before an unfortunate incident occurs and we find ourselves in a most uncomfortable and serious situation.
>
> I encourage the superintendents at festival park [sic] to discuss this matter in greater detail with their staff. We must give this matter considerable thought and think of ways in which we might overcome this problem. Otherwise the festival program in the Southern Arizona Group may come to a sudden halt.[1084]

Indeed, the overwhelming number of problems that arose in 1989 were enough to bring the program to a sudden halt. Scrawled in the margin of the file copy of the Draft Public Service Announcement postponing the 1989 event is the note "CANCEL FOR 89!"[1085]

One more requirement was pointed out at the March 1989 meeting. Food vendors had to meet health codes and be licensed to serve the public. Other parks also maintained the right of approval of menus and prices.[1086] The fact that Coronado Memorial and its fellow parks in southern Arizona were unaware of simple health code requirements for food vendors highlights the casual nature of Festival organization. Through seventeen years of the annual event, the Coronado staff never developed a formal procedure for putting the Borderlands Festival together that would address legal codes, liability, and other ongoing issues such as translation. Yet, the entire process was a learning experience.

In part, the reason behind the failure to firmly resolve problems which continued year after year was simply that there was no staff and little budget dedicated solely to the Festival. Left to their own devices, with minimal budgetary and administrative support, the Coronado staff did their best to do what they could with the modest time and resources available. In a way, the unprofessional production values of the Festival are probably what ensured that it survived for as long as it did. If it had been approached professionally at an earlier date, the legal and liability requirements that were discussed in 1989 would have been discovered and, probably, would have spelled its doom at that time. Thus, there was, perhaps, an absolute contradiction between the Festival existing and it being done right. Nonetheless, the ongoing popularity of the event attests to the quality of the productions that the Memorial presented.

In 1989, Coronado's era of big interpretive programs came to an end, but interpretive programs continued to develop, sometimes in concert with other Memorial projects. After mining property was acquired by the Memorial it had to cleaned and made safe. That created both responsibilities and opportunities. For example, the State of Texas property was acquired in late 1986. The next summer the old buildings were removed and trash cleaned up. In 1988, a mine safing team came from Death Valley to install safety netting across most of the openings, shafts, and adits. At that point, the property was considered "an excellent interpretive area and a detailed prospectus" was drafted.[1087] A State of Texas Mine Trail was considered, which would provide new scenic vistas and highlight the historical role of mining in the region.[1088]

Defunct mines in Montezuma Canyon became habitat for bats. Throughout the National Park Service are more than ten thousand abandoned mines. Because of ongoing concern for public safety they are often sealed. Over the last decade, the nonprofit Bat Conservation International has held some twenty Bats and Mines Workshops with federal and state agencies in the west to help employees combine concerns for mine safety and bat conservation. It is estimated that three to thirty thousand long-nosed bats spend part of the year at Coronado National Memorial.[1089] A study in cooperation with the National Forest Service and the University of Arizona Department of Ecology and Evolutionary Biology has monitored the use of gated mines on the Memorial by endangered long-nosed bats.[1090]

The endangered status of the long-nosed bat came up at Coronado in another context as well. A new grazing management plan in 2000 expressed concern about the consumption of agave by cattle and its impact on nectar eating lesser long-nosed and Mexican long-tongued bats.[1091] The grazing plan mentioned a few other affected species. Among them were the barking frog, loggerhead shrike, elegant trogon, Mexican spotted owl, and peregrine falcon.[1092] At the founding of the Memorial, of course, the privileges of grazing allotment holders were protected above all else. However, recent environmental concerns have been added to the equation over the history of the Memorial.

When Coronado National Memorial was created in 1952, permanent grazing rights were included in the package as a legacy of the 1941 bill and Senator Hayden's promises to the state's ranchers. It was quickly determined that the best way to handle the matter was for the Forest Service to continue to administer grazing permits, as was done at Saguaro National Monument.[1093] Of the three existing grazing allotments on the new Memorial, the vast majority of two, the Grubstake and the Lone Mountain, were still on National Forest land, while the third, the Montezuma, was split fifty-fifty between the Memorial and Forest Service lands. The Lone Mountain allotment was held by Henry D. Lee and the Grubstake by Alex D'Albini, neither of whom were friends of the Memorial.[1094] However, they were reported to be in excellent condition in the early years of the Memorial's existence. The Montezuma allotment seemed to be more prone to showing the effects of overuse.[1095] It belonged to Joe Zaleski and later to John Jones, both of whom got along well with the new park and its staff. In 1961, Jones agreed voluntarily to cut back the number of his cattle grazed on the Memorial when drought conditions required it.[1096]

By the 1970s, grazing was seen as a problem by NPS planners. Only minimal fencing had been constructed to protect specific areas, such as the picnic area and visitor center. Cattle were generally free to wander the Memorial grounds at will, posing sanitation problems and damaging the vegetation during the dry season. In addition, bulls and cows with calves could be a hazard to visitors as well as the staff and their families. Consultation between the Forest Service and Memorial superintendents was sporadic and the founding legislation gave neither sufficient leeway for making policy. In 1973, more fencing was planned to solve part of the problem.[1097]

The grazing issue also contributed to planning for the boundary adjustment of 1978. Most of the grazing within the Memorial took place west of Montezuma Pass.[1098] Of particular concern was the Yaqui Springs area, which had become damaged as the whole area had been overgrazed. Planners came to recognize that the formation of the Memorial, in extent, shape, and organization, had been shaped for concern for outside interests. By trading away the lands west of Montezuma Pass, the Memorial would give away much of the headache of grazing.[1099] After 1978, the portions of the Grubstake and the Lone Mountain allotments still within the Memorial were retired. The Joe's Spring allotment was brought into the Memorial's boundaries with the addition of the north side of Montezuma Canyon.[1100]

An agreement between the Forest Service and NPS in 1988 allowed the Memorial to control rotation of herds and to add fencing to protect vegetation and resources.[1101] The Montezuma allotment changed hands several times over the last few decades and became inactive in 1990. In 1992, the Park Service finally began to administer its grazing permits for itself. Following a new 1999 agreement with the National Forest Service, the two agencies share responsibility administering and monitoring the Joe's Spring allotment, which extends across their boundary. They also share grazing fees collected from the permit holder. Relying on the 1941 legislation's wording that specified that grazing shall continue as long as it did not interfere with recreational development, NPS now is able to more stringently regulate grazing within the Memorial.[1102] In addition, as noted above, other concerns, such as environmental protection, are now important issues, that were not even considered in 1941 or 1952.

Throughout this work, a tension in planning between the historical significance originally ascribed to the Memorial by Congress and its natural resource base has been an ongoing theme. The beauty of the Huachuca Mountains has been the primary attraction for many visitors. For them, hiking trails, which provide access to the outdoor experience have been of paramount importance. Hiking trails on Coronado Memorial began with the simple trail from the Montezuma Pass parking lot to the viewpoint on Coronado Peak. In 1963-64, a longer trail was cut through Joe's Canyon to Coronado Peak, where it connected with the trail from the pass. In December 1961, it was projected for construction in fiscal year (FY) 1963.[1103] In the objectives for FY 1964, stabilization of the trail was still to be accomplished.[1104]

A smaller spur trail, added much later, runs from Joe's Canyon Trail and Coronado Peak, south down Yaqui Ridge to the border at International Boundary Marker Number 102. It was planned as a segment of the Arizona Trail which, when finished, will provide an unbroken trail between the north and south borders of the state. The Arizona Trail was first conceived in the mid-1980s. When it was proposed at Coronado, several alternatives were considered. It is interesting to note that one would have followed close to the alignment of the road once planned for ingress to the ill-fated museum/visitor center on the international border.[1105] A Heritage Grant, funded by the Arizona state lottery, was awarded to the Memorial for trail construction in 1995 and construction began. Crews from Saguaro National Park and the Huachuca Hiking Club continued work on the trail until 1997. The Yaqui Ridge Trail was officially dedicated on National Trails Day, June 6, of 1998.[1106]

As the twenty-first century began, Coronado National Memorial had evolved into a multi-use area serving many recreational demands. The historical theme is still featured in the visitor center and other interpretive sites. The small network of hiking trails now includes a short trail to Coronado Cave, which can also be explored by any visitor with a permit and a flashlight. Bird watching is a rapidly growing diversion for which the Huachuca Mountains are appropriately famous. In addition, the Memorial staff and a crew of energetic and able volunteers are exploring the ranching and mining history of the Memorial and taking oral histories from residents throughout the local area. They are expanding the base of knowledge about the Memorial and of southeastern Arizona and northeastern Sonora in general.

The population of the region continues to expand, increasing demand for the kinds of recreational opportunity that the Memorial provides. In 1972, "a major urban development" was planned by the Prescott Valley Corporation.[1107] In August 1973, the first phase of Prescott Valley's Sierra Grande development, four miles northeast of the Memorial, consisting of 3,800 lots, was approved by the Cochise County Planning and Zoning Board.[1108] By 1976, Prescott Valley Development was marked on a map as an "Obsolete Proposal." However, the Tenneco West Land Development, to the north of it, was still seen as viable.[1109] As specific development schemes came and went, the local population grew steadily. Between 1980 and 1995, the population of Cochise County was estimated to have increased by thirty per cent, a trend that can be expected to continue. That growth is approaching the Memorial as the Sierra Vista area expands to the south. Visitation reflects regional population growth, going up by thirty per cent during the 1990s.[1110] By the turn of the century, however, it was evident that the trend had reversed itself, for visitation had fallen in the few previous years.

As southwestern Cochise County grows and urbanizes, more people will continue to find their way to Coronado National Memorial. They will find a Memorial that is evolving to meet their needs. Beginning with a mission that was limited to the commemoration of Coronado's 1540 expedition, the Memorial has expanded its focus, experimenting with various methods of interpretation along the way. The natural resource of the southern Huachuca Mountains has grown in importance as it becomes more important to an approaching urban sprawl. The effort to administer, preserve, and interpret the area of the Montezuma Canyon will, no doubt, continue to evolve to meet the challenges and opportunities presented in the future. Given its long, and sometimes slow history, Coronado National Memorial has come of age. It is hoped that this history will play a small part in that continuing process.

A view down Montezuma Canyon into the San Pedro Valley. (Coronado National Memorial Archives, National Park Service)

Appendix A

Land Acquisitions and Transfers with references to Associated Structures

Appendix A Contents
1. Introduction
2. Intra-Governmental Transfers
3. Homestead Entry Survey 311
4. Homestead Entry Survey 310
5. Pyeatt Homestead (Montezuma Ranch)
6. Kudzmi Homestead
7. State of Texas mine property
8. Victorio mine property

1. Introduction
The following appendix traces the ownership of the land that makes up Coronado National Memorial. Because its focus is the acquisition of land for the Memorial, the majority of the material is presented on the later transactions, during the period of the Memorial's existence. However, land now within the Memorial is also traced through previous owners in summary form. Its history is discussed more fully in the pertinent chapters.

The appendix is organized topically. All transfers from other governmental agencies, primarily the National Forest Service, are included in the first section. The Homestead Entry Surveys are arranged in the order in which they were claimed. William Ratliff's claim, H.E.S. 311, precedes his son's claim, H.E.S. 310, because William was the first permanent settler in the area. The Pyeatt Homestead (Montezuma Ranch) and Kudzmi Homestead follow.

The larger blocks of mining land are separated into two sections, State of Texas Mine and Victorio Company property. The latter is so designated because that company had come to own all of the land before the creation of the Memorial. Other mine claims are not addressed because the land belonged to the Coronado National Forest even though others may have had rights to minerals on the properties.

Within each block of Homestead land the material is addressed chronologically until such time as it came to be assigned tract numbers (beginning with 101-). At that point it is organized numerically by tract number, and transfers of tracts are ordered in chronological sequence.

2. Intra-Governmental Transfers
Original Memorial Land – 1952
A November 5, 1952, Proclamation by the President of the United States defined the original land included in Coronado National Memorial. The proclamation specified that it was based upon "section 1 of the act of August 18, 1941, 55 Stat. 630 (16 U.S.C. 450 y) as amended by Public Law 478, 82nd Congress, approved July 9, 1952." The Memorial was described as follows:

>Township 24 South, Range 20 East,
>>Section 10: South half of the Southwest quarter, and South half of the Southeast quarter;
>>Section 11: South half of the Southwest quarter;
>>Section 13: Southwest quarter of the Northwest quarter, and South half;
>>Section 14: Northwest quarter of the South half, and Northwest quarter of the Northeast quarter, and South half of the Northeast quarter;
>>all of Section 15;
>>all of Section 22;
>>all of Section 23;
>>all of Section 24;
>Township 24 South, Range 21 East,
>>Section 17: lots 5 and 6;
>>Section 18:, lots 3, 4, 8, 9, 10 and the Southeast quarter of the Southwest quarter;
>>all of Section 19;
>>Section 20: lots 3 and 4.

The area described aggregate approximately 2,745.33 acres. The deed is marked "Deed No. 1."[1111] A map that accompanied the proclamation illustrates the original boundaries of the Memorial.

1960
The boundaries of Coronado National Memorial changed in accordance with legislation passed in September 1960. Senate Bill 2806 of the 86th Congress, 2nd Session created Public Law 689, which adjusted the Memorial boundary in four ways. The legislation added 3.6 acres of National Forest Service land in lots 5 and 6 of Section 20, Township 24 South, Range 21 East, that were apparently intended to be included within the original boundaries but were inadvertently excluded. That land comprised a narrow strip along the international border in the southeast corner of the Memorial. It also transferred lots 2 and 7 of Section 18, Township 24 South, Range 21 East, Gila and Salt River Base and Meridian, comprising 75.33 acres, from Coronado National Forest, National Forest Service, to the Memorial.

Some mining land was excluded from the Memorial by the 1960 legislation, including the Billy Boy claim in the State of Texas group of claims and the Z.T. Parker claim, later of the Victorio Company properties. The land reverted to Coronado National Forest, National Forest Service. The mining claims remained with their owners. This property was described as the north half of the southwest quarter of the northwest corner of Section 13, and the north half of the southeast quarter of the northeast quarter of Section 14, Township 24 South, Range 20 East, Gila and Salt River Base and Meridian. Each section contained 20 acres, for a total deletion of 40 acres.

This legislation also authorized the purchase of a 49.856 acre portion of Homestead Entry Survey 310 from Southwest Monuments Association.[1112] [See Homestead Entry Survey 310 material for summary and citations.]

1964

In the early 1960s, the United States Section of the International Boundary and Water Commission acted to divest itself of land within a 60 foot wide strip running along the border. The National Park Service moved to obtain those portions within the Coronado National Memorial and Organ Pipe Cactus National Monument, both in Arizona. The land within that strip was specifically included in the International Memorial by the 1941 act that established it. However, NPS was required to obtain authorization from the Secretary of State before initiating "recreational or other development" within the strip.[1113] The affected land within Coronado National Memorial was:

> A strip 60 feet wide north of the International Boundary between the east and west boundaries of Coronado National Memorial, more particularly described as the southerly 60 feet of the following subdivisions:
> Township 24 South, Range 20 East (Gila and Salt River Meridian)
> Section 22, Lots 1, 2, 3, and 4;
> Section 23, Lots 1, 2, 3, and 4;
> Section 24, Lots 1, 2, 3, and 4;
> Township 24 South, Range 21 East (Gila and Salt River Meridian)
> Section 19, Lots 1, 2, 3, and 4;
> Section 20, Lots 3 and 4;
> Totaling 32.504 acres more or less.[1114]

Given that the described land is now within the boundaries of the Memorial, which extend to the International border, it appears that the transfer did take place. Note above and below that adjacent tracts of this border strip were transferred to the Memorial in 1960 and 1978.

1978

In 1978, federal legislation again altered the boundaries of Coronado National Memorial through an exchange with the National Forest Service. Public Law 95-625, created on November 10, 1978, by the National Parks and Recreation Act of 1978, revised the boundaries of many units of the National Park Service, including Coronado National Memorial.

Transferred from the Memorial to Coronado National Forest was 1,247 acres comprising:

> The South half of the South half of Section 10, the Southwest quarter of the Southwest quarter of Section 11; the West half of the West half of Section 14; All of Sections 15 and 22; and the West half of the West half of Section 23, of Township 24 South, Range 20 East, Gila and Salt River Base and Meridian.

Added to the Memorial from the National Forest was approximately 3,326 acres, including approximately 569 acres of private land, were:

> portions of Sections 2, 11, 12, 13, and 14 of Township 24 South, Range 20 East; and Sections 5, 6, 7, 8, 17, 18, and 20 of Township 24 South, Range 21 East; Gila and Salt River Base and Meridian. It was more specifically described as follows:
> Beginning at a point on the northerly boundary of Coronado National Memorial, said point also being the northwest corner of the Southeast quarter of the Southwest quarter of Section 11, Township 24 South, Range 20 East; thence North, along the west line of the East half of the West half of said Section 11, to the northwest corner of said East half of the West half of Section 11; thence East, along the north line of said Section 11; to the northwest corner of the Northeast quarter of the Northeast quarter of said Section 11, thence southeasterly to the northwest corner of the North half of the Southwest quarter of the Northwest quarter of Section 12, said township and range; thence East, along the north line of said North half of the Southwest quarter of the Northwest quarter, to the northeast corner of said North half of the Southwest quarter of the Northwest quarter of Section 12; thence South, along the east line of said North half of the Southwest quarter of the Northwest quarter, to the southeast corner of said North half of the Southwest quarter of the Northwest quarter of Section

12; thence East, along the north line of the South half of the South half of the North half of said Section 12, to the southeast corner of the North half of the Southwest quarter of the Northeast quarter of said Section 12; thence North, along the North-South centerline of the Northeast quarter of Section 12, to the northwest corner of the South half of the Northeast quarter of the Northeast quarter of said Section 12; thence East, along the north line of said South half of the Northeast quarter of the Northeast quarter, to the northeast corner of said South half of the Northeast quarter of the Northeast quarter of Section 12; thence northeasterly, through Sections 7 and 6, Township 24 South, Range 21 East, to the northwest corner of the South half of the Southeast quarter of said Section 6; thence East, along the north line of said South half of the Southeast quarter, to the northeast corner of said South half of the Southeast quarter of Section 6; thence southeasterly, through Sections 5 and 8, said township and range, to the northeast corner of the South half of the Southeast quarter of said Section 8; thence South, along the east line of Sections 8, 17 and 20, said township and range, to the southeast corner of said Section 20; thence West, along the south line of said Section 20, to a point on the easterly boundary of Coronado National Memorial, said point also being the south quarter corner of said Section 20; thence northerly and westerly, along the existing boundary of Coronado National Memorial, to the point of beginning.[1115]

The land excluded from the Memorial was all on the west side of Montezuma Pass. Added lands extended the Memorial to the north and to the east. It included National Forest Service lands that had been part of the Kudzmi Homestead and Homestead Entry Surveys 310 and 311. In the extreme southeast corner of the Memorial, and making up the southeast corner of the land transferred in 1978, was a square tract labeled 101-19, 137.31 acres in size. It included the 133.67 acre Kudzmi Homestead plus 3.64 acres. That 3.64 acres was very likely a strip directly along the international border, much like the 3.6 acre border strip in the 1960 land transfer. That land was relinquished by the United States Section of the International Boundary and Water Commission [see above]. Also added to the Memorial was a 1.03 acre strip running the length of the boundary between Homestead Entry Survey No. 311 and the Pyeatt Homestead. These small additions filled in between lands claimed earlier in the century.[1116]

The transfer also encompassed private land within Homestead Entry Surveys 310 and 311, the State of Texas mine properties, and the Doredor/Victorio mining properties. Such lands would later be added by purchase.

3. William Ratliff -- Homestead Entry Survey 311

According to documents filed by the Surveyor General's office in 1917, William Ratliff officially applied for a 160 acre homestead claim on October 22, 1911. The survey was executed March 12-13, 1914 and approved August 8, 1917 for 158.23 acres. Ratliff's homestead consisted of the south half of the northwest quarter and north half of the southwest quarter of Section 17, Township 24 South, Range 21 East, Gila and Salt River Meridian. Montezuma Wash ran through the southwest corner of property from northwest to southeast.[1117]

William Ratliff died in 1917, leaving the land to be split among his heirs. William's son Ed was the executor of his will and representative of all the heirs. In 1932, nine Ratliffs by name or marriage transmitted their claims to George Ratliff, another son of the elder William. Ed and his wife Ira quit claimed an unspecified tract, evidently Homestead Entry Survey 310 to George in a separate transaction. On 30 September 1933, George and Annie Ratliff transferred both Homestead Entry Surveys, 310 and 311, to Marko Vucinich. On 21 November 1933, Vucinich transferred all of 310 and 311 to Joe Zaleski.[1118]

Joe Zaleski also bought the Pyeatt Homestead and the Simon Kudzmi Homestead to the south. During the 1930s and 1940s, Zaleski operated a dude ranch with headquarters on the Pyeatt Homestead. In October 1950, Joe Zaleski transferred ownership of the ranch, not including the Pyeatt Homestead, to his son Frank by way of a Gift Deed. In 1956, Frank quit-claimed it back to Joe. Included in these two transfers were both Ratliff homesteads, numbered Homestead Entry Surveys 310 and 311, and the Kudzmi Homestead.[1119] In April 1957, Joe Zaleski sold the same property to John A. and Inez Z. Jones along with some cattle and horses, "miscellaneous tools, equipment, and furniture," and a stock brand.[1120]

In May 1959, a 49.856 acre portion of Homestead Entry Survey 310 was purchased by Southwest Monuments Association (now Southwest Parks and Monuments Association) from the Jones family.[1121] The remainder of Homestead Entry Survey 310, all of Homestead Entry Survey 311, and the Kudzmi Homestead, were given by John A. and Inez Z. Jones to John Z. and Lawrence D. Jones, "for and in consideration of the love and affection" of parents for their children, in 1962.[1122] They sold the total amount to the Baumkirchner brothers, Everett and Fred, and their wives, Margaret E. and Mary Ann, respectively, in 1965. The purchase price was not recorded, but the Jones brothers carried a $45,000 mortgage on the property.[1123]
In 1973, the Baumkirchners traded 541.43 acres, including most of their land in the area of the Memorial, to the National Forest Service for other land of equal value. Included in the land exchange was the entire Kudzmi Homestead, the remainder of H.E.S. 310 not already within the Memorial, and a 50 acre portion of the southwest corner of H.E.S. 311.[1124] The remainder of H.E.S. 311 was subdivided, most into residential sized tracts. Those properties came to be known collectively as Montezuma Estates. They are examined individually below.

Tract 101-10 94.23 acres
After the Baumkirchner's sold 50 acres of H.E.S. 311 and subdivided they rest, they kept the biggest piece, tract 101-10. This property was sometimes listed as two separate parcels although they were transferred together.
Description
A 1979 appraisal listed 94.23 acres to be acquired in fee. The described property contained several building improvements, including rental units, residences, barns, sheds, etc. Access was by paved highway. The property was generally located in Section 17, Township 24 South, Range 21 East, Gila and Salt River Meridian.[1125]
Parcel 1 89.85 acres
AKA Parcel No. 13.
AKA P-2.[1126]
Description
Homestead Entry Survey No. 311, on file in the Bureau of Land Management as granted by Patent recorded in Book 79 of Deeds, of Real Estate, page 54, records of Cochise County, Arizona;
> EXCEPT beginning at the Southwest corner of said survey; thence North along the West line of said survey, 1650 feet; thence East parallel with the South line of said survey,
> 1320 feet;
> thence South parallel with the West line of said survey;
> 1650 feet to point on the South line of said survey;
> thence West along the South line to the Point of Beginning;
> and
> EXCEPT beginning at the Northwest corner of Homestead Entry Survey No. 311;
> thence East along the North line of said Survey, 2022.20 feet
> to the True Point of Beginning;
> thence South 56° 10' 31" East 583.61 feet;
> thence South 0° 13' East 377.1 feet;
> thence South 89° 47' West 483.6 feet;
> thence North 0° 13' West 703.8 feet to the True Point of
>   Beginning; and
> EXCEPT beginning at the Northwest corner of said Homestead

Entry Survey No. 311;
thence North 89° 47' East 1813.48 feet along the North line of said survey to the True Point of Beginning;
thence South 0° 13' East 417.44 feet;
thence North 89° 47' East 208.72 feet;
thence North 0° 13' West 417.44 feet to a point on the North line of said survey;
thence West to the True Point of Beginning; and
EXCEPT beginning at the Northwest corner of said Homestead Entry Survey No. 311;
thence East along the North line of said survey, 1773.48 feet to the True Point of Beginning;
thence South 0° 13' East 417.44 feet;
thence South 89° 47' West 1083.6 feet;
thence North 0° 13' West 417.44 feet to the North line of said survey;
thence East along the North line to the True Point of Beginning, containing 89.85 acres more or less.[1127]

Parcel 2 4.38 acres
AKA Parcel No. 12.
AKA P-17.[1128]

Description
That portion of Homestead Entry Survey No. 311, on file in the Bureau of Land Management as granted by Patent recorded in Book 79 of Deeds of Real Estate, page 54, records of Cochise County, Arizona, described as follows:
BEGINNING at the Northwest corner of said survey;
thence East 1147.32 feet along the North line of said survey to the True Point of Beginning.
thence South 0° 13' East 417.44;
thence South 89° 47' West 457.44 feet;
thence North 0° 13' West 417.44 feet to a point on the North line of said survey;
thence East the True Point of Beginning, containing 4.38 acres, more or less.[1129]

Ownership/Disposition of Tract 101-10
An undated appraisal of property which NPS wished to acquire for Coronado National Memorial reflected the subdivision of H.E.S. 311, and of Tract 101-10, and continued ownership by the Baumkirchners. It listed Parcel Numbers 12 and 13, which together made up Tract 101-10, separately. The owners of both parcels were shown as Fred E. and Mary Ann Baumkirchner, of Hereford, Arizona, as joint tenants with right of survivorship, as to an undivided ½ interest; and Everett M. and Margaret E. Baumkirchner, of Bisbee, Arizona, as joint tenants with right of survivorship, as to an undivided ½ interest.[1130]
On 20 March 1980, Fred E. Baumkirchner and Mary Ann Baumkirchner, husband and wife, and Everett M. Baumkirchner and Margaret E. Baumkirchner, husband and wife, sold 94.23 acres to NPS for $471,200. The deed listed and described the two separate parcels that made up Tract 101-10.[1131]

Tract 101-11 4 acres
Tract 101-11 was two separate land parcels that became a single tract when both came to be owned by the Tyras in 1971. They were later sold, together, to NPS.

Description
A 1979 appraisal described 4 acres to be acquired in fee. The property was improved with a single family residence and miscellaneous outbuildings. It was located in the North half of Section 17, Township 24 South, Range 21 East, Gila and Salt River Meridian.[1132]
Parcel 1 2 acres
AKA Parcel No. 6.
AKA P-4.[1133]
Description
That portion of Homestead Entry Survey No. 311, on file in the Bureau of Land Management, as granted by Patent recorded in Book 79 of Deeds of Real Estate, page 54, records of Cochise County, Arizona, described as follows:
> BEGINNING at corner No. 2 of said survey;
> thence North 89° 47' East a distance of 1356.04 feet along the North line of said survey, to the true point of beginning;
> thence North 89° 47' East a distance of 208.72 feet;
> thence South 0° 13' East a distance of 417.44 feet;
> thence South 89° 47' West a distance of 208.72 feet;
> thence North 0° 13' West a distance of 417.44 feet to the True Point of Beginning.[1134]

Ownership of Parcel 1
The Baumkirchners sold the two acre property that came to be known as Tract 101-11, Parcel 1, to Lawrence Edward Ray in July 1967. The deed marked the property as "Parcel No. 3."[1135] Ray borrowed $14,400 from the Farmers Home Administration of the United States Department of Agriculture for the purchase and they held the deed to the property as collateral.[1136] Ray sold the same property to James M. and Billie Jean Tyra in August 1971.[1137] Evidently, the Tyras borrowed money from the Baumkirchners that was repaid in full when all of Tract 101-11 was sold to NPS in 1980.[1138] [See Ownership/Disposition of Tract 101-11 below]

Parcel 2 2 acres
AKA Parcel No. 11.[1139]
Description
That portion of Homestead Entry Survey No. 311, on file in the Bureau of Land Management, as granted by Patent recorded in Book 79 of Deeds of Real Estate, page 54, records of Cochise County, Arizona, described as follows:
> BEGINNING at the Northwest corner of said survey;
> thence East along the North line 1147.32 feet to the point of beginning.
> thence continuing East 208.72 feet;
> thence South 0° 13' East 417.44 feet;
> thence South 89° 47' West 208.72 feet;
> thence North 0° 13' West 417.44 feet to the Point of Beginning.[1140]

Ownership of Parcel 2
The Baumkirchners sold the two acre Parcel 2 of Tract 101-11 to the Tyras in September 1971, at about the same time that the Tyras purchased Parcel 1 from Ray.[1141] The Tyras seem to have borrowed money from the Baumkirchners which they repaid when they sold Tract 101-11 to NPS in 1980.[1142] Those two purchases placed the Tyras in possession of four acres, which came to be labeled Tract 101-11.

Ownership/Disposition of Tract 101-11
By the end of 1971 James M. Tyra and Billie Jean Tyra owned four acres of H.E.S. 311 that was called Tract 101-11. They purchased half of it from the Baumkirchners and the other half from Lawrence Edward Ray, but seem to have borrowed the money for all of it from the Baumkirchners. They held the land in Joint Tenancy Deeds until the time that they sold it to

NPS. On 25 March 1980, the Tyras sold the four acres of Tract 101-11, in two parcels, to NPS for $62,000. A hand written note on the deed identified it as "DEED # 11."[1143] On the same day, a Warranty Deed for both parcels of Tract 101-11 was transferred from the Baumkirchners to the Tyras, signifying that the mortgage on the property had been paid and clearing the title for ownership by NPS and inclusion into Coronado National Memorial.[1144]

Tract 101-12 1 acre
AKA #104-60-7 or #104-60-8.[1145]
AKA Parcel No. 9.
AKA P-5.[1146]
Description
That portion of Homestead Entry Survey No. 311, on file in the Bureau of Land Management, as granted by Patent recorded in Book 79 of Deeds of Real Estate, page 54, records of Cochise County, Arizona, described as follows:

> BEGINNING at Corner No. 2 of said Homestead Entry Survey;
> thence North 89° 47' East, a distance of 1564.76 feet along the North line of said Homestead Entry Survey, to the TRUE POINT OF BEGINNING.
> thence North 89° 47' East, a distance of 208.72 feet;
> thence South 0° 13' East, a distance of 208.72 feet;
> thence South 89° 47' West, a distance of 208.72 feet;
> thence North 0° 13' West, a distance of 208.72 feet to the

TRUE POINT OF BEGINNING.[1147]

A 1979 appraisal described one acre to be acquired in fee. It was a vacant 1-acre homesite with access on ¼ mile dirt road off Coronado Memorial Highway, located in the North half of Section 17, Township 24 South, Range 21 East, Gila and Salt River Meridian.[1148]

Ownership/Disposition
In August 1971, the Baumkirchner brothers and their wives sold two one-acre parcels of land to Dewitt and Doretta Ruth Green.[1149] These two parcels became Tracts 101-12 and 101-14. On 3 April 1980 Dewitt Green and Doretta Ruth Green, husband and wife, sold 2 acres to NPS for $19,000. That sale included Tracts 101-12 and 101-14. A hand written note on the deed identified at as "DEED # 10."[1150]

Tract 101-13 1 acre
AKA #104-60-6.[1151]
AKA Parcel No. 7.
AKA P-6.[1152]
Description
That portion of the Homestead Entry Survey No. 311, on file in the Bureau of Land Management, as granted by Patent recorded in Book 79 of Deeds of Real Estate, page 54, records of Cochise County, Arizona, described as follows:

> BEGINNING at Corner No. 2 of said Homestead Entry Survey;
> thence North 89° 47' East, a distance of 1564.76 feet, along the North line of said Homestead Entry Survey;
> thence South 0° 13' East a distance of 208.72 feet, to the TRUE POINT OF BEGINNING;
> thence North 89° 47' East, a distance of 208.72 feet;
> thence South 0° 13' East, a distance 208.72 feet;
> thence South 89° 47' West, a distance 208.72 feet
> thence North 0° 13' West, a distance of 208.72 feet to the
> TRUE POINT OF BEGINNING.[1153]

A 1979 appraisal described one acre to be acquired in fee. It was improved with an 1120 square foot residential structure and miscellaneous outbuildings. Access was off a dirt road, from Coronado Memorial Highway. The tract was located in the Northeast quarter of the Northwest quarter of Section 17, Township 24 South, Range 21 East, Gila and Salt River Meridian.[1154]

Ownership/Disposition

The Baumkirchners sold the portion of H.E.S. 311 known as Tract 101-13 to William and Eloise Archie in July 1967. The deed for the sale was marked "Parcel No. 15."[1155] The Archies held the land until November 1972 and then sold it to Robert G. and Betty J. Chavez.[1156] They, in turn, sold the property to Eileen Owens in April 1978.[1157] In January 1985, Owens sold it to Allan and Leona Cerkowniak.[1158] As of June 2000, the Cerkowniaks still reside in this house and property.

Tract 101-14 1 acre
AKA #104-60-7 or #104-60-8.[1159]
AKA Parcel No. 8.
AKA P-7.[1160]

Description

That portion of Homestead Entry Survey No. 311, on file in the Bureau of Land Management, as granted by Patent recorded in Book 79 of Deeds of Real Estate, page 54, records of Cochise County, Arizona, described as follows:

>BEGINNING at Corner No. 2 of said Homestead Entry Survey;
>thence North 89° 47' East, a distance of 1813.48 feet along the North line of said Homestead Entry Survey, to the TRUE POINT OF BEGINNING.
>thence North 89° 47' East, a distance of 208.72 feet;
>thence South 0° 13' East, a distance of 208.72 feet;
>thence South 89° 47' West, a distance of 208.72 feet;
>thence North 0° 13' West, a distance of 208.72 feet to the
>TRUE POINT OF BEGINNING.[1161]

A 1979 appraisal listed one acre to be acquired in fee. This was a vacant rural one-acre homesite, with access from Coronado Memorial Highway on a ¼ mile dedicated dirt road. The tract was located in the Northeast quarter of the Northwest quarter of Section 17, Township 24 South, Range 21 East, Gila and Salt River Meridian.[1162]

Ownership/Disposition

In August 1971, the Baumkirchner brothers and their wives sold two one-acre parcels of land to Dewitt and Doretta Ruth Green.[1163] These two parcels became Tracts 101-12 and 101-14. On 3 April 1980 Dewitt Green and Doretta Ruth Green, husband and wife, sold 2 acres to NPS for $19,000. That sale included Tracts 101-12 and 101-14. A hand written note on the deed identified at as "DEED # 10."[1164]

Tract 101-15 1 acre
AKA #104-60-3.[1165]
AKA Parcel No. 5.
AKA P-8.[1166]

Description

That portion of Homestead Entry Survey No. 311, on file in the Bureau of Land Management, as granted by Patent recorded in Book 79 of Deeds of Real Estate, page 54, records of Cochise County, Arizona, described as follows:

>BEGINNING at corner No. 2 of said Survey;
>thence North 89° 47' East a distance of 1813.48 feet, along
>the North line of said survey;
>thence South 0° 13' East a distance of 208.72 feet to the True Point of Beginning;
>thence North 89° 47' East a distance of 208.72 feet;
>thence South 0° 13' East a distance of 208.72 feet;

thence South 89° 47' West a distance of 208.72 feet;
thence North 0° 13' West a distance of 208.72 feet to the
True Point of Beginning.[1167]

A 1979 appraisal described one acre to be acquired in fee. It was improved with a 1316 square foot residence and access was good. The tract was located in Northeast quarter of the Northwest quarter of Section 17, Township 24 South, Range 21 East, Gila and Salt River Meridian.[1168]

Ownership/Disposition

The Baumkirchners sold Tract 101-15 to Calvin R. and Esther Teague in September 1966.[1169] The Teagues sold it to William L. Cashman and Ramona E. Cashman in April 1971.[1170] As of June 2000, the Cashmans still reside in this house and property.

Tract 101-16 6 acres
AKA Parcel No. 10.
AKA P-9.[1171]

Description

That portion of Homestead Entry Survey No. 311, on file in the Bureau of Land Management, as granted by Patent recorded in Book 79 of Deeds of Real Estate, page 54, records of Cochise County, Arizona, described as follows:

BEGINNING at the Northwest corner of Homestead Entry Survey No. 311;
thence East along the North line of said survey 2022.20 feet to the True Point of Beginning;
thence South 56° 10' 31" East 583.61 feet;
thence South 0° 13' East 377.10 feet;
thence South 89° 47' West 483.6 feet;
thence North 0° 13' West 703.8 feet to the True Point of Beginning.[1172]

A 1979 appraisal described six vacant acres with good access to be acquired in fee. The property was located in the Northeast quarter of the Northwest quarter of Section 17, Township 24 South, Range 21 East, Gila and Salt River Meridian.[1173]

Ownership/Disposition

The Baumkirchners sold this six-acre tract to a son of one of the brothers, Everett M. Baumkirchner Jr. In October 1971 the property was transferred pending payments totaling $6,000.[1174] On 19 March 1980 Everett M. Baumkirchner Jr. sold 6 acres to NPS for $36,000. A hand written note on the deed identified at as "DEED # 8."[1175] On the same day, another Warranty Deed for Tract 101-16 was transferred from the Baumkirchner brothers and their wives to Everett M. Baumkirchner Jr. The second Warranty Deed was probably given after the last money owed on the property was paid to the sellers and cleared the title for ownership by NPS and inclusion into Coronado National Memorial.[1176]

4. Edward Ratliff -- Homestead Entry Survey 310

According to 1917 documents filed by the Surveyor General's office, Ed Ratliff officially applied for his 160 acre homestead claim on February 3, 1911. The survey was executed March 11-12, 1915 and approved August 8, 1917 for 157.72 acres. Ed Ratliff's homestead consisted of the south half of the northeast quarter and north half of the southeast quarter of Section 18, Township 24 South, Range 21 East, Gila and Salt River Base and Meridian. Montezuma Wash ran through the property from northwest to southeast.[1177]

Ed and his wife, Ira, quit claimed an unspecified tract, evidently Homestead Entry Survey 310, to Ed's brother, George, in 1932. At the same time, all of the heirs of William Ratliff transmitted their claims to Homestead Entry Survey 311 to George. On 30 September 1933, George and Annie Ratliff tranferred Homestead Entry Surveys 310 and 311 to Marko Vucinich. On 21 November 1933, Vucinich transferred both 310 and 311 to Joe Zaleski.[1178] Zaleski owned at least four homestead entry surveys at the mouth of Montezuma Canyon. He operated the property as a dude ranch. Its center of operations was the Pyeatt homestead, later the Richards property.

In October 1950, Joe Zaleski transferred ownership of much of the property, not including the Pyeatt Homestead, to his son Frank by way of a Gift Deed. In 1956, Frank quit-claimed it back to Joe. Included in these two transfers were both Ratliff homesteads, numbered Homestead Entry Surveys 310 and 311, and the 133.67 acre Kudzmi Homestead.[1179] In April 1957, Joe Zaleski sold the same property to John A. and Inez Z. Jones along with some cattle and horses, "miscellaneous tools, equipment, and furniture," and a stock brand.[1180]

In May 1959, a 49.856 acre portion of Homestead Entry Survey 310 was purchased by Southwest Monuments Association (now Southwest Parks and Monuments Association) from the Jones family for a total cost of $3,000. The property was:

> A roughly triangular tract of land lying in the South Half (S½) of the tract currently or formerly known as Homestead Entry Survey 310 (H.E.S. 310) except for a small portion which lies in the Southwest (SW) corner of the North Half (N½) of said H.E.S. 310 in Cochise County, Arizona, in the North Half (N½) of the Southeast Quarter (SE¼) of Section 18, Township 24 South, Range 21 East, Gila and Salt River Base and Meridian, and more particularly described as follows:
>
> BEGINNING at the Southwest corner (identified as corner number 1), of Homestead Entry Survey 310, said point being located on the present boundary of Coronado National Memorial and marked by an iron pipe with a brass cap and a rock cairn placed by the United States Bureau of Land Management in 1955; thence North zero degrees thirty-three minutes west, one thousand two-hundred ninety-four and twenty-six hundredths feet, more or less, along the west boundary of said tract, which line is also the present boundary of sadi Memorial, to the northwest corner of Lot 8, Section 18, said point being marked by an iron pipe with a brass cap and a rock cairn placed by the United States Bureau of Land Management in 1955;
>
> thence north zero degrees twenty-three minutes east, two hundred thirty and eight-tenths feet, more or less, along the west boundary of Homestead Entry Survey 310 to a point on a circular curve marked by an iron pipe with a National Park Service brass cap, said point being located south eight-one degrees forty-four minutes east, exactly one hundred forty feet from the point of curvature of said curve;
>
> thence southeasterly five hundred forty-eight and two-tenths feet along said circular curve to the right of radius one thousand seven-hundred thirty-two and four-tenths feet and having a beginning tangent bearing of south eighty-four degrees three minutes east (from point of courvature to point of intersection) to the point of tangency of said curve;
>
> thence south sixty-one degrees sixteen minutes east, two hundred twenty-four and eight-tenths feet to the point of curvature of a circular curve to the right;
>
> thence southeasterly two hundre ninety-two and six-tenths feet along said circular curve to the right of radius six thousand twenty-nine and six-tenths feet to the point of tangency of said curve;
>
> thence south fifty-eight degrees twenty-nine minutes east, five hundred eighty-eight and seven-tenths feet to the point of curvature of a circular curve to the right;
>
> thence southeasterly two hundred twenty-five and nine-tenths feet along said circular curve to the right of radius two thousand two-hundred nine and nine-tenths feet to the point of tangency of said curve;
>
> thence south fifty-two degrees thirty-eight minutes east, twenty-eight and eight-tenths feet to the point of curvature of a circular curve to the left;
>
> thence southeasterly two hundred sixteen and nine-tenths feet along said circular curve to the left of radius one thousand six-hundred nine and nine-tenths feet to the point of tangency of said curve;

thence south sixty degrees twenty-one minutes east, thirty and seven-tenths feet to the point of curvature of a circular curve to the right;

thence southeasterly seven hundred thirteen and six-tenths feet, more or less, along said circular curve to the right of radius one thousand two-hundred fifty-four and nine-tenths feet to a point on the southern boundary line of Homestead Entry Survey 310 marked by an iron pipe with a National Park Service brass cap, said point also being located on the present northern boundary line of Coronado National Memorial;

thence north eighty-nine degrees forty-nine minutes west two thousand three-hundred and sixty-one feet, more or less, along the southern boundary line of Homestead Entry Survey 310 which line is also the present northern boundary of the said Memorial, to the point of beginning (all bearings referred to the true meridian); containing 49-856 acres, more or less.[1181]

That tract was conveyed by Southwestern Monuments Association to NPS for inclusion in the Memorial in May 1962 for $3,000.[1182]

The remainder of Homestead Entry Survey 310, all of Homestead Entry Survey 311, and the Kudzmi Homestead, were given by John A. and Inez Z. Jones to John Z. and Lawrence D. Jones "for and in consideration of the love and affection" of parents for their children in 1962.[1183] They sold the total amount to the Baumkirchner brothers, Everett and Fred, and their wives, Margaret E. and Mary Ann, respectively, in 1965. The purchase price was not recorded, but the Jones brothers carried a $45,000 mortgage on the property.[1184]

In 1973, the Baumkirchners traded 541.43 acres, including most of their land in the area of the Memorial, to the National Forest Service for other land of equal value. Included in the land exchange was the entire Kudzmi Homestead, the remaining 107.864 acres of H.E.S. 310 not already within the Memorial, and an approximately 50 acre portion of the southwest corner of H.E.S. 311.[1185] While negotiations were going on between the Baumkirchners and the National Forest Service, the Forest Service was also discussing the acquisition with the National Park Service and Coronado National Memorial. NPS lacked the funding to purchase the land itself and supported Forest Service acquisition.[1186] That land eventually entered the Memorial via exchange with the National Forest Service. [See National Forest Service Land section.]

5. The Pyeatt Homestead

Cornelius N. Driscoll first claimed the Montezuma Ranch land in July 1913.[1187] By the middle of 1914, Driscoll had moved to another tract, east of the San Pedro River, which he claimed under the Homestead Act in September 1914.[1188] John Pyeatt settled the later Montezuma Ranch in November 1915 and applied for a claim in June 1917.[1189] Pyeatt's claim to the Montezuma Ranch property was eventually approved, and a deed was granted in July 1921, with final recording of Pyeatt's patent number 814549 having "been established and duly consummated, in conformity to law," taking place on December 4, 1925. The 160 acre property was described as the south half of northeast quarter and north half of the southeast quarter of Section 17, Township 24 South, Range 21 East of the Gila and Salt River Base and Meridian, Arizona.[1190]

John Pyeatt married Inez, "Tiny," Ratliff, the adopted daughter of the family that owned, at least, two claims west of his new homestead. Pyeatt was dead within four years of his receiving final approval for his second homestead. His widow moved to Paso Robles, California, and in March 1929 she sold the lot to Joseph Zaleski.[1191] During the 1930s and 1940s, Zaleski, who owned adjacent property as well, operated a dude ranch with its headquarters on the Pyeatt Homestead. Zaleski's son, Frank, came to own the property and he kept it until the end of 1949. After World War II, around 1946 or 1947, Harry H. and Ruth Ethlyn Peterson began to manage the Montezuma Ranch. The Petersons purchased the ranch from Frank Zaleski, described as portions of Township 24, Range 21, Sections 17 and 18, on December 13, 1949. On the same day they transferred title to the property to Nancy Carter Nelms.[1192]

Nancy Nelms and manager Don Brooks ran Montezuma as a dude ranch and a summer camp for young girls for a few years.[1193] Nelms put Montezuma Ranch on the market in 1955, listing it with realtor George Howe of Tucson. On November 21, 1955, Howe himself purchased Montezuma Ranch from Nelms, thus ending the guest ranch period of its history. In April 1973, the ranch passed into the hands of George F. and Elsie R. Weick.[1194] [See Tract 101-18 below.]

Tract 101-18 160 acres
AKA #104-60-2.[1195]
AKA Parcel No. 4.
AKA P-10.[1196]
Description
     A 1979 appraisal described Tract 101-18 as 160 acres to be acquired in fee. The appraisal specified that the tract was improved with several buildings, including residences, barns, sheds, and miscellaneous outbuildings, including a pool. There was excellent access to the property. Its location was described as in the west half of Section 17, Township 24 South, Range 21 East, Gila and Salt River Meridian, Arizona.[1197]
     On 25 May 1979, new owner Richard Richards added that the land contained his permanent residence, three other houses, a swimming pool, a 48'x 100' green house, a 35'x 40' storage building, a 35'x 36' carrot juice factory, a 30 acre apple orchard containing approximately 5000 trees and a well, and a crop of carrots.[1198] George Brown thought that Richard Richards added the second story to the house on the east.[1199]
     A title insurance company report placed Tract 101-18 in the south half of the northeast quarter; and the north half of the southeast quarter of Section 17, Township 24 South, Range 21 East of the Gila and Salt River Base and Meridian, Cochise County, Arizona.[1200]
Ownership/Disposition
     George and Martha Howe purchased the Pyeatt Homestead, then known as the Montezuma Ranch, in 1955 [see Pyeatt Homestead above]. A deed recorded on April 27, 1973 recorded the sale of the property to George F. and Elsie R. Weick, of Wood Dale, Illinois.[1201] In March 18, 1974, the Weicks were listed as the owners of Section 17, Township 24 South, Range 21 East, also known as Parcel #104-60-2.[1202]
According to information gleaned from real estate tracking books in the Cochise County Assessor's Office, Bisbee, Arizona, in 1975 the Weicks sold the property to Patricia H. Hughes, who, in turn, sold the ranch to Richard B. Richards and his wife, Cheryl, in March 1979.[1203] The Transamerica Title Company Preliminary Report, one copy of which was filed with documents from 1980-1981, listed both Patricia H. Hughes, of Mesa, Arizona, and Richard Weick, of Hereford, Arizona, as owners of this tract, without details or explanation.[1204] A May 1979 NPS list of land owners showed Tract 101-18 as owned by Patricia H. Hughes. That name was crossed out and written in was "Richard B. Richards (Ryan; Weick)".[1205] Given that Richard B. Richards is known to be the son of Elsie Weick, it is likely that both Weick and Ryan are other names used by the same man.
     On June 8, 1979, the owner of Tract 101-18 was shown as "Hughes/Richards." The same letter went on to state that Tract 101-18 had been conveyed to Mr. Richard Richards of Hereford, Arizona, and was subsequently subdivided into three parcels. It was as yet unknown how the land was subdivided, the size of resultant tracts, or to whom two of the tracts were sold.[1206] Even before then, on 25 May 1979, Richards gave oral permission for appraisal as owner of the property.[1207] A July 1979 list of landowners shows Richards and his wife (et ux.) as owners Tract 101-18.[1208]
     Some confusion remained as to the ownership of Tract 101-18, even after it was subdivided. A listing of the status of lands as of February 29, 1980, showed Hughes owner.[1209] A similar listing one month later indicated that Richards was the owner.[1210] A July 30, 1979, memorandum by Paul R. Thompson, Acting Superintendent, Coronado National Memorial,

discussed land owners within the proposed new boundaries of the Memorial. It listed Richard B. Richards among those agreeable to the land acquisition plan.[1211]

A handwritten note describes a call from Leland Auslander (sic, proper spelling is Auslender) from Los Angeles, California, to Robert D. (Bob) Gibbons, Western Region, NPS. Auslender said that he had purchased 25 vacant acres of Tract 101-18, the deed being recorded one month earlier.[1212]

At this point Tract 101-18 was divided into two tracts. At first, they were labeled Tracts 101-23 and 101-24. Later, those designations were deleted and replaced by Tracts 101-25 and 101-26. [See Tracts 101-23, 101-24, 101-25, and 101-26]

Tract 101-23 deleted

Leland Auslender of Los Angeles, California, called Bob Gibbons on September 24, 1979 to inform him that he had purchased 25 acres of Tract 101-18. He described the property as being in the south half of the northwest quarter of the northwest quarter of the southeast quarter, and the south half of the northwest quarter of the southeast quarter of Section 17, Township 24 South, Range 21 East, Gila and Salt River Base and Meridian, Arizona. Auslender assigned Richards as his agent.[1213]

A March 31, 1980, list of properties showed Tract 101-23, belonging to R. Richards, containing 135 acres and Tract 101-24, belonging to L. Oslander (sic), with 25 acres.[1214] A memo of May 12, 1980, deleted Tracts 101-18, 101-23, and 101-24. It noted that Tracts 101-23 and 101-24 "were listed with erroneous acreages so were deleted." It also recorded the establishment of two parcels from Tract 101-18: Tract 101-25, with 95 acres, belonging to Richards and Tract 101-26, with 65 acres, belonging to Auslender.[1215] [See Tract 101-25]

Tract 101-24 deleted

When Tract 101-18 was subdivided in late 1979, the resulting tracts were first recorded as numbers 101-23 and 101-24. A 31 March 1980 list of properties showed Tract 101-23 containing 135 acres and belonging to Richard Richards, and Tract 101-24, with 25 acres, belonging to Leland Auslender.[1216] A memo of 12 May 1980 recorded that Tracts 101-23 and 101-24 "were listed with erroneous acreages so were deleted." It also noted the establishment two parcels from Tract 101-18: Tract 101-25, with 95 acres, belonging to Richards and Tract 101-26, with 65 acres, belonging to Auslender.[1217] [See Tract 101-26]

Tract 101-25 95 acres
Description

When Tract 101-18 was subdivided, the northern part became Tract 101-25.

Ownership/Disposition

Richard B. Richards retained ownership of Tract 101-25 when Tract 101-18 was divided and Tract 101-26 sold to Leland Auslender. Tract 101-15 was subsequently subdivided into Tracts 101-27, 101-28, 101-29, and 101-30. [See Tracts 101-27, 101-28, 101-29, and 101-30]

Tract 101-26 65 acres
Description

Tract 101-26 was made up of the southern part of Tract 101-18. When Tract was sold to NPS it was described as follows:

> The North half of the Northwest quarter of the Northwest quarter of the Southeast quarter; and
> The Northeast quarter of the Northwest quarter of the Southeast quarter; and
> The South half of the Northwest quarter of the Northeast quarter of the Southeast quarter; and
> The South half of the Northeast quarter of the Southeast quarter; and

The South half of the Northwest quarter of the Northwest quarter of the Southeast quarter; and the
South half of the Northwest quarter of the Southeast quarter of Section 17, Township 24 South, Range 21 East of the Gila and Salt River Base and Meridian.[1218]

Ownership/Disposition

A memo of May 12, 1980, recorded the creation of Tracts 101-25 and 101-26 from Tract 101-18. Tract 101-26 contained 65 acres and belonged to Leland I. Auslender.[1219]

On April 21, 1980, Auslender sold 65 acres to NPS for $325,000. The document notes that this was also known at one time as 101-24. A hand written note on the deed identified it as "DEED # 6".[1220]

Tract 101-27 5 acres
Description

Tract 101-27 was formerly the northeast corner of 101-25. It remained in the possession of Richard B. Richards and his wife when Tract 101-25 was subdivided.[1221] Tract 101-27 was transferred to NPS together with Tract 101-28. [See Tract 101-28]

Tract 101-28 5 acres
Description

Tract 101-28 was formerly the southeast corner of 101-25.[1222]
When Tracts 101-27 and 101-28 were sold, together, to NPS, the deed described the combined property as:

the north half of the northeast quarter of the southeast quarter of the northeast quarter and the south half of the northeast quarter of the northeast quarter of the southeast quarter, Section 17, Township 24 South, Range 21 East, Gila and Salt River Base and Meridian, Arizona.[1223]

Ownership/Disposition of 101-27 and 101-28

On 15 December 1981 Richard B. Richards and Cheryl Richards (AKA Cheryl A. Richards), husband and wife, sold 10 acres to NPS for $50,000. That sale comprised Tracts 101-27 and 101-28 combined. A hand written note on the deed identified it as "DEED # 9".[1224]

Tract 101-29 82.5 acres
Description

When 95 acre Tract 101-25 was divided, 82.5 acre Tract 101-29 retained most of its land.[1225] It was the home of Sunrise Farm. Tract 101-29 was also listed once in 1982 as 85 acres.[1226] It was described as:

The southwest quarter of the northeast quarter, the northwest quarter of the northwest quarter of the southeast quarter of the northeast quarter; the south half of the north half of the southeast quarter of the northeast quarter; the south half of the southeast quarter of the northeast quarter; and the north half of the north half of the northeast quarter of the southeast quarter, Township 24 South, Range 21 East, Section 17, Gila and Salt River Meridian, Cochise County, Arizona.[1227]

Ownership/Disposition

On 4 February 1985 Richard Richards and Cheryl Richards, husband and wife, sold scenic easement to NPS for $549,000. The conditions are spelled out in attachments. A handwritten note on the deed identifies it as "DEED # 14." The easement agreement read as follows:

THE scenic easement granted to the United States of America of the above described land consists of a covenant on the part of the Grantors to refrain from doing, severally and collectively, on behalf of themselves, their heirs, executor and assigns, the various acts hereinafter mentioned, it being hereby agreed that these restrictions shall constitute a servitude upon said land and will be for the benefit of the Grantee through the preservation of the scenic values of the land controlled by this easement.

THE RESTRICTIONS HEREBY IMPOSED ON THE LAND, THE ACTS WHICH THE GRANTOR PROMISES TO DO OR REFRAIN FROM DOING UPON THE LAND, AND THE RIGHTS IN AND TO THE LAND GRANTED TO THE UNITED STATES OF AMERICA AND ITS ASSIGNS BY THE GRANTOR ARE AS FOLLOWS: There shall be no new construction of any improvements, as of the date of this easement. No additions or alterations shall be made on existing structures. Any building or structure damaged or destroyed by fire or other casualty or deteriorated by the elements or wear and tear may be maintained, repaired, renovated, remodeled or reconstructed so long as the basic character of the building or structure is not materially altered.

The general topography of the landscape shall remain in its present condition. There shall be no cutting or permitting of cutting, destroying or removing any trees, brush or other flora, provided, however, that existing and seedling trees, shrubbery and other flora may be pruned or cut down to maintain the premises consistent with good management practices. Reserving, to the Grantor, herein, the right and privilege to clear and restore trees and shrubs that are damaged or disturbed by the forces of nature; the right and privilege to gather, remove and use dead wood.

Grantors within 6 months shall purchase 100 five gallon Arizona Cypress trees. The Grantee will be responsible for the planting in locations which will be agreed upon by both parties. The Grantee shall be allowed to plant additional trees in the future if deemed necessary and appropriate by the Superintendent.

Any additional trees beyond the original 100 shall be purchased by the Grantee. Maintenance of all trees will be the responsibility of the Grantor.

No signs, billboards or advertisements shall be displayed or placed upon the property.

Mobile homes or recreational vehicles over 20 feet in length shall only be allowed on the property if they do not remain longer than 90 days.

At all times the property shall be kept in a neat and orderly condition and no trash or debris shall be placed upon the land or allowed to accumulate.

All efforts shall be made to screen personal property from the park visitor.

Park personnel shall be permitted, upon giving reasonable verbal or written notice to the landowner, to enter upon said property to ascertain compliance with the restrictions and covenants of this easement. Prior arrangement for entrance on said land is not necessary for reasons of emergency or safety.

No additional easements or other rights of way of any kind shall be granted to any other party by the Grantor.

There shall be no construction of new roadways or changing the course of existing roads on the property covered hereby.

This property shall not be used for any industrial, mining or similar use or for the accommodation of any paying guests for a period of less than 90 days.

All animals must be adequately restrained and shall not be permitted to stray from the property.

The Grantors in the use of this property shall conform to all applicable laws, ordinances, and regulations in effect in the area, including but not limited to all applicable general National Park Service regulations and general and special regulations for the area in particular.

This grant of scenic easement is only for the purpose of preserving and protecting the scenic value of the said lands, and does not grant the general public any right of ingress or egress over or across said, or any other rights of usage.

THESE INTERESTS in land are being acquired by the National Park Service of the

United States Department of the Interior for the use and benefit of the Coronado National Memorial and are appurtenant to said park lands.

SUBJECT to existing easements for public roads and highways, public utilities, railroads and pipelines.

TO HAVE AND TO HOLD the herein-described estate in land unto the Grantee and its assigns forever.[1228]

Despite the restrictions contained in the scenic easement agreement signed by NPS and Mr. and Ms. Richards, the landowners soon floated several development schemes for Tract 101-29. They included fee sale of 25 acres, including all structures; contracting with the state to run a halfway house for paroled felons; operating a nursing home; developing a mini-RV park; and subdividing the property into five new building sites. Richards also brought up selling the property to NPS with the stipulation that he be allowed to remain.[1229]

Another issue involving the scenic easement on Tract 101-29 and relations between Richards and the Memorial was waste disposal on the property. In May 1990, new superintendent Edward Lopez conducted a Level I Hazardous Waste Inspection Survey of the Richards property and submitted a report expressing concern about dumps and recommending that a Level II Hazardous Waste Survey be performed.[1230] On the request of Bob Cousins, Regional Director, Western Region, NPS, the Arizona Department of Environmental Quality inspected Richards's 82½ acre property on 19 June 1990. They issued a report on 16 August 1990. They identified "Several Solid Waste issues" including "three unapproved refuse landfills, diesel fuel leaks, fiberglass resin discharges, and various waste containers of oil and paint, and waste batteries."[1231] While some dump sites, litter, and abandoned vehicles were present before the easement, it was clear that the property had deteriorated since it was signed.[1232]

Subsequent to the easement agreement, Richard Richards began attempting to sell Tract 101-29. He claimed financial hardship, partly due to the restrictions in the easement, adding in 1990 that he was by then divorced and otherwise in debt as well. In 1988, Richards first suggested that NPS purchase the property, stipulating that he wanted to continue living there and using the land for agriculture. Given his ongoing circumvention of the scenic easement and degeneration of Tract 101-29, some NPS officials supported the idea. Superintendent Joseph L. Sewell recommended fee acquisition by NPS and renewable one-year special use permits that allowed Richards to stay on the land.[1233]

It was, belatedly, recognized by NPS officials that the scenic easement was ineffective as written. There seemed to be no enforcement mechanisms which specified consequences for violations. In addition, NPS had no pictures or descriptions of the property to document the appearance of the property at the time of the agreement in order to prove that violations had occurred. Obvious violations of specific items in the easement agreement had already taken place without retribution. One example was the granting of right-of-way to the Sulfur Springs Valley Electrical Cooperative. Now, Richards was prepared to pursue further development, unconcerned about the seemingly unenforceable easement. In addition, stipulated screening efforts had been ineffective and would likely continue to be so. Finally, Richards was determined to sell the property, and probably subdivide it. If NPS did not acquire it the same problems were likely to continue with the new owners.[1234]

Requests to Washington, D.C., for acquisition funding raised concerns. The Director's office noted that the landowner was claiming a hardship based upon an easement for which he had already been paid. Fee acquisition would then be used as a remedy for repeated violations of the easement. Even after acquisition, the violator would remain on the property under a special use permit. In effect, NPS would pay for the land twice and it would still be under the control of a private landowner who had proven uncooperative in the past. Such a course would be inconsistent with existing policy and set a dangerous precedent for future acquisitions.[1235] When hardship funds were requested to allow immediate acquisition, a Congressional Subcommittee also expressed concern that purchase was proposed as a means of preventing development that was specifically prohibited by the already purchased easement.[1236]

When Edward Lopez met Richard Richards in December 1989 Richards introduced himself as "the person that 'had taken the NPS for over $500,000 and was in the process of taking another one half million from them again.'"[1237] Thereafter, Richards continued his attempts to subdivide and sell Tract 101-29, promising prospective buyers that they could build as long as they were replacing one of the many buildings already on the property. He also continued to plead hardship to NPS. On October 16, 1990, Acting Regional Director, Western Region, Lewis S. Albert explained that the Richards family was losing all their equity through possible bankruptcy and hadn't marketed the property because they were counting on NPS to buy it. He went on to discuss the insufficient regulation that allowed Richards to violate easement and the mess that he has had already created and would likely exacerbate.[1238] By early 1991, NPS was negotiating purchase with a Chapter 13 Trustee, suggesting that the property had been foreclosed. However, funding was not then available and was not thought likely to be until after October 1, 1992.[1239]

On the evening of 25 July 1991 the status and fate of the Richards property was suddenly changed. As Superintendent Edward Lopez was leaving the Memorial he was flagged down by Linda Sorenson, who lived with Richards on the property. At her request, Lopez contacted the Cochise County Sheriff's Department. Sorenson had been assaulted by Richards and retaliated by turning him in for marijuana cultivation. Together, Sheriff's deputies and Park Rangers searched the Richards property and the adjacent area of the Memorial. They found marijuana growing within the house as well as thirty- eight marijuana plants on NPS land.[1240] According to Coronado Superintendent Edward Lopez, the Department of Justice, United States Attorney's Office, and Drug Enforcement Agency approached him shortly after the drug bust to assess NPS interest in obtaining the property through the seizure process. NPS discussed the offer and then responded that they would be interested in acquisition.[1241] In August 1991, the U.S. Attorney's Office filed for seizure of Tract 101-29 in its entirety.[1242] Subsequently, Richards pled guilty to domestic violence. As part of his plea bargain, Richards agreed not to contest the seizure. As part of the forfeiture he also agreed not to have any later interest in the land. Richards continued to live on the property until April 1993, paying rent to the U.S. Marshal Service.[1243] Superintendent Lopez recalled that the property came under the custodial ownership of the Department of Justice, U.S. Marshal Service, some six weeks after the arrest.[1244] In May 1992, NPS was informed by the U.S. Attorney's office that the land had been seized as part of the plea bargain with Richards. NPS was offered the opportunity to acquire it for the price of all existing liens plus interest, taxes, and expenses incurred by the Marshal's Service. NPS agreed to a stipulated total, projected for August 5, 1992, of $227,016.34. They wanted a guarantee that Richards and certain property, including trees and a carrot harvest but not fencing, would be off the property before the Memorial took possession.[1245]

However, between the arrest and seizure of the land by the Department of Justice Richards's mother, Elsie Weick, had filed a lien on a portion of the property for money owed to her. The Department of Justice contested the Weick lien. According to NPS employees, the general feeling was that Ms. Weick filed the lien so that her son would come out of the process without losing everything. The eventual settlement provided for Ms. Weick and the Department of Justice to split the proceeds from the sale of the parcel determined to be covered by the lien.[1246] Because of uncertainty about the outcome of the Weick lien and its value, NPS could not guarantee payment of outstanding claims and expenses. Therefore, the Asset Forfeiture Office of the Department of Justice could not continue its efforts to transfer Tract 101-29 to NPS.[1247]

There were two other outstanding liens on Tract 101-29 as well, belonging to Western Farm Credit Bank and Citibank. There was some confusion regarding exactly what land secured what loan. That confusion stemmed from the legal descriptions defining the land base of the collateral.[1248] A September 1992 notice of impending Trustee's Sale described one of the tracts. It specified that the land, Tax Parcel Number 104-60-002D-6, secured a principal amount of $120,000, as per agreement of 9 December 1988. The original Trustor was Richard Richards; the beneficiary was Western Farm Credit Bank; and the Successor Trustee was Melinda S. Barnett.[1249] This property became known as Tract 101-39. The remaining 25.59 acres of the original 82.5

were eventually assigned to lien-holders as well. Elsie Weick and the Department of Justice were to split the proceeds from the sale of 20.47 acres, while Citibank was assigned 5.12 acres. Both properties contained residential structures.

From that point on, the 82.5 acre Tract 101-29, also labeled Tract 101-04 at times, was usually considered as three separate tracts numbered 101-39 (56.91 acres), 101-40 (5.12 acres), and 101-41 (20.47 acres). For the next few years, however, it was still, sometimes, discussed and dealt with as one large lot, particularly when the issue was hazardous waste. During 1996, NPS conducted "Level I Survey: Contaminant Survey Checklist of Proposed Real Estate Acquisition" inspections on all of the 82.5 acres which formerly made up tract 101-29.[1250] Subsequently, in 1997, Coronado National Memorial took bids for clean-up of the properties that had made up Tract 101-29 as part of the process of acquiring all of them.[1251]

[See Tracts 101-39, 101-40, and 101-41]

Tract 101-30 2.5 acres
Description
Tract 101-30 was made up of land formerly on the north side of Tract 101-25.[1252]
When sold to NPS, Tract 101-30 was only described as follows:
> The east half of the north half of the northwest quarter of the southeast quarter of the northeast quarter of Section 17, Township 24 South, Range 21 East, Gila and Salt River Base and Meridian, Arizona.[1253]

Ownership/Disposition
On 3 August 1982 Richard B. Richards and Cheryl Richards, husband and wife, sold 2.5 acres to NPS for $12,500. A hand written note identifies the deed as "DEED # 13".[1254]

Tract 101-39 56.91 acres
Description
When it was sold to NPS, Tract 101-39 was described as:
> The Northeast quarter of the Southwest quarter of the Northeast quarter; and the Southeast quarter of the Southwest quarter of the Northeast quarter; and the South half of the Southeast quarter of the Northeast quarter; and the South half of the North half of the Southeast quarter of the Northeast quarter; and the Northwest quarter of the Northwest quarter of the Southeast quarter of the Northeast quarter; and the North half of the North half of the Northeast quarter of the Southeast quarter of Section 17, Township 24 South, Range 21 East of the Gila and Salt River Base and Meridian, Cochise County, Arizona;
> Except the following described parcels (A) and (B):
> Parcel (A):
> Beginning at the Northwest corner of the South half of the Northeast quarter of said Section 17;
> Thence South 100.00 Feet;
> Thence East 100.00 Feet;
> Thence North 60.00Feet;
> Thence East 200.00 Feet;
> Thence South 260.00 Feet;
> Thence East 150.00 Feet;
> Thence North 200.00 Feet;
> Thence East 70.00 Feet;
> Thence South 35.00 Feet;
> Thence East 800.00 Feet to a point on the West line of
> the Northwest quarter of the Northwest quarter of the Southeast quarter of the Northeast quarter;
> Thence North along said West line, 135.00 Feet to a point on the North line of the

South half of the Northeast quarter;
Thence West along said North line of the South half of the Northeast quarter, 1,320.00 Feet, more or less, to the Point of Beginning.
Parcel (B):
Beginning at the Northwest corner of the South half of the Northeast quarter of said Section 17;
Thence South 100.00 Feet;
Thence East 100.00 Feet;
Thence North 60.00 Feet;
Thence East 200.00 Feet;
Thence South 260.00 Feet;
Thence East 150.00 Feet;
Thence North 200.00 Feet; To the True Point of Beginning;
Thence East 70.00 Feet;
Thence South 35.00 Feet;
Thence East 630.00 Feet;
Thence South 315.00 Feet;
Thence West 700.00 Feet;
Thence North 350.00 Feet to the True Point of Beginning;
Excepting Therefrom any portion lying within the West half of the Southwest quarter of the Northeast quarter of said Section 17.[1255]

Ownership/Disposition

The origin of Tract 101-39 was in a $120,000 loan to Richard Richards from Western Farm Credit Bank on 9 December 1988. According to Bob Cousins, there was some confusion regarding the land base used as collateral for this and another loan from United Bank of Arizona unspecified Western Farm Credit Bank. After that conundrum was sorted out, Western Farm Credit Bank was able to foreclose on 56.91 acres, which became Tract 101-39.[1256]

In November 1994, NPS was contacted by an agent for Western Farm Credit Bank regarding the sale of Tract 101-39. In December, Sondra S. Humphries, Chief, Division of Land Resources for the Western Region, responded with an offer for $24,000. Her letter detailed some intermediate steps which would have to precede.[1257] It was not until April 22, 1996, that the property was cleared by a Level 1 hazardous waste inspection.[1258] Subsequently, in May 1996, an executed copy of an Offer to Sell was transmitted to Western Farm Credit Bank.[1259]

On June 17, 1996, a DOI Certificate of Inspection and Possession for Tract 101-39, 56.91 acres, was signed by Ed Lopez, Park Superintendent.[1260] The sale was recorded on 18 June 1996. At that time it was also identified as Coronado National Memorial Deed No. 20.[1261] In May 1997 Notification of Closing for Tract 101-39 was received at CORO. It showed that the title for 56.91 acres passed from Western Farm Credit Bank to the United States Government on June 18, 1996. The purchase price was $24,000.[1262]

Tract 101-40 5.12 acres

Description

Tract 101-40 was described in NPS correspondence as:
PARCEL I:
That portion of the South half of the Northeast quarter of Section 17, Township 24 South, Range 21 East of the Gila and Salt River Base and Meridian, Cochise County, Arizona, described as follows:
BEGINNING at the Northwest corner of the South half of the Northeast quarter of said Section 17;
thence South 100 feet;
thence East 100 feet;
thence North 60 feet;

thence East 200 feet;
thence South 260 feet;
thence East 150 feet;
thence North 200 feet to the TRUE POINT OF BEGINNING;
thence East 70 feet;
thence South 35 feet;
thence East 630 feet;
thence South 315 feet;
thence West 700 feet;
thence North 350 feet to the TRUE POINT OF BEGINNING;
Excepting therefrom any portion lying within the West half of the Southwest quarter of the Northeast quarter of said Section 17.
PARCEL II:
That portion of the following described Parcel A lying within the West half of the Southwest quarter of the Northeast quarter of Section 17, Township 24 South, Range 21 East of the Gila and Salt River Base and Meridian, Cochise County, Arizona;
PARCEL A:
Beginning at the Northwest corner of the South half of the Northeast quarter of said Section 17;
thence South 100 feet;
thence East 100 feet;
thence North 60 feet;
thence East 200 feet;
thence South 260 feet;
thence East 150 feet;
thence North 200 feet to the TRUE POINT OF BEGINNING;
thence East 70 feet;
thence South 35 feet;
thence East 630 feet;
thence South 315 feet;
thence West 700 feet;
thence North 350 feet to the TRUE POINT OF BEGINNING.
PARCEL III:
An easement for ingress and egress over the following described property;
That portion of the South half of the Northeast quarter of Section 17, Township 24 South, Range 21 East of the Gila and Salt River Base and Meridian, Cochise County, Arizona, described as follows:
BEGINNING at the Northwest corner of the South half of the Northeast quarter of said Section 17;
thence South 100 feet;
thence East 100 feet;
thence North 60 feet;
thence East 200 feet;
thence South 260 feet;
thence East 150 feet;
thence North 200 feet to the TRUE POINT OF BEGINNING;
thence West 75 feet;
thence North 100 feet;
thence West 10 feet;
thence South 110 feet;
thence East 85 feet;
thence North 10 feet to the TRUE POINT OF BEGINNING.[1263]

Ownership/Disposition

The origin of Tract 101-40 was in a Deed of Trust recorded July 11, 1988. It was collateral for a $26,500 loan to Richard Richards from United Bank of Arizona which came due June 7, 1989. According to Bob Cousins, there was some confusion regarding the land base used as collateral for this and another loan from Western Farm Credit Bank. Once that was sorted out, Citibank, the successor to the United Bank of Arizona was able to foreclose on 5.12 acres, which became Tract 101-40. In April 1994, Citibank made notice of a Trustee's Sale to be held the following July. The Tax Parcel Number of the property was given as 104-60-002.[1264]

On March 26, 1997, Citibank, as successor to United Bank of Arizona, conveyed a 5.12 acre property whose description fits Tract 101-40 to Elsie Weick, Richard Richards's mother, for undisclosed considerations. The property was held under a deed of trust dated 8 July 1988 in which the Trustors were Richard and Cheryl Richards, the Trustee and Beneficiary was the United Bank of Arizona.[1265] Within a few months, Richards was acting as an agent for Weick in marketing Tract 101-40, which NPS opposed, considering it a violation of the plea agreement in which Richards was prohibited from acquiring interest in the property.[1266] Late in 1997, NPS was still working to acquire the remainder of the Montezuma Ranch properties and was accepting bids for clean-up as part of the appraisal process.[1267]

On February 5, 1998, Tract 101-40 was transferred from Elsie Weick to "Sunrise, A Trust," which was located at Weick's Wood Dale, Illinois, address, for the sum of ten dollars. Elsie Weick was the only "co-trustee" listed on the document.[1268] The title company did not show a change in the ownership of the property and Elsie Weick and her representatives continued to act as they had before the transfer.[1269] Negotiations dragged on through 1998 and 1999. Weick's representatives tried to drive the price up and NPS countered by promising condemnation.[1270]

In 1999, NPS continued to address other issues, like clean-up, that arose from violations of the scenic easement agreement. In February, an administrative waiver was signed by Superintendent Jim Bellamy which would allow acquisition in spite of the existence of a competing easement for transmission lines.[1271] In May, Bellamy filed a complaint with the Cochise County Planning Department, Building & Zoning Division. It reported extensive renovation to the two story house without a permit. The property was identified by Tax parcel identification number 104-60-2H.[1272] Bellamy was concerned that such improvements would increase the price which NPS would eventually pay for the property, after which the buildings would likely be demolished.[1273] As 1999 came to an end, Tract 101-40 was still for sale. A potential buyer contacted Coronado National Memorial for information about NPS acqusition plans and existing easements. Meanwhile, condemnation proceedings were instituted against the property by NPS after they were unable agree with the owners on a fair price. NPS offered $41,000, which they considered a just value. Weick made no counter-offer. The final price was to be determined by an administrative court.[1274] Superintendent Bellamy reported in July 2001 that "a settlement has been reached on the remaining 5.12 acres of the old Montezuma Ranch property, and it looks like we will receive title very soon."[1275]

Tract 101-41 20.47 acres
Description
In a 1996 forfeiture judgement Tract 101-41 was described as follows:
> *Parcel I*:
> That portion of the South half of the Northeast quarter of Section 17, Township 24 South, Range 21 East of the Gila and Salt River Base and Meridian, Cochise County, Arizona, described as follows:
> BEGINNING at the Northwest corner of the South half of the Northeast quarter of said Section 17;
> thence South 100 feet;
> thence East 100 feet;
> thence North 60 feet;

thence East 200 feet;
thence South 260 feet;
thence East 150 feet;
thence North 200 feet;
thence East 70 feet;
thence South 35 feet;
thence East 800 feet to a point on the West line of the Northwest quarter of the Northwest quarter of the Southeast quarter of the Northeast quarter;
thence North along said West line 135 feet to a point on the North line of the South half of the Northeast quarter; thence West along said North line of the South half of the Northeast quarter, 1320 feet, more or less, to the Point of Beginning.

Parcel II:
That portion of the West half of the Southwest quarter of the Northeast quarter of Section 17, Township 24 South, Range 21 East, Gila and Salt River Base and Meridian, Cochise County, Arizona, lying Southerly of the following described lines:
Commencing at the Northwest corner of the South half of the Northeast quarter of Section 17;
thence South 100 feet to the Point of Beginning;
thence East 100 feet;
thence North 60 feet;
thence East 200 feet;
thence South 260 feet;
thence East 150 feet;
thence South 150 feet;
thence East to a point in the East line of the West half of the Southwest quarter of the Northeast quarter of said Section 17, being the point of terminus.[1276]

Ownership/Disposition
When the owner of Tract 101-29, Richard Richards, was arrested in July 1991, the Department of Justice moved to seize his property. Within weeks, his mother, Elsie Weick, had filed a lien on a portion of the property for money owed to her. According to Coronado Superintendent Edward Lopez and Western Regional Director Bob Cousins, both NPS and the Justice Department doubted the validity of the Weick lien but it was approved by the court.[1277] The agreement between Weick and the Department of Justice was reflected in an order dated January 6, 1996. The U.S. Marshall's office was directed to seize and sell the property; the proceeds, after expenses, were to be split between Weick and the U.S. Marshall's Service.[1278]

On April 19, 1996, Richard Richards's attorney, Ethan Steele, wrote to Paul Tatham, I.R.P. District Headquarters, Sierra Vista, regarding his interest in listing the property for the Marshal's Service. Steele described three appraisals of $80,000, $220,000, and $60,000 and expressed his opinion that the last was the most accurate. He also mentioned the scenic easement, deteriorated structures, and approximately $20,000 in back taxes as liabilities to the tract. The U.S. Forest Service was then offering $60,000 for the property.[1279]

On 13 January 1998, Ed Lopez, Coronado National Memorial Superintendent, signed a Department of the Interior Certificate of Inspection and Possession for 20.47 acre Tract 101-41.[1280] On 23 January 1998 Alfred W. Madrid, United States Marshall for the District of Arizona, sold 20.47 acres of described land to DOI, NPS, for $56,500. According to the deed, the land was forfeited by Richard Richards on 21 December 1992. On 8 January 1996, "a Forfeiture Judgement was entered pursuant to written stipulation by the parties as to claimant Elsie Weick, declaring the interest of Elsie Weick, in the above described real estate, was forfeited to the United States of America." The United Sates Marshall was then charged with the duty to dispose of the property. The deed was labeled "CORONADO NM DEED NO. 22."[1281] The title was officially passed on February 2, 1998.[1282]

6. Kudzmi Homestead

The Kudzmi Homestead was made up of the South half of the Southeast quarter of Section 17 and Lots 1 and 2 of Section 20, Township 24 South, Range 21 East, Gila and Salt River Base and Meridian, Cochise County, Arizona. It was first claimed within the 160 acre homestead claim of Elmer L. Hertel, as reflected in field notes dated March 3, 1915. The map accompanying the claims shows that the Hertel claim extended further west than the later Kudzmi homestead and west of the mid-line of Sections 17 and 20.[1283] Simon Kudzmi, a naturalized immigrant from Russia, settled on the 133.67 acre claim in October 1928 and built a house in February 1929. Joe Zaleski was one of the witnesses for Kudzmi when he filed his final proofs.[1284]

Evidently, Zaleski then bought the claim from Kudzmi at some point before 1950. In October 1950, Joe Zaleski transferred ownership of all of his considerable property, except the Pyeatt Homestead, to his son Frank by way of a Gift Deed. In 1956, Frank quit-claimed it back to Joe. Included in these two transfers were Homestead Entry Surveys 310 and 311 and the Kudzmi Homestead.[1285] In April 1957, Joe Zaleski sold the same property to John A. and Inez Z. Jones along with some cattle and horses, "miscellaneous tools, equipment, and furniture," and a stock brand.[1286]

The Kudzmi Homestead, along with some of of Homestead Entry Survey 310 and all of Homestead Entry Survey 311, was given by John A. and Inez Z. Jones to John Z. and Lawrence D. Jones "for and in consideration of the love and affection" of parents for their children in 1962.[1287] They sold the total amount to the Baumkirchner brothers, Everett and Fred, and their wives, Margaret E. and Mary Ann, respectively, in 1965. The purchase price was not recorded, but the Jones brothers carried a $45,000 mortgage on the property.[1288] In 1973, the Baumkirchners traded 541.43 acres, including most of their land in the area of the Memorial, to the National Forest Service for other land of equal value. Included in the land exchange was the entire Kudzmi Homestead, the remainder of HES 310 not already within the Memorial, and a 50 acre portion of the southwest corner of HES 311.[1289]

7. The State of Texas Mine Property

The State of Texas Mine occupies the site of the "oldest historic mine claim in Montezuma Canyon," the Lena claim. The Lena mine was located in May 1878 by George J. Rasking and John L. Harris and recorded the next month by D.B. Ren. The Lena was renamed the Chicago Mine in 1885 under the ownership of Peter Connor and A.W. Emanuel.[1290] Connor (or Conner) and his partners filed several claims in Montezuma Canyon in 1879, among which was the Lookout, also thought to be on land later occupied by the State of Texas and its companion claims.[1291] The State of Texas Mine itself was founded in the same location in 1889. There is some disagreement as to the exact ownership of the State of Texas during its first few years of operation. Geoffrey T. Bohrer cites an 1889 claim by August Baron that reported a find of "mineral bearing quartz."[1292] However, Peter M. Van Cleve, using Deeds of Mines in the Cochise County Recorders Office in Bisbee, Arizona, writes that Richard C. Van Dorn made the first State of Texas claim in 1889. According to Van Cleve, Van Dorn soon sold a one-third share of the mine to Peter Connor, who, in turn, sold it and other local mine interests to William Graf in 1892. In the meantime, in 1891, August Baron, exercising Power of Attorney for Van Dorn, sold the remaining two-thirds share of the State of Texas Mine and another mine to Graf. Then, in 1893, Baron, a banker and miner from Tombstone, purchased all of Graf's interests, including the State of Texas.[1293]

In any case, by the middle of the 1890s, the State of Texas Mine belonged to August Baron. Baron had the claim surveyed in 1897 and the plat was approved in 1898.[1294] In 1902, over forty mines in Montezuma and Copper canyons, including the State of Texas, were leased by the Mitchell Mining Company, of Ishpeming, Michigan, which mined copper at the site. Mitchell relinquished the leases in 1906 and they reverted to their former owners.[1295] Almost immediately, the Gray Metals Company began to operate the mine, which was still owned by Baron. By 1914, the Texas No. 2, Extension, Bonita, Josephine, and New York mines had been added to the operation.[1296] August Baron died in 1913 and his mine properties were passed on to his wife, Christine. She promptly sold them to Douglas Gray of Tombstone, the owner of Gray Metals Company. In 1920, Gray took on two partners, Maurice Clark, of Douglas, and William H. Stilwell, of Phoenix, and incorporated a new incarnation of the Gray Metals Company as a publicly owned corporation. Gray sold his mines to the new corporation in 1920 fo $20,000. Only two years later, the State of Texas, Texas No. 2, Extension, Bonita, Josephine, and New York mines were sold at public auction as part of a court judgement against Gray. Nathan L. Amster bought them in August 1922 for $9,370.90.[1297]

In September 1926, T.J. Sparkes, of Prescott, Arizona, and Burdett Moody, of Los Angeles, California, purchased several mining claims in the Hartford Mining District from Nathan L. and Estelle D. Amster for $5,000. The purchase included the State of Texas, State of Texas No. 2, Extension, Bonita, Josephine, and New York mines.[1298] In a January 1939 letter, Grace Sparkes told Burdett Moody that her father, T.J. Sparkes, had recently died, which left her in control of his portion.[1299] She shared ownership of a half interest in the State of Texas property with her siblings as joint heirs to their father, T.J. Sparkes. However, she was the most active partner. In June 1942, Grace Sparkes was given total control of the State of Texas mine property when Moody quit-claimed his share with the stipulation that he would receive half of future net profits or half of the net proceeds of any future sale.[1300] In September, the other Sparkes heirs quit-claimed their shares to Grace as well.[1301] Burdett Moody died in 1946. It is unclear what the relationship between he and Sparkes was at the time and whether his widow retained an interest in the property.[1302]

In 1960, forty acres were excluded from Coronado National Memorial and added to the Coronado National Forest. Half of that land made up the Billy Boy mine claim, owned by Grace Sparkes [see Intra-Governmental Transfers].[1303] Grace Sparkes died in 1963, leaving the State of Texas mine property to her four nephews. During the previous few years she had improved the property and offered it for sale to NPS as well as on the open market.[1304] The State of Texas properties were designated Tracts 101-06, 101-07, and 101-08. They were eventually sold together by William Sparkes. However, they were not consistently described as separate entities. The three tracts were combined in different ways in various documents. Therefore, each will be briefly described and transactions unique to each will be presented; then they will be dealt with as a group.

Tract 101-06 20.59 acres
Description
A 1979 appraisal described 20.59 acres to be acquired by fee. This property consisted of one patented mining claim, State of Texas No. 2. The property was described in National Park Service records as vacant of building improvements. The property was generally located in the Southwest quarter of the Southwest quarter of Section 12, Township 24 South, Range 20 East, Gila and Salt River Base and Meridian. The terrain was mountainous.[1305]

Tract 101-07 20.66 acres
AKA Parcel No. 14.
AKA P-12.[1306]
Description
Tract 101-07 was the State of Texas Lode Mining Claim in the Hartford Mining District, being shown on Mineral Survey No. 1280 on file in the Bureau of land Management, as granted by Patent recorded in Book 14 of Deeds of Mines, page 481, records of Cochise County, Arizona.[1307]

In a 1979 appraisal it was described as 20.66 acres to be acquired by fee. The property contained a 10' x 18' unoccupied wood cabin. The property was mountainous terrain, generally bisected by the section line between Sections 12 and 13, Township 24 South, Range 20 East, Gila and Salt River Base and Meridian.[1308]

Ownership/Disposition

Tract 101-07, the State of Texas Lode Mining Claim, was shared by four heirs of Grace Sparkes until 1980. Charles J. Sparkes, Jack M. Sparkes, Thomas Frederick Sparkes, and William J. Sparkes each held an undivided quarter interest as their sole and separate property.[1309]

In April 1980 the State of Texas Lode, encompassing 20.66 acres, was transferred by Charles J. Sparkes, Jack M. Sparkes, and Thomas F. Sparkes, to William J. Sparkes. Thomas F. Sparkes acknowledged the quit claim before a notary on the same day, the other two did so in 1986.[1310]

Tract 101-08 10 acres

Description

Tract 101-08 was described in 1979 as 10 acres to be acquired by fee. This property consists of one patented mining claim, "State of Texas No. 2 Millsite." According to National Park Service records, the property was improved with several residential/cabin structures, utility buildings, and other miscellaneous improvements. The property was generally located in the South half of the Northwest quarter of the Northwest quarter of Section 13, Township 24 South, Range 20 East, Gila and Salt River Base and Meridian. It was bisected by the paved Coronado Memorial Highway (62).[1311]

Tracts 101-06 and 101-08
AKA Parcel No. 1.
AKA P-11.[1312]

These two tracts were often consolidated because of common ownership although they are not directly adjacent.

Description

Appraisal documents described Tracts 101-06 and 101-08 together as Parcel No. 1:

> The State of Texas No. 2 Lode Mining Claim; and The State of Texas Mill Site; and The State of Texas No. 2 Mill Site Millsite Claims in the Hartford Mining District, being shown on Mineral Survey Nos. 4335A and 4335B on file in the Bureau of Land Management, as granted by Patent recorded in Docket 71, page 181 to 184, records of Cochise County, Arizona;
>
> Except all that portion within the boundaries of the property shown on Mineral Survey No. 3642, and all veins, lodes and ledges, throughout their entire depth, the tops or apexes of which be inside of said excluded portion, as set forth in said Patent; and
>
> Except from the State of Texas No. 2 Mill Site, Millsite Claim, all uranium, thorium or any other material which is or may be determined to be peculiarly essential to the production of fissionable materials, whether or not of commercial value, as reserved in Patent from the United States of America.[1313]

Ownership/Disposition

Ownership of this parcel was described as divided between William J. Sparkes, of Hereford, Arizona, a married man, as his sole and separate property, as to an undivided ¼ interest; and William J. Sparkes, a married man as to an undivided ¾ interest. The rights of Patricia, as the spouse of William J. Sparkes on July 18, 1974, to an undivided ¾ interest were protected. "Spouse failed to disclaim at time of acquisition of an interest in the property by instrument recorded in Docket 948, page 457 to 460)."[1314] Parenthetically, a September 1979 newspaper article identified Sparkes's wife at that time as "Dean."[1315]

Tracts 101-06 and 101-07.

These two tracts of the State of Texas Mine property were appraised for mineral value together. An April 1980 memorandum reported that appraisers of the Western Regional Office had prepared an estimate "for the purpose of providing a basis for ceiling increase for the 1982 fiscal year. Appraiser Robert F. Temple included within the Sparkes appraisals (Tracts 101-06 and 101-

07) a mineral value of $119,540 as furnished by the Division of Mining and Minerals." The letter mentions a very unstable silver market and added that, with the exceptions of lead and zinc, the precious metal market was expected to remain volatile.[1316]

Tracts 101-06, 101-07, and 101-08
Ownership/Disposition
On 29 December 1986, William J. and Patricia M. Sparkes sold 51.25 acres to NPS for $540,000. The land was described as Tract Numbers 101-06, 101-07, and 101-08. The deed was labeled "CORONADO NM DEED NO. 21."[1317]

8. Victorio Company mining property
In 1978, the date that the Memorial expanded to the north side of Montezuma Canyon via a land exchange with the National Forest Service, thirteen claims were owned by The Victorio Company. Most of them had once been owned by Bruce Doredor. The claims were in two groups separated by the State of Texas mine properties. To the east were Doredor, Paring No. 1, Paring No. 2, Paring No. 3, and Paring No. 4. To the west were Z.T. Parker, Chief, Fraction, Rubio, Tunnelsite, Miss Stake, Grub Stake No. 2, and Grub Stake No. 3.
According to a summary of mine claims compiled at Coronado National Memorial, the Miss Stake, Grub Stake No. 2, and Grub Stake No. 3 mine claims, along with three others in their immediate vicinity, were claimed by Felix Livericio in March 1899. The Doredor, Paring No. 1, Paring No. 2, Paring No. 3, Paring No. 4, Z.T. Parker, Chief, Fraction, Rubio, and Tunnelsite were claimed by Bruce Doredor. The four Paring mines were claimed in 1901 and the Doredor in 1920. The western group are said to have been claimed in 1909.[1318] All thirteen claims were patented by Bruce Doredor on April 10, 1920.[1319]
The same summary of mine claims cited above lists purchase of Z.T. Parker, Chief, Fraction, Rubio, Tunnelsite, Grub Stake No. 2, and Miss Stake by "Clark/Smith" in 1938.[1320] Bill Clark was on the Board of Supervisors and was said to have purchased the property for back taxes.[1321] In 1960, forty acres were removed from Coronado National Memorial and added to the Coronado National Forest in order to exclude current mining claims from the Memorial. Half of that land was on and around the Z.T. Parker claim [see Intra-Governmental Transfers].
In July 1970, Ruth M. Clark, a widow, and Charles A. and Paquita C. Smith, sold several mining properties, including the thirteen Doredor claims in the Hartford Mining District of the Montezuma Mountains that fell within the eventual boundaries of Coronado National Memorial. The sellers were, evidently, Bill Clark's widow and his partner. The buyers were Coronado Investment Company, a partnership comprised of Peter G. Wray and H. Wayne Pruett.[1322] In 1973, the properties were transferred to Pruett-Wray Cattle Company, made up of the same partners.[1323] By 1979, Pruett-Wray had changed its name to "Victorio Land and Cattle Company" and then to "The Victorio Company."[1324]
In 1979, the Victorio properties were considered as two separate tracts, which were separated by the State of Texas mine properties. The westernmost tract, called Tract 101-05, consisted of the Z.T. Parker, Chief, Fraction, Rubio, Tunnelsite, Miss Stake, Grub Stake No. 2, and Grub Stake No. 3 claims. It held a total area of 154.54 acres [See Tract 101-05]. The eastern properties, Doredor, Paring No. 1, Paring No. 2, Paring No. 3, and Paring No. 4, made up Tract 101-09, 84.31 acres. Tract 101-09 was further divided by sale in 1979. The western half of that property was sold to James J. and Jacqueline S. Wardle and became known as Tract 101-22.[1325] The remaining property was designated Tract 101-21. [See Tracts 101-21 and 101-22 below.]

Tract 101-05 154.54 acres
AKA Parcel No. 3.
AKA P-14.[1326]

Description
A 1979 appraisal described 154.54 acres to be acquired by fee. It was improved with an approximately 756 square foot frame building, an approximately 590 square foot rock building, and an approximately 280 square foot corrigated metal shed, all of which were believed to be unoccupied. Access to the property was judged difficult.[1327]
When Tract 101-05 was sold to NPS in 1980, it was described as follows:
> THE Z.T. PARKER, CHIEF, FRACTION, RUBIO, TUNNELSITE, MISS TAKE, GRUB STAKE NO. 2 and GRUB STAKE NO. 3 LODE MINING CLAIMS in the Hartford Mining District, being shown on Mineral Survey No. 3642, on file in the Bureau of Land Management, as granted by Patent recorded in Book 30 of Deeds of Mines, page 326, records of Cochise County, Arizona.[1328]

Ownership/Disposition
Tract 101-05 was purchased by ownership that became the Victorio Company in 1970 [See above]. On 26 March 1980, The Victorio Company sold 196.73 acres to NPS for $340,000. That sale comprised Tracts 101-05 and 101-21 [See Tract 101-21 below]. A hand written note identified the deed as "DEED # 5."[1329]

Tract 101-09 84.31 acres
AKA Parcel No. 2.
AKA P-13.[1330]

Description:
Tract 101-09 was made up of the eastern bloc of mining properties owned by the Victorio Company, including the Doredor, Paring No. 1, Paring No. 2, Paring No. 3, and Paring No. 4 Lode Mining Claims in Hartford Mining District, being shown on Mineral Survey No. 3641 on file in the Bureau of Land Management, as granted by Patent recorded in Book 30 of Deeds of Mines, page 332, records of Cochise County, Arizona.[1331]
A 1979 appraisal described it as 84.31 acres to be acquired in fee. According to National Park Service records, the property was vacant and unimproved of structures. Access was by an undescribed jeep road. The property was generally located in Northeast quarter of Section 13, and South half of the Southeast quarter of Section 12, Township 24 South, Range 20 East, Gila and Salt River Meridian.[1332]

Ownership/Disposition
Tract 101-09 was purchased by ownership that became the Victorio Company in 1970 [See above]. It was split into Tracts 101-21 and 101-22 in 1979. [See Tracts 101-21 and 101-22 below.]

Tract 101-21 42.16 acres
Description
Tract 101-21 was made up of the eastern part of 101-09. When it was sold to NPS in 1980, it was described as follows:
> THE DOREDOR, PARING NO. ONE, PARING NO. TWO, PARING NO. THREE and PARING NO. 4 LODE MINING CLAIMS, in Hartford Mining District, being shown on Mineral Survey No. 3641 on file in the Bureau of Land Management, as granted by Patent recorded in Book 30 of Deeds of Mines, page 332, records of Cochise County, Arizona; EXCEPT those portions of PARING NO. 1, PARING NO. 2, and PARING NO. 3 and all of THE DOREDOR MINING CLAIMS, located in the Hartford Mining District and situated in portions of Sections 12 and 13, Township 24 South, Range 20 East of the Gila and Salt River Base and Meridian, Cochise County, Arizona, being shown on mineral survey No. 3641 on file in the Bureau of Land Management as granted by Patent recorded June 10,

1922 in Book 30 of Deeds of Mines, page 332, records of Cochise County, Arizona, more particularly described as follows:

> BEGINNING at the Southwest corner of PARING NO. 3 LODE;
> thence North 01° 32' 00" East coincident with the Westerly line of PARING NO. 3 LODE, a distance of 617.40 feet to a point on the Southerly line of PARING NO. 2 LODE;
> thence North 74° 47' 00" West coincident with said line, a distance of 500.00 feet to the Southwest corner of PARING NO. 2 LODE:
> thence North 01° 32' 00" East coincident with the Westerly line of PARING NO. 2 LODE, a distance of 617.40 feet to the Southwest corner of DOREDOR LODE;
> thence North 00° 11' 00" West coincident with the Westerly line of THE DOREDOR LODE, a distance of 622.20 feet to the Northwest corner of THE DOREDOR LODE;
> thence South 74° 47' 00" East coincident with the Northerly line of THE DOREDOR LODE, a distance of 881.00 feet to the Northeast corner of PARING NO. 1 LODE;
> thence continuing South 74° 47' 00" East coincident with the Northerly line of PARING NO. 1 LODE, a distance of 254.60 feet;
> thence South 02° 24' 29" East a distance of 1883.25 feet to a point on the South line of PARING NO. 3 LODE;
> thence North 74° 47' 00" West coincident with the South line of PARING NO. 3 LODE, a distance of 750.00 feet to the POINT OF BEGINNING.[1333]

Ownership/Disposition
The Victorio Company retained ownership of Tract 101-21 when Tract 101-09 was subdivided. On 26 March 1980, The Victorio Company sold 196.73 acres to NPS for $340,000. That sale comprised Tracts 101-05 and 101-21. A hand written note identified the deed as "DEED # 5."[1334]

Tract 101-22 42.15 acres
AKA Parcel A of the Doredor Claim.[1335]
Description
Tract 101-22 was the western part of Tract 101-09. When it was sold to James J. and Jacqueline S. Wardle, it was described as follows:

> Those portions of Paring No. 1, Paring No. 2 and Paring No. 3 and all of the Doredor Mining Claims, located in the Hartford Mining District, and situated in portions of Sections 12 and 13 Township 24 South, Range 20 East of the G. & S. R. B. & M., Cochise County, Arizona, being shown on Mineral Survey No. 3641 on file in the Bureau of Land Management as granted by patent recorded June 10, 1922, in Book 30 of Deeds of Mines, at Page 332, more particularly described as follows:
> Beginning at the Southwest corner of Paring No. 3 lode,   Thence North 01 Degrees 32' 00" East coincident with the Westerly line of Paring No. 3 Lode a distance of 617.40 feet to a point on the Southerly line of Paring No. 2 Lode;
> Thence North 74 Degrees 47' 00" West coincident with said line a distance of 500.00 feet to the Southwest corner of Paring No. 2 Lode;
> Thence North 01 Degrees 32' 00" East coincident with the Westerly line of Paring No. 2 Lode a distance of 617.40 feet to the Southwest corner of Doredor Lode;
> Thence North 00 Degrees 11' 00" West coincident with the Westerly line of the Doredor Lode a distance of 622.20 feet to the Northwest corner of the Doredor Lode;
> Thence South 74 Degrees 47' 00" East coincident with the Northerly line of the Doredor Lode a distance of 881.00 feet to the Northeast corner of Paring No. 1 Lode;
> Thence continuing South 74 Degrees 47' 00" East coincident with the Northerly line of Paring No. 1 Lode a distance of 254.60 feet;
> Thence South 02 Degrees 24' 29" East a distance of 1883.25 feet to a point on the

South line of Paring No. 3 Lode;

Thence North 74 Degrees 47' 00" West coincident with the South line of Paring No. 3 Lode a distance of 750.00 feet to the point of beginning.

Reserving unto the Grantors herein an Easement for Ingress, Egress and Utility purposes in and over a strip of land 50 feet in width, the centerline of which is described as follows:

Beginning at a point on the South line of Paring No. 3 Lode, being also the South line of Parcel A from which the Southwest corner of said Paring No. 3 Lode, being also the Soutwest corner of Parcel A, Bears North 74 Degrees 47 Minutes 00 Seconds West 454.21 Feet distant, Thence North 30 Degrees 20 Minutes 00 Seconds East a distance of 161.06 Feet, Thence North 19 Degrees 43 Minutes 15 Seconds East a distance of 72.89 Feet, Thence South 57 Degrees 59 Minutes 52 Seconds East a distance of 108.84 Feet, Thence North 89 Degrees 53 Minutes 03 Seconds East a distance of 77.61 Feet to its Point of Termination being also a point on the East line of said Parcel A from which the Southwest corner of said Paring No.3 Lode bears South 02 Degrees 24 Minutes 29 Seconds East 227.94 Feet distant and North 74 Degrees 47 Minutes 00 Seconds West 750.00 Feet distant the Side Lines of said 50 Foot Easement to be extended or shortened to meet at Angle points and to Terminate at the East line of said Parcel A.[1336]

Ownership/Disposition

The Victorio Company, an Arizona Corporation; formerly Victorio Land and Cattle Company, an Arizona Corporation; formerly Pruett-Wray Cattle Company, an Arizona Corporation, divided Tract 101-09 and sold half, consisting of Tract 101-22, to James J. Wardle and Jacqueline S. Wardle, husband and wife, in December 1979.[1337] Tract 101-22 was subdivided to create Tracts 101-33 through 101-37 [see below].

Tract 101-33 13.05 acres

Description

Tract 101-33 was made up of the southeast section of Tract 101-22.[1338] In August 1983, James J. and Jacqueline Wardle sold a property, which came to be known as Tract 101-33, to Richard D. and Judy L. Compton. It was described as:

Those portions of the Paring No. 2 and No. 3 Mining Claims, located in the Hartford Mining District, and situated in Portions of Sections 12 and 13, Township 24 South, Range 20 East, of the G. & S. R. B & M., Cochise County, Arizona, being shown on Mineral Survey No. 3641 on file in the Bureau of Land Management as granted by patent recorded June 10, 1922, in Book 30 of Deeds of Mines at Page 332, more particularly described as follows:

Beginning at the North Quarter Corner of said Section 13;

Thence South 6 Degrees 40 Minutes 10 Seconds East, a distance of 351.84 feet to the Beginning of an access easement as described in Docket 1671 at Page 161, Cochise County Records;

Thence North 75 Degrees 13 Minutes 06 Seconds West, a distance of 15.09 feet;

Thence South 8 Degrees 25 Minutes 14 Seconds West, a distance of 59.00 feet being on the Westerly side line of said access easement, also being the True Point of Beginning;

Thence South 75 Degrees 13 Minutes 06 Seconds East, a distance of 776.69 feet to a point being on the Easterly line of that parcel as described in Docket 1388 at Page 333, Cochise County Records;

Thence South 3 Degrees 01 Minutes 10 Seconds East along said Easterly line, a distance of 885.08 feet to a half inch rebar capped L.S. 9086 being the Southeast corner of said parcel as recorded in Docket 1388 at Page 333, Cochise County Records;

Thence North 75 Degrees 13 Minutes 06 Seconds West, a distance of 747.31 feet (whose record is 750.00 feet) to a half inch rebar capped L.S. 9086 being the Southwest corner

of said parcel as recorded in Docket 1388 at Page 333, Cochise County Records;
Thence North 0 Degrees 50 Minutes 28 Seconds East along the Westerly line of said Paring No. 3, a distance of 471.01 feet;
Thence South 75 Degrees 13 Minutes 06 Seconds East, a distance of 78.80 feet to an angle point on the Westerly side line of said access easement;
Thence North 26 Degrees 08 Minutes 24 Seconds East, a distance of 177.00 feet;
Thence North 15 Degrees 30 Minutes 04 Seconds West, a distance of 120.28 feet;
Thence North 68 Degrees 18 Minutes 58 Seconds West, a distance of 170.87 feet;
Thence North 30 Degrees 21 Minutes 04 Seconds West, a distance of 95.37 feet;
Thence North 8 Degrees 25 Minutes 14 Seconds East, a distance of 20.48 feet to the True Point of Beginning.[1339] Tract 101-33 was sold to NPS in 1984 as three parcels and an access easement. They were described as follows:

PARCEL 1

A metes and bounds description of a parcel of land being a portion of the Paring Number 3 Mining Claim, Mineral Survey No. 3641, in Section 13, T24S, R20E, Gila and Salt Meridian, Cochise County, Arizona and more specifically described as follows:
BEGINNING at the North ¼ corner of said Section 13; thence S 4° 05' 29" E a distance of 1298.63 feet to a ½" rebar capped L.S. 9086, being the Southwest corner of that parcel as described in Docket 1388, Page 337, Cochise County Records, also being the TRUE POINT OF BEGINNING; thence N 0° 50' 28" E along the Westerly line of said Paring No. 3 a distance of 471.01 feet; thence S 75° 13' 06" E a distance of 78.80 feet to an angle point on the Westerly side line of an access easement as described in Docket 1671, Page 161, Cochise County Records; thence N 26° 08' 24" E along said Westerly side line a distance of 36.47 feet; thence N 81° 28' 45" E a distance of 122.74 feet to an angle point on the Northerly side line of said access easement; thence S 72° 44' 18" E a distance of 82.69 feet to an angle point on said Northerly side line; thence S 75° 13' 06" E a distance of 76.75 feet; thence S 3° 01' 10" E a distance of 564.92 feet to the South line of said parcel as described in Docket 1388, Page 337, Cochise County Records; thence N 75° 13' 06" W a distance of 417.31 feet to the TRUE POINT OF BEGINNING.
Containing 4.69 Acres more or less.
Included in the above described parcel is a portion of an access easement recorded in Docket 1671, Page 161, Cochise County Records, leaving a net Acreage of 4.02 Acres more or less.

PARCEL 2

A metes and bounds description of a parcel of land being a portion of the Paring Number 3 Mining Claim, Mineral Survey No. 3641, in Section 13, T24S, R20E, Gila and Salt River Meridian, Cochise County, Arizona and more specifically described as follows:
BEGINNING at the North ¼ corner of said Section 13; thence S 4° 05' 29" E a distance of 1298.63 feet to a ½" rebar capped L.S. 9086, being the Southwest corner of that parcel as described in Docket 1388, Page 337, Cochise County Records; thence S 75° 13' 06" E along the South line of said Parcel as described in Docket 1388, Page 337, Cochise County Records a distance of 417.31 feet to the TRUE POINT OF BEGINNING; Thence N 3° 01' 10" W a distance of 564.92 thence S 75° 13' 06" E a distance of 330.00 feet to the Easterly line of said parcel as described in Docket 1388, Page 337, Cochise County Records; thence S 3° 01' 10" E a distance of 564.92 feet to a ½" rebar capped L.S. 9086 being the Southeast corner of said parcel as described in Docket 1388, Page 337, Cochise County Records; thence N 75° 13' 06" W a distance of 330.00 feet to the TRUE POINT OF BEGINNING.
Containing 4.07 Acres more or less.
Included in the above described parcel is a portion of an access easement recorded in Docket 1671, Page 161, Cochise County Records. Leaving a net acreage of 4.04 Acres more or less.

PARCEL 3

A metes and bounds description of a parcel of land being portions of the Paring Numbers 2 and 3 Mining Claims, Mineral Survey No. 3641, in Section 13, T24S, R20E, Gila and Salt River Meridian, Cochise County, Arizona and more specifically described as follows:

BEGINNING at the North ¼ corner of said Section 13; thence S 6° 40' 10" E at a distance of 351.84 feet to the beginning of an acess (sic) easement as described in Docket 1671, Page 161, Cochise County Records;

thence N 75° 13' 06" W a distance of 15.09 feet;

thence S 8° 25' 14" W a distance of 59.00 feet being on the Westerly side line of said access easement, also being the TRUE POINT OF BEGINNING;

thence S 75° 13' 06" E a distance of 776.69 feet to a point being on the Easterly line of that parcel as described in Docket 1388, Page 337, Cochise County Records;

thence S 3° 01' 10" E along said Easterly line a distance of 320.16 feet;

thence N 75° 13' 06" W a distance of 406.75 feet to an angle point on the Northerly side line of said access easement; thence N 72° 44' 18" W a distance of 82.69 feet to an angle point on said Northerly side line;

thence S 81° 28' 45" W a distance of 122.74 feet to the Westerly side line of said access easement;

thence along said side line the following courses and distances: N 26° 08' 24" E a distance of 140.53 feet; thence N 15° 30' 04" W a distance of 120.28 feet;

thence N 68° 18' 58" W a distance of 170.87 feet;

thence N 30° 21' 04" W a distance of 95.37 feet;

thence N 8° 25' 14" E a distance of 20.48 feet to the TRUE POINT OF BEGINNING.

Containing 4.29 Acres more or less.

Included in the above described parcel is a portion of an access easement recorded in Docket 1671, Page 161, Cochise County Records, leaving a net acreage of 4.06 Acres more or less.

ACCESS EASEMENT

A metes and bounds description of an access easement being portions of the Paring No. 2 and Doredor Mining Claims, Mineral Survey No. 3641 in Sections 12 and 13, T24S, R20E, Gila and Salt River Meridian, Cochise County, Arizona, said access easement being 30.00 feet wide and more specifically described as follows:

BEGINNING at the North ¼ corner of said Section 13 being the TRUE POINT OF BEGINNING of said access easement; thence N 85° 39' 12" E a distance of 30.00 feet; thence S 4° 20' 48" E a distance of 349.93 feet; thence S 8° 25' 14" W a distance of 6.73 feet to the beginning of the Easterly side line of an access easement as described in Docket 1671, Page 161, Cochise County Records; thence N 75° 13' 06" W a distance of 30.18 feet to the beginning of the Westerly side line of said easement as described in Docket 1671, Page 161, Cochise County Records; thence N 4° 20' 48" W a distance of 346.61 feet to the TRUE POINT OF BEGINNING.[1340]

Ownership/Disposition

In August 1983, James J. and Jacqueline Wardle sold Tract 101-33 to Richard D. and Judy L. Compton.[1341] On 12 February 1985, the Comptons sold 13.05 acres in three parcels to NPS for $118,750.[1342]

Tracts 101-34, 101-35, and 101-36

Description

In January 1980, James J. and Jacqueline S. Wardle entered into an agreement with Jacques and Audrey C. O'Keefe which transferred the western 456.82 feet of the Wardles' property, Tract 101-22, to the O'Keefes. The description was as follows:

> The most Westerly 456.82 feet of the following described property;
>
> Those portions of Paring No. 1, Paring No. 2 and Paring No. 3 and all of the Doredor

Mining Claims, located in the Hartford Mining District, and situated in portions of Sections 12 and 13, Township 24 South, Range 20 East of the Gila and Salt River Base and Meridian, Cochise County, Arizona, being shown on Mineral Survey Number 3641 on file in the Bureau of Land Management as granted by Patent recorded June 10, 1922, in Book 30 of Deeds of Mines, at page 332, more particularly described as follows:

Beginning at the Southwest corner of Paring No. 3 Lode;

Thence North 01 Degrees 32 Minutes 00 Seconds East, coincident with the Westerly line of Paring No. 3 Lode, a distance of 617.40 feet to a point on the Southerly line of Paring No. 2 Lode;

Thence North 74 Degrees 47 Minutes 00 Seconds West, coincident with said line , a distance of 500.00 feet to the Southwest corner of Paring No. 2 Lode;

Thence North 01 Degrees 32 Minutes 00 Seconds East, coincident with the Westerly line of Paring No. 2 Lode, a distance of 617.40 feet to the Southwest corner of Doredor Lode;

Thence North 00 Degrees 11 Minutes 00 Seconds West, coincident with the Westerly line of the Doredor Lode, a distance of 622.20 feet to the Northwest corner of the Doredor Lode;

Thence South 74 Degrees 47 Minutes 00 Seconds East, coincident with the Northerly line of the Doredor Lode, a distance of 881.00 feet to the Northeast corner of Paring No. 1 Lode;

Thence continuing South 74 Degrees 47 Minutes 00 Seconds East, coincident with the Northerly line of Paring No. 1 Lode, a distance of 254.60 feet;

Thence South 02 Degrees 24 Minutes 29 Seconds East, a distance of 1888.25 feet to a point on the South line of Paring No. 3 Lode;

Thence North 74 Degrees 47 Minutes 00 Seconds West, coincident with the South line of Paring No. 3 Lode, a distance of 750.00 feet to the Point of Beginning.

Ownership/Disposition

In January 1980, James J. and Jacqueline S. Wardle entered into an agreement with Jacques and Audrey C. O'Keefe transferring this property. It became Tracts 101-34, 101-35, and 101-36.[1343] [See Tracts 101-34, 101-35, and 101-36].

Tract 101-34 4.02 acres

Description

Tract 101-34 was made up of the northwest section of Tract 101-22.[1344] It was divided out of the property sold by Wardle to O'Keefe. It was described as follows:

> That portion of the DOREDOR MINING CLAIM, located in the Hartford Mining District, and situated in portions of Section 12, Township 24 South, Range 20 East of the Gila and Salt River Base and Meridian, Cochise County, Arizona, being shown on Mineral Survey Number 3641, on file in the Bureau of Land Management, as granted by Patent recorded June 10, 1922, in Book 30 of Deeds of Mines, at page 332, more particularly described as follows:
> BEGINNING at the South quarter corner of said Section 12;
> thence North 00° 52' 32" East parallel with the West line of said Doredor, a distance of 118.53 feet to the TRUE POINT OF BEGINNING;
> thence North 75° 13' 06" West parallel with the North line of said Doredor, a distance of 385.95 feet to the West line of said Doredor;
> thence North 00° 52' 32" West, a distance of 471.41 feet to Corner No. 3 of said Doredor;
> thence South 75° 13' 06" East along the North line of said Doredor, a distance of 385.95 feet;

thence South 00° 52' 32" East parallel with said West line of the Doredor, a distance of 471.41 feet to the TRUE POINT OF BEGINNING.[1345]

Ownership/Disposition

The Wardles sold a property that included Tract 101-34 to Jacques and Audrey O'Keefe in January 1980 as part of an All-Inclusive Agreement.[1346] The O'Keefe's sold it to Richard D. and Judy L. Compton in December 1983.[1347] On 12 February 1985 Richard D. Compton and Judy L. Compton, husband and wife, sold the 4.02 acre Tract 101-34 to NPS for $33,400.[1348]

Tract 101-35 4.03 acres

Description

Tract 101-35 was the southwest section of Tract 101-22.[1349] It was described as follows when sold to NPS:

> Those portions of the PARING NOS. 2 and 3 MINING CLAIMS, Hartford Mining District, in Section 13, Township 24 South, Range 20 East of the Gila and Salt River Base and Meridian, Cochise County of Arizona, being shown on Mineral Survey No. 3641 on file in the Bureau of Land Management as granted by patent recorded in Book 30 Deeds of Mines page 332, more specifically described as follows:
> BEGINNING at the North one-quarter corner of said Section 13; thence South 04° 20' 48" East, a distance of 346.61 feet to the
> beginning of the Westerly side line of an access easement as recorded in Docket 1671 at page 161, Cochise County Records, being the TRUE POINT OF BEGINNING;
> thence South 08° 25' 14" West, a distance of 79.48 feet;
> thence South 30° 21' 04" East, a distance of 95.37 feet;
> thence South 68° 18' 58" East, a distance of 170.87 feet;
> thence South 15° 30' 04" East, a distance of 120.28 feet;
> thence South 26° 08' 24" West, a distance of 177.00 feet;
> thence North 75° 13' 06" West, a distance of 78.80 feet to the
> West line of said PARING No. 3;
> thence North 00° 50' 28" East, a distance of 145.69 feet to the
> Corner No. 3 of said PARING NO. 3;
> thence North 75° 13' 06" West, a distance of 500.00 feet to
> Corner No. 2 of said PARING NO. 2;
> thence North 00° 50' 28" East along the West line of said PARING NO. 2, a distance of 312.00 feet;
> thence South 75° 13' 06" East parallel with the South line of
> said PARING NO. 2, a distance of 417.24 feet to the TRUE POINT OF BEGINNING.[1350]

Ownership/Disposition

The Wardles sold a property that included Tract 101-35 to Jacques and Audrey O'Keefe in January 1980 as part of an All-Inclusive Agreement.[1351] Tract 101-35 was sold to Paul E. and Laurel A. Froelich in April 1983. A Joint Tenancy Deed was signed naming the Froelichs as tenants and the O'Keefe's as "Grantor, Mortgagor or Trustor." On the same day, a Warranty Deed transferring the property from the Wardles to the O'Keefes was also signed. These linked transactions imply that the O'Keefes had still owed the Wardles as part of the 1980 All-Inclusive Agreement.[1352] On 5 July 1985 Paul E. Froelich and Laurel A. Froelich, husband and wife, sold the 4.03 acre Tract 101-35 to NPS for $32,250. The deed was labeled "CORONADO N.M. DEED NO. 19."[1353]

Tract 101-36 4.04 acres

Description

Tract 101-36 was the western section of Tract 101-22.[1354] The tract was described as follows:
> Those portions of the Doredor, PARING NO. 2 and 3 MINING CLAIMS, located in the Hartford Mining District, and situated in portions of Section 12 and 13, Township 24 South,

Range 20 East of the Gila and Salt River Base and Meridian, Cochise County, Arizona, being shown on Mineral Survey No. 3641 on file in the Bureau of Land Management as granted by patent recorded June 10, 1922, in Book 30 of Deeds of Mines at page 332, more particularly described as follows:

BEGINNING at the North quarter corner of said Section 13, being the TRUE POINT OF BEGINNING;

thence South 4° 20' 48" East, a distance of 346.61 feet to the beginning of the Westerly side line of an access easement as recorded in Docket 1700 at page 292, Cochise County Records;

thence North 75° 13' 06" West parallel with the South line of said Paring No. 2, a distance of 417.24 feet to the West line of said Paring No. 2;

thence North 0° 50' 28" East, a distance of 305.40 feet to corner No. 3 of said Paring No. 2;

thence North 0° 52' 32" West along the West line of said DOREDOR, a distance of 150.79 feet;

thence South 75° 13' 06" East parallel with the North line of said DOREDOR, a distance of 385.95 feet;

thence South 0° 52' 32" East parallel with said West line of the DOREDOR, a distance of 118.53 feet to the TRUE POINT OF BEGINNING.

Except one half of all the mineral rights as reserved in Deed recorded in Docket 1708 page 40, records of Cochise County, Arizona.[1355]

Ownership/Disposition

The Wardles sold a property that included Tract 101-36 to Jacques and Audrey O'Keefe in January 1980 as part of an All-Inclusive Agreement.[1356] The O'Keefes sold Tract 101-36 to Valentin Castro III and Deborah Castro in August 1983.[1357] On 25 February 1985 Valentin Castro III and Deborah Castro, husband and wife, sold Tract 101-36, 4.04 acres. to NPS for $33,400.[1358]

Tract 101-37 16.75 acres

Description

Tract 101-37 was formerly the northeast section of Tract 101-22.[1359] When it was sold to NPS it was described as follows:

That portion of THE DOREDOR, PARING NO. ONE, PARING NO. 2, PARING NO. THREE and PARING NO. 4 LODE MINING CLAIMS, in Hartford Mining District, being shown on Mineral Survey No. 3641 on file in the Bureau of Land Management, as granted by Patent recorded in Book 30 of Deeds of Mines, page 332, records of Cochise County, Arizona, described as follows:

BEGINNING at the Southwest corner of PARING NO. 3 LODE;

thence North 01° 32' 00" East coincident with the Westerly line of PARING NO. 3 LODE, a distance of 617.40 feet to a point on the Southerly line of PARING NO. 2 LODE;

thence North 74° 47' 00" West coincident with said line, a distance of 500.00 feet to the Southwest corner of PARING NO. 2 LODE;

thence North 01° 32' 00" East coincident with the Westerly line of PARING NO. 2 LODE, a distance of 617.40 feet to the Southwest corner of DOREDOR LODE;

thence North 00° 11' 00" West coincident with the Westerly line of THE DOREDOR LODE, a distance of 622.20 feet to the Northwest corner of THE DOREDOR LODE;

thence South 74° 47' 00" East coincident with the Northerly line of THE DOREDOR LODE, a distance of 881.00 feet to the Northeast corner of PARING NO. 1 LODE;

thence continuing South 74° 47' 00" East coincident with the Northerly line of PARING NO. 1 LODE, a distance of 254.60 feet;

thence South 02° 24' 29" East a distance of 1883.25 feet to a point on the South line of PARING NO. 3 LODE;

thence North 74° 47' 00" West coincident with the South line of PARING NO. 3 LODE, a distance of 750.00 feet to the POINT OF BEGINNING.

EXCEPT those portions conveyed in Deeds recorded in Docket 1667, page 419 and in Docket 1700, page 285, records of Cochise County, Arizona.[1360]

Ownership/Disposition

The NPS purchased all the tracts subdivided from 101-22 in 1985. On 6 February 1985 James J. Wardle and Jacqueline S. Wardle, husband and wife, sold Tract 101-37, 16.75 acres, to NPS for $120,600. A handwritten note on the deed identifies it as "DEED # 15."[1361]

Appendix B

Grazing

1940: Three grazing allotments within the area being considered for Coronado National Memorial were described in 1940:

H.D. Lee, who had a yearlong term permit to graze 650 head of cattle as well as a temporary permit that covered a short period for any natural increase to his herd.

Alex D'Albini had a yearlong term permit for 88 head of stock and a yearlong term permit for 42 cattle on the Grubstake allotment. D'Albini declared a short drift fence of 31 chains in Section 13, and another drift fence of one and a half mile in sections 11 and 4 as well as a 500 foot pipeline from a spring that flowed in Section 13.

Joe Zaleski had a yearlong term permit on the Montezuma allotment for 30 head of cattle. The National Park Service planned to interfere with the continued use of the range only on "the two small fenced areas surrounding the observation point and the Museum site."[1362]

1941: The 1941 legislation authorizing Coronado International Memorial contained language specifically protecting the rights of ranchers and miners to pursue their vocations within the park. Of the two pages that made up the statute, one focused almost exclusively on the topic. Rights to water then used for stock were protected along with grazing privileges. Future road and fence construction would have to include access routes for cattle in order to ensure that development of the park did not threaten existing grazing and water rights.[1363]

1952: The Memorial that was proclaimed by the President on November 5, 1952, was based upon the act of August 18, 1941, 55 Stat. 630 (16 U.S.C. 450 y) as amended by Public Law 478, 82nd Congress, approved July 9, 1952, which did nothing more than change the Memorial from international to national.[1364] Thus, grazing privileges were still protected. It was quickly determined that the best way to handle the administration of grazing permits was for the Forest Service to continue to handle it within the Memorial as well as in the surrounding Forest Service lands. This was the same procedure used at Saguaro National Monument.[1365]

1953: In 1953, the National Park Service and National Forest Service signed a Memorandum of Agreement regarding grazing permits.[1366]

1955: The Soil and Moisture Conservation segment of a Master Plan Development Outline compiled in July 1955 discussed erosion. Even though soil erosion was classed as slight on 90% of the Memorial and "moderate in the remainder," much of the erosion had been caused by grazing. It was therefore agreed that fencing to exclude livestock would be enough of a measure to restore the brush, grass, and woodland vegetation and ultimately return the area to its natural state.[1367]

Grazing Preferences Involving Use of National Park Lands in 1955:[1368]

	Preference Yearlong	Percent National Forest	Percent National Park	Total Livestock Total	Total Livestock N.P.S.
Lone Mountain Henry Lee	650	94.5	5.5	614	36
Grubstake Alex D'Albini	133	83.5	16.5	111	22
Montezuma Frank Zaleski	11/15 to 4/30 44	50	50	22	22

Of the three existing grazing allotments on the Memorial in 1955, the vast majority of two, the Grubstake and the Lone Mountain, were still on National Forest land, while the third, the Montezuma, was split fifty-fifty between the Memorial and Forest Service lands. The Lone Mountain allotment was owned by Henry D. Lee and the Grubstake by Alex D'Albini, neither of whom were friends of the Memorial.[1369] However, they were reported to be in excellent condition in the early years of the Memorial's existence. The Montezuma allotment seemed to be more prone to showing the effects of overuse.[1370]

1961: Mission 66 planners discussed livestock and the cattle industry as an interpretive issue, because it was "an aspect of Spanish culture" and Coronado was the first European to introduce horses, cattle, goats, and sheep into the region.[1371]

A Monthly Report for July 1961 discussed grazing and current drought conditions: "The drought conditions have made it most evident that the Jones Joint Park -- forest allotment has been over-grazed. Since there is no fence between the private and state leased land and the federal lands, it is difficult to control the numbers of cattle on Park-Forest lands. The superintendent talked the matter over with Mr. Jones who has agreed to cut down the present numbers as soon as his old and dry cows are marketable. Meanwhile the range is greening up well and providing good ground cover. Since we have no gully-washers, no dangerous signs of erosion have been observed."[1372]

1965: In 1965, three grazing allotments were described:

Permittee	No. of Cattle	Animals Unit Months	Allotment Name
Henry D. Lee	36	430	Lone Mountain
Alex D'Albini	22	264	Grub Stake
Frank Zaleski	22	121	Montezuma

The same document continued that Frank Zaleski's allotment was grazed from November 15 to April 30 and was the one most heavily utilized and prone to overgrazing. Fences separated the three allotments. More fencing was planned to keep cattle out of trails and facilities. After those areas were fenced, it was thought that allotments might have to be reduced.[1373]

1969: A 1969 letter from NPS to Fred Baumkirchner gave him permission to run a temporary water line from State of Texas mine to Baumkirchner lands, through the Memorial. A subsequent Memorandum Of Agreement between the National Park Service, National Forest Service, and Baumkirchner set conditions for agreeing to allow him to use water from the NPS tank to water his cattle.[1374]

1973: In 1973, more fencing was planned to solve part of the grazing problem. Only minimal fencing had been constructed to protect specific areas, such as the picnic area and visitor center. Cattle were generally free to wander the Memorial grounds at will, posing sanitation problems and damaging the vegetation during the dry season. In addition, bulls and cows with calves could be a hazard to visitors as well as the staff and their families. Consultation between the Forest Service and Memorial superintendents was sporadic and the founding legislation gave neither sufficient leeway for making policy.[1375]

The grazing issue also contributed to planning for the boundary adjustment of 1978. A planning document specified that most of the grazing within the Memorial took place in the western, west of Montezuma Pass, and eastern portions of the Memorial; it itemized that it was in Sections 10, 15, and 22, and Sections 17-20.[1376]

The Annual Report for 1993 stated: "Grazing continues to be a spotty problem. As a result of substantial range damage on the west side the Forest Service has reduced the allottees AUM's by 20% for the next five years.
"Location of a cattle feeding station in the canyon bottom 1,000 feet from CORO's well has caused concern for contamination of the area water supply. The 1973 U.S. Public Health Survey backed this concern up. Thus, through the assistance of the Forest Service, the allottee was required to move the site an additional 1,000 feet upstream. The problem may still exist."[1377]

1974: The 1974 Annual Report said that grazing inside the Memorial continued to be a spotty problem; particularly west of Montezuma Pass in the Yaqui Springs area. The U.S. Forest Service, which managed the grazing, instituted a new management program with the permittee in 1973 – which entailed reductions in animal units per month.[1378]

1976: The Final general management plan of September 1976 highlighted a particular concern with the Yaqui Springs area, which had become damaged as the whole area had been overgrazed.[1379] It also included maps of current grazing allotments.[1380]

A 1976 Environmental Review discussed grazing: "All alternatives considered will allow continued grazing under Forest Service jurisdiction. The objective of their range management is to maintain or restore excellent range condition while properly harvesting and utilizing the optimum amount of high quality forage (Arizona Inter-Agency Range Committee, 1972). Within limits imposed by soil and climatic conditions, improvements in the range resource at Coronado National Memorial will be directed toward maximum production of desirable forage species, optimum plant density and vigor, adequate mulch cover, greater water infiltration, reduced soil-surface evaporation, minimum soil erosion, and reduction of sediment pollution."[1381]

ca. 1978: The anonymous, undated, memo entitled "Boundary Adjustment–a Radical Proposal" discussed reasons for making significant adjustments to the boundaries of the Memorial. The portion of the Memorial west of Montezuma Pass, according to the memo, was not really enjoyed by the visiting public except as a scenic backdrop in any case. In addition, it represented seventy percent of the grazing land within the Memorial. Both land and water resources had been damaged by overgrazing. Withdrawal of that land would relieve NPS personnel of the duty of patrolling and administering the overgrazing of the unused land.[1382]

1978: The 1978 boundary adjustment which reconfigured the Memorial also changed the shape of grazing allotments within the Memorial.[1383]

1986: A briefing statement on grazing management of October 1986 summarized grazing privileges: "The latest Memorandum of Agreement on file was written in 1955 and established that the US Forest Service would continue 1) to issue permits and 2) to receive and account for grazing within the Memorial, the National Park Service to receive its proportionate part of fees collected. No increase of livestock number is permitted with concurrence of NPS." It went on, "There are two [sic] allotments in the park. Past records show a history of overgrazing, continued yearlong grazing for decades, and large AUM's. No longterm (five years) or annual operating plans have been done for either allotment. Portions of both allotments are overgrazed. No record has been found of NPS receiving a proportion of the grazing fees."[1384]

The 1986 Annual Statement for Interpretation and Visitor Services said that two grazing allotments were actively using Memorial lands and only the Montezuma allotment used the "developed and heaviest public use areas." It went on: "Livestock now graze freely throughout this allotment and could present a safety and sanitation problem in these high visitor use areas as well as damage vegetation and landscaping around the picnic area and visitor center." It continued with specific recommendations to end grazing in some areas and limit and control it in others.[1385]

According to the Annual Report for 1986: "During 1986, one hundred twenty-eight cattle were grazed on 2,495 acres of Memorial lands on three separate allotments. The U.S. Forest Service administers the grazing permits through a cooperative agreement. There are indications (erosion, loss of native grasses and intrusion of exotic species) of deterioration of the resource from overgrazing, especially on the southwestern portion of the Memorial. The Superintendent and SOAR Resource Management Specialist worked closely with the U.S. Forest Service District Ranger in documenting the damage to the resource and attempting to improve range management. In March, 1986, the U.S. Forest Service notified the permittee of a proposed reduction of the 40% in the grazing capacity on the Montezuma allotment. The permittee has filed an appeal which was denied by the Coronado National Forest Supervisor in Tucson and is now under consideration at the regional level in Albuquerque, N.M."[1386]

1987: A January 1987 situation report: "During 1986, one hundred and twenty eight head of cattle were grazed on 2,495 acres of Memorial lands on three separate allotments. The U.S. Forest Service administers the grazing permits through a cooperative agreement. There are indications (loss of native grasses and encroachment of exotic species) of deterioration of the resource from over-grazing on nearly half of the area grazed, especially on the southeastern portion of the Memorial. A range analysis study will be initiated this year in order to properly document the extent of the problem. A new grazing plan which will include pasture rotation will require the construction of nearly two miles of drift fence to implement."[1387]

In the summer of 1987 a new Interagency Agreement regarding grazing was negotiated between the National Park Service and the National Forest Service under which the Forest Service would continue to issue permits for existing allotments. A new interagency agreement and memoranda of understandings for grazing allotments, individually and collectively, were signed in the summer of 1987.[1388]

In the process, a letter stated that the National Forest Service had conducted a production utilization study for one allotment in 1985 and planned to do the same for the others within a year. In addition, an ongoing vegetation study covered long-term trends.[1389]

1988: According to the Annual Statement for Interpretation and Visitor Services of February 1988, an agreement between the Forest Service and NPS in 1988 allowed the Memorial to control rotation of herds and to add fencing to protect vegetation and resources. In general it improved Memorial control of grazing and increased its share of fees collected.[1390]

1990s: According to a summary provided in a Draft Livestock Management Plan, the Montezuma allotment changed hands several times and then became inactive in 1990. In 1992, the Park Service finally began to administer its grazing permits for itself. Following a new 1999 agreement with the National Forest Service, the two agencies share responsibility administering and monitoring the Joe's Spring allotment, which extends across their boundary. They also share grazing fees collected from the permit holder. Relying on the 1941 legislation's wording that specified that grazing could continue as long as it did not interfere with recreational development, NPS now is able to more stringently regulate grazing within the Memorial.
A new grazing management plan in 2000 expressed concern about the consumption of agave by cattle and its impact on nectar eating lesser long-nosed and Mexican long-tongued bats. The grazing plan mentioned a few other affected species. Among them were the barking frog, loggerhead shrike, elegant trogon, Mexican spotted owl, and peregrine falcon. At the founding of the Memorial, of course, the rights of grazing allotment holders were protected above all else. However, recent environmental concerns have been added to the equation over the history of the Memorial.[1391]

All of the WACC Folders which carry the number L 3019 contain data on grazing, most separated by allotment and owner. They include:
WACC Folder L 3019: Grazing D'Albini F 28
WACC Folder L 3019: Grazing Joe's Spring F 29
WACC Folder L 3019: Baumkirchner F 30
WACC Folder L 3019: Baumkirchner F 31
WACC Folder L 3019: Logan F 32
WACC Folder L 3019: Marco F 33
WACC Folder L 3019: Marco F 34
WACC Folder L 3019: Watkins Sierra Vista Realty F 35
WACC Folder L 3019: Grazing Control F 36
WACC Folder L 3019: Annual Graze Reports F 37

Appendix C

Mining

General
1940: In 1940, as the Memorial was under consideration, the Arizona Small Miners Association approved of the project because there was little evidence of valuable minerals.[1392]

1941: The 1941 legislation authorizing Coronado International Memorial contained language specifically protecting the rights of ranchers and miners to pursue their vocations within the park. Of the two pages that made up the statute, one focused almost exclusively on the topic.[1393]

1953: In 1953, NPS considered limiting future mining from parts of Coronado National Memorial in consideration of possible development plans.[1394]

1966: In 1966, it was noted that there was then no mining occurring with the Memorial, although the possibility of such activity existed because of the language of the founding legislation. There were claims nearby and had been discussions of building access roads which could affect the Memorial.[1395]

1969: In 1969, a mining claim within Memorial boundaries in the Montezuma Pass area raised fears regarding environmental destruction and road maintenance.[1396]

1970: In 1970, exploratory drilling was, at least, planned, within Memorial boundaries west of Montezuma Pass.[1397]

1971: In 1971, an effort was conceived to acquire all outstanding mining claims within Coronado National Memorial by whatever means possible.[1398]

1973: In the early 1970s, NPS considered pending actions to end the possibility of further mining within Coronado National Memorial.[1399] Meanwhile, several, evidently short-lived, claims were filed to the west of Montezuma Pass.[1400]

According to the 1973 Annual Report, no mining activity existed within the Memorial; however, at least one new claim was established one mile northeast of park headquarters during January.[1401]

1976: In 1976, Congress changed the law which allowed mining with NPS lands.[1402] In a note included with material related to this legislation, it was stated that there had been no mining activity with Coronado National Memorial since it opened in 1952.[1403]
Elimination of mining from the memorial would preclude future exploration and discovery of minerals. However, a document concluded, there was no indication that future mining ventures would have been any more productive than those in the past, which have been of little economic significance. Therefore, very little adverse impact to the mining industry or area economy should result from excluding mining.[1404]

1978: The 1978 Boundary Adjustment excluded land which had been claimed and explored for mineral resources while including some other such lands.[1405]

1979-1984: From 1979 to 1984, Wilbert P. Witkopp of Sierra Vista, Arizona, disputed with the National Park Service, National Forest Service, and Bureau of Land Management over the status and fate of several claims which he had filed in 1971. After the Boundary Adjustment of 1978, some of them came within Coronado National Memorial.[1406]

1988: Beginning in 1987, a mine-safing project was begun with the help of a team from Death Valley National Monument. Subsequently, an inspection and mapping trip was conducted to Coronado Memorial.[1407] During September 1988, ten openings were covered at Coronado National Memorial. Further recommendations were made for additional mine safing at the Memorial.[1408]

State of Texas Mine

The Lena mine, the "oldest historic mine claim in Montezuma Canyon," was located in May 1878 by George J. Rasking and John L. Harris and recorded the next month by D.B. Ren. The original papers located the Lena next to older mine workings whose origins were unknown. An 1880 newspaper article noted that there were then nine mines working in Montezuma Canyon. The Lena was renamed the Chicago Mine in 1885 under the ownership of Peter Connor and A.W. Emanuel.[1409] Connor (or Conner) and his partners filed several claims in Montezuma Canyon in 1879, among which was the Lookout, also thought to be on land later occupied by the State of Texas and its companion claims.[1410]

The State of Texas Mine was founded in the same location as the Lena in 1889. There is some disagreement as to the exact ownership of the State of Texas during its first few years of operation. Geoffrey T. Bohrer cites an 1889 claim by August Baron that reported a find of "mineral bearing quartz."[1411] However, Peter M. Van Cleve, using Deeds of Mines in the Cochise County Recorders Office in Bisbee, Arizona, writes that Richard C. Van Dorn made the first State of Texas claim in 1889. According to Van Cleve, Van Dorn soon sold a one-third share of the mine to Peter Connor, who, in turn, sold it and other local mine interests to William Graf in 1892. In the meantime, in 1891, August Baron, exercising Power of Attorney for Van Dorn, sold the remaining two-thirds share of the State of Texas Mine and another mine to Graf. Then, in 1893, Baron, a banker and miner from Tombstone, purchased all of Graf's interests, including the State of Texas.[1412]

By the middle of the 1890s, the State of Texas Mine belonged to August Baron. Baron had the claim surveyed in 1897 and the plat was approved in 1898.[1413] Some time later, Charles Gerdes, then of Gleeson, Arizona, stated that he had been Baron's partner and "did the greater part of the development work on the claim" at some time.[1414] According to reports, twenty-five tons of high grade lead-silver-zinc ores were shipped to Canon City, Colorado, in 1897. Forty-two tons were shipped in 1898-1899.[1415]

In 1902, over forty mines in Montezuma and Copper canyons, including the State of Texas, were leased by the Mitchell Mining Company, of Ishpeming, Michigan, which mined copper at the site. Mitchell relinquished the leases in 1906 and they reverted to their former owners.[1416] Almost immediately, the Gray Metals Company began to operate the mine, which was still owned by Baron. By 1914, the Texas No. 2, Extension, Bonita, Josephine, and New York mines had been added to the operation.[1417] A new 350-foot vertical shaft near the main workings around the same time. Records indicate that ore was cut at varying depths, but do not indicate the quality of ore. This shaft has been caved in for many years. The *Arizona Mining Journal* of 1920 reported that ore containing silver, lead, and zinc was shipped by Gray Metals Company.[1418]

August Baron died in 1913 and his mine properties were passed on to his wife, Christine. She promptly sold them to Douglas Gray of Tombstone, the owner of Gray Metals Company. In 1920, Gray took on two partners, Maurice Clark, of Douglas, and William H. Stilwell, of Phoenix, and incorporated a new incarnation of the Gray Metals Company as a publicly owned corporation. Gray sold his mines to the new corporation in 1920 fo $20,000. Only two years later, the State of Texas, Texas No. 2, Extension, Bonita, Josephine, and New York mines were sold at public auction as part of a court judgement against Gray. Nathan L. Amster bought them in August 1922 for $9,370.90.[1419]

In September 1926, T.J. Sparkes, of Prescott, Arizona, and Burdett Moody, of Los Angeles, California, purchased several mining claims in the Hartford Mining District from Nathan L. and Estelle D. Amster for $5,000. The purchase included the State of Texas, State of Texas No.

2, Extension, Bonita, Josephine, and New York mines.[1420] The partners did little or no mining over the next fifteen years.[1421]

In a January 1939 letter, Grace Sparkes told Burdett Moody that her father, T.J. Sparkes, had recently died and discussed her family's efforts to reopen the State of Texas Mine. She added that she had not visited the property in two years.[1422] Moody replied that he and T.J. Sparkes had been hoping to sell the property and that he still wished to do so. He estimated that he had $8,000 to $9,000 invested in the mine property, though he also wrote a few months later that he was "in around $5000 to $6000 altogether."[1423] Given that the property had only cost $5,000 and had not been operated since its purchase, it can be guessed that Moody had put up the vast majority of the partners' investment. T.J. Sparkes, a mining engineer, supplied expertise for the moribund enterprise.[1424]

Over the next few years, Grace Sparkes continued to pursue loans to reopen the mine and encouraged Moody to support her. She shared ownership of a half interest in the State of Texas property with her siblings as joint heirs to their father, T.J. Sparkes. However, she seemed to be the most active partner. Meanwhile, Moody persisted in his desire to divest of the State of Texas properties.[1425] Others saw the potential for turning a profit from the State of Texas as did Sparkes, and she and Moody received many offers from miners wishing to lease the property. None were accepted, as Sparkes was determined to keep the property and make it pay off.[1426]

In 1942, Grace Sparkes was given total control of the State of Texas mine property. In June, Moody quit-claimed his share with the stipulation that he would receive half of future net profits or half of the net proceeds of any future sale.[1427] In September, the other Sparkes heirs quit-claimed their shares to Grace as well.[1428] She finally obtained a loan from the federal government in connection with the World War II effort, also in 1942, and the mine produced zinc from 1943-1946.[1429] Burdett Moody died in 1946. It is unclear what the relationship between he and Sparkes was at the time and whether his widow retained an interest in the property.[1430]

In 1960, forty acres were excluded from Coronado National Memorial and added to the Coronado National Forest. Half of that land made up the Billy Boy mine claim, owned by Grace Sparkes. The land reverted to Coronado National Forest, National Forest Service while the mine claims remained with Sparkes.[1431]

Grace Sparkes died in 1963, leaving the State of Texas mine property to her four nephews. During the previous few years she had improved the property and offered it for sale to NPS as well as on the open market.[1432] The State of Texas properties were designated Tracts 101-06, 101-07, and 101-08. For details of the sale of those tracts and other related transactions, see the Land Appendix and Chapters VIII and IX.

A 1988 Interpretive Prospectus included a history of the State of Texas property. Itstated that in 1987, the property was cleared, old buildings torn down, and trash removed. In 1988, it was mine-safed. It was, at the time, considered an excellent interpretive area, for which a prospectus had been drafted.[1433]

Victorio Properties
According to a summary of mine claims compiled at Coronado National Memorial, the Miss Stake, Grub Stake No. 2, and Grub Stake No. 3 mine claims, along with three others in their immediate vicinity, were claimed by Felix Livericio in March 1899. The Doredor, Paring No. 1, Paring No. 2, Paring No. 3, Paring No. 4, Z.T. Parker, Chief, Fraction, Rubio, and Tunnelsite were claimed by Bruce Doredor. The four Paring mines were claimed in 1901 and the Doredor

in 1920. The western group are said to have been claimed in 1909.[1434] All thirteen claims were patented by Bruce Doredor on April 10, 1920.[1435] One source placed Doredor in the canyon and on those claims much earlier, probably before 1900.[1436]

According to an 1979 NPS appraisal report on the properties, then owned by the Victorio Company, there had "been no recorded production from any of the claims."[1437]

The same summary of mine claims cited above lists purchase of Z.T. Parker, Chief, Fraction, Rubio, Tunnelsite, Grub Stake No. 2, and Miss Stake by "Clark/Smith" in 1938.[1438] Bill Clark was on the Board of Supervisors and was said to have purchased the property for back taxes.[1439]

In 1960, forty acres were removed from Coronado National Memorial and added to the Coronado National Forest in order to exclude current mining claims from the Memorial. Half of that land was on and around the Z.T. Parker claim. The land reverted to Coronado National Forest, National Forest Service. The mining claims remained with their owners.[1440]

In July 1970, Ruth M. Clark, a widow, and Charles A. and Paquita C. Smith, sold several mining properties, including the thirteen Doredor claims in the Hartford Mining District of the Montezuma Mountains that fell within the eventual boundaries of Coronado National Memorial. The sellers were evidently Bill Clark's widow and his partner. The buyers were Coronado Investment Company, a partnership comprised of Peter G. Wray and H. Wayne Pruett.[1441] In 1973, the properties were transferred to Pruett-Wray Cattle Company, made up of the same partners.[1442] By 1979, Pruett-Wray had changed its name to "Victorio Land and Cattle Company" and then to "The Victorio Company."[1443]

In 1979, the Victorio properties were considered as two separate tracts, which were separated by the State of Texas mine properties. The westernmost tract, called Tract 101-05, consisted of the Z.T. Parker, Chief, Fraction, Rubio, Tunnelsite, Miss Stake, Grub Stake No. 2, and Grub Stake No. 3 claims. It held a total area of 154.54 acres [See Tract 101-05]. The eastern properties, Doredor, Paring No. 1, Paring No. 2, Paring No. 3, and Paring No. 4, made up Tract 101-09, 84.31 acres. For details of the sale of those tracts and other related transactions, see the Land Appendix and Chapters VIII and IX.

Bibliography of Published Sources

"Abandoned mines a danger to humans, a home to bats," CNN.com nature, August 28, 2000, http://www.cnn.com/2000/NATURE/08/28/mines.bats.ap/.

Alessio Robles, Vito (ed.). *Nicolás de Lafora, relación del viaje que hizo a los presidios internos situados en la frontera de la América septentrional*. México D.F.: Editorial Pedro Robredo, 1939.

Almada, Francisco R. *Diccionario de historia, geografía y biografía sonorense*. Hermosillo: Instituto Sonorense de Cultura, 1990.

Anderson, Clinton P., with Milton Viorst. *Outsider in the Senate: Senator Clinton Anderson's Memoirs*. New York: The World Publishing Company, 1970.

Aranda, Rigoberto. "El río San Pedro, entre Sonora y Arizona, corre el riesgo de secarse debido a la sobreexplotación a que lo somete EU," *La Crónica de Hoy*, June 23, 1999, http://www.cronica.com.mx/cronica/1999/jun/23/.

August, Jack L., Jr. *Vision in the Desert: Carl Hayden and Hydropolitics in the American Southwest*. Fort Worth: Texas Christian University Press, 1999.

Bakker, Elna and Richard G. Lillard. *The Great Southwest: The Story of a Land and Its People*. Palo Alto: American West Publishing Company, 1972.

Bancroft, Hubert Howe. *History of Arizona and New Mexico, 1530-1888*. San Francisco: The History Company, Publishers, 1890.

Bantjes, Adrian A. *As If Jesus Walked on Earth: Cardenismo, Sonora, and the Mexican Revolution*. Wilmington: Scholarly Resources Books, 1998.

Barkan, Elliot. "New Origins, New Homeland, New Region: American Immigration and the Emergence of the Sunbelt, 1955-1985," *Searching for the Sunbelt: Historical Perspectives on a Region*, edited by Raymond A. Mohl. Knoxville: The University of Tennessee Press, 1990, pp. 124-148.

Barrera, Mario. *Race and Class in the Southwest: A Theory of Racial Inequality*. Notre Dame: University of Notre Dame Press, 1979.

Bartra, Armando. *Los Herederos de Zapata: Movimientos Campesinos Posrevolucionarios en México. 1920-1980*. México, D.F.: Ediciones Era, 1985.

Bassols Batalla, Angel. *El Noroeste de México: Un estudio geográfico-económico*. México, D.F.: Universidad Nacional Autónoma de México, 1972.

Bohrer, Geoffrey T. "Siamese Triplets: Grace Sparkes, The State of Texas Mine, and the Coronado National Memorial," National Park Service, 1993.

Bolton, Herbert E. *Coronado on the Turquoise Trail: Knight of Pueblos and Plains*. Albuquerque: The University of New Mexico Press, 1949.

Bolton, Herbert Eugene. *Rim of Christendom: a Biography of Eusebio Francisco Kino, Pacific Coast Pioneer*. New York: The MacMillan Company, 1936.

Bowden, J.J. *Private Land Claims in the Southwest*. Master's Thesis: Southern Methodist University, 1969.

Briggs, Vernon M., Jr. *Immigration Policy and the American Labor Force*. Baltimore: The John Hopkins University Press, 1984.

Burgess, Opie Rundle. "Bisbee: Portrait of a Copper Camp, Proud Queen City of County of Cochise," *Arizona Highways*, photography by Esther Henderson and Chuck Abbott, Vol. 28, No. 2 (February 1952), pp. 12-13, 32-35.

Carlson, Alvar W. "Environmental Overview," *Borderlands Sourcebook: A Guide to the Literature on Northern Mexico and the American Southwest*. Norman, University of Oklahoma Press, 1983, pp. 75-80.

Celis, Lourdes, Catherine Macotela, Rosario Rico, Victor M. Ruíz, and Elena Ulloa. *historia de la acción pública: adolfo lópez mateos 1958-1964. I – las ideas*. México, D.F.: Fondo para la Historia de las ideas Revolucionarias en México, 1978.

Centro de Investigaciones Agrarias, Comite Interamericano de Desarrollo Agricola. *Estructura Agraria y Desarrollo Agrícola en México: Estudio sobre las Relaciones entre la Tenencia y uso de la Tierra y el Desarrollo Agrícola de México*. México, D.F.: Centro de Investigaciones Agrarias, 1970.

Day, Arthur Grove. *Coronado's Quest: The Discovery of the Southwestern States*. Berkeley: University of California Press, 1940.

Di Peso, Charles C. *The Babocomari Village Site on the Babocomari River, Southeastern Arizona*. Dragooon: The Amerind Foundation, Inc., 1951.

Di Peso, Charles C. *The Sobaipuri Indians of the Upper San Pedro River Valley, Southeastern Arizona*. Dragoon: The Amerind Foundation, Inc., 1953.

Di Peso, Charles C., John B. Rinaldo, and Gloria J. Fenner. *Casas Grandes: A Fallen Trading Center of the Gran Chichimeca*. Dragoon, Arizona: The Amerind Foundation, Inc., 1974.

Eckstein, Salomón. *El ejido colectivo en México*. México, D.F.: Fondo de Cultura Económica, 1966.

Eidsvik, H. K. "The Status of Wilderness: An International Overview" *Natural Resources Journal*, vol. 29, No. 1 (1989), pp. 57-82.

Emory, William H. *Report on the United States and Mexican Boundary Survey: Made Under the Direction of the Secretary of the Interior*. Washington, D.C.: A.O.P. Nicholson, 1857-1859.

Faulk, Odie B. *Tombstone: Myth and Reality*. New York: Oxford University Press, 1972.

Fergusson, Erna. *Our Southwest*. New York: Alfred A. Knopf, 1940.

Fogel, Walter. "Twentieth-Century Mexican Migration to the United States," *The Gateway: U.S. Immigration Issues and Policies*, edited by Barry R. Chiswick. Washington: American Enterprise Institute for Public Policy Research, 1982.

Garreau, Joel. *The Nine Nations of North America*. Boston: Houghton Mifflin Company, 1981.

Garza Salazar, Florentino. *Propuesta al Ejecutivo del Estado para Decretar la Zona de Amortiguamiento de la Actual Reserva Forestal Nacional y Refugio de Fauna Silvestre, de las Sierras los Ajos, Buenos Aires y la Púrica con la Categoría de Zona Sujeta a Conservación Ecológica, en los Municipios de Cananea, Bacoachi, Fronteras, Naco y Nacozari, Sonora, México*. Hermosillo: Gobierno del Estado de Sonora; Centro de Ecológico de Sonora, 1993.

Gladwin, Harold Sterling. *Excavations at Snaketown. IV. Reviews and Conclusions*. Medallion Papers, No. XXXVIII. Globe, Arizona: Gila Pueblo, 1948.

Gladwin, Harold Sterling. *A History of the Ancient Southwest*. Portland, Maine: The Bond Wheelwright Company, 1957.

Granger, Byrd Howell. *Arizona's Names (X Marks the Place)*. The Falconer Publishing Company, 1983.

Hadley, Diana and Thomas E. Sheridan. *Land Use History of the San Rafael Valley, Arizona (1540-1960)*. Fort Collins: National Forest Service, 1995.

Hammond, George P. and Agapito Rey (trans. and eds.). *Narratives of the Coronado Expedition 1540-1542*. Albuquerque: University of New Mexico Press, 1940.

Hart, John Mason. *Revolutionary Mexico: The Coming and Process of the Mexican Revolution*. Berkeley: University of California Press, 1987.

Haury, Emil W. "The Search for Chichilticale," *Arizona Highways*, Vol. 60, No. 4 (April 1984), pp. 14-19.

Heald, Phyllis W. "Coronado National Memorial," *Desert Magazine*, Vol. 22, No. 3 (March 1959), pp. 13-15.

Heyman, Josiah McC. *Life and Labor on the Border: Working People of Northeastern Sonora, Mexico, 1886-1986*. Tucson: The University of Arizona Press, 1991.

Hodge, Frederick Webb. "The First Discovered City of Cibola," *American Anthropologist*, Vol. 8

Huizer, Gerrit. *La Lucha Campesina en México*. México, D.F.: Centro de Investigaciones Agrarias, 1970.

Huizer, Gerrit. "Peasant Organization in the Process of Agrarian Reform in Mexico," *Studies in Comparative International Development*, Vol. IV, No. 6 (1968-1969), pp. 115-145.

Humphrey, Robert R. *90 Years and 535 Miles: Vegetation Changes Along the Mexican Border*. Albuquerque: University of New Mexico Press, 1987.

International Boundary and Water Commission, United States and Mexico. *Boundary between the United States and Mexico, as surveyed and marked by the International Boundary Commission under the Convention of July 29th, 1882: revived February 18th, 1899*. Washington, D.C.: Government Printing Office, 1899.

International Boundary and Water Commission, United States and Mexico. *Report of the Boundary Commission upon the survey and re-marking of the boundary between the United States and Mexico west of the Rio Grande*, aka: *Views of the monuments and characteristic scenes along the boundary between the United States and Mexico west of the Rio Grande*. Washington, D.C.: Government Printing Office, 1899.

Karns, Harry J. (trans.). *Unknown Arizona and Sonora 1693-1721: From the Francisco Fernández del Castillo version of Luz de Tierra Incógnita by Captain Juan Mateo Manje. An English Translation of Part II*. Tucson: Arizona Silhouettes, 1954.

Kaye, Glen. "The Mexico-U.S.A. Border Region: The Filling of an Empty Land," *Transboundary Resources Report*, Vol. 9, no. 1, (1995), pp. 1-8.

Kessell, John L. *Friars, Soldiers, and Reformers: Hispanic Arizona and the Sonora Mission Frontier 1767-1856*. Tucson: The University of Arizona Press, 1976.

Kessell, John L. *Mission of Sorrows: Jesuit Guevavi and the Pimas, 1671-1767*. Tucson: The University of Arizona Press, 1970.

Kessell, John L. "The Puzzling Presidio: San Phelipe de Guevavi, Alias Terrenate," *New Mexico Historical Review*, Vol. XLI, No. 1 (January 1966), pp. 21-39.

Kinnaird, Lawrence (trans. and ed.). *The Frontiers of New Spain: Nicolas de Lafora's Description, 1766-1768*. Berkeley: The Quivira Society, 1958.

Knight, Alan. "The rise and fall of Cardenismo, c. 1930 – c. 1946," *Mexico Since Independence*, edited by Leslie Bethell. Cambridge: Cambridge University Press, 1994.

Laird, Wendy, Joaquin Murrieta-Saldivar, and John Shepard, "Cooperation across Borders: A Brief History of Biosphere reserves in the Sonoran Desert" *Journal of the Southwest*, Vol. 39, Nos. 3-4 (1997), pp. 307-313.

Longwell, Alden Richard. *The Cananea Ejidos: From Private Ranch to Collective in Sonora*. Ph.D. Dissertation: University of Nebraska, 1974.

Lorey, David E. *The U.S.—Mexican Border in the Twentieth Century: A History of Economic and Social Transformation*. Wilmington, Del.:SR Books, 1999.

Machado, Manuel A., Jr. *The North Mexican Cattle Industry, 1910-1975: Ideology, Conflict, and Change*. College Station: Texas A&M University Press, 1981.
McCroskey, Mona Lange. *Grace Marion Sparkes: Matriarch of the Early Arizona Tourist Industry*. M.A. Thesis, Arizona State University, 1987.
Memorandum of Understanding Between National Park Service of the Department of the Interior, United States of America and Secretariat of Urban Development and Ecology, United Mexican States on Cooperation in Management and Protection of National Parks and Other Protected Natural and Cultural Heritage Sites. Signed at Mexico and Washington, November 30, 1988 and January 24, 1989 (TIAS 11599).
Migration Between Mexico & the United States, México—Estados Unidos Sobre Migración: A Report of the Binational Study on Migration, vii, http://www.utexas.edu/lbj/uscir/binpap-v.html.
Myers, John L. *The Arizona Governors 1912-1990*. Phoenix: Heritage Publishers, Inc., 1989.
Naylor, Thomas H. and Charles W. Poltzer (eds.). *The Presidio and Militia on the Northern Frontier of New Spain, Volume I, A Documentary History: 1570-1700*. Tucson: The University of Arizona Press, 1986.
Office of Science and Technology, National Park Service. *State of the Parks, 1980: A Report to the Congress*. Washington, D.C.: Government Printing Office, 1980.
Officer, James E. *Hispanic Arizona, 1536-1856*. Tucson: The University of Arizona Press, 1987.
Officer, James E. "Yanqui Forty-Niners in Hispanic Arizona: Interethnic Relations on the Sonora Frontier," *Journal of Arizona History*, Vol. 29, No. 2 (Summer 1987), pp. 101-134.
Peña, Elsa M. y J. Trinidad Chávez. "Ganadería y agricultura en la sierra: 1929-1980," *Historia General de Sonora, Historia Contemporánea de Sonora 1929-1984*, Segunda edición, edited by Gerardo Cornejo Murrieta. Hermosillo: Colegio de Sonora, 1988, pp. 469-504.
Riley, Carroll L. "The Location of Chichilticale," *Southwestern Culture History: Collected Papers in Honor of Albert H. Schroeder*, edited by Charles H. Lange. Santa Fe: Ancient City Press, 1985, pp.145-161.
Riley, Carroll L. and Joni L. Manson. "The Cíbola-Tiguex Route: Continuity and Change in the Southwest," *New Mexico Historical Review*, Vol. 58, No. 4 (October 1983), pp. 347-368.
Ruiz, Ramón Eduardo. *The People of Sonora and Yankee Capitalists*. Tucson: The University of Arizona Press, 1988.
Sánchez, George J. *Becoming Mexican American: Ethnicity, Culture and Identity in Chicano Los Angeles, 1900-1945*. New York, Oxford University Press, 1993.
Sánchez, Joseph P. Sánchez, "The Route of the Expedition of Francisco Vázquez de Coronado: A Historiographical Overview," Spanish Colonial Research Center, National Park Service, Albuquerque (Unpublished Ms., 1990).
Sanderson, Steven E. *Agrarian Populism and the Mexican State: The Struggle for Land in Sonora*. Berkeley: University of California Press, 1981.
Sanderson, Susan R. Walsh. *Land Reform in Mexico: 1910-1980*. Orlando: Academic Press, Inc., 1984.
San Pedro Riparian National Conservation Area. Washington, D.C.: Bureau of Land Management, Safford District, Arizona; U.S. Government Printing Office: 1995.
Sauer, Carl. "The Road to Cibola," *University of California Publications Ibero-Americana*, Vol. 3 (1932).
Saugey, David A. "U.S. National Forests: Unsung Home to America's Bats," *Bats*, Vol. 9, No. 3 (Fall 1991), pp. 3-6.
Sayles, E.B. *The San Simon Branch: Excavations at Cave Creek in the San Simon Valley. I. Material Culture*. Medallion Papers, No. XXXIV. Globe, Arizona: Gila Pueblo, 1945.
Schmitt, Karl M. *Communism in Mexico: A Study in Political Frustration*. Austin: University of Texas Press, 1965.

Schroeder, Albert H. "Fray Marcos de Niza, Coronado and the Yavapai," *New Mexico Historical Review*, Vol. XXX, No. 4 (October 1955), pp. 265-296; Vol. XXXI, No. 1 (January 1956), pp. 24-37.

Seis Años de Política Agraria del Presidente Adolfo López Mateos. México, D.F.: Departamento de Asuntos Agrarios y Colonización, 1964.

Simpson, James H. "Coronado's march in search of the 'Seven Cities of Cibola' and discussion of their probable location," *Annual Report of the Board of Regents of the Smithsonian Institution*. Washington, D.C.: Government Printing Office, 1872.

Smith, Cornelius C., Jr. *Fort Huachuca: The story of a frontier post*. Washington, D.C.: Department of the Army, United States Government Printing Office, 1981.

Sonnichsen, Charles Leland. *Colonel Greene and the Copper Skyrocket; The Spectacular Rise and Fall of William Cornell Greene: Copper King, Cattle Baron, and Promoter Extra-ordinary in Mexico, the American Southwest, and the New York Financial District*. Tucson: The University of Arizona Press, 1974.

State of the Environment: An Assessment at Mid-Decade. Washington D.C.: The Conservation Foundation, 1984.

Steinbeck, John. *Travels with Charley: In Search of America*. New York: Bantam Books, 1963.

Stewart, Yvonne G. "Montane Cochise Culture Sites in Coronado National Memorial," *Proceedings of the First Conference on Scientific Research in the National Parks, Volume II*, New Orleans, Louisiana, November 9-12, 1976, edited by Robert M. Linn; Sponsored by National Park Service and American Institute of Biological Sciences. Washington, D.C.: United States Department of the Interior, National Park Service Transactions and Proceedings Series, Number 5, 1979.

Szekely, Alberto. "The Development of Mexico-U.S. Cooperation: The Conservation of Wildlife Transboundary Resources" *Transboundary Resources Report*, Vol 3, no. 1, (1989), pp. 1-8.

Toops, Connie "Going to Bat for Bats," *National Parks: The Magazine of the National Parks and Conservation Association*, Vol. 75, No. 1-2 (January-February 2001), pp. 28-31.

Tucker, Edwin A. and George Fitzpatrick. *Men Who Matched the Mountains: The Forest Service in the Southwest*. Washington, D.C.: U.S. Department of Agriculture, Forest Service, Southwest Region; U.S. Government Printing Office, 1972

Tuthill, Carr. *The Tres Alamos Site on the San Pedro River, Southeastern Arizona*. Dragooon, Arizona: The Amerind Foundation, Inc., 1947.

Udall, Stewart L. "In Coronado's Footsteps," *Arizona Highways*, photography by Jerry Jacka, Vol. 60, No. 4 (April 1984), pp. 3-13, 20-45.

Udall, Stewart L. *Majestic Journey: Coronado's Inland Empire*, photography by Jerry Jacka. Santa Fe: Museum of New Mexico Press, 1987.

UNESCO Man and the Biosphere (MAB) Programme, http://cons-dev.univ-lyon1.fr/madagascar/MANANARA/mamanet/TEXTE/annexes/mab/home.htm.

UNESCO Man and the Biosphere (MAB) Programme. The Seville Strategy for Biosphere Reserves. The Biosphere Reserve Concept, http://cons-dev.univ-lyon1.fr/madagascar/MANANARA/mamanet/TEXTE/annexes/mab/stry_1.htm.

Valencia Ortega, Ismael. *Cananea*. Hermosillo: Centro Regional del Noroeste, Instituto Nacional de Antropología e Historia – SEP, Secretaria de Fomento Educativo y Cultura, 1984.

Wagoner, Jay J. *Early Arizona: Prehistory to Civil War*. Tucson: The University of Arizona Press, 1975.

"What is Your Favorite Park Doing for Bats," *Bats*, Vol. 13, No. 1 (Spring 1995), p. 10.

Wilson, John P. *Islands in the Desert: A History of the Uplands of Southeastern Arizona*. Albuquerque: University of New Mexico Press, in cooperation with the Historical Society of New Mexico, 1995.

Winship, George P. *The Coronado Expedition, 1540-1542*. Washington, D.C.: Fourteenth Annual Report of the Bureau of Ethnology, 1896.

Footnotes

[1] Resume of the Coronado Project, probably authored by Odd S. Halseth in 1951, Hayden Papers, AC, ASU, Box 201, folder 3. The entry for 1939 reads: "United States Congress passed a bill creating the United States Coronado Exposition Commission, with an appropriation of $200,000 for a program of Folk Festivals, publication of historical material and pageants to celebrate the Coronado Entrada in the various states supposed to have been visited by his expedition, namely Arizona, New Mexico, Colorado, Oklahoma, Texas and Kansas. These states set up 'Coronado Commissions' to plan for participation in this program, but received no share of the federal appropriation, except for the sum of 'not more that $10,000 for the establishment of a suitable monument' at or near the place where Coronado crossed the present border between Mexico and the United States."

[2] Ibid.

[3] Ibid.

[4] Charles M. Morgan to the President of the United States, Phoenix, Arizona, September 1, 1939, Carl Hayden Papers, Arizona Collection, Arizona State University, Tempe (Hereinafter cited as Hayden Papers, AC, ASU, Box 591, folder 2.

[5] R. T. Jones to Carl Hayden, Phoenix, Arizona, September 13, 1939, Hayden Papers, AC, ASU Box 591, folder 2.

[6] Carl Hayden to The Secretary of State, Washington, D.C., September 21, 1939, Hayden Papers, AC, ASU Box 591, folder 2.

[7] Hayden to The Secretary of the Interior, Washington, D.C., October 12, Hayden Papers, AC, ASU Box 591, folder 2.

[8] Ibid., Hayden Papers, AC, ASU Box 591, folder 2.

[9] Cordell Hull to Carl Hayden, October 10, 1939, Hayden Papers, AC, ASU Box 591, folder 2.

[10] John W. Finch to Carl Hayden, Washington, D.C., October 20, 1939, Hayden Papers, AC, ASU Box 591, folder 2.

[11] Hayden to Jones, October 21, 1939, Hayden Papers, AC, ASU Box 591, folder 2.

[12] Jones to Hayden, Phoenix, Arizona, October 19, 1939, Hayden Papers, AC, ASU Box 591, folder 2.

[13] Ibid., Hayden Papers, AC, ASU Box 591, folder 2.

[14] Hull to Hayden, November 1, 1939, Hayden Papers, AC, ASU Box 591, folder 2. Hayden promptly informed Governor Jones on the situation, see Hayden to Jones, November 2,

1939, Hayden Papers, AC, ASU Box 591, folder 2.
[15] Hull to Hayden, November 25, 1939, Hayden Papers, AC, ASU Box 591, folder 2.
[16] Hull to Hayden, December 29, 1939, AC, ASU Box 591, folder 2.
[17] Clinton P. Anderson to G.C. Dickens, Albuquerque, New Mexico, February 2, 1940, Hayden Papers, AC, ASU Box 591, folder 2.
[18] Ibid., Hayden Papers, AC, ASU Box 591, folder 2.
[19] Ibid., Hayden Papers, AC, ASU Box 591, folder 2.
[20] Ibid., Hayden Papers, AC, ASU Box 591, folder 2.
[21] Ibid., Hayden Papers, AC, ASU Box 591, folder 2.
[22] Ibid., Hayden Papers, AC, ASU Box 591, folder 2.
[23] Hayden to Anderson, Telegram dated February 15, 1940, Hayden papers, AC, ASU Box 591, folder 2.
[24] Hayden to Anderson (Telegram) February 12, 1940, Hayden Papers, AC, ASU Box 591, folder 2.
[25] Hayden to the Secretary of the Interior, February 8, 1940, Hayden Papers, AC, ASU Box 591, folder 2.
[26] Oscar L. Chapman to Hayden, Washington, D.C., January 4, 1940, Hayden Papers, AC, ASU Box 591, folder 2.
[27] Emil W. Haury to Aubrey Neasham, Tucson, December 19, 1939, AC, ASU, Box 591, folder 2.
[28] Report of Vernon A. Neasham in Special Report covering the Proposed Coronado International Monument submitted by Region III Headquarters, national Park Service, Department of the Interior, Santa Fe, New Mexico, February, 1940, Hayden Papers, AC, ASU, Box 591, folder 2.
[29] A.J. Wirtz to Carl Hayden, Washington, D.C., February 14, 1940, Hayden Papers, AC, ASU, Box 591, folder 2.
[30] Ibid., p. 1, Hayden Papers, AC, ASU, Box 591, folder 2.
[31] Ibid., p. 3, Hayden Papers, AC, ASU, Box 591, folder 2.
[32] Ibid., pp. 4-5, Hayden Papers, AC, ASU, Box 591, folder 2.
[33] Ibid., p. 5, Hayden Papers, AC, ASU, Box 591, folder 2.
[34] Ibid., p. 6, Hayden Papers, AC, ASU, Box 591, folder 2.
[35] Ibid., p. 6, Hayden Papers, AC, ASU, Box 591, folder 2.
[36] Ibid., p. 6, Hayden Papers, AC, ASU, Box 591, folder 2.
[37] Harold L. Ickes, Secretary of the Interior to Hon. Carl Hayden, Washington, D.C., February 27, 1940, Hayden Papers, AC, ASU, Box 591, folder 2.
[38,39] Hayden to Ickes, Washington, D.C., February 29, 1940, Hayden Papers, AC, ASU, Box 591, folder 2. The "Texas Mine" is a reference to the State of Texas Mine.
[40] Ibid.
[41] Hayden to Ickles, Washington, D.C., March 8, 1940, Hayden Papers, AC, ASU, Box 591, folder 2.
[42] Arno B. Cammerer to Hayden, Washington, D.C., March 14, 1940, Hayden Papers, AC, ASU, Box 591, folder 2.
[43] Anderson to Hayden, Albuquerque, New Mexico, March 15, 1940, Hayden Papers, AC, ASU, Box 591, folder 2.
[44] Ibid.
[45] Ibid.
[46] E.K. Burlew, First Assistant Secretary, to Hayden, Washington, D.C., March 18, 1940, Hayden Papers, AC, ASU, Box 591, folder 2.
[47] Hayden to Anderson, March 18, 1940, Hayden Papers, AC, ASU, Box 591, folder 2.
[48] Hayden to Stuart M. Bailey, Postal Telegraph, March 22, 1940, Hayden Papers, AC, ASU, Box 591, folder 2.
[49] Hayden to Frank C.W. Pooler, Regional Forester, March 8, 1940, Hayden Papers, AC, ASU, Box 591, folder 2.

50 Ibid.
51 Franck C.W. Pooler to Hayden, Albuquerque, New Mexico, March 21, 1940, Hayden Papers, AC, ASU, Box 591, folder 2.
52 Ibid.
53 G.M. Butler to Hayden, Tucson, March 31, 1940, Hayden Papers, AC, ASU, Box 591, folder 2.
54 Ibid.
55 Hayden to Butler, April 6, 1940, Hayden Papers, AC, ASU, Box 591, folder 2.
56 Frank C.W. Pooler to Chief, Forest Service, Albuquerque, New Mexico, April 5, 1940. Hayden Papers, AC, ASU, Box 591, folder 2.
57 Ibid.
58 Ibid.
59 Ibid.
60 Ibid.
61 *Report* signed by John A. Adams, Albuquerque, New Mexico April 4, 1940, Hayden Papers, AC, ASU Box 591, folder 2.
62 Ibid., pp. 2-3.
63 Ibid., p. 2.
64 Hayden to Cammerer, Washington, D.C., April 8, 1940, Hayden Papers, AC, ASU, Box 591, folder 2.
65 Ibid.
66 Ibid.
67 Ibid.
68 Ibid.
69 Ibid.
70 Cammerer to Hayden, Washington, D.C., April 9, 1940, Hayden Papers, AC, ASU, Box 591, folder 2.
71 Hayden to Colonel John R. White, April 12, 1940, Hayden Papers, AC, ASU, Box 591, folder 2.
72 Hayden to Pooler, April 12, 1940, Hayden Papers, AC, ASU, Box 591, folder 2.
73 Ibid.
74 Anderson to Hayden, Albuquerque, New Mexico, April 11, 1940, Hayden Papers, AC, ASU, Box 591, folder 2.
75 Ibid.
76 Ibid.
77 Ibid.
78 Hayden to Anderson, Washington, D.C., April 16, 1940, Hayden Papers, AC, ASU, Box 591, folder 2.
79 Ibid.
80 Fred Winn to Hayden, Tucson, Arizona, April 12, 1940, Hayden Papers, AC, ASU, Box 591, folder 2.
81 Hayden to Winn, Washington, April 17, 1940, Hayden Papers, AC, ASU, Box 591, folder 2.
82 Hayden to Hull, Washington, D.C., April 16, 1940, Hayden Papers, AC, ASU, Box 591, folder 2.
83 Hull to Hayden, Washington, D.C., April 16, 1940, Hayden Papers, AC, ASU, Box 591, folder 2.
84 Hull to Hayden, Washington, D.C., April 17, 1940, Hayden Papers, AC, ASU, Box 591, folder 2.
85 Hayden to Hull, Washington, D.C., April 22, 1940, Hayden Papers, AC, ASU, Box 591, folder 2. Copies with the same date were sent to Fred Winn,, Mrs. J.M. Keith, Secretary of the Arizona Cattle Growers Association in Phoenix, Charles F. Willis, State Secretary of the Arizona Small Mine Operators Association, Phoenix, Arizona, and William Alberts, State Land Commissioner, Phoenix, Arizona, Ibid.
86 A Bill to provide for the establishment of the Coronado International Monument, in the

State of Arizona, Committee on Public lands and Surveys, 76th Congress, 3rd Session, April 20, 1940, no Senate Bill number assigned, Hayden Papers, AC, ASU, Box 591, folder 2.

87 A Bill to provide for the establishment of the Coronado International Monument in the State of Arizona, Revised Committee Print, May 28, 1940, Hayden Papers, AC, ASU, Box 591, folder 2.

88 Cammerer to Anderson, Washington, D.C., April 22, 1940, Hayden Papers, AC, ASU, Box 591, folder 3.

89 Charles F. Willis to Hayden, Phoenix, May 2, 1940, Hayden Papers, AC, ASU, Box 591, folder 3.

90 Mrs. J.M. Keith to Hayden, Phoenix, May 2, 1940, Hayden Papers, AC, ASU, Box 591, folder 3.

91 Alex D'Albini to Hayden, Hereford, April 26, 1940, Hayden Papers, AC, ASU, Box 591, folder 3.

92 Henry Davis Lee to Hayden, Ft. Huachuca, May 28, 1940, Western Union Telegram, Hayden Papers, AC, ASU, Box 591, folder 3.

93 W.E. Clark to Hayden, Bisbee, May 11, 1940, Western Union Telegram, Hayden Papers, AC, ASU, Box 591, folder 3.

94 Wm. Alberts to Hayden, Phoenix, May 8, 1940, Hayden Papers, AC, ASU, Box 591, folder 3.

95 Mrs. J.M. Keith to Hayden, Phoenix, May 11, 1940, Hayden Papers, AC, ASU, Box 591, folder 3.

96 Hayden to Mrs. J.M. Keith, May 15, 1940, Hayden Papers, AC, ASU, Box 591, folder 3. Regarding this proposal Hayden wrote: "First, I suggested that the western boundary of the Monument be moved one section east so as to eliminate all of Sec. 15, T. 24 W., R. 20 E., as well as those portions of Sections 10 and 22 which were included within the boundaries as shown on the map which I sent you and in the draft of bill previously transmitted for your information. Since the only developments within the Monument which are proposed by the Park Service would be located at the look out point and at the probable museum site (marked on the map which I sent you and located, respectively, on the mountain peak in about the center of Section 14, T. 24 S., R. 29 E. and in the N½ of the NW¼ of Sec. 20, T. 24 S., R. 21 E.), it seems to me that if the area is reduced the most reasonable reduction could be brought about by, as I suggested, moving the boundary one section east. However, I am told the purpose of including within the Monument Section 15 and the fractional portions of Sections 10 and 22, T. 24 S., R. 20 E. is to provide a suitable location for a proposed circle road which will leave the existing Copper Canyon Road at about the northwest corner of the proposed Monument (near the northwest corner of the southwest quarter of section 10), go down through about the middle of Section 15 and cross into Mexico, making a circle and returning to the existing road via the museum, through a right-of-way lying between patented lands in Section 17, T. 24 S., R. 21 E. Because of the topography of the country, Section 15 is apparently about the only suitable location for such a loop road going into Mexico and returning, and my suggestion was, therefore not acceptable to the National Park Service."

97 Ibid.
98 Ibid.
99 Editorial, Arizona Daily Star, Phoenix, May 5, 1940, Hayden Papers, AC, ASU, Box 591, folder 3..
100 Henry Davis Lee to Ms. J.M. Keith, Lone Mountain Ranch, Patagonia, May 15, 1940, Hayden Papers, AC, ASU, Box 591, folder 3.
101 Davis to Hayden, Patagonia, May 15, 1940, Hayden Papers, AC, ASU, Box 591, folder 3.
102 Ibid.
103 D'Albini to Hayden, Hereford, May 16, 1940, Hayden Papers, AC, ASU, Box 591, folder 3.
104 Don Smith to Hayden, Nogales, May 17, 1940, Hayden Papers, AC, ASU, Box 591, folder 3.
105 Hayden to Smith, May 22, 1940, Hayden Papers, AC, ASU, Box 591, folder 3.

[106] D'Albini to Hayden, Hereford, May 21, 1940, Hayden Papers, AC, ASU, Box 591, folder 3.
[107] Hayden to Colonel John R. White, May 24, 1940, Hayden Papers, AC, ASU, Box 591, folder 3.
[108] Lee to Hayden, Patagonia, May 23, 1940, Hayden Papers, AC, ASU, Box 591, folder 3.
[109] Report, Committee on Public Lands and Surveys, Calendar No. 2220, September 10 (legislative day, August 5), 1940, Hayden Papers, AC, ASU, Box 591, folder 3.
[110] W.E. Clark, Clerk Board of Supervisors, to Hon. Carl Hayden, Bisbee, Postal Telegraph dated Arizona, May 3, 1940, 12:55 PM in Hayden Papers, AC, ASU Box 591, folder 3. Clark wrote: "REPLYING YOUR LETTER APRIL TWENTY SECOND STOP BOARD OF SUPERVISORS HEARTILY APPROVES PROJECT AND BELIEVES BILL PROPOSED BY YOU ADEQUATELY PROTECTS PRIVATE INTERESTS STOP ONLY PROTESTS WE HAVE HEARD ARE FROM TWO HOLDERS OF NATIONAL FOREST GRAZING PERMITS WE BELIEVE THAY ARE NOT INJURED STOP LETTER FOLLOWS."
[111] Hayden to Charles F. Willis, September 30, 1940, Western Union Telegram, Hayden Papers, AC, ASU, Box 591, folder 3.
[112] Congressional Record—House, November 18, 1940, Hayden Papers, AC, ASU, Box 591, folder 3.
[113] Ibid.
[114] Ibid.
[115] Ibid.
[116] G.E. Michaels to Pete Riley, October 25, 1941, WACC, Folder H 14: Area and Service History (41-52) F3.
[117] Congressional Record—Senate, November 1940, 13645.
[118] Southwest to Celebrate Four Hundredth Anniversary of Coronado's March. Extension of Remarks of Hon. John M. Houston of Kansas in the House of Representatives, Tuesday, March 26, 1940. Includes article by Martelle W. Trager, Washington Post of March 24, 1940 in Appendix to the Congressional Record, 1677.
[119] Martelle W. Trager, "Southwest to Celebrate Four Hundredth Anniversary of Coronado's March—Traveling Pageant to Follow Trail Spaniard Blazed in Quest for Riches," Washington Post, March 24, 1940 in appendix to the Congressional Record, 1677.
[120] Herbert E. Bolton, *Coronado, Knight of Pueblos and Plains*, (Albuquerque: University of New Mexico Press, 1949). Actually, A. Grove Day in 1940 suggested Naco as the entry point. See A. Grove Day, *Coronado's Quest: The Discovery of the American Southwest.* (Berkeley and Los Angeles, 1940) for his full account of the Coronado Expedition.
[121] Mrs. J.M. Keith to Mr. Chas. M. Morgan, May 9, 1940, Phoenix, Arizona, Coronado National Memorial Collection, Box 4.
[122] Charles M. Morgan, "Autobiographical Notes, 1960," Coronado National Memorial Collection, WACC, Folder H 14: Area and Service History (1939) F1.
[123] Ibid.
[124] Ibid.
[125] Charles M. Morgan to Herbert E. Bolton, November 4, 1939, Coronado National Memorial Collection, WACC, Folder H 14: Area and Service History (1939) F1.
[126] Clinton P. Anderson to Congressman John R. Murdock, October 10, 1939, University of New Mexico Archives, Box 1.
[127] Comments of Dr. R. K. Wyllys, History and Social Studies Depts., Arizona State Teachers Collee, Tempe, Arizona in Karl E. Kilby to President Zimmerman and Gilberto Espinosa, Albuquerque, NM., University of New Mexico Archives (hereinafter cited as UNM Archives, Box 7).
[128] Comments of J. Manuel Espinosa, St. Louis University in Karl E.Kilby to President Zimmerman and Gilberto Espinosa (undated), UNM Archives, Box 7.
[129] G.R. Michaels to Aubrey Neasham, Bisbee, Arizona, February 6, 1940, Hayden Papers, AC, ASU Box 591, folder 2.

[130] United States Coronado Exposition Commission to The Minister for Foreign Relations, The Republic of Mexico, 1940, Coronado National Memorial Collection, WACC, Folder H 14: Area and Service History (1939) F1.

[131] Ibid..

[132] An Act, to provide the establishment of Coronado National Memorial in the State of Arizona, House of Representatives, Committee On Interior and Insular Affairs, Subcommittee on Public Lands. H.R. 7553, June 16, 1952, Unpublished U.S. House of Representatives Committee Hearings, 1947-1954.

[133] Quoted in Tolson to Sparkes, Washington, D.C., February 21, 1952, Hayden Papers, AC, ASU, Box 201, folder 3.

[134] Charles DiPeso, Casas Grandes (Dragoon: The Amerind Foundation, Inc. 1974), Vol. 4, p. 39.

[135] George P. Hammond and Agapito Rey, eds. and trans. Narratives of the Coronado Expedition (Albuquerque, University of New Mexico, 1940), p. 240.

[136] James H. Simpson, "Coronado's march in search of the `Seven Cities of Cibola' and discussion of their probable location" in Annual Report of the Board of Regents of the Smithsonian Institution, (Washington, D.C.: Government Printing Office, 1872), p. 329.

[137] Charlie R. Steen, "The First European Explorers of the Southwest." Article VI, United States Department of the Interior Memorandum for the Press. On file, Coronado National Memorial, Arizona.

[138] Frederick Webb Hodge, "The First Discovered City of Cibola," American Anthropologist, (1895) 8:142-252.

[139] George J. Undreiner, "Fray Marcos de Niza and his Journey to Cibola," in The Americas, Vol. III, no. 4, April 1947, pp. 415-486.

[140] Undreiner, op. cit., 1947, pp. 415-486.

[141] Adolph F. Bandelier, "Historical Introduction to Studies among the Sedentary Indians of New Mexico" in Papers of the Archaeological Institute of America (Boston, American Series I, 1881), p. 1 and "An Outline of the Documentary History of the Zuni Tribe," Journal of American Archaeology and Ethnology, 1892, pt. II:407; George P. Winship, The Coronado Expedition, 1540-1542 (Washington, D.C.: Fourteenth Annual Report of the Bureau of Ethnology, 1896), p. 387. Bolton, Coronado1(949), 105; Carl Sauer, "The Road to Cibola," Ibero-Americana, Berkeley, 1932, p. 36.

[142] Albert H. Shroeder, "Fray Marcos de Niza, Coronado and the Yavapai," New Mexico Historical Review, 30: 265.

[143] Ibid., p. 267.

[144] Hammond and Rey, Narratives, p. 166.

[145] Ibid., p. 251.

[146] Ibid., p. 165.

[147] DiPeso, Casas Grandes, p. 100.

[148] Ibid.

[149] Schroeder, "Fray Marcos de Niza," New Mexico Historical Review (1956), 31:32.

[150] Ibid., p. 33.

[151] Ibid., p. 32.

[152] Carroll L. Riley and Joni L. Manson, "The Cíbola-Tiguex Route: Continuity and Change in the Southwest," New Mexico Historical Review (October 1983), pp. 349.

[153] Riley, "The Location of Chichilticale" in Charles H. Lange, ed., Collected Papers in Honor of Albert H. Schroeder (Santa Fe: Ancient City Press, 1985), 153.

[154] Hammond and Rey, Narratives, 284.

[155] Bolton, Coronado, 108-117.

[156] DiPeso, Casas Grandes, p. 102.

157 Sauer, "The Road to Cibola," Ibid., pp. 36-37.
158 Master Plan Development Outline Coronado National Memorial, November 1954, D18, Master Plans [1954] F2.pdf, WACC, Archives CD Box 3.
159 Resume of the Coronado Project, probably written by Odd S. Halseth in 1951, Hayden Papers, AC, ASU, Box 201, folder 3.
160 Tolson to Sparkes, Washington, July 18, 1951, Hayden Papers, AC, ASU, Box 201, folder 3. In this correspondence, Tolson gives these dates and place of the 1942 meeting.
161 Ibid., Also see Tolson to G.R. Michaels, Chicago, January 29, 1944, WACC, H14: Area & Service, History 41-42 F3.
162 Ibid.
163 Ibid.
164 Ibid.
165 Tolson to Sparkes, Washington, D.C., December 6, 1950, Hayden Papers, AC, ASU, Box 201, folder 3.
166 Tolson to Hayden, Chicago, May 27, 1944, WACC, Folder H 14: Area and Service History (41-52) F3.
167 Ibid.
168 Ibid.
169 E.T. Scoyen to Gus Michaels, Santa Fe, June 8, 1944, WACC, Folder H 14: Area and Service History (41-52) F3.
170 Tolson to Sparkes, Washington, D.C., July 18, 1951, Hayden Papers, AC, ASU, Box 201, folder 3. Here, Tolson quotes from his letter to Halseth dated August 19, 1944.
171 Ibid.
172 Ibid.
173 Tolson to Hayden, Washington, D.C., September 6, 1944, WACC, Folder H 14: Area and Service History (41-52) F3.
174 Tolson to Villas Perez, Chicago, February 1, 1944, WACC, Folder H 14: Area and Service History (41-52) F3.
175 Ibid.
176 Tolson to Hayden, Chicago, December 26, 1944, WACC, Folder H 14: Area and Service History (41-52) F3.
177 Tolson to Hayden, Chicago, January 15, 1945, WACC, Folder H 14: Area and Service History (41-52) F3.
178 Tolson to Michaels, Chicago, February 8, 1946, WACC, Folder H 14: Area and Service History (41-52) F3.
179 Tolson to Michaels, Chicago, March 8, 1946, WACC, Folder H 14: Area and Service History (41-52) F3.
180 Michaels to Tolson, Bisbee, November 4, 1946, WACC, Folder H 14: Area and Service History (41-52) F3.
181 Tolson to Tillotson, Chicago, November 20, 1946, WACC, Folder H 14: Area and Service History (41-52) F3.Also see, Dean Acheson, Acting Secretary, Department of State, to Julius A. Krug, Secretary of the Interior, November 8, 1946, WACC, Folder H 14: Area and Service History (41-52) F3. Other members were P.V. Wood head, U.S. Forest Service, Albuquerque; William H. Zeh, Office of Indian Affairs, Phoenix; and John C. Gatlin, Regional Director, U.S. Fish and Wildlife Service, Albuquerque.
182 Tolson to Sparkes, Washington, D.C., July 18, 1951, Hayden Papers, AC, ASU, Box 201, folder 3.
183 Ibid. Also see entry for 1947 in Resume of the Coronado Project, probably authored by Odd S. Halseth in 1951, Hayden papers, AC, ASU, Box 201, folder 3. In this summary report, probably written by Halseth it is stated that the United States Commission sent a member to visit Secretary of Agriculture, Nasario Ortiz Garza and Ing. Villas Perez resulting in the establishment of, a new Commission for Mexico. On July 16, 1947, the Mexican Commis-

sioners Ing. Jesús Merino Fernandez Delgado, Ing. Federico Sanchez, Lic. Silvestre Aguilar, Ing. Carlos Villas Perez, and Ing. Luis de la Fuente met with members of the U.S. Commission in Mexico City. This is obviously the same meeting that Tolson reported on in his July 18, 1951 letter to Sparkes, op. cit.

184 Tolson to Sparkes, July 18, 1951, ibid. The Mexican Commission was reorganized with the following members: Ing. Eulogio de la Garza, Director General, Forestry, Wildlife, and Fisheries Service; Ing. David Herrera Jordan, Mexican Representative of the International Boundary and Water Commission; Ing., Luis Macias Arellano, Chief Wildlife Division, Forest and Wildlife Service; and Ing. Humerto Ortega Gattaneo, Chief, Division of Forest Protection. Minister of Agriculture Nazario S. Ortiz Garza was the ex officio member of the Commission.

185 Ibid.

186 Ibid.

187 Memorandum from Assistant Director Tolson, National Park Service to Assistant Secretary Davidson, Department of the Interior, Washington, D.C., January 12, 1949, Hayden Papers, AC, ASU, Box 201, folder 3.

188 Tolson to Sparkes, Washington, D.C., July 18, 1951, Hayden Papers, AC, ASU, Box 201, folder 3.

189 Ibid., Toldon informed Davidson of Department of State "Assistant Secretary Peurifoy's reply of December 3, 1948, stating that, because of the American interests involved in thes proposed park areas, the Department of Stte hesitates to make further inquiry of the Mexican Government, at this time, concerning the status of the two decrees. Mr. Peurifoy also stated that the state Department would be glad to have its representatives discuss this matter further with representatives of the Interior Department, and, if this was desired, to get in touch with Mr. Paul J. Reveley, Chief, Division of Mexican Affairs, to arrange for a time and place for the meeting." Hayden to Halseth, Washington, D.C., February 14, 1949, Hayden Papers, AC, ASU, Box 201, folder 3.

190 On January 28, 1949, Hayden wrote a form letter to those he believed still interested in the Coronado International Memorial. For copies of the letter, see Hayden to Grace Sparkes, Gus R. Michaels, H.H. Peterson (Montezuma Ranch), and Odd S. Halseth, January 28, 1949, Hayden Papers, AC, ASU, Box 201, folder 3. Also see, Halseth to Hayden, Phoenix, February 7, 1949, Hayden Papers, AC, ASU, Box 201, folder 3.

191 Halseth to Hayden, Phoenix, February 7, 1949, Ibid.

192 Memorandum from Assistant Director Tolson to Assistant Secretary Davidson, January 12, 1949, Hayden Papers, AC, ASU, Box 201, folder 3.

193 Ibid.

194 Hayden to Halseth, Washington, D.C., February 14, 1949, Hayden Papers, AC, ASU, Box 201, folder 3.

195 Ibid.

196 Ibid.

197 Sparkes to Hayden, July 28, 1949, Hayden Papers, AC, ASU, Box 201, folder 3.

198 Dan E. Garvey to Hayden, Phoenix, March 2, 1949, Hayden Papers, AC, ASU, Box 201, folder 3.

199 Garvey to Tolson, Phoenix, July 19, 1949, Hayden Papers, AC, ASU, Box 201, folder 3. The terms of office for the commissioners were: "Ray Busey, term expiring first Monday in January 1950; Alex Jacome-January 1951; J.V. Robbins-January 1952; Art [Odd?] Halseth-January 1953; J. Howard Pile-January 1954."

200 Tolson to Hayden, Washington, D.C., March 11, 1949, Hayden Papers, AC, ASU, Box 201, folder 3.

201 Sparkes to Hayden, Bisbee, April 14, 1949; and, Hayden to Sparkes, April 23, 1949, Hayden Papers, AC, ASU, Box 201, folder 3.

202 Hayden to Folsom Moore, May 3, 1949, Hayden Papers, AC, ASU, Box 201, folder 3.

[203] Ibid.
[204] Garvey to Tolson, Phoenix, July 19, 1949, Hayden Papers, AC, ASU, Box 201, folder 3.
[205] Tolson to Garvey, Washington, D.C., October 28, 1949, Hayden Papers, AC, ASU, Box 201, folder 3.
[206] Garvey to Tolson, Phoenix, November 14, 1949, Hayden Papers, AC, ASU, Box 201, folder 3.
[207] Ibid.
[208] Memorandum from Assistant Director Tolson to Regional Director, Region Three, November 30, 1949, Hayden Papers, AC, ASU, Box 201, folder 3.
[209] Hayden to Sparkes, August 2, 1949, Hayden Papers, AC, ASU, Box 201, folder 3.
[210] Hayden to Sparkes, Phoenix, September 15, 1950, Hayden Papers, AC, ASU, Box 201, folder 3. Also see, Hayden to Sparkes, July 3, 1950, ibid.
[211] Telegram, Sparkes to Hayden, Bisbee, Hayden Papers, AC, ASU, Box 201, folder 3.
[212] Sparkes to Hayden, Phoenix, September 25, 1950, Hayden Papers, AC, ASU, Box 201, folder 3.
[213] Sparkes to Tolson, Bisbee, September 5, 1950, Hayden Papers, AC, ASU, Box 201, folder 3.
[214] Tolson to Sparkes, Washington, D.C., September 15, 1950, Hayden Papers, AC, ASU, Box 201, folder 3.
[215] Ibid.
[216] Memorandum, D.M. Lyons to Paul, United States Senate (Letterhead), Hayden Papers, AC, ASU, Box 201, folder 3.
[217] C. Edgar Goyette to Hayden, Tucson, July 14, 1950, Hayden Papers, AC, ASU, Box 201, folder 3.
[218] Sparkes to Hayden, Bisbee, September 25, 1950, Hayden Papers, AC, ASU, Box 201, folder 3.
[219] Ibid.
[220] Ibid.
[221] Tillotson to Sparkes, Santa Fe, New Mexico, October 28, 1950, Hayden Papers, AC, ASU, Box 201, folder 3.
[222] Sparkes to Tolson, Bisbee, November 27, 1950, Hayden Papers, AC, ASU, Box 201, folder 3.
[223] Ibid.
[224] Tolson to Sparkes, Washington, D.C., December 6, 1950, Hayden Papers, AC, ASU, Box 201, folder 3.
[225] Memorandum from Regional Director to Director, Santa Fe, December 14, 1950, Hayden Papers, AC, ASU, Box 201, folder 3.
[226] Ibid.
[227] Ibid.
[228] Ibid.
[229] Ibid.
[230] Ibid. Tillotson's amendment, in part, read: "That section 1 of the Act…be, and the same is hereby, amended by striking the word 'size' from the proviso at the end of the said section 1 and inserting in lieu thereof the following: `of such size as may be determined by the Secretary of the Interior to be necessary." See, "'A Bill…To Amend…An Act to provide for the establishment of the Coronado International Memorial, in the State of Arizona,' approved August 18, 1941," Hayden Papers, AC, ASU, Box 201, folder 3.
[231] Ibid.
[232] Ibid.
[233] Hayden to Wiswall, December 21, 1950, Hayden Papers, AC, ASU, Box 201, folder 3.
[234] Tillotson to Wiswall, Washington, D.C., December 29, 1950, Hayden Papers, AC, ASU, Box 201, folder 3.
[235] Ibid.
[236] Tillotson to NPS Director, December 21, 1950, Hayden Papers, AC, ASU, Box 201, folder 3.
[237] Telegram Sparkes to Hayden, Bisbee, December 22, 1950, Hayden Papers, AC, ASU, Box 201, folder 3.

238 Telegram Hayden to Sparkes, December 26, 1950, Hayden Papers, AC, ASU, Box 201, folder 3.
239 Memorandom Tolson to Tillotson, Washington, D.C., December 26, 1950, Hayden Papers, AC, ASU, Box 201, folder 3.
240 Ibid.
241 Mary Contreras to Hayden, Cananea, January 31, 1951.
242 Tolson to Eaton, Washington, D.C., February 15, 1951, Hayden Papers, AC, ASU, Box 201, folder 3. Throughout its history, the words "Memorial" and "Monument" were used interchangeably in the Arizona Commission's name in both official and informal contexts.
243 Minutes of the Arizona International Memorial Commission Meeting, February 25, 1951, Hayden Papers, AC, ASU, Box 201, folder 3
244 Handwritten note from Halseth to Hayden transmitting the Minutes, Phoenix, February 28, 1951, Hayden Papers, AC, ASU, Box 201, folder 3.
245 Memorandum from Sparkes to Arizona Coronado International Memorial Commission, March 20, 1951, Hayden Papers, AC, ASU, Box 201, folder 3.
246 Sparkes to Williams, Hereford, March 19, 1951, Hayden Papers, AC, ASU, Box 201, folder 3. Ing. Nazario S. Ortiz Garza, Minister of Agriculture, was an ex officio member of the Mexican Commission, Memorandum Tolson to Tollitson, Washington, D.C., March 29, 1951, Hayden Papers, AC, ASU, Box 201, folder 3.
247 Telegram Sparkes to Pyle, Bisbee, Hayden Papers, AC, ASU, Box 201, folder 3.
248 Hayden to Sparkes, April 24, 1951, Hayden Papers, AC, ASU, Box 201, folder 3.
249 Halseth to Hayden, Phoenix, June 21, 1951, Hayden Papers, AC, ASU, Box 201, folder 3.
250 Emilio Segura, Jr. to Grace Sparkes, June 18, 1951, Ranchos de Cananea, Hayden Papers, AC, ASU, Box 201, folder 3.
251 Sparkes to Hayden Hereford, September 3, 1951, Hayden Papers, AC, ASU, Box 201, folder 3.
252 Ibid.
253 Hayden to Chapman, September 5, 1951, Hayden Papers, AC, ASU, Box 201, folder 3.
254 Dale E. Doty to Pyle, Washington, D.C., (no date) Hayden Papers, AC, ASU, Box 201, folder 3.
255 Howard Pyle to Miguel Aleman Valdis, Phoenix, August 31, 1951, Hayden Papers, AC, ASU, Box 201, folder 3.
256 Hayden to President Aleman, Washington, D.C., September 12, 1951, Hayden Papers, AC, ASU, Box 201, folder 3.
257 Pyle to Sparkes, Phoenix, November 29, 1951, Hayden Papers, AC, ASU, Box 201, folder 3.
258 Manuel Pello to Pyle, Mexico City, November 16, 1951, Hayden Papers, AC, ASU, Box 201, folder 3.
259 Pyle to Manuel Pello, December 13, 1951, Hayden Papers, AC, ASU, Box 201, folder 3.
260 Tolson to Sparkes, Washington, D.C., January 28, 1952, Hayden Papers, AC, ASU, Box 201, folder 3.
261 "C.E. Wiswall, Rancher, Dies in Cananea," The Bisbee Daily Review, Saturday March 1, 1952, Hayden Papers, AC, ASU, Box 201, folder 3.
262 Tolson to Sparkes, Washington, D.C., October 19, 1951, Hayden Papers, AC, ASU, Box 201, folder 3.
263 Tolson to Sparkes, Washington, D.C., December 7, 1951, Hayden Papers, AC, ASU, Box 201, folder 3.
264 Ibid.
265 Hayden to Sparkes, Washington, D.C., January 2, 1952, Hayden Papers, AC, ASU, Box 201, folder 3.
266 Sparkes to Tolson, Hereford, January 12, 1952, Hayden Papers, AC, ASU, Box 201, folder 3.
267 Tolson to Wiswall, Washington, D.C., January 28, 1952, Hayden Papers, AC, ASU, Box 201, folder 3.

268 Tolson to Sparkes, Washington, D.C, January 28, 1952, Hayden Papers, AC, ASU, Box 201, folder 3.
269 Hayden to Sparkes, February 11, 1952, Hayden Papers, AC, ASU, Box 201, folder 3.
270 Ibid.
271 Sparkes to Hayden, State of Texas Mine, February 1952, Hayden Papers, AC, ASU, Box 201, folder 3.
272 Ibid.
273 *Brief Digest Bisbee Chamber of Commerce—National Parks and Monuments* Committee Meeting, Bisbee, February 25, 1952, 2 p.m., Hayden Papers, AC, ASU, Box 201, folder 3.
274 "C.E. Wiswall, Rancher, Dies, in Cananea, The Bisbee Daily Review, Saturday, March 1, 1952; also see, Emile Segura, Jr. to Tolson, Cananea, March 11, 1952; and, Sparkes to Tolson, Hereford, March 18, 1952, Hayden Papers, AC, ASU, Box 201, folder 3.
275 Sparkes to Hayden, Hereford, March 6, 1952, Hayden Papers, AC, ASU, Box 201, folder 3.
276 Ibid.; also see, Hayden to Sparkes, March 12, 1952, Hayden Papers, AC, ASU, Box 201, folder 3.
277 Tolson to Sparkes, Washington, D.C., March 13, 1952, Hayden Papers, AC, ASU, Box 201, folder 3.
278 National Park Service PBS dated March 18, 1952, Tolson to Sparkes, Care of Mrs. Margaret Rockwell, Adams Hotel, Phoenix, Hayden Papers, AC, ASU, Box 201, folder 3.
279 Segura to Tolson, Cananea March 11, 1952, Hayden Papers, AC, ASU, Box 201, folder 3.
280 Sparkes to Hayden, telegram, March 18, 1952, Hayden Papers, AC, ASU, Box 201, folder 3.
281 Tolson to Sparkes, Washington, D.C., March 19, 1952, AC, ASU, Box 201, folder 3.
282 Ibid.
283 H.R. 7553 in the House of Representatives, April 23, 1952, introduced by Congressman Patten, Hayden Papers, AC, ASU, Box 201, folder 3.
284 Sparkes to Hayden, Hereford, April 2, 1952, Hayden Papers, AC, ASU, Box 201, folder 3.
285 Hayden to Sparkes, June 23, 1952, and Hayden to Father Bonaventure Oblasser, O.F.M. June 28, 1952, Hayden Papers, AC, ASU, Box 201, folder 3.
286 Hayden to Sparkes, telegram, July 2, 1952, Hayden Papers, AC, ASU, Box 201, folder 3.
287 Hayden to Sparkes, August 26, 1952, Hayden Papers, AC, ASU, Box 201, folder 3.
288 Note on desk calendar for October 24; also see, George Brubaker to Hayden, November 3, 1952, Hayden Papers, AC, ASU, Box 201, folder 3.
289 Brubaker to Hayden, Washington, D.C. November 3, 1952, Hayden Papers, AC, ASU, Box 252, folder 39.
290 Sparkes to Hayden, July 3, 1952, Hayden Papers, AC, ASU, Box, 201, folder 3.
291 Charles S. Murphy to Hayden, The White House, July 10, 1952, Hayden Papers, AC, ASU, Box 201, folder 3.
292 George A. Brubaker, Assistant Sectetary to Senator Hayden to Senator Carl Hayden, Western Union Telegraph November 7 1952, Hayden Papers, AC, ASU, Box 252 folder 38.
293 Hayden to Sparkes, November 14, 1952, Hayden Papers, AC, ASU, Box 537, folder 30.
294 Sparkes to Hayden, July 28, 1952, Hayden Papers, AC, ASU, Box 201, folder 3.
295 G.R. Michaels, Secretary, Bisbee Chamber of Commerce, to Frank Pinkley, National Park Service, Bisbee, April 3, 1936, WACC, Folder H 14: Area and Service History 1939 F1.
296 Senator Carl Hayden to W.E. Clark, Clerk, Cochise County Board of Supervisors, April 22, 1940, WACC, Folder H 14: Area and Service History 1940 F2.
297 Clinton P. Anderson to Hayden, Albuquerque, April 11, 1940, Hayden Papers, AC, ASU, Box 591, Folder 2.
298 Hayden to Clark, April 22, 1940.
299 An Act to Provide for the establishment of the Coronado International Memorial, in the State of Arizona, approved August 18, 1941 (55 Stat. 630).
300 Charles Leland Sonnichsen, Colonel Greene and the Copper Skyrocket; The Spectacular Rise and Fall of William Cornell Greene: Copper King, Cattle Baron, and Promoter

Extra-ordinary in Mexico, the American Southwest, and the New York Financial District (Tucson: The University of Arizona Press, 1974), 4, 54.

[301] Ibid, 268-269. As an interpreter of the region, Sonnichsen is described on the title page of his book on Greene as aiming "to express the attitudes and assumptions of his fellow Americans in their thinking about the Western experience."

[302] Josiah McC. Heyman, Life and Labor on the Border: Working People of Northeastern Sonora, Mexico, 1886-1986 (Tucson: The University of Arizona Press, 1991) 29-30.

[303] John Mason Hart, Revolutionary Mexico: The Coming and Process of the Mexican Revolution (Berkeley: University of California Press, 1987) 63-68; Sonnichsen, Colonel Greene and the Copper Skyrocket, 177-206.

[304] Sonnichsen, Colonel Greene and the Copper Skyrocket, 206.

[305] Heyman, Life and Labor on the Border, 29.

[306] Sonnichsen, Colonel Greene and the Copper Skyrocket, 233-234.

[307] Ibid, 272.

[308] Ibid, 233-234; Centro de Investigaciones Agrarias, Comite Interamericano de Desarrollo Agricola, Estructura Agraria y Desarrollo Agrícola en México: Estudio sobre las Relaciones entre la Tenencia y uso de la Tierra y el Desarrollo Agrícola de México (México, D.F.: Centro de Investigaciones Agrarias, 1970), 220.

[309] Elsa M.Peña y J. Trinidad Chávez, "Ganadería y agricultura en la sierra: 1929-1980," Historia General de Sonora, Historia Contemporánea de Sonora 1929-1984, Segunda edición, edited by Gerardo Cornejo Murrieta (Hermosillo: Colegio de Sonora, 1988), 488-489.

[310] Specific estimates vary, but fall into this range, Alan Knight, "The rise and fall of Cardenismo, c. 1930 – c. 1946," Mexico Since Independence, edited by Leslie Bethell (Cambridge: Cambridge University Press, 1994), 258; Steven E. Sanderson, Agrarian Populism and the Mexican State: The Struggle for Land in Sonora (Berkeley: University of California Press, 1981), 114-115.

[311] See Adrian A. Bantjes, As If Jesus Walked on Earth: Cardenismo, Sonora, and the Mexican Revolution (Wilmington: Scholarly Resources Books, 1998), "Introduction," for a summary of different views.

[312] Ibid, xvi.

[313] Ibid, 225.

[314] Ibid, 67.

[315] Ibid, 59-67, 210-211.

[316] Knight, "The rise and fall of Cardenismo," 285.

[317] Manuel A. Machado Jr., The North Mexican Cattle Industry, 1910-1975: Ideology, Conflict, and Change (College Station: Texas A&M University Press, 1981), 52-54; Adrian A. Bantjes, As If Jesus Walked on Earth, 132. Machado and Bantjes, citing the same source, provide different figures for the original limit but agree on the final figure.

[318] Heyman, Life and Labor on the Border, 37; Ismael Valencia Ortega, Cananea (Hermosillo: Centro Regional del Noroeste, Instituto Nacional de Antropología e Historia – SEP, Secretaria de Fomento Educativo y Cultura, 1984), 85.

[319] Bantjes, As If Jesus Walked on Earth, 98-99.

[320] Armando Bartra, Los Herederos de Zapata: Movimientos Campesinos Posrevoluciones en México. 1920-1980 (México: Ediciones Era, 1985), 22-24, 65.

[321] Bantjes, As If Jesus Walked on Earth, 98-99; Gerrit Huizer, "Peasant Organization in the Process of Agrarian Reform in Mexico," Studies in Comparative International Development, Vol. IV, No. 6 (1968-1969), 129.

[322] Bantjes, As If Jesus Walked on Earth, 224.

[323] Knight, "The rise and fall of Cardenismo, 302.

[324] Gerrit Huizer, La Lucha Campesina en México (México: Centro de Investigaciones Agrarias, 1970), 90-91.

[325] Sanderson, Agrarian Populism and the Mexican State, 141.

326 Huizer, "Peasant Organization in the Process of Agrarian Reform in Mexico," 134.
327 Peña y Trinidad Chávez, "Ganadería y agricultura en la sierra: 1929-1980," 491-492.
328 Huizer, "Peasant Organization in the Process of Agrarian Reform in Mexico," 139.
329 Peña y Trinidad Chávez, "Ganadería y agricultura en la sierra: 1929-1980," 492-493.
330 Ibid.
331 Sanderson, Agrarian Populism and the Mexican State, 156-157.
332 Among the radical leaders of a Sonoran affiliate of the CTM was longtime activist Jacinto López. López had been jailed, with several other CTM leaders, by Governor Yocupicio in 1938 in a dispute involving the reformed lands, or ejidos, of the Yaqui and Mayo Valleys. He went on to found his own party, the Popular Socialist Party (Partido Popular Socialista, PPS) and, in 1949, appeared to win the governorship of Sonora. The ruling party, by then refounded as the Institutional Revolutionary Party (Partido Revolucionario Institucional, PRI), imposed its candidate and repression followed, focusing on the ejidos of Sonora, Sanderson, Agrarian Populism and the Mexican State, 117, 139-140
333 Karl M. Schmitt, Communism in Mexico: A Study in Political Frustration (Austin: University of Texas Press, 1965), 180; Ibid; Centro de Investigaciones Agrarias, Comite Interamericano de Desarrollo Agricola, Estructura Agraria y Desarrollo Agrícola en México, 220; Gerrit Huizer, La Lucha Campesina en México, 94; Huizer, "Peasant Organization in the Process of Agrarian Reform in Mexico," 139; Peña y Trinidad Chávez, "Ganadería y agricultura en la sierra: 1929-1980," 492-493.
334 Schmitt, Communism in Mexico, 181.
335 Susan R. Walsh Sanderson, Land Reform in Mexico: 1910-1980 (Orlando: Academic Press, Inc., 1984) 149.
336 Lourdes Celis, Catherine Macotela, Rosario Rico, Victor M. Ruíz, and Elena Ulloa, historia de la acción pública: adolfo lópez mateos 1958-1964. I – las ideas (México: Fondo para la Historia de las ideas Revolucionarias en México, 1978), 191.
337 Sanderson, Agrarian Populism and the Mexican State, 157; Centro de Investigaciones Agrarias, Comite Interamericano de Desarrollo Agricola, Estructura Agraria y Desarrollo Agrícola en México, 220.
338 Wiswall to J.H. Morgan, July 11, 1950.
339 Minutes of Meeting, Bisbee Chamber of Commerce, National Parks and Monuments Committee, July 18, 1950, WACC, Folder H 14: Area Service and History 41-52 F3.
340 Wiswall to J.H. Morgan, July 11, 1950.
341 Emilio Segura, Jr., Secretary, Ranchos de Cananea, to Sparkes, Bisbee Chamber of Commerce, Ranchos de Cananea, June 18, 1951, WACC, Folder H 14: Area Service and History 41-52 F3.
342 Hillary A. Tolson to Margaret Rockwell, Washington, D.C., February 1, 1951, Ibid.
343 Tolson to Grace M. Sparkes, Washington, D.C., July 30, 1951, WACC, Folder H 18: Biographical Data F11.
344 Charles M. Morgan to Arizona Cattle Growers Association, Phoenix, May 8, 1940.
345 Minutes of Meeting, Bisbee Chamber of Commerce, National Parks and Monuments Committee, July 18, 1950.
346 Minutes of Meeting, Bisbee Chamber of Commerce, National Parks and Monuments Committee, December 8, 1950, WACC, Folder H 18: Biographical Data F11.
347 Minutes of the Arizona International Memorial Commission Meeting, February 24, 1951, WACC, Folder H 14: Area and Service History 41-52 F3.
348 Tolson to Sparkes, Washington, D.C., July 18, 1951, WACC, Folder H 18: Biographical Data F11.
349 Ibid.
350 Tolson to Paul A. Sexson, Executive, Office of the Governor, Washington, D.C., September 28, 1951, WACC, Folder H 14: Area and Service History 41-52 F3.
351 Tolson to Rockwell, Washington, D.C., February 1, 1951, Ibid.

352 Tolson to Assistant Secretary Davis, NPS, Washington, D.C., January 12, 1949, Ibid.
353 Tolson to Rockwell, February 1, 1951.
354 Sparkes to Hayden, Hereford, September 3, 1951, Hayden Papers, AC, ASU, Box 201, folder 3.
355 Hayden to Sparkes, January 2, 1952, WACC, Folder H 18: Biographical Data F11.
356 Letter, unidentified, NPS (probably Hillory Tolson), to Sparkes, Washington, D.C., March 19, 1952, Ibid.
357 Alden Richard. Longwell, The Cananea Ejidos: From Private Ranch to Collective in Sonora (Ph.D. Dissertation: University of Nebraska, 1974), 141-145.
358 Odd S. Halseth, to Sparkes, Phoenix, July 21, 1951, WACC, Folder H 18: Biographical Data F11.
359 "Last Testament Upheld Here, Suit to Break Will of Greene's Wife Denied," April 2, 1952.
360 Seis Años de Política Agraria del Presidente Adolfo López Mateos, 2. Mexican President Adolfo López Mateos, Seis Años de Política Agraria del Presidente Adolfo López Mateos (México: Departamento de Asuntos Agrarios y Colonización, 1964), 2.
361 Larry Dale, "The Coronado International Memorial Project," n.d., WACC, Folder H 14: Area and Service History, General F6.
362 Minutes of Meeting, Bisbee Chamber of Commerce, National Parks and Monuments Committee, December 8, 1950.
363 Regional Director, NPS, to Director, NPS, Santa Fe, December 14, 1950, Hayden Papers, AC, ASU, Box 201, folder 3.
364 Aubrey Neasham, to Tolson, San Francisco, March 26, 1952, WACC, Folder H 18: Biographical Data F11.
365 Tolson to Pyle, Washington, D.C., May 9, 1952, Hayden Papers, AC, ASU, Box 201, folder 3.
366 Sparkes to Hayden, Prescott, August 20, 1952, Hayden Papers, AC, ASU, Box 201, folder 3.
367 Hayden to Sparkes, Washington, D.C., June 3, 1954, Hayden Papers, AC, ASU, Box 537, folder 30.
368 Hayden to Folson Moore, Editor Bisbee Daily Review, June 3, 1954, Hayden Papers, AC, ASU, Box 537, folder 30.
369 Sparkes to Hayden, June 5, 1954, Hayden Papers, AC, ASU, Box 537, folder 30.
370 Hayden to Sparkes, June 9, 1954, Hayden Papers, AC, ASU, Box 537, folder 30.
371 Hayden to Sparkes, June 29, 1954, Hayden Papers, AC, ASU, Box 537, folder 30.
372 Luis A. Gastellum to Sparkes, October 15, 1954, D18, Master Plans [1954] F2.pdf, WACC, Archives CD Box 3.
373 Ibid.
374 Ibid.
375 Ibid.
376 Burroughs to Sparkes, Flagstaff, November 5, 1954, D18, Master Plans [1954] F2.pdf, WACC, Archives CD Box 3.
377 Gastellum to Burroughs, Memorandum, Globe, November 9, 1954, D18, Master Plans [1954] F2.pdf, WACC, Archives CD Box 3.
378 Sparkes to Burroughs, Hereford, November 12, 1954, D18, Master Plans [1954] F2.pdf, WACC, Archives CD Box 3.
379 Sparkes to Tolson, November 10, 1954, D18, Master Plans [1954] F2.pdf, WACC, Archives CD Box 3.
380 Tolson to Sparkes, November 17, 1954, D18, Master Plans [1954] F3.pdf, WACC, Archives CD Box 3.
381 Ibid.
382 Master Plan Development Outline, Coronado National Memorial, General Information Section, p. 3, D 18 Master Plans [1954] F3.pdf, WACC, Archives CD Box 3.
383 Ibid., Interpretation Section, p. 7.
384 Ibid., Interpretation Section, p. 2.

[385] Ibid., Interpretation Section, p. 6.
[386] Ibid.
[387] Ibid., Interpretation Section, p. 5.
[388] Ibid., Interpretation Section, p. 6.
[389] Ibid., Interpretation Section, p. 4.
[390] Ibid., Interpretation Section, p. 5.
[391] Ibid., Development Section 4a2, p. 1.
[392] Ibid.
[393] Ibid.
[394] Ibid.
[395] General Superintendent, SWNM to Chief, Western Office, Division of Design and Construction, August 10, 1954, D18, Master Plans [1954] F2.pdf, WACC, Archives CD Box 3.
[396] Ibid.
[397] Ibid., Development, p. 5
[398] Ibid.
[399] Ray B. Ringenbach, Superintendent, Tumacacori to John M. Davis, General Superintendent, Tumacacori, April 27, 1954, D18, Master Plans [1954] F2.pdf, WACC, Archives CD Box 3.
[400] Hillory A. Tolson, Acting Director, NPS, to Senator Barry Goldwater, Washington, D.C., September 6, 1955; Tolson to Hayden August 26, 1955, WACC, Folder H 14: Area & Service History 50s F5.
[401] Hayden to Tolson, August 1, 1955, Hayden Papers, AC, ASU, Box 537, folder 30.
[402] Nogales Petitioners to Hayden, Nogales, May 24, 1955, AC, ASU, Box 537, folder 30. Among the signers were Ross Middleton, J.E. McDonald, Sr., E.H. McClanahan, Arnold Arvizu, Howard Morgan, H.J. Brunswicker, Mrs. Jeanne Immoff, Mrs. Ross Middleton, Mr. Paige B. Forman, Jr., E. Burger, F.C. Stephenson, Mr. and Mrs. Robert Henley, Betty Rae Hart, Joe D. Warren, Mrs. E.W. Siddell, Ernest Morton, and N. Chamberlain.
[403] Tolson to Hayden, Washington, D.C., August 25, 1955, Hayden Papers, AC, ASU, Box 537, folder 30.
[404] Anderson to Congressman John R. Murdock, October 10, 1939, University of New Mexico Archives, Box 1.
[405] Murdock to Anderson, Washington, D.C., October 6, 1939, University of New Mexico Archives, Box 1.
[406] Hayden to Mr. And Mrs. Ross Middleton, Washington, D.C., September 2, 1955, Hayden Papers, AC, ASU, Box 537, folder 30.
[407] Hayden to Mrs. Jeanne Imhoff, September 2, 1955, Hayden Papers, AC, ASU, Box 537, folder 30.
[408] Twenty eight petitioners to Barry Goldwater, June 6, 1955, Hayden Papers, AC, ASU, Box 537, folder 30.
[409] Ibid.
[410] Halseth to Hayden, Phoenix, October 7, 1955, Hayden Papers, AC, ASU, Box 537, folder 30.
[411] Sparkes to Tolson, Hereford, September 12, 1955, Hayden Papers, AC, ASU, Box 537, folder 30.
[412] Ibid.
[413] Moore to Hayden, Bisbee, October 12, 1955, Hayden Papers, AC, ASU, Box 537, folder 30.
[414] Carroll A. Burroughs, Acting Superintendent, Coronado National Memorial, to General Superintendent, July 21, 1955, WACC, Folder H 14: Area & Service History 50s F5.
[415] Ibid.
[416] Chamber of Commerce Newsletter, Bisbee, May 31, 1955, Hayden Papers , AC, ASU, Box 537, folder 30.
[417] Sparkes to Hayden, Bisbee, February 11, 1957, Hayden Papers, AC, ASU, Box 537, folder 30.
[418] Wirth to Hayden, Washington, D.C., March 1, 1957, Hayden Papers AC, ASU, Box 537, folder 30.

[419] Memorandum, Superintendent, CORO to Regional Director, SWR, Hereford, February 27, 1958, Hayden Papers, AC, ASU, Box 537, folder 30.

[420] Folsom Moore to Hayden, Bisbee, February 28, 1958, Hayden Papers, AC, ASU, Box 537, folder 30. The text of his letter is as follows: Yesterday, I went with Wilkins of the Phoenix office, Bureau of Public Roads, Jacob Erickson of the same office and Bill Willey, to the Coronado National Memorial.

After we had gone to the top, we stopped at the Superintendent's office and had a look at his maps, and discussed with him the plans of the Park Service pertaining to the Memorial. My purpose in taking these men to the Memorial was to give them an idea of the urgent necessity of road construction form the Forest Boundary to the parking area in Montezuma Pass.

Mr. Philip Welles, the Superintendent of the Memorial, showed us the land recently acquired by the Park Service for the erection of permanent buildings, and told us that contracts were called for opening on March 17th, for an aerial survey of that particular ground.

I asked Mr. Welles if it would be possible to have the park Service extend the aerial survey to cover the canon from the Forest Boundary to the western end of the Memorial limits on the west slope of Huachuca mountains. He demurred, saying that he doubted seriously whether the Park Service would want to spend more money that for the survey of the ground on which it is planned to begin erection of permanent buildings.

Then, I asked that he write the Regional Director at Albuquerque about the matter, and that he send me a copy of his letter.

Since the Park Service is bringing in an aerial survey party for the small survey outlined in the call for bids, it would seem to me that the same survey party could make the survey of the road—at least to the Pass—for but little more expenditure.

…..Would you be good enough to contact the Park Service immediately, asking that they obtain the services of the successful bidder at the March 17 opening….It will speed the possibility of road construction at least five years. And it should be of material benefit in the laying out of trails, a labor which is now being done by Memorial personnel on foot.

[421] Township 24 south, range 20 east, section 10, south half southwest quarter, south half southeast quarter; section 11, south half, southwest quarter; section 13, southwest quarter northwest quarter, south half; section 14, northwest quarter, south half, northwest quarter northeast quarter, south half northeast quarter; section 15, all; section 23, all; section 24, all; township 24 south, range 21 east, section 17, south half southwest quarter; section 18, southwest quarter, south half southeast quarter; section 19, all; section 20, lots 3 and 4; aggregating approximately two thousand eight hundred and eighty acres.

[422] Rickard E. Klinck, "In the Land of Coronado," Arizona Highways (September 1957), p. 35.

[423] Ibid. p. 35-36.

[424] Ibid. p. 36.

[425] Ibid. p. 37.

[426] Ibid, p. 37.

[427] Master Plan for the Conservation and Use of Coronado National Memorial (1961), "Park Organization Brief," Vol. I, Chapter 3, p. 3, WACC, Folder D 18: Master Plans (Mission 66) F1.

[428] Mission 66 for Coronado National Memorial, National Park Service, United States Department of the Interior (1957), p. 2, WACC, Folder D 18: Master Plans (Mission 66) F1.

[429] Ibid.

[430] Ibid.

[431] Ibid.

[432] Ibid., p. 3.

[433] Ibid., p. 3.

434 Memorandum from W.G. Carnes, Chief, Mission 66 Staff to Regional Director, Region Three, Washington, D.C., October 1, 1957, WACC, Folder D 18: Master Plans (Mission 66) F1.

435 Wirth to Regional Director, Region Three, Memorandum, May 15, 1957, Washington, D.C., WACC, Folder D 18: Master Plans (Mission 66) F1.

436 Notice of Approval Coronado National Memorial signed by Conrad Wirth, Washington, D.C., May 15, 1957, p. 1. WACC, Folder D 18: Master Plans (Mission 66) F1.

437 Ibid., p. 2.

438 Ibid., p. 2.

439 Ibid., p. 2.

440 Mission 66 Prospectus, Coronado National Memorial, April 1956, p. 2.

441 Ibid., p. 3.

442 Ibid., p. 3.

443 Master Plan Development Outline, Coronado National Memorial, Arizona, Land Status, March 1957, WACC, Folder D 18: Master Plans (Mission 66) F1.

444 Ibid.

445 Ibid., see marginal noted signed by Reshoft dated 5-1-57.

446 Master Plan, May 1957, Buildings, p. 2, WACC, Folder D 18: Master Plans (Mission 66) F1..

447 Master Plan for Preservation and Use of Coronado National Memorial, Volume III—General Park Information Section G—Construction Data, May 1963, p. 3, WACC, Folder D 18: Master Plans (Mission 66) F1. Also see Completion Report of Construction Project, Contract 14-10-333-509, Signed by Philip Welles, Superintendent, Coronado National Memorial, n.d., WACC, Folder D 3415: Buildings Constructon and Maintenance 1960 F25.

448 Ibid.

449 Telephone interview with former NPS Intermountain Regional Director John Cook, Page, Arizona, by Joseph P. Sánchez, Jerry L. Gurulé, and Bruce Erickson, February 6, 2002.

450 Master Plan, May 1957, p. 4.

451 Ibid., Soil and Moister Conservation (S&MC) section, p. 2

452 Master Plan for the Preservation and Use of Coronado National Memorial, Arizona, Chapter 5 Design Analysis, General Development and Developed Areas, Revised 1964 (from 1961, 1962 and 1963 plans), p. 2, WACC, Folder D 18: Master Plans (Mission 66) F1.

453 Ibid.

454 Ibid.

455 Ibid., p. 2; also see p. 5.

456 Ibid., p. 4.

457 Ibid., p. 2.

458 Ibid., p. 4.

459 Ibid.

460 Ibid.

461 Construction Data report, Volume III, Section G, p. 3, WACC, Folder D 18: Master Plans (Mission 66) F1..

462 Ibid., p. 5.

463 Master Plan for the Conservation and Use of Coronado National Memorial (1961), "Objectives and Policies", Vol. I, Chapter 1, p. 6.

464 Ibid., p. 6.

465 Ibid., p. 6.

466 Hillary A. Tolson, Assistant Director, NPS, to Mrs. Margaret Rockwell, Washigton, D.C., February 1, 1951, WACC, Folder H 14: Area and Service History 41-52 F3.

467 Gus R. Michaels to Frank Pinkley, Bisbee, April 3, 1936, WACC, Folder H 14: Area and Service History 1939 F1.

468 Coronado Cuarto Centennial Commission of Arizona, Secretary's Report of Progress, Phoenix, February 17, 1940, WACC, Folder H 14: Area and Service History 1940 F2.

[469] Mrs. Clyda F. Markhama and Fr. Martin Knauf, O.F.M., Director, Third Order of St. Francis, to Bisbee Chamber of Commerce, c/o F.C. Bledsoe, Phoenix, February 1, 1938, WACC, Folder H 14: Area History de Niza F8.

[470] Bledsoe to M.J. Cunningham, John Wood, Rev. J. Davis, S.S. Shattuck, Folsom Moore, John Ball, Mrs. Macia, Bisbee, March 28, 1938, ibid.

[471] Minutes of the "Meeting of the Fray Marco de Niza Association Held in Bisbee Chamber of Commerce on April Fourth at 10:00 A.M.," ibid.

[472] Michaels to Plans and Designs Division, State Parks, Tucson, Bisbee, April 8, 1938, ibid.

[473] Minutes of the "Meeting of Four Hundredth Anniversary Committee, Held August Ninth, Bisbee Chamber of Commerce Office, at 10:30 P.M.," ibid.

[474] Minutes of the "Meeting of the Marco de Niza Monument Committee, November 3, at 9:30 A.M.," ibid.

[475] Fr. Bonaventure Oblasser, O.F.M., Executive Secretary, Fray Marcos de Niza Monument Association, Mission San Antonio de Pala, March 3, 1941, to Michaels, ibid.

[476] Oblasser to The Secretary, Bisbee Chamber of Commerce, Komatke, February 27, 1941, ibid.

[477] George Brown, interview by Thomas B. Carroll, September 20, 1974, CORO Files; Byrd Howell Granger, Arizona's Names (X Marks the Place) (The Falconer Publishing Company, 1983), 367-368.

[478] Oblasser to The Secretary, Bisbee Chamber of Commerce, Komatke, February 27, 1941.

[479] Michaels to Oblasser, Bisbee, March 26, 1941, ibid.

[480] Grace M. Sparkes to Arthur R. Williams, American Consul, Agua Prieta, Hereford, March 19, 1951, WACC, Folder H 14: Area and Service History 41-52 F3.

[481] Hayden to W.E. Clark, Clerk, Cochise County Board of Supervisors, April 22, 1940, WACC, Folder H 14: Area and Service History 1940 F2.

[482] "Cuarto Centennial Commission Named By Governor Jones," Arizona Republic, July 27, 1939; Charles M. Morgan's Autobiographical Notes, WACC, Folder H 14: Area and Service History 1939 F1.

[483] Tolson, Acting Director, NPS, to Hayden, Chicago, September 6, 1944, WACC, Folder H 14: Area and Service History 41-52 F3.

[484] "State Advisory Board Selected for Coronado Anniversary," Press Release, Coronado Cuarto Centennial Commission of Arizona, Phoenix, August 11, 1939, ibid.

[485] "Charles M. Morgan Interview, May 14, 1974, Phoenix, AZ," by Tom White, WACC, Folder H 14: Area and Service History F7.

[486] Charles M. Morgan to Superintendent, Coronado National Monument, Tucson, December 11, 1975, WACC, Folder L 76: Environmental Impact/Assessment – Public Response 1975 F53.

[487] "Charles M. Morgan Interview, May 14, 1974, Phoenix, AZ."

[488] "Cuarto Centennial Commission Named By Governor Jones," July 27, 1939.

[489] "State Advisory Board Selected for Coronado Anniversary," August 11, 1939.

[490] "Notes for the Gazette," n.d. (seems to go with "Secretary's Report of Progress," Coronado Cuarto Centennial Commission of Arizona, Phoenix, February 17, 1940), WACC, Folder H 14: Area and Service History 1940 F2.

[491] "Coronado Events in Arizona," dated 1540-1940 (can also be identified as no later than 1940 by some of the officials listed in United States Coronado Exposition Commission), ibid.

[492] Ibid.

[493] Ethel M. Macia to Gus Michaels, February 11, 1940, WACC, Folder H 14: Area and Service History 1940 F2.

[494] Sparkes to Williams, March 19, 1951.

[495] Macia to Michaels, February 11, 1940.

[496] Sparkes to Williams, March 19, 1951.

[497] Sparkes to Williams, March 19, 1951.

498 Michaels to Aubrey Neasham, Bisbee, February 29, 1940, WACC, Folder H 14: Area and Service History 1940 F2.
499 Morgan to Secretaries, Chambers of Commerce, Bisbee, Douglas, Nogales, Tombstone, Tucson, Phoenix, February 29, 1940, ibid.
500 Michaels to M.J. Cunningham, John Wood, Rev. James P. Davis, S.S. Shattuck, Folsom Moore, John Ball and Mrs. J.H. Macia, Bisbee, March 1, 1940, WACC, Folder H 14: Area and Service History 1940 F2.
501 Telegram, W.K. Caley, S.S. Shattuck, M.J. Cunningham, to Hayden, n.d., ibid.
502 Sparkes gave the date of this delegation as March 6, but the evidence suggests that it visited on March 5. Sparkes to Williams, March 19, 1951.
503 Caley, Shattuck, Cunningham, to Hayden, n.d.
504 Michaels to Fred Guirey, Arizona Highway Department, March 6, 1940, WACC, Folder H 14: Area and Service History 1940 F2.
505 Morgan to Michaels, Phoenix, April 30, 1940, ibid.
506 Michaels to Morgan, Bisbee, May 7, 1940, ibid.
507 Michaels to Mrs. J.M. Keith, Secretary, Arizona Cattle Growers' Association, Bisbee, May 7, 1940, ibid. Michaels addressed his letter to "Mrs. A. Keith" and signed his letter "G.R. Michaels," Mrs. J.M. Keith's reply was addressed to "J.R. Michaels," Keith to Michaels, Phoenix, May 11, 1940, ibid.
508 Michaels to Keith, May 7, 1940.
509 Senator Carl Hayden to Keith, May 16, 1940, ibid.
510 Keith to Morgan, May 9, 1940, ibid.
511 Keith to Michaels, Phoenix, May 11, 1940, ibid.
512 Keith to Morgan, May 9, 1940, ibid.
513 Paul Roca to Folsom Moore, Washington, D.C., June 28, 1940, ibid.
514 Italics added, Clark to Hayden, Bisbee, June 21, 1970, ibid.
515 Hayden to Cunningham, Washington, D.C., July 31, 1940; Hayden to Caley, Washington, D.C., July 31, 1940; Hayden to Shattuck, Washington, D.C., July 31, 1940, ibid.
516 Michaels to Rockwell, Bisbee, October 26, 1941, WACC, Folder H 14: Area and Service History 41-52 F3.
517 E.T. Scoyen Acting Regional Director, NPS, to Michaels, Santa Fe, June 8, 1944, ibid.
518 Sparkes to Hayden, State of Texas Mine, October 25, 1947, ibid.
519 Sparkes to Moody, Prescott, January 30, 1939, Sparkes Collection, Arizona Historical Society (AHS), Box 7, Folder 294.
520 Moody to Sparkes, Los Angeles, August 1, 1941, Sparkes Collection, AHS, Box 7, Folder 296, and others in the same folder.
521 Sparkes to Moody, April 22, 1940, Sparkes Collection AHS, Box 7 Folder 295, and others in the same folder.
522 Sparkes, to Rockwell, Prescott, April 11, 1940, Sparkes Collection, AHS, Box 23, Folder 956.
523 Sparkes to Moody, April 7, 1942, Sparkes Collection, AHS, Box 7, Folder 297. The Montezuma Canyon Road was built from 1933 to 1935, Laurel Dale, Superintendent, Coronado National Memorial, to Thomas Mulhern, Historic Preservation, Western Regional Office, Hereford, February 23, 1976, Re: Historic Structures at Coronado National Memorial, CORO Files. George Brown is given as the main source of information for this report.
524 Danny Freeman, Chairman, Centennial Book, Prescott, to Laurel Bale [sic - Dale], Prescott, August 20, 1985, WACC, Folder K 14: Information Requests F1.
525 Erna Fergusson, Our Southwest (New York: Alfred A. Knopf, 1940), 181-188.
526 Mona Lange McCroskey, Grace Marion Sparkes: Matriarch of the Early Arizona Tourist Industry (M.A. Thesis, Arizona State University, 1987), 66-67.
527 Tolson to Hayden, Chicago, May 27, 1944, WACC, Folder H 14: Area and Service History 41-52 F3.

[528] Hayden to Sparkes, September 9, 1944, WACC, Folder H 18: Biographical Data F11; Hayden to Sparkes, Washington, D.C., January 2, 1945, WACC, Folder H 14: Area and Service History 41-52 F3.
[529] McCroskey, Grace Marion Sparkes, 116-117.
[530] Ibid, 136-137.
[531] Ibid, 139.
[532] Peter M. Van Cleve, "History of Mining in the Coronado National Memorial" (1997), pp. 2-8, Coronado National Memorial Files.
[533] McCroskey, Grace Marion Sparkes, 140.
[534] Hayden to Sparkes, January 3, 1946; Tolson to Sparkes, Chicago, October 25, 1946, WACC, Folder H 18: Biographical Data F11.
[535] Sparkes to Hayden, October 25, 1947.
[536] Ibid.
[537] Ibid.
[538] Sparkes to Hayden, State of Texas Mine, June 28, 1947, ibid.
[539] Tolson to Hayden, Washington, D.C., March 11, 1949, WACC, Folder H 18: Biographical Data F11.
[540] Odd S. Halseth to Sparkes, Phoenix, July 21, 1951, ibid.
[541] Governor Dan E. Garvey to Sparkes, Phoenix, December 9, 1950, ibid.
[542] Minutes of Meeting, Bisbee Chamber of Commerce, National Parks and Monuments Committee, December 8, 1950, ibid; "After Many Years of Effort, Coronado National Memorial Becomes Reality Long Dreamed," Bisbee Daily Review, July 20, 1952, n.p., Hayden Papers, AC, ASU, Box 201, Folder 3.
[543] M.R. Tillotson, Regional Director, NPS, to Governor Howard Pyle, Santa Fe, February 6, 1951, ibid.
[544] Pyle to Sparkes, Phoenix, March 9, 1951, ibid.
[545] "After Many Years of Effort, Coronado National Memorial Becomes Reality Long Dreamed."
[546] George Brown, interview by Barbara Alberti, August 18, 1998; Bart Barbour, "Dude Ranches at Coronado National Memorial: A Brief History," n.d., CORO Files.
[547] Barbour, "Dude Ranches," from Tracking Book, Cochise County Assessor's Office, Bisbee, Arizona; Quit-Claim Deed, Frank Zaleski to Jose Zaleski, Signed January 3, 1956, CCR, Deeds of Real Estate, Docket 142, pages 239-241.
[548] Carroll A. Burroughs, Acting Superintendent, Coronado National Memorial, to General Superintendent, July 21, 1955, WACC, Folder L 14: Area & Service History 50s F5.
[549] Grace Sparkes, "Coronado National Memorial Report," Feruary 13, 1957, WACC, Folder H 14: Area and Service History 1940 F2.
[550] Untitled, undated, copy of Congressional debate on bill, H.R. 7553, WACC, Folder H 18: Biographical Data, General F11.
[551] Senator Carl Hayden to Grace Sparkes, Washington, D.C., July 2, 1954, ibid.
[552] Ray Ringenbach, Superintendent, Tumacacori National Monument, to Grace Sparkes, October 24, 1954, Tumacacori; Sparkes to Ringenbach, November 16, 1954, ibid
[553] Ray B. Ringenbach, Superintendent, Tumacacori National Monument, to Grace Sparkes, Tumacacori, August 10, 1954, ibid.
[554] Sparkes to Ringenbach, Prescott, July 7, 1954, ibid.
[555] John M. Davis, General Superintendent, Southwestern National Monuments, NPS, to Sparkes, Globe, November 17, 1954, ibid.
[556] Davis to Sparkes, Globe, November 23, 1954, ibid.
[557] D.D. Crumley, Chief Clerk, Southwestern National Monuments, NPS, to Sparkcs, Globe, December 7, 1954; Lease between Grace M. Sparkes and the United States of America, January 1, 1955, ibid.
[558] Purchase Order, July 12, 1957, ibid.

559 Memorandums to Acting Superintendent Don Jackson, Coronado National Memorial, February 13 to March 6, 1960, WACC, Folder A 26: Reports, daily logs 1960 F3.

560 Philip Welles, Superintendent, Coronado National Memorial, to Sparkes, Hereford, May 15, 1959, WACC, Folder H 18: Biographical Data, General F11.

561 Department of the Interior, Notice of Appointment, Grace M. Sparkes, Effective 9/11/55, ibid.

562 Daily Report, Sparkes to Welles, Coronado National Memorial, March 30, 1958, WACC, Folder A 26: Reports, Daily Logs 57,58 F1.

563 McCroskey, *Grace Marion Sparkes*, 144.

564 Superintendent, Coronado, to Director, NPS, Narrative Report for September 1963, Hereford, October 1, 1973, WACC, Folder A 2615: Monthly Reports F6.

565 Superintendent, Coronado, to Director, NPS, Narrative Report for October 1963, Hereford, October 28, 1973, ibid.

566 Notice of Appointment, Philip Welles, as member of the Coronado International Monument Commission of Arizona, March 15, 1965, WACC, Folder H 14: Area and Service History 50-69 F4.

567 George P. Hammond and Agapito Rey (eds.), *Narratives of the Coronado Expedition 1540-1542* (Albuquerque: University of New Mexico Press, 1940), 7.

568 Superintendent, Coronado, to Director, NPS, February, 1962, Monthly Narrative Report, Hereford, February 27, 1962, WACC, Folder A 2615: Monthly Reports F6.

569 Letterhead of "The Coronado International Monument Commission of Arizona," dated March 15, 1967, WACC, Folder H 14: Area and Service History 50-69 F4.

570 Unsigned letter, Welles to D. Tenny Lemoreaux, Bisbee, September 20, 1965, ibid.

571 "Plan Memorial with Mexico," unidentified newspaper clipping, ca. October 14, 1965; John H. McCarroll to Welles, Wickenburg, August 16, 1965, ibid.

572 Philip Welles to Mrs. Margaret Adams Rockwell, Bisbee, August 12, 1965, ibid.

573 Welles to Rockwell, September 23, 1965, ibid.

574 Welles to Governor Samuel P. Goddard, Bisbee, October 18, 1965, ibid.

575 Fernando Pesqueira to Welles, Hermosillo, November 24, 1965; Héctor Sánchez Encinas to Welles, Hermosillo, October 21, 1966, ibid.

576 Welles to Governor Raul H. Castro, Tucson, January 20, 1976, WACC, Folder L 62: International Parks F51.

577 Welles to Governor Jack Williams, December 12, 1969, WACC, Folder H 14: Area and Service History 50-69 F4.

578 Dale to Ben Avery, Hereford, January 2, 1976, WACC, Folder H 14: Area and Service History General F6.

579 Ibid.

580 John Clay, General Superintendent, Southern Arizona Group, NPS, to Regional Director, Western Region, NPS, Phoenix, March 24, 1976, ibid.

581 "Cochise County overlooked," Bisbee Review, March 18, 1976, 2, WACC, Folder L 62: International Parks F51; John L. Myers, *The Arizona Governors 1912-1990* (Phoenix: Heritage Publishers, Inc., 1989), 139.

582 Thomas B. Carroll, Interpretative Specialist, to Superintendent, Coronado National Memorial, Hereford, October 3, 1976, WACC, Folder L 62: International Parks F51.

583 Robert C. Milne, Chief, International Park Affairs Division, NPS, to Associate Regional Director, Operations, Western Region, NPS, October 28, 1977, ibid.

584 Bernard L. Fontana, Chairman, Coronado International Monument Commission , to Sergio Bribiesca E., Phoenix, November 18, 1977, ibid.

585 Fontana to Governor Bruce Babbit, Phoenix, June 2, 1978, ibid.

586 Fontana to Rosalynn Carter, February 21, 1978, WACC, Folder A 8215: Special Events F9.

587 Fontana to Dale, Tucson, August 24, 1977, ibid.

588 Ibid; Fontana to Carter, February 21, 1978.

589 James Officer to Dale, Tucson, October 3, 1982, WACC, Folder A 8215: Special Events F15.
590 "Charles M. Morgan Interview, May 14, 1974, Phoenix, AZ," by Tom White
591 E.B. Sayles, The San Simon Branch: Excavations at Cave Creek in the San Simon Valley. I. Material Culture, Medallion Papers, No. XXXIV (Globe, Arizona: Gila Pueblo, 1945), iv; Jay J. Wagoner, Early Arizona: Prehistory to Civil War (Tucson: The University of Arizona Press, 1975), 11-13.
592 Harold Sterling Gladwin, Excavations at Snaketown. IV. Reviews and Conclusions, Medallion Papers, No. XXXVIII (Globe, Arizona: Gila Pueblo, 1948), 127-131.
593 Yvonne G. Stewart, "Montane Cochise Culture Sites in Coronado National Memorial," Proceedings of the First Conference on Scientific Research in the National Parks, Volume II, New Orleans, Louisiana, November 9-12, 1976, Edited by Robert M. Linn; Sponsored by National Park Service and American Institute of Biological Sciences. Washington, D.C.: United States Department of the Interior, National Park Service Transactions and Proceedings Series, Number 5, 1979, CORO MAX 1 - Archeology, Folder 75a: Archeological Survey, CORO Files.
594 Carr Tuthill, The Tres Alamos Site on the San Pedro River, Southeastern Arizona (Dragoon, Arizona: The Amerind Foundation, Inc., 1947), 15,83-86; Charles C. Di Peso, The Babocomari Village Site on the Babocomari River, Southeastern Arizona (Dragoon, Arizona: The Amerind Foundation, Inc., 1951), 224-241; Charles C. Di Peso, The Sobaipuri Indians of the Upper San Pedro River Valley, Southeastern Arizona (Dragoon: The Amerind Foundation, Inc., 1953), 1-4.
595 Archeologist, Division of Archeology, Western Archeological and Conservation Center (WACC), to Chief, Division of Archeology, WACC, Tucson, December 10, 1990, CORO MAX 1 - Archeology, Folder 90a: Montezuma Cave Artifacts, CORO Files.
596 Harold Sterling Gladwin, A History of the Ancient Southwest (Portland, Maine: The Bond Wheelwright Company, 1957), 337.
597 Di Peso, The Babocomari Village Site on the Babocomari River, 5,239.
598 Di Peso, The Sobaipuri Indians of the Upper San Pedro River Valley, 263-268.
599 Francisco R. Almada, Diccionario de historia, geografía y biografía sonorense (Hermosillo: Instituto Sonorense de Cultura, 1990), 612.
600 Herbert Eugene Bolton, Rim of Christendom: a Biography of Eusebio Francisco Kino, Pacific Coast Pioneer (New York: The MacMillan Company, 1936), 248,n.2; 269. There has been inconsistency between authors in the placement of accents in the name of the Sobaipuri and their village, Quiburi; following Di Peso, neither name is accented here.
601 James E. Officer, Hispanic Arizona, 1536-1856 (Tucson: The University of Arizona Press, 1987), 31.
602 Harry J. Karns (trans.), Unknown Arizona and Sonora 1693-1721: From the Francisco Fernández del Castillo version of Luz de Tierra Incógnita by Captain Juan Mateo Manje. An English Translation of Part II (Tucson: Arizona Silhouettes, 1954), 74-75.
603 Herbert Eugene Bolton, Rim of Christendom, 266-269.
604 Karns, Unknown Arizona and Sonora 1693-1721, 77-79.
605 Di Peso, The Sobaipuri Indians of the Upper San Pedro River Valley, 26,55-63.
606 Karns, Unknown Arizona and Sonora 1693-1721, 79-83.
607 Di Peso, The Sobaipuri Indians of the Upper San Pedro River Valley, 32,41.
608 John L. Kessell, "The Puzzling Presidio: San Phelipe de Guevavi, Alias Terrenate," New Mexico Historical Review, XLI:1 (January 1966):38-39; Di Peso, The Sobaipuri Indians of the Upper San Pedro River Valley, 35.
609 Vito Alessio Robles (ed.), Nicolás de Lafora, relación del viaje que hizo a los presidios internos situados en la frontera de la América septentrional (México D.F.: Editorial Pedro Robredo, 1939), 124-125.
610 "Itinerario de el sr. Marques de Rubi Mariscal de Campo de los exercitos de S.M. en la Inspeccion que de Su Rl. orden hizo de los Presidios internos de esta Nva. españa en

1766 hasta 1768," Thorn Family Spanish Colonial Documents Collection, The Center for American History, The University of Texas at Austin.

[611] John P. Wilson, Islands in the Desert: A History of the Uplands of Southeastern Arizona (Albuquerque: University of New Mexico Press, in cooperation with the Historical Society of New Mexico, 1995), 158.

[612] J.J. Bowden, Private Land Claims in the Southwest, (Thesis for degree of Master of Laws in Oil and Gas, Southern Methodist University, 1969), II:1927-1937.

[613] Ibid, 1910-1926.

[614] Ibid, 1881-1898.

[615] Ibid, 1917-1926.

[616] Jay J. Wagoner, Early Arizona, 192-197; Sonnichsen, Colonel Greene and the Copper Skyrocket, 237-239;290,n.14. The complex saga of San Rafael de la Zanja Grant is worthy of a chapter of its own; for a summary, see Bowden, Private Land Claims in the Southwest, 1819-1830.

[617] Wagoner, Early Arizona, 192-197.

[618] One local source recalled that Ratliff arrived in the late 1890s, George Brown, interview by Thomas B. Carroll, September 20, 1974; another thought it was about 1885, Buck D'Albini, "Presentation," n.d., CORO Files.

[619] George Brown, 1974.

[620] Buck D'Albini, "Presentation"

[621] Cochise Chapter of The Arizona Archeological Society, "The Ratliff Ranch: A Chronology," n.d., CORO Files.

[622] Laurel Dale, Superintendent, Coronado National Memorial, to Thomas Mulhern, Historic Preservation, Western Regional Office, Hereford, February 23, 1976, Re: Historic Structures at Coronado National Memorial, Ibid; George Brown is given as the main source of information for this report.

[623] Approval of field notes of Homestead Entry Survey No. 311, Office of the U.S. Surveyor General, Phoenix, Arizona, August 8, 1917, Ibid.

[624] Approval of field notes of Homestead Entry Survey No. 310, Office of the U.S. Surveyor General, Phoenix, Az., August 8, 1917, Ibid.

[625] Sketch map of homestead claims, n.d., Ibid.

[626] Jack Ratliff, interview by Sandra Tate and Ellen Bolduc, n.d., Ibid.

[627] Cochise Chapter of The Arizona Archeological Society, "The Ratliff Ranch," n.d.

[628] Application for Second Entry, John Pyeatt, U.S. Land Office, Phoenix, Arizona, June 4, 1917, WACC, Folder L 1425: Land Holdings – Pyeatt F6; Bart Barbour, "Dude Ranches at Coronado National Memorial: A Brief History," n.d., CORO Files.

[629] Testimonies of Witnesses Zeno Aston and Robert Fourr, Homestead Entry, Final Proof, April 14, 1921, WACC, Folder L 1425: Land Holdings – Pyeatt F6; Homestead Entry Application, John Pyeatt, Received U.S. Land Office, Phoenix, Arizona, WACC, Folder L 1425: Land Holdings – Pyeatt F6.

[630] Office of the Acting Secretary of Agriculture to Office of the Secretary of the Interior, Washington, D.C., December 27, 1913, Ibid.

[631] Application for Amendment, Cornelius N. Driscoll, September 23, 1914, WACC, Folder L 1425: Land Holdings – Driscoll F7.

[632] Final Certificate, Homestead, John Pyeatt, Approved June 29, 1921, WACC, Folder L 1425: Land Holdings – Pyeatt F6; Barbour, "Dude Ranches."

[633] Jack Ratliff, interview by Sandra Tate and Ellen Bolduc, n.d., CORO Files

[634] Rufus D'Albini, interview by Peter Van Cleve, December 3, 1997; Buck D'Albini, "Presentation;" Jack Ratliff, n.d.; Barbour, "Dude Ranches;" George Brown, interview by Barbara Alberti, August 18, 1998, Ibid.

[635] Barbour, "Dude Ranches;" George Brown 1998.

[636] Betty Peterson-Stowe and Frank Peterson, interview by Donna B. Bertolini and Scott Sticha, July 16, 1999, CORO Files.
[637] Barbour, "Dude Ranches."
[638] Field Notes, Coronado National Forest, Elmer L. Hertel, March 3, 1915, WACC, Folder L 1425: Land Holdings – Kudzmi F8.
[639] Notice of Publication, Simon Kudzmi, August 29, 1929; Testimony of Claimant, Simon Kudzmi, Final Proof, December 28, 1929; Testimonies of Witnesses William Norick and Joseph Zaleski, Homestead Entry, Final Proof, December 28, 1929, Ibid.
[640] Barbour, "Dude Ranches;" George Brown 1998; Betty Peterson-Stowe and Frank Peterson 1999; Tyne Turrie, "Riding the Range at Border Ranch," Highway Traveler (June/July 1937), 12-13,40-44, CORO Files.
[641] Turrie, "Riding the Range at Border Ranch."
[642] George Brown 1998.
[643] George Brown 1998; Barbour, "Dude Ranches."
[644] Barbour, "Dude Ranches."
[645] H.H. Petersen to Sidney P. Osborn, Governor of Arizona, June 28, 1947, WACC, H 14: Area and Service History 41-52 F3.
[646] George Brown 1998; Barbour, "Dude Ranches."
[647] Barbour, "Dude Ranches," from Tracking Book, Cochise County Assessor's Office, Bisbee, Arizona.
[648] Barbour, "Dude Ranches;" George Brown 1998; Grace Sparks, "Huachuca Area," Bisbee Daily Review, June 18, 1950, n.p.; Pete Van Cleve, "List of Classified Structures, CCC/WPA, Coronado Establishment and Land Acquisitions," 1996, CORO Files. The names Jean Faye and Rex Watts were supplied by CORO staff, personal communication, July 2001.
[649] Wilson Islands in the Desert, 158.
[650] Peter M. Van Cleve, "History of Mining in the Coronado National Memorial" (1997), pp. 2-8, CORO Files.
[651] Wilson, Islands in the Desert, 43,158.
[652] Van Cleve, "History of Mining in the Coronado National Memorial," 2-8.
[653] "A Summary of the Abandoned Mineral Lands (AML) on the Coronado National Memorial," April 19, 1996, CORO Files.
[654] Baron claim, 1/1/1889, and Baron claim papers, 4/4/1898, from Geoffrey T. Bohrer, "Siamese Triplets: Grace Sparks, The State of Texas Mine, and the Coronado National Memorial," (National Park Service, 1993), pp. 1-2.
[655] Van Cleve, "History of Mining," pp. 3-4.
[656] Bohrer, "Siamese Triplets," pp. 1-2.
[657] Gerdes identified his former partner as "August Barron of Tombstone." Charles Gerdes to Mssrs. Sparks [sic] and Moody, Gleeson, April 15, 1939, Sparkes Collection, AHS, Box 7, Folder 294.
[658] Robert D. O'Brien, "Appraisal of Mineral Interests Inherent in the State of Texas Mine Tracts No. 101-06, 101-07, 101-08 Coronado National Monument," (San Francisco: National Park Service, Western Region, 1979), p. 3.
[659] Van Cleve, "History of Mining," p. 5; Bohrer calls it the Mitchell Development Company, Bohrer, "Siamese Triplets, p. 2.
[660] Van Cleve, "History of Mining," pp. 5-6.
[661] O'Brien, "Appraisal of Mineral Interests," p. 4.
[662] Van Cleve, "History of Mining," pp. 6-7.
[663] Sale Agreement, Nathan L. and Estelle D. Amster to T.J. Sparkes and Burdett Moody, September 1, 1926, Sparkes Collection, AHS, Box 12, Folder 464, Arizona Historical Society; Mining Deed, Nathan L. and Estelle D. Amster to T.J. Sparkes and Burdett Moody, September 27, 1926, Sparkes Collection, AHS, Box 12, Folder 470.
[664] Van Cleve, "History of Mining," p. 8.

665 Grace Sparkes Burdett Moody, c/o The Bureau Light, Water and Power, Los Angeles, Ca., Prescott, January 30, 1939, Sparkes Collection, AHS, Box 7, Folder 294.

666 Burdett Moody to Grace M. Sparkes, Los Angeles, February 1, 1939; Burdett Moody to Grace M. Sparkes, Los Angeles, May 4, 1939, Ibid. The Sparkes papers contain sales contracts, never executed, from this period that confirm that the property was in negotiation for sale. See especially Box 12, Folders 465-467.

667 Van Cleve, "History of Mining," p. 7.

668 Burdett Moody to Grace M. Sparkes, Los Angeles, August 1, 1941, Sparkes Collection, AHS, Box 7, Folder 296, and others in the same folder.

669 See, in particular, Sparkes Collection, AHS, Box 7, Folder 294.

670 Grace M. Sparkes to Burdett Moody, April 22, 1940, Sparkes Collection AHS, Box 7 Folder 295, and others in the same folder.

671 Letter, Grace M. Sparkes, to Mrs. Foster Rockwell (Margaret), Vice Chairman, Arizona Commission, Coronado Cuarto Centennial Exposition, Prescott, April 11, 1940, Sparkes Collection, AHS, Box 23, Folder 956.

672 Grace M. Sparkes to Burdett Moody, April 7, 1942, Sparkes Collection, AHS, Box 7, Folder 297.

673 Mining Deed, Burdett and Sarah C. Moody sell and quit claim to Grace Sparkes, June 9, 1942, Sparkes Collection, AHS, Box 12, Folder 470; also see Folder 468.

674 Mining Deed, Thomas J. Sparkes Jr. and wife Maybelle; Charity S. and Perry L. Bones; and Genevieve Sparkes, widow of John G. Sparkes; all of Yavapai County, sell and quit claim all of the mine claims to Grace Sparkes, September 21, 1942, Sparkes Collection, AHS, Box 12, Folder 470.

675 Van Cleve, "History of Mining," p. 8.

676 Sarah Moody to Grace Sparkes, Los Angeles, 1946, Sparkes Collection, AHS, Box 7, Folder 299.

677 George Brown 1998.

678 "A Summary of the Abandoned Mineral Lands;" "Abandoned Mineral Lands (AML) and Related List of Classified Structure (LCS)," n.d., CORO Files.

679 "A Summary of the Abandoned Mineral Lands."

680 Dale to Mulhern, Hereford, February 23, 1976.

681 "A Summary of the Abandoned Mineral Lands."

682 Dale to Mulhern, February 23, 1976.

683 Establishment of the Coronado National Memorial (Name change from International Memorial), Arizona, By the President of the United States, A Proclamation (No. 2995), November 5, 1952, ILRPC Files.

684 "Boundary Adjustment – a Radical Proposal," n.d., WACC, Folder L 1417: Boundary Adjustments – Surveys & Reports F1.

685 George Brown 1998; Bart Barbour, "Dude Ranches."

686 Barbour, "Dude Ranches," from Tracking Book, Cochise County Assessor's Office, Bisbee, Arizona; Quit-Claim Deed, Frank Zaleski to Jose Zaleski, Signed January 3, 1956, CCR, Deeds of Real Estate, Docket 142, pages 239-241.

687 Warranty Deed, Joe Zaleski, aka José, and wife Lucy, to John A. and Inez Z. Jones, Signed April 19, 1957, CCR, Deeds of Real Estate, Docket 166, pages 587-588.

688 Untitled, undated, copy of Congressional debate on bill, H.R. 7553, WACC, Folder H 18: Biographical Data, General F11.

689 Senator Carl Hayden to Grace Sparkes, Washington, D.C., July 2, 1954, Ibid.

690 Ray B. Ringenbach, Superintendent, Tumacacori National Monument, to Grace Sparkes, Tumacacori, August 10, 1954, Ibid.

691 Sparkes to Ringenbach, Prescott, July 7, 1954, Ibid.

692 Recognition of Right of Way, Signed by Grace M. Sparkes, June 15, 1951, WACC, Folder L 1425: Land Holdings – Sparkes & Acquisition F17.

[693] John M. Davis, General Superintendent, Southwestern National Monuments, NPS, to Sparkes, Globe, November 17, 1954, WACC, Folder H 18: Biographical Data, General F11.
[694] Davis to Sparkes, Globe, November 23, 1954, Ibid.
[695] D.D. Crumley, Chief Clerk, Southwestern National Monuments, NPS, to Sparkes, Globe, December 7, 1954, Ibid.
[696] Lease between Grace M. Sparkes and the United States of America, January 1, 1955, Ibid.
[697] Lease between Grace M. Sparkes and the United States of America, July 1, 1955, Ibid.
[698] Department of the Interior, Notice of Appointment, Grace M. Sparkes, Effective 9/11/55, Ibid.
[699] Lease between Grace M. Sparkes and the United States of America, July 1, 1956, Ibid.
[700] Purchase Order, July 12, 1957, Ibid.
[701] Purchase Order, July 24, 1958; Purchase Order, July 23, 1959, ibid.
[702] Completion Report of Construction Project, Contract 14-10-333-509, Signed by Philip Welles, Superintendent, Coronado National Memorial, n.d., WACC, Folder D 3415: Buildings Construction and Maintenance 1960 F25.
[703] Memorandums to Acting Superintendent Don Jackson, Coronado National Memorial, February 13 to March 6, 1960, WACC, Folder A 26: Reports, daily logs 1960 F3.
[704] Welles to Sparkes, Hereford, May 15, 1959, WACC, Folder H 18: Biographical Data, General F11.
[705] William H. Woods, Jr., Forest Supervisor, National Forest Service, to Director, National Park Service, Tucson, July 26, 1956, WACC, Folder L 1417: Boundary Adjustments – Surveys & Reports F1.
[706] "Report of Jerome C. Miller, Associate Landscape Architect," Special Report Covering the Proposed Coronado International Monument, Submitted by Region III Headquarters, National Park Service, Department of the Interior, Santa Fe, February 1940, WACC, Folder H 14: Area and Service History, General F6.
[707] Regional Chief, Cooperative Activities Division, NPS, to Acting Regional Director, NPS, Santa Fe, October 14, 1954, WACC, Folder D 18: Master Plans (1954) F2.
[708] National Park Service Boundary Status Report, August 7, 1956, WACC, Folder L 1417: Boundary Adjustments – Surveys & Reports F1.
[709] National Park Service Boundary Status Report, August 7, 1956.
[710] Welles to Earl Jackson, Executive Secretary, Southwestern Monuments Association, Hereford, December 8, 1958, WACC, Folder L 1425: Land Holdings – "Jones Property" & Acquisition of (SWPM Association) F12.
[711] A.M. Koehler, Acting Regional Chief of Operations, NPS, to Earl Jackson, Santa Fe, December 4, 1958, Ibid.
[712] Deed, John A. and Inez Z. Jones to Southwestern Monuments Association, Signed and recorded May 22, 1959, CCR, Deeds of Real Estate, Docket 217, pages 129-130.
[713] An Act to Revise the Boundaries of the Coronado National Memorial and to Authorize the Repair and Maintenance of an Access Road Thereto, in the State of Arizona, and for Other Purposes, Approved September 2, 1960 (74 Stat 736). (Public Law 86-689), CORO Files.
[714] Acting Director, NPS, to Regional Director, Region Three, NPS, Washington, D.C., August 22, 1958, WACC, Folder L 1417: Boundary Adjustments – Proposed/Enacted Legislation F2.
[715] Regional Chief, NPS Planning, Region Three, to Superintendent, Coronado National Memorial, Santa Fe, n.d. (possibly September 12, 1958), Ibid.
[716] Acting Director, NPS, to Regional Director, Region Three, NPS, Washington, D.C., August 22, 1958.
[717] Request for Transfer of Excess Real Property and Related Personal Property, from Director, NPS, to Commissioner, United States Section, International Boundary and Water Commission, Washington, D.C., February 1964, WACC, Folder L 1417: Boundary Adjustments – Proposed/Enacted Legislation F2.

718 An Act to Provide for the Establishment of the Coronado International Memorial, in the State of Arizona, Approved August 18, 1941 (55 Stat) 630), CORO Files.

719 Acting Regional Director, Region Three, NPS, to Director, NPS, Santa Fe, n.d. (possibly October 8, 1958), WACC, Folder L 1417: Boundary Adjustments – Proposed/Enacted Legislation F2.

720 Request for Transfer of Excess Real Property and Related Personal Property, February 1964. See also, Donald E. Lee, Chief, Division of Land and Water Rights, NPS, to Bernard L. Boutin, Administrator, General Services Administration, March 5, 1964, and Boundary Status Map, October 1958, Ibid; Alphabetical listing by landowner's name, NPS Division of Land Acquisitions, July 10, 1979; Land Acquisition Plan, Coronado National Memorial, January 18, 1980 (and attached maps), ILRPC Files; Land Ownership Record, NPS, September 2, 1960, WACC, Folder L 1425: Land Holdings – Sparkes & Acquisition F17.

721 Welles to Regional Director, NPS, Hereford, September 15, 1957, Ibid.

722 Sparkes to Senator Barry Goldwater, Hereford, September 11, 1958, WACC, Folder L 1425: Land Holdings – Sparkes & Acquisition F17.

723 Sparkes to Welles, Hereford, March 1950, Ibid.

724 Gentry, McNulty & Tori, Attorneys at Law, to Acting Superintendent, Coronado National Memorial, Bisbee, October 14, 1965, Ibid; also see other memos and letters in the same folder for improvements and sales prospects.

725 Warranty Deed, Ruth M. Clark, a widow, and Charles A. Smith and Paquita C. Smith, his wife, to Coronado Investment Company, a partnership comprised of Peter G. Wray and H. Wayne Pruett, co-partners, Recorded July 2, 1970, CCR, Deeds of Real Estate, Docket 645, pages 543-545.

726 Warranty Deed, Coronado Investment Company to Pruett-Wray Cattle Company, Signed May 1, 1973, CCR, Deeds of Real Estate, Docket 871, pages 481-483.

727 Deed (Joint Tenancy), The Victorio Company, an Arizona Corporation; formerly Victorio Land and Cattle Company, an Arizona Corporation; formerly Pruett-Wray Cattle Company, an Arizona Corporation, to James J. Wardle and Jacqueline S. Wardle, husband and wife, Signed December 18, 1979, CCR, Deeds of Real Estate, Docket 1388, pages 333-334.

728 Deed of Gift, John A. and Inez Z. Jones, of Santa Cruz County, Arizona, to John Z. and Lawrence D. Jones, Signed April 24, 1962, CCR, Deeds of Real Estate, Docket 300, pages 406-407.

729 Joint Tenancy Deed, John Z. Jones and Lawrence D. Jones to Everett Baumkirchner and Margaret E. Baumkirchner, husband and wife, an undivided half interest, Signed May 26, 1965, CCR, Deeds of Real Estate, Docket 389, page 21; Joint Tenancy Deed, John Z. Jones and Lawrence D. Jones to Fred and Mary Ann Baumkirchner, husband and wife, an undivided half interest, Signed May 26, 1965, CCR, Deeds of Real Estate, Docket 389, page 22; Realty Mortgage, Everett Baumkirchner and Margaret E. Baumkirchner, his wife, and Fred Baumkirchner and Mary Ann Baumkirchner, his wife, with John Z. Jones and Lawrence D. Jones, Signed June 1, 1965, CCR, Deeds of Real Estate, Docket 389, page 23.

730 Jac Hein, Sierra Vista: its people and neighbors: a narrative history (Sierra Vista, Az.: Banner Printing Center, 1983), unidentified photocopied pages, CORO Files.

731 Joint Tenancy Deed, Fred E. and Mary Ann Baumkirchner, and Everett M. and Margaret E. Baumkirchner, to Calvin R. and Esther Teague, Signed September 30, 1966, CCR, Deeds of Real Estate, Docket 456, page 215.

732 Warranty Deed, Calvin R. Teague and Esther Teague, his wife, to William L. Cashman and Ramona E. Cashman, his wife, Signed April 29, 1971, CCR, Deeds of Real Estate, Docket 767, page 168.

733 Warranty Deed, Fred E. Baumkirchner and Mary Ann Baumkirchner, husband and wife, and Everett M. Baumkirchner and Margaret E. Baumkirchner, husband and wife, to William Arthur Archie and Eloise Archie, husband and wife, Signed July 21, 1967, CCR, Deeds of Real Estate, Docket 493, page 280.

[734] Warranty Deed, William A. Archie and Eloise Archie, his wife, to Robert G. Chavez and Betty J. Chavez, his wife, Signed November 17, 1972, CCR, Deeds of Real Estate, Docket 831, page 427.
[735] Warranty Deed, Robert G. Chavez and Betty J. Chavez, husband and wife, to Eileen G. Owens, an unmarried woman, Signed April 28, 1978, CCR, Deeds of Real Estate, Docket 1250, page 147.
[736] Warranty Deed, Fred E. Baumkirchner and Mary Ann Baumkirchner, husband and wife, and Everett M. Baumkirchner and Margaret E. Baumkirchner, husband and wife, to Lawrence Edward Ray, an unmarried man, Signed July 21, 1967, CCR, Deeds of Real Estate, Docket 491, page 525.
[737] Real Estate Mortgage for Arizona, Lawrence Edward Ray and Farmers Home Administration of the United States Department of Agriculture, September 27, 1967, CCR, Deeds of Real Estate, Docket 502, pages 478-479.
[738] Joint Tenancy Deed, Lawrence Edward Ray, husband of Maria T. Ray, as his sole and separate property, to James M. Tyra and Billie Jean Tyra, his wife, Signed August 13, 1971, CCR, Deeds of Real Estate, Docket 713, page 392.
[739] Joint Tenancy Deed, Fred E. Baumkirchner and Mary Ann Baumkirchner, his wife, an undivided half interest, and Everett M. Baumkirchner and Margaret E. Baumkirchner, his wife, an undivided half interest, to James M. Tyra and Billie Jean Tyra, his wife, Signed September 30, 1971, CCR, Deeds of Real Estate, Docket 1221, page 457.
[740] Warranty Deed, Fred E. and Mary Ann Baumkirchner, and Everett M. and Margaret E. Baumkirchner, to James M. and Billie Jean Tyra, March 25, 1980, CCR, Deeds of Real Estate, Docket 1413, pages 456-457.
[741] Joint Tenancy Deed, Fred E. and Mary Ann Baumkirchner, and Everett M. and Margaret E. Baumkirchner, to Dewitt and Doretta Ruth Green, August 23, 1971, CCR, Deeds of Real Estate, Docket 862, pages 10-11.
[742] Warranty Deed, Fred E. Baumkirchner and Mary Ann Baumkirchner, husband and wife, and Everett M. Baumkirchner and Margaret E. Baumkirchner, husband and wife, to Everett M. Baumkirchner, Jr., Signed October 11, 1971, CCR, Deeds of Real Estate, Docket 940, page 71; Agreement, Fred E. Baumkirchner and Mary Ann Baumkirchner, his wife, as to an undivided ½ interest; and Everett M. Baumkirchner and Margaret E. Baumkirchner, his wife, as to an undivided ½ interest, and Everett M. Baumkirchner, Jr., a single man, Signed October 11, 1971, CCR, Deeds of Real Estate, Docket 732, page 107.
[743] Warranty Deed, Fred E. and Mary Ann Baumkirchner, and Everett M. and Margaret E. Baumkirchner, to Everett M. Baumkirchner, Jr., Signed March 19, 1980, CCR, Deeds of Real Estate, Docket 1410, page 2.
[744] Warranty Deed, Fred E. Baumkirchner and Mary Ann Baumkirchner, husband and wife, and Everett M. Baumkirchner and Margaret E. Baumkirchner, husband and wife, to Transamerica Title Insurance Company, as Trustee, Signed March 11, 1972, CCR, Deeds of Real Estate, Docket 841, pages 215-216; Warranty Deed, Transamerica Title Insurance Company to United States of America, Signed March 1, 1973, CCR, Deeds of Real Estate, Docket 841, page 218.
[745] Request for bids for appraisal of properties by A.W. Gray, Division of Land Acquisition, Western Region, NPS, May 4, 1979, ILRPC Files.
[746] Joint Tenancy Deed, George H. Howe and Martha J. Howe, his wife, to George F. Weick and Elsie R. Weick, his wife, Wood Dale, Illinois, Recorded April 27, 1973, CCR, Deeds of Real Estate, Docket 853, page 84.
[747] "Boundary Adjustment – a Radical Proposal," n.d.
[748] Hugo H. Huntzinger, Superintendent, Coronado National Memorial, to Director, Southwest Region, Subject: Boundary Changes for Existing NPS Areas, Hereford, August 31, 1970, WACC, Folder L 1417: Boundary Adjustments – Surveys & Reports F1.

[749] Frederick J. Brower, Acting Team Manager, Western Team, Denver Service Center, to Regional Director, Western Region, February 19, 1974, WACC, Folder L 1417: Boundary Adjustments – Surveys & Reports F1.

[750] Environmental Review Proposal, General Management Plan, Coronado National Memorial, Initial Draft, n.d., WACC, Folder L 7617: Environmental Review Study/Statement 1976 F55.

[751] Boundary Status Map, October 1958; Alphabetical listing by landowner's name, July 10, 1979; Land Acquisition Plan, January 18, 1980 (and attached maps).

[752] Several descriptions can be found scattered through WACC, Folder L 76: Environmental Impact/Assessment – Public Response 1975 F53; Folder L 76: Environmental Impact/Assessment – Public Response 1976 F54; Folder L 7617: Environmental Review Study/Statement 1976 F55; Folder L 7617: Environmental Impact Statement (EIS) F56.

[753] It should be noted that there was also more than one adjustment package considered. One particularly interesting plan offered the following alternatives:
1. Transfer all of the Memorial's land, except part of Section 18 (T24S R21E), to the National Forest Service in return for Sections 1 and 12 (R20E) and 6 and 7 (R21E), surrounding Montezuma Peak. Ash Canyon Road would be paved to provide primary access. A chair lift to Montezuma Peak or Ash Peak would be installed and visitor facilities constructed at the parking lot below the tram.
2. All land would revert to the Forest Service and a new site would be selected. Possible site suggestions included "Hawikuh, Acoma, Tiguex, and Pecos in Arizona [sic, all are in New Mexico] and other locations as far north as Kansas."
3. Status quo would be maintained, but the international angle would be pursued with Mexico.
4. No Action. "This action would negate all impacts associated with implementing the proposal. No effort would be expended to exemplify the implications of the Coronado Expedition and its influence on our Hispanic heritage. In essence, this alternative would question the worthiness of the Memorial being represented within the system."
5. Return the area west of Montezuma Pass to the Forest Service with no land being returned in exchange.

WACC, Folder L 7617: Environmental Impact Statement (EIS) F56.

[754] For comments, see WACC, Folder L 76: Environmental Impact/Assessment – Public Response 1975 F53; Folder L 76: Environmental Impact/Assessment – Public Response 1976 F54.

[755] Robert A. Jantzen, Director, Arizona Game and Fish Department, to Laurel Dale, Superintendent, Coronado National Memorial, Phoenix, December 17, 1975, WACC, Folder L 76: Environmental Impact/Assessment – Public Response 1975 F53.

[756] Comments by Mr. Ted H. Eyde, Secretary, Southwestern Minerals Explorations Association, Tucson, October 29, 1975, ibid.

[757] John E. Kinnison to Superintendent, Coronado National Monument, Tucson, December 8, 1975, ibid.

[758] D.A. Heatwole, Regional Project Geologist, The Anaconda Company, to Superintendent, Coronado National Monument, Tucson, December 9, 1975, ibid.

[759] Charles M. Morgan to Superintendent, Coronado National Monument, Tucson, December 11, 1975, ibid.

[760] Robert L. Coshland, Southwest Representative, National Parks and Conservatioon Association, to Superintendent, Coronado National Memorial, Tucson, December 3, 1975, WACC, Folder L 76: Environmental Impact/Assessment – Public Response 1976 F54.

[761] An Act to Provide for the Regulation of Mining Activity Within, and to Repeal the Application of Mining Laws to Areas of the National Park System, and for Other Purposes. (90 Stat 1342) (Public Law 94-429) Approved September 28, 1976, CORO Files.

[762] Laurel Dale to Regional Director, Western Regional Office, NPS, Hereford, June 13, 1977, WACC, Folder L 1425: Land Holdings – Pruett-Wray/Victorio (LaFevre) F13.

763 A.P. LeFevre, Vice President, Land Resources, The Victorio Company, to A.W. Gray, Phoenix, September 27, 1978, ibid.
764 Gray to Wayne Pruett, The Victorio Company, December 19, 1979, ibid.
765 Constance M. Dochas to Coronado Memorial, Bisbee, December 20, 1975, WACC, Folder L 76: Environmental Impact/Assessment – Public Response 1975 F53.
766 Bessie J. Payne to Coronado National Memorial, Hereford, December 15, 1975, ibid.
767 Comments by Fred E. and Everett M. Baumkirchner, November 24, 1975, ibid.
768 From the introduction to Land Acquisition Plan, Coronado National Memorial, April 15, 1980, ILRPC Files.
769 John H. Clay, General Superintendent, Southern Arizona Group, NPS, to Regional Director, Western Region, Phoenix, July 25, 1978, ibid.
770 Acting Deputy Director, NPS, to Regional Director, Western Region, Washington, D.C., June 29, 1978, ibid.
771 Clay, to Regional Director, Western Region, Phoenix, July 25, 1978.
772 "Boundary Adjustment – a Radical Proposal," n.d.
773 Howard Fischer, "His aunt helped build park that could dispossess him," The Arizona Daily Star, September 13, 1979, D:1, WACC, Folder L 1425: Land Holdings – Sparkes & Acquisition F17.
774 "We, the undersigned, do hereby protest the acquisition by the National Park Service of that property owned by William J. Sparkes, which property is situated in Montezuma Canyon, Coronadom National Memorial, Cochise County, Arizona, and which property is commonly referred to as the State of Texas Mine," received, Coronado National Memorial, April 1, 1980, ibid.
775 Ullrich to Dale, March 27, 1980.
776 Huachuca Conservation Council, Resolution, Coronado National Memorial, Adopted March 5, 1980, ILRPC Files.
777 Jerome J. Pratt, Secretary-Treasurer, Huachuca Conservation Council to Cecil D. Andrus, Secretary of the Interior, Sierra Vista, March 10, 1980, ibid.
778 Dale to Regional Director, Western Region, Hereford, March 17, 1980, ibid.
779 Paul R. Thompson, Supervisory Park Technician, Maintenance Supervisor, to Registrar of Contractors, Hereford, October 5, 1976, WACC, Folder K 14: Information Requests F1.
780 Dale to Will Sparkes, Hereford, December 27, 1974, WACC, Folder A 34: Commendations F13.
781 Dale to Regional Director, Western Region, Hereford, February 5, 1980, WACC, Folder L 1425: Land Holdings – Sparkes & Acquisition F17.
782 Request for bids for appraisal of properties by A.W. Gray, May 4, 1979.
783 Transamerica Title Insurance Company Preliminary Report, n.d., ILRPC Files.
784 Request for bids for appraisal of properties by A.W. Gray, May 4, 1979.
785 Ibid.
786 Transamerica Title Insurance Company Preliminary Report, n.d.
787 Quit Claim Deed, Charles J. Sparkes, Jack M. Sparkes, and Thomas F. Sparkes, to William J. Sparkes, Dated April 9, 1980, ILRPC Files.
788 Transamerica Title Insurance Company Preliminary Report, n.d.
789 Fischer "His aunt helped build park that could dispossess him."
790 Annual Statement for Interpretation and Visitor Services, Coronado National Memorial, 1988, WACC, Folder K 1817: Annual Statement For Interpretation F9.
791 Regional Director, Western Region, to Associate Director, Management and Operations, NPS, Subject: Legislative Cost Estimate, Coronado National Memorial, April 1, 1980, ILRPC Files.
792 Grant Deed, William J. and Patricia M. Sparkes, to NPS, Signed December 29, 1986, ibid.
793 Grant Deed, The Victorio Company, an Arizona Corporation which acquired title as Pruett-Wray Cattle Company, an Arizona Corporation, to NPS, Executed March 26, 1980, ibid.

[794] Request for bids for appraisal of properties by A.W. Gray, May 4, 1979.
[795] Joint Tenancy Deed, The Victorio Company, an Arizona Corporation; formerly Victorio Land and Cattle Company, an Arizona Corporation; formerly Pruett-Wray Cattle Company, an Arizona Corporation, to James J. Wardle and Jacqueline S. Wardle, husband and wife, Signed December 18, 1979, CCR, Deeds of Real Estate, Docket 1388, pages 333-334.
[796] Grant Deed, The Victorio Company, to NPS, Executed March 26, 1980.
[797] Howard Chapman, Regional Director, Western Region, to Associate Director, Management and Operations, NPS, July 10, 1980, WACC, Folder L 1425: Land Holdings – Wardle & Acquisition F14.
[798] All-Inclusive Agreement, James J. Wardle and Jacqueline S. Wardle, husband and wife, to Jacques O'Keefe and Audrey C. O'Keefe, husband and wife, Signed January 5, 1980, CCR, Deeds of Real Estate, Docket 1395, pages 484-487.
[799] Dale to Regional Director, Western Region, Hereford, May 27, 1980, WACC, Folder L 1425: Land Holdings – Wardle & Acquisition F14.
[800] Bob Cousins, Realty Specialist, Division of Land Acquisition, Western Region, to Acting Chief, Division of Land Acquisition, Western Region, March 10, 1981, ILRPC Files.
[801] Dale to Regional Director, Western Region, Hereford, March 22, 1983, WACC, Folder L 1425: Land Holdings – Wardle & Acquisition F14.
[802] Bill English, State Representative, to U.S. Senator Barry Goldwater, June 29, 1982, ibid.
[803] Ira J. Hutchison, Director, Acting, NPS, to Barry Goldwater, Washington, D.C., November 4, 1982, ibid.
[804] Dale to Regional Director, Western Region, Hereford, March 22, 1983.
[805] Dale to Chief, Energy, Mining and Minerals Division, Minerals Overview Report and Map, Hereford, March 20, 1986; Grant Deed, Paul E. Froelich and Laurel A. Froelich, his wife, to NPS, Signed July 5, 1985, ILRPC Files.
[806] Joint Tenancy Deed, Jacques O'Keefe and Audrey C. O'Keefe, husband and wife, to Paul E. Froelich and Laurel A. Froelich, husband and wife, Signed April 8, 1983, CCR, Deeds of Real Estate, Docket 1671, pages 164-166.
[807] Warranty Deed, James J. Wardle and Jacqueline S. Wardle, husband and wife, to Jacques O'Keefe and Audrey C. O'Keefe, husband and wife, Signed April 8, 1983, and recorded April 29, 1983, CCR, Deeds of Real Estate, Docket 1671, page 162.
[808] Dale to Chief, Energy, Mining and Minerals Division, Hereford, March 20, 1986; Grant Deed, Valentin Castro III and Deborah Castro, husband and wife, to NPS, Signed February 25, 1985, ILRPC Files.
[809] Joint Tenancy Deed, Jacques O'Keefe and Audrey C. O'Keefe, husband and wife, to Valentin Castro III and Deborah Castro, husband and wife, Signed August 29, 1983, CCR, Deeds of Real Estate, Docket 1708, pages 40-43.
[810] Joint Tenancy Deed, James J. Wardle and Jacqueline Wardle (aka Jacqueline S. Wardle), husband and wife, to Richard D. Compton and Judy L. Compton, husband and wife, Signed August 29, 1983, CCR, Deeds of Real Estate, Docket 1700, pages 285-286.
[811] Dale to Chief, Energy, Mining and Minerals Division, Hereford, March 20, 1986; Grant Deed, Richard D. Compton and Judy L. Compton, husband and wife, to NPS, February 12, 1985, ILRPC Files.
[812] Joint Tenancy Deed, Jacques O'Keefe and Audrey O'Keefe, husband and wife, to Richard D. Compton and Judy L. Compton, husband and wife, Signed December 28, 1983, CCR, Deeds of Real Estate, Docket 1730, pages 579-580.
[813] Dale to Chief, Energy, Mining and Minerals Division, Hereford, March 20, 1986; Grant Deed, Richard D. Compton and Judy L. Compton, husband and wife, to NPS, Signed February 12, 1985, ILRPC Files.
[814] Dale to Regional Director, Western Region, November 9, 1983, WACC, Folder L 1425: Land Holdings – Wardle & Acquisition F14.
[815] Ibid.

816 Anna Hirst, President, Huachuca Audubon Society, to Barry Goldwater, January 10, 1984, ibid.
817 Clay to Regional Director, Western Region, February 2, 1984, ILRPC Files.
818 Chapman to Gordon Douglas, Coronado Resource Conservation and Development, November 19, 1981, WACC, Folder L 1425: Land Holdings – Wardle & Acquisition F14.
819 Grant Deed, James J. Wardle and Jacqueline S. Wardle, his wife, to NPS, Signed February 6, 1985, ILRPC Files.
820 Grant Deed, Richard D. and Judy L. Compton, to NPS, Signed February 12, 1985.
821 Grant Deed, Valentin Castro III and Deborah Castro, to NPS, Signed February 25, 1985.
822 Grant Deed, Paul E. and Laurel A. Froelich, to NPS, Signed July 5, 1985.
823 Wilbert P. Witkopp to Unknown, July 26, 1979, ILRPC Files.
824 Witkopp to Unknown, November 7, 1983, ILRPC Files.
825 U.S. Department of the Interior, Office of Hearings and Appeals, Interior Board of Land Appeals, Ruling, Tako Mining, Arlington, April 9, 1982, ILRPC Files.
826 U.S. Department of the Interior, Office of Hearings and Appeals, Interior Board of Land Appeals, Ruling, Tako Mining, Arlington, October 31, 1983, ILRPC Files.
827 Witkopp to President Reagan, Sierra Vista, July 13, 1984, ILRPC Files.
828 Witkopp to Unknown, July 26, 1979.
829 Chapman to Congressman Morris K. Udall, San Francisco, September 25, 1979, ILRPC Files.
830 Witkopp to Reagan, Sierra Vista, July 13, 1984.
831 Chapman to Witkopp, Draft, September 17, 1984, ILRPC Files.
832 Witkopp to Unknown, November 7, 1983.
833 Grant Deed, Everett M. Baumkirchner Jr., to NPS, Signed March 19, 1980, ILRPC Files.
834 Warranty Deed, Fred E. and Mary Ann Baumkirchner, and Everett M. and Margaret E. Baumkirchner, to Everett M. Baumkirchner Jr., Signed March 19, 1980, CCR, Deeds of Real Estate, Docket 1410, page 2.
835 Grant Deed, Fred E. Baumkirchner and Mary Ann Baumkirchner, his wife, as joint tenants, and Everett M. Baumkirchner and Margaret E. Baumkirchner, his wife, as joint tenants, to NPS, Signed March 20, 1980, ILRPC Files.
836 Grant Deed, James M. Tyra and Billie Jean Tyra, his wife, as joint tenants, to NPS, March 25, 1980, ILRPC Files.
837 Warranty Deed, Payoff Deed for Agreement recorded in Docket 726 page 258. Fred E. Baumkirchner and Mary Ann Baumkirchner, husband and wife, and Everett M. Baumkirchner and Margaret E. Baumkirchner, husband and wife, to James M. Tyra and Billie Jean Tyra, Husband and Wife. Signed March 25, 1980, CCR, Deeds of Real Estate, Docket 1413, pages 456-457
838 Grant Deed, Dewitt Green and Doretta Ruth Green, his wife, as joint tenants, to NPS, April 3, 1980, ILRPC Files.
839 Warranty Deed, Robert G. and Betty J. Chavez to Eileen G. Owens, Signed April 28, 1978, CCR, Deeds of Real Estate, Docket 1250, page 147.
840 Joint Tenancy Deed, Eileen G. Owens, an unmarried woman, to Allan Cerkowniak and Leona Cerkowniak, husband and wife, Signed January 4, 1985, CCR, Deeds of Real Estate, Listing number 860406690.
841 Barbour, "Dude Ranching".
842 Request for bids for appraisal of properties by A.W. Gray, May 4, 1979.
843 Handwritten note re: telephone call, Leland Auslander (sic) to Bob Gibbons, September 24, 1979, ILRPC Files.
844 NPS Division of Land Acquisition Master Deed Listing, May 31, 1980, ibid.
845 Division of Land Acquisition, Western Region, NPS, to Chief, Coordination and Control Branch, NPS, May 12, 1980, ibid.
846 Grant Deed, Leland I. Auslender to NPS, April 21, 1980, ibid.

847 Untitled map of Coronado National Memorial, July 1982; Dale to Chief, Energy, Mining and Minerals Division, March 20, 1986, ibid.
848 Grant Deed, Richards and Richards to NPS, December 15, 1981, ibid.
849 Grant Deed, Richard B. Richards and Cheryl Richards to NPS, August 3, 1982, ibid.
850 Untitled map of Coronado National Memorial, July 1982.
851 Henry Ruiz, Chief of Maintenance, Coronado National Memorial, interview by Jerry G. Gurulé and Bruce A. Erickson, May 4, 2000.
852 Grant Deed, Richard Richards and Cheryl Richards to NPS, scenic easement, February 4, 1985, ILRPC Files.
853 Memorandum, Joseph L. Sewell, Superintendent, Coronado National Memorial, to Regional Director, Western Region, NPS, May 3, 1988; Memorandum, Joseph L. Sewell, Superintendent, Coronado National Memorial, to Regional Director, Western Region, NPS, March 7, 1989, CORO Files.
854 Ed Lopez, "Montezuma Ranch Acquisition Process Briefing Paper," n.d., ibid.
855 Dale A. Anderson, Manager, Hazardous Waste Inspection Unit, Office of Waste Programs, Arizona Department of Environmental Quality, to Bob Cousins, Regional Director, Western Region, NPS, Phoenix, August 16, 1990, ibid.
856 Clay Cunningham, General Superintendent, Southern Arizona Group, NPS, to Regional Director, Western Region, NPS, Phoenix, July 31, 1990, ibid.
857 Addendum to the Land Protection Plan for Coronado national Memorial, October 26, 1988, ILRPC Files; Cunningham to Regional Director, Western Region, NPS, July 18, 1990, CORO Files.
858 Cunningham to Regional Director, Western Region, July 18, 1990; Edward Lopez, Superintendent, Coronado National Memorial, to Regional Director, Western Region, August 15, 1990, CORO Files.
859 Draft Memorandum, Director, NPS, to Regional Director, Western Region, NPS, Washington, D.C., n.d., ILRPC Files.
860 Acting Director, NPS, to Regional Director, Western Region, NPS, Washington, D.C., October 31, 1990, CORO Files.
861 Lopez, "Montezuma Ranch Acquisition Process Briefing Paper," n.d.
862 Lewis S. Albert, Acting Regional Director, Western Region, NPS, to Associate Director, Operations, NPS, September 28, 1990, CORO Files; Lopez to Regional Director, Western Region, August 15, 1990; Lopez, "Montezuma Ranch Acquisition Process Briefing Paper," n.d.
863 Edward R. Haberlin, Chief, Division of Land Resources, Western Region, NPS, to Margo Martin, Chapter 13 Trustee, San Francisco, January 14, 1991, CORO Files.
864 Criminal Incident Record, Case/Incident Number 910056, filed by William R. Smith, July 29, 1991; Supplemental Criminal Incident Record, Case/Incident Number 910056, filed by Edward Lopez, July 29, 1991; Supplemental Criminal Incident Record, Case/Incident Number 910056, filed by William R. Smith, July 27, 1991; Supplemental Criminal Incident Record, Case/Incident Number 910056, filed by Michael D. Walden, July 26, 1991, ibid.
865 Lopez, "Montezuma Ranch Acquisition Process Briefing Paper," n.d.
866 Complaint for Forfeiture, United States District Court, District of Arizona, United States of America, Plaintiff vs. 82.5 acres of real property located in Cochise County, Arizona and known as the Montezuma Ranch, DBA The Sunrise Farms, Inc. with all improvements, fixtures and appurtenances thereto and thereon; Defendant, August 16, 1991, CORO Files.
867 Lopez, "Montezuma Ranch Acquisition Process Briefing Paper," n.d.
868 Ibid.
869 Haberlin to Linda A. Akers, United States Attorney, Department of Justice, District of Arizona, San Francisco, May 26, 1992, CORO Files.

[870] Lopez, "Montezuma Ranch Acquisition Process Briefing Paper," n.d.; c.c. mail, Bob Cousins to Harlan Hobbs, Edward A. Lopez, and Sondra S. Humphries, Subject: CORO acquisitions, August 12, 1996, ibid.
[871] Cindy K. Jorgenson, Assistant U.S. Attorney, Department of Justice, District of Arizona, to Melinda S. Barnett of James S. Marlar, P.C., and Jeffrey A. Bernick of Ridenour, Swenson, Cleer & Evans, Tucson, August 16, 1993, ibid.
[872] Cousins to Hobbs, Lopez, and Humphries, August 12, 1996.
[873] Jim Walters, Southwest Hazardous Waste Program Agent, to Southwest Land Resources Program Center, April 3, 1997, CORO Files.
[874] Montezuma Ranch Update, probably written by Edward Lopez, July 1, 1997; Proposal for Clean-up, Eads Construction Redi-Mix, Inc., Bisbee, September 16, 1997; Proposal for Clean-up, B-R Constructors, Inc., Huachuca City, September 18, 1997, ibid.
[875] Notice of Trustee's Sale, filed by Melinda S. Barnett of James S. Marlar, P.C., Phoenix, September 30, 1992, ibid; Cousins to Hobbs, Lopez, and Humphries, August 12, 1996.
[876] Sondra S. Humphries, Chief, Division of Land Resources, Western Region, NPS, to Gary L. Buntrock, Garmar Enterprises, Inc., San Francisco, December 13, 1994, CORO Files.
[877] c.c. mail, Jim Walters to Edward A. Lopez and Bob Cousins, April 22, 1996; Sondra S. Humphries, Chief, Pacific Land Resources Program Center, NPS, to Michael Morris, Western Farm Credit Bank, San Francisco, May 22, 1996, ibid.
[878] U.S. Department of the Interior Certificate of Inspection and Possession, Tract 101-39, filed by Edward Lopez, June 17, 1996, ibid.
[879] Grant Deed, Western Farm Credit Bank to NPS, June 3, 1996, ILRPC Files.
[880] Notification of Closing, Tract 101-39, May 22, 1997, CORO Files.
[881] Notice of Trustee's Sale, filed by Ronald M. Horowitz of Anderson, Brody, Levinson, Weiser & Horwitz, P.A., Phoenix, April 21, 1994, Cochise County, Arizona, CORO Files; Cousins to Hobbs, Lopez, and Humphries, August 12, 1996.
[882] Assignment of Beneficial Interest Under Deed of Trust to Elsie Weick, from Citibank (Arizona), Trustee, as successor to United Bank of Arizona, March 26, 1997, CORO Files.
[883] Ethan Steele, Attorney at Law for Richard Richards, to Janet Martin, Office of United States Attorney, Tucson, June 23, 1997, ibid.
[884] Description of Tract No. 101-40, November 19, 1997, ibid; Montezuma Ranch Update, July 1, 1997; Proposal for Clean-up, Eads Construction Redi-Mix, Inc., September 16, 1997; Proposal for Clean-up, B-R Constructors, Inc., September 18, 1997.
[885] Grant Deed, Elsie Weick to Sunrise, A Trust, February 5, 1998, CORO Files.
[886] Handwritten note, re: Tract 101-40, September 13, 1999, ibid.
[887] c.c.mail, Julian Trujillo, Southwest Regional Office, NPS, to William Smith, Coronado National Memorial, June 9, 1998, ibid.
[888] Administrative Waiver, signed by Jim Bellamy, Superintendent, Coronado National Memorial, February 17, 1999, ibid.
[889] Complaint Form, Cochise County Zoning Regulations, Cochise County Planning Department, Building & Zoning Division, Sierra Vista, filed by Jim Bellamy, Superintendent, Coronado National Memorial, May 25, 1999, ibid.
[890] Bellamy to Regional Director, Intermountain Region, NPS, Hereford, May 27, 1999, ibid.
[891] Ann MacNeill, Zoning Enforcement Officer, Cochise County Planning Department, Building and Zoning Division, to Sunrise-A Trust, Wooddale [sic], Il., Sierra Vista, August 12, 1999, Copy, ibid.
[892] Robert Wierzal to Bellamy, Scottsdale, October 7, 1999; Bellamy to Wierzal, Hereford, October 18, 1999; Barbara A. Sulhoff, Chief, Land Resources Program Center, Intermountain Region, NPS, to Field Solicitor, NPS, Santa Fe, November 30, 1999, ibid.
[893] Bellamy to Joseph P. Sánchez, Spanish Colonial Research Center (SPCO), NPS, Hereford, July 27, 2001, SPCO Files.
[894] Steele to Paul Tatham, I.R.P. District Headquarters, Tucson, April 19, 1996, ibid.

[895] U.S. Department of the Interior Certificate of Inspection and Possession, Tract 101-40, signed by Edward Lopez, January 13, 1998, ibid.
[896] United States Marshal's Special Warranty Deed, Alfred E. Madrid, United States Marshal for the District of Arizona, to The United States of America for the United States Department of the Interior, National Park Service, January 3, 1998, ILRPCenter Files.
[897] Notification of Closing, Tract 101-41, February 2, 1998, CORO Files.
[898] Henry Ruiz, May 4, 2000.
[899] Bellamy to Regional Director, Intermountain Region, Subject: Condemnation of Montezuma Ranch, Hereford, May 27, 1999, CORO Files.
[900] Ibid, 88.
[901] Mario Barrera, Race and Class in the Southwest: A Theory of Racial Inequality, (Notre Dame: University of Notre Dame Press, 1979), 116-118.
[902] Walter Fogel, "Twentieth-Century Mexican Migration to the United States," in The Gateway: U.S. Immigration Issues and Policies ed. Barry R. Chiswick (Washington: American Enterprise Institute for Public Policy Research, 1982), 193-197.
[903] Lorey, The U.S.—Mexican Border in the Twentieth Century…, 107-108.
[904] Ibid, 170-171.
[905] Vernon M. Briggs, Jr. Immigration Policy and the American Labor Force (Baltimore: The Johns Hopkins University Press, 1984), 1.
[906] Migration Between Mexico & the United States, México—Estados Unidos Sobre Migración: A Report of the Binational Study on Migration, vii. This report and other papers accessible at: http://www.utexas.edu/lbj/uscir/binpap-v.html.
[907] The Arizona Republic, "State is pipeline for illegal drugs," Monday, January 17, 2000. CORO Files.
[908] Ibid.
[909] Ibid.
[910] Sierra Vista Herald/Bisbee Daily Review, "Flow of illegal immigrants wearing down park land" no date.CORO Files.
[911] Ibid.
[912] John Steinbeck, Travels with Charley: In Search of America. (New York: Bantam Books, 1963), 214.
[913] Alvar W. Carlson, "Environmental Overview," Borderlands Sourcebook: A Guide to the Literature on Northern Mexico and the American Southwest, (Norman:University of Oklahoma Press, 1983), 75-80.
[914] Alberto Szekely, "The Development of Mexico-U.S. Cooperation: The Conservation of Wildlife Transboundary Resources," Transboundry Resources Report, 3:1, (1989), 5-6
[915] Ibid, 5
[916] Memorandum of Understanding Between National Park Servcie of the Department of the Interior, United States of America and Secretariat of Urban Development and Ecology, United Mexican States on Cooperation in Management and Protection of National Parks and Other Protected Natural and Cultural Heritage Sites. Signed at Mexico and Washington, November 30, 1988 and January 24, 1989, (TIAS 11599). An update to this agreement was signed on May 18, 2000 between the National Park Service of the Department of the Interior of the United States of America and the Secretariat of Environment, Natural Resources and Fisheries of the United Mexican States through its National Institute of Ecology.
[917] H. K. Eidsvik, "The Status of Wilderness: An International Overview," Natural Resources Journal, 29:1, (1989), 57-82.
[918] Ibid, 22, 41.
[919] State of the Environment: An Assessment at Mid-Decade, (Washington D.C.:The Conservation Foundation, 1984), 190.

[920] Office of Science and Technology, National Park Service, State of the Parks, 1980: A Report to the Congress, (Washington D.C.: Government Printing Office, 1980), viii.
[921] Glen Kaye, "The Mexico-U.S.A. Border Region: The Filling of an Empty Land," Transboundry Resources Report, 9:1, (Spring, 1995), 4-7
[922] UNESCO Man and the Biosphere (MAB) Programme. More information on this subject is accessible at: http://cons-dev.univ-lyon1.fr/madagascar/MANANARA/mamanet/TEXTE/annexes/mab/home.htm
[923] UNESCO Man and the Biosphere (MAB) Programme. The Seville Strategy for Biosphere Reserves. The Biosphere Reserve Concept. at: http://cons-dev.univ-lyon1.fr/madagascar/MANANARA/mamanet/TEXTE/annexes/mab/stry_1.htm
[924] Letter from Director José María Guerra Limón of the Reserva Forestal Nacional y Refugio de Fauna Silvestre Sierra Los Ajos, Buenas Aires y La Púrica, to Regional Director John Cook, National Park Service, Mountain Region, May 27, 1997. CORO Files.
[925] Letter from Regional Director John Cook, National Park Service, Intermountain Region to Director José María Guerra Limón, Reserva Forestal Nacional y Refugio de Fauna Silvestre Sierra Los Ajos, Buenas Aires y La Púrica, June 9, 1997. CORO Files.
[926] Letter of Agreement between Reserva Forestal Nacional y Refugio de Fauna Silvestre Sierra Los Ajos, Buenas Aires y La Púrica-Bavispe, Chiricahua National Monument, and Coronado National Memorial signed February 3, 1998. CORO Files.
[927] Arizona Range News "Mexican Officials Study Local Monument" October 22, 1997. CORO Files.
[928] "Three Year Plan (1997-2000) between Chiricahua National Monument, Coronado National Memorial, Reserva Nacional Forestal (National Forest Reserve) Sierra los Ajos, Buenos Aires, y la Púrica." CORO Files
[929] Draft of Letter of Agreement between Reserva Forestal Nacional y Refugio de Fauna Silvestre Ajos-Bavispe, Chiricahua National Monument, and Coronado National Memorial. CORO Files.
[930] San Pedro Riparian National Conservation Area. (Washington D.C.:Bureau of Land Management, Safford District, Arizona;U.S. Government Printing Office, 1995).
[931] Connie Toops, "Going to Bat for Bats" National Parks: The Magazine of The National Parks Conservation Association 75:1-2, (January/February 2001), 29-31.
[932] Coronado. (Washington D.C.:Coronado National Memorial, Arizona. National Park Service, U.S. Department of the Interior; U.S. Government Printing Office: 1994).
[933] La Crónica de Hoy, "El río San Pedro, entre Sonora y Arizona, corre el riesgo de secarse debido a la sobreexplotación a que lo somete EU" (translation: "The San Pedro River, between Sonora and Arizona, is in danger of drying up, due to overexploitation by the U.S.") by Rigoberto Aranda. Wednesday, June 23, 1999, México. *http://www.cronica.com.mx/cronica/1999/jun/23/*.
[934] Joint Declaration between the Secretariat of Environment, Natural Resources and Fisheries (SEMARNAP) of the United States of Mexico and the Secretary of the Department of the Interior (DOI) of the United States of America, to work jointly in the Upper San Pedro River Basin. June 22, 1999.
[935] La Crónica de Hoy, "El río San Pedro, entre Sonora y Arizona…" by Rigoberto Aranda. Wednesday, June 23, 1999, México. *http://www.cronica.com.mx/cronica/1999/jun/23/* . The quoted text above is a translation of the original which follows: "No se substrae el agua y hay poca presión de población. Este convenio es un caso especial, ya que por primera vez se toman acciones de conservación que consideran a los ecosistemas en su conjunto. No se enfocan a un sólo recurso, como el agua, que es el caso del río Bravo."
[936] Ejidos are lands held in common by communities of an area, sometimes reapportioned to individuals for their use and sometimes worked by the communites as a whole.

[937] Joint Declaration between the Secretariat of Environment, Natural Resources and Fisheries (SEMARNAP) of the United States of Mexico and the Secretary of the Department of the Interior (DOI) of the United States of America, to work jointly in the Upper San Pedro River Basin. June 22, 1999.

[938] Ibid.

[939] An Act to Provide for the establishment of the Coronado International Memorial, in the State of Arizona, approved August 18, 1941 (55 Stat. 630).

[940] E.K. Burlew, Acting Secretary of the Interior, to Alva B. Adams, Chairman, Committee on Public Lands and Surveys, United States Senate, Washington, D.C., July 27, 1940, Report [To accompany S. 4130], 76th Congress, 3rd Session, Senate Report No. 2107, WACC, Folder H 14: Area & Service History 1940 F2.

[941] Grace M. Sparkes to Hillory Tolson, Acting Director, NPS, State of Texas Mine, October 28, 1950, WACC, Folder H 18: Biographical Data F11.

[942] Letter from eighteen residents of Nogales to Hayden, Nogales, May 24, 1955; The same letter to Goldwater from twenty-eight residents of southern Arizona, June 6, 1955, WACC, Folder H 14: Area and Service History 1940 F2.

[943] Untitled, undated, copy of Congressional debate on bill, H.R. 7553, WACC, Folder H 18: Biographical Data, General F11.

[944] Senator Carl Hayden to Grace Sparkes, Washington, D.C., July 2, 1954, ibid.

[945] Luis A. Gastellum, Assistant General Superintendent, Southwestern National Mounuments (SWNM), NPS, to Sparkes, Globe, October 15, 1954, ibid.

[946] Ray B. Ringenbach, Superintendent, Tumacacori National Monument, to Grace Sparkes, Tumacacori, August 10, 1954, ibid.

[947] Sparkes to Tolson State of Texas Mine, October 28, 1950.

[948] Cornelius C. Smith, Jr. Fort Huachuca: The story of a frontier post (Washington, D.C.: Department of the Army, United States Government Printing Office, 1981), 17-18.

[949] Ibid, 277-278.

[950] Ibid, 311.

[951] Ibid, 315; Establishment of the Coronado National Memorial (Name change from International Memorial), Arizona, By the President of the United States, A Proclamation (No. 2995), November 5, 1952, ILRPC Files.

[952] Smith, Fort Huachuca, 315.

[953] Master Plan Development Outline, Coronado National Memorial, November 1954, WACC, Folder D 18: Master Plans (1954) F2.

[954] Smith, Fort Huachuca, 318-332.

[955] Mission 66 for Coronado National Memorial, n.d. (filed among documents from 1956-1957), WACC, Folder D 18: Master Plan (Mission 66) F1.

[956] Ibid.

[957] Master Plan for the Conservation and Use of Coronado National Memorial, March 12, 1961, ibid.

[958] Regional Chief, Cooperative Activities Division, NPS, to Acting Regional Director, NPS, Santa Fe, October 14, 1954, WACC, Folder D 18: Master Plans (1954) F2.

[959] National Park Service Boundary Status Report, August 7, 1956, WACC, Folder L 1417: Boundary Adjustments – Surveys & Reports F1.

[960] Mission 66 for Coronado National Memorial, n.d. (ca. 1956-1957).

[961] Minutes of Meeting, Bisbee Chamber of Commerce, National Parks and Monuments Committee, December 8, 1950, WACC, Folder H 18: Biographical Data F11.

[962] Tolson to Governor Howard Pyle, Washington, D.C., May 9, 1952, Hayden Papers, AC, ASU, Box 201, folder 3; Master Plan Development Outline, Coronado National Memorial, November 1954.

[963] Master Plan Development Outline, Coronado National Memorial, March 1956, WACC, Folder D 18: Master Plans (56,57,58) F4.

964 Daily log, December 1, 1958, and passim, WACC, Folder A 26: Reports Daily logs 57,58 F1.
965 George Brown, interview by Thomas B. Carroll, September 20, 1974, CORO Files.
966 "Report of Jerome C. Miller, Associate Landscape Architect," Special Report Covering the Proposed Coronado International Monument, Submitted by Region III Headquarters, National Park Service, Department of the Interior, Santa Fe, February 1940, WACC, Folder H 14: Area and Service History, General F6.
967 Sparkes to Hayden, State of Texas Mine, June 28, 1947, WACC, Folder H 18: Biographical Data F11.
968 Rex King, Acting Regional Forester, NFS, to Carl Hayden, Albuquerque, March 2, 1948, ibid.
969 Recognition of Right of Way, Signed by Grace M. Sparkes, June 15, 1951, WACC, Folder L 1425: Land Holdings – Sparkes & Acquisition F17.
970 An Act to Revise the Boundaries of the Coronado National Memorial and to Authorize the Repair and Maintenance of an Access Road Thereto, in the State of Arizona, and for Other Purposes, Approved September 2, 1960 (74 Stat. 736). (Public Law 86-689), CORO Files.
971 Sparkes to Thomas J. Allen, Director, Region III, NPS, State of Texas Mine, June 17, 1961; Sparkes to Allen, State of Texas Mine, June 27, 1961, WACC, Folder H 18: Biographical Data F11.
972 Easement and Recognition of Road Right-of-Way, Signed by Grace M. Sparkes, August 15, 1961, WACC, Folder L 1425: Land Holdings – Sparkes & Acquisition F17.
973 "Boundary Adjustment – a Radical Proposal," n.d., WACC, Folder L 1417: Boundary Adjustments – Surveys & Reports F1.
974 Ibid.
975 Huntzinger to Director, Southwest Region, Subject: Boundary Changes for Existing NPS Areas, Hereford, August 31, 1970.
976 Frederick J. Brower, Acting Team Manager, Western Team, Denver Service Center, to Regional Director, Western Region, February 19, 1974, WACC, Folder L 1417: Boundary Adjustments – Surveys & Reports F1.
977 Environmental Review Proposal, General Management Plan, Coronado National Memorial, Initial Draft, n.d., WACC, Folder L 7617: Environmental Review Study/Statement 1976 F55.
978 E.W. Watkins, Acting Regional Director, Southwest Region, NPS, to Superintendent, Coronado National Memorial, Santa Fe, February 11, 1966, WACC, Folder K 26: Interpretive Reports F10.
979 Ibid.
980 William E. Brown, "Interpretive Prospectus for Coronado National Memorial," Revised April 1967, WACC, Folder K 18: Interpretive Prospectus F2.
981 Ibid.
982 Ibid, underlined in the original.
983 Hugo H. Huntzinger, Superintendent, Coronado National Memorial, to Director, Southwest Region, Subject: Boundary Changes for Existing NPS Areas, Hereford, August 31, 1970, WACC, Folder L 1417: Boundary Adjustments – Surveys & Reports F1.
984 William E. Brown, "Interpretive Prospectus Coronado National Memorial - Arizona," March 1974, WACC, Folder K 18: Interpretive Prospectus F2.
985 Ibid, underlined in the original.
986 Superintendent, Coronado National Memorial, to The Director, Report 10A2 – Annual Report on Information and Interpretive Services, Calendar Year 1958; Acting Superintendent, Coronado, to Director, Report NPS(CN)-1 - Annual Report on Information and Interpretive Services for 1964, WACC, Folder K 26: Interpretive Reports F10.
987 Terry R. Carlstrom, "Coronado National Memorial Master Plan," Draft, March 1974, 9, WACC, Folder D 18: Master Plan (1974) F10.
988 Brown, "Interpretive Prospectus Coronado National Memorial - Arizona," March 1974.

989 Huntzinger to General Superintendent, Southern Arizona Group (SOAR), Completion Report, CORO Centennial Arts Festival, Hereford, May 23, 1972, WACC, Folder A 8215: Special Events F1.
990 Ibid.
991 Ibid.
992 Centennial Art Festival Program, May 13–14, 1972, ibid.
993 Brown, "Interpretive Prospectus Coronado National Memorial - Arizona," March 1974.
994 Outline of Consolidated Comments by Staff on Coronado National Memorial Master Plan, January 31, 1974, WACC, Folder D 18: Master Plan (1974) F10.
995 Huntzinger to George Hunter, President, Sierra Vista Exchange Club, Hereford, February 8, 1973, WACC, Folder A 82: Special Events F3.
996 Huntzinger to Director, Western Region, through General Superintendent, Southern Arizona Group, Hereford, July 2, 1973, ibid.
997 Coronado Superintendent Laurel W. Dale to Regional Director, Western Region, NPS, through General Superintendent, SOAR, NPS, Hereford, December 18, 1974, WACC, Folder A 8215: Special Events F5.
998 Southwest Mission Research Center Newsletter, Vol. VIII, No. 23 (August 1974), 2, ibid.
999 Dale to Regional Director, through General Superintendent, SOAR, Hereford, December 18, 1974.
1000 Dale to Mrs. Louise C. Tester, Executive Director, Arizona Commission on the Arts & Humanities, Hereford, August 25, 1975, WACC, Folder A 8215: Special Events F6.
1001 Thomas B. Carroll, "Report on Bicentennial Activities at Coronado National Memorial, Cochise County, Arizona," September 23, 1976, 2; "Report on Bicentennial Activities, Western Region, National Park Service," n.d., WACC, Folder A 82: Bicentennial F42.
1002 Ibid, 7.
1003 "Report on Bicentennial Activities, Western Region, National Park Service," n.d.
1004 Dale to Sergio Bribiesca Elvira, Hereford, June 14, 1976, WACC, Folder A 8215: Special Events F7.
1005 Dale to Charles Polzer, Hereford, May 19, 1978, WACC, Folder A 8215: Special Events F9.
1006 Dale to Earl Jackson, Hereford, May 16, 1978, ibid.
1007 Dale to Bernard Fontana, Hereford, May 17, 1978, ibid.
1008 Brown, "Interpretive Prospectus Coronado National Memorial - Arizona," March 1974.
1009 Mary Lou Baldi, Untitled Environmental Living Handbook (probably December 1974), WACC, Folder A 98: Environmental Living Handbooks F50.
1010 Environmental Living Agenda, Coronado National Memorial, March 1–3, 1974; Carroll to Coronado Superintendent, Hereford, March 4, 1974, WACC, Folder A 98: Environmental Living Program F48.
1011 Ben Salazar, Acting Superintendent, Coronado National Memorial, to Clay Holland, Principal, Carmichael Elementary School, Sierra Vista, Az., Hereford, n.d., ibid. Ben Salazar wrote several similar, undated, letters; he also identified himself as Education Program Specialist/Historian, see the same file. "Staff Historian" Salazar left Coronado National Memorial in July 1973, so this program was obviously in the works before that date, WACC, Folder A 2621: Annual Reports F11.
1012 Huntzinger to Jackson, Hereford, March 5, 1974, WACC, Folder A 98: Environmental Living Program F48.
1013 "The Environmental Living Program, Coronado National Memorial," n.d. (probably written by Mary Lou Baldi), 3-10, WACC, Folder A 98: Environmental Living Handbooks F50.
1014 See WACC, Folder A 98: Environmental Living Program F49 and WACC, Folder A 98: Environmental Living Handbooks F50 for material from various programs.
1015 Laura Barry to Teachers, Environmental Living Program Coordinator, Hereford, September 9, 1976, WACC, Foler A 98: Environmental Living Program F49.

[1016] Environmental Living Program Coordinator, Western Region, to Staff Historian, Coronado, San Francisco, March 19, 1976, ibid.
[1017] Dale to unnamed principal, Hereford, April 22, 1976, ibid.
[1018] Environmental Living Program Coordinator, Western Region, to Staff Historian, Coronado, San Francisco, March 19, 1976.
[1019] Requisition to Vendor Laura Barry, Coronado National Memorial, July 1, 1977, WACC, Folder A 98: Environmental Living Program F49.
[1020] Requisition to Vendor Mary Lou Baldi, Coronado National Memorial, July 1, 1977; July 10, 1977 (apparently for the same contract), ibid.
[1021] Baldi, Untitled Environmental Living Handbook (probably December 1974); Environmental Living Workshop Agenda, March 1-3, 1974, WACC, Folder A 98: Environmental Living Program F48.
[1022] Dale to Mrs. Cecilia Gross, Smith Middle School, Hereford, May 17, 1977, WACC, Folder A 98: Environmental Living Program F49.
[1023] Peg White, "Unique program: Students reenact history, cultural environments," Fort Huachuca Scout, pictures by Jim Gross, May 26, 1977, ibid.
[1024] Coronado National Memorial School Outreach Program overview, March 31, 1988, ibid.
[1025] Undated "Budget – Environmental Living Program," filed with material from 1982-1984, WACC, Folder A 98: International Education Program F52.
[1026] Arizpe/Palominas Environmental Cultural Exchange Program –- Tentative Agenda, May 11-12, 1984, ibid.
[1027] Dale to Regional Director, Western Region, NPS, Hereford, May 10, 1983, ibid.
[1028] John Clay, General Superintendent, SOAR, to Regional Director, Western Region, NPS, Phoenix, April 6, 1984, ibid.
[1029] Annual Statement for Interpretation and Visitor Services, July 23, 1985, WACC, Folder K 1817: Annual Statement for Interpretation F9.
[1030] Carroll to General Superintendent, SOAR, Hereford, June 27, 1974, WACC, Folder A 34: Commendations F13.
[1031] Brown, "Interpretive Prospectus for Coronado National Memorial," Revised April 1967.
[1032] Brown, "Interpretive Prospectus Coronado National Memorial - Arizona," March 1974.
[1033] Carlstrom, "Coronado National Memorial Master Plan," Draft, March 1974, 32-37.
[1034] Master Plan of Coronado National Memorial, Chapter 3: Management Programs Narrative, 1965, WACC, Folder D 18: Master Plans (65,66,72) F7.
[1035] Philip S. Romigh, Denver Service Center, NPS, to Huntzinger, Denver, March 13, 1973, WACC, Folder D 18: Master Plan (1973) F8; Untitled Proposal for land exchange, n.d., 78-85, WACC, Folder L 7617: Environmental Impact Statement (EIS) F56.
[1036] Dale to "Friend of Coronado," Hereford, n.d. (1976), WACC, Folder D 18: Master Plan (1976) F12; "Public favors larger Coronado Memorial; Nixes Amphitheatre," Bisbee Review, March 25, 1976, WACC, Folder D 18: General Management Plan (1976) F17.
[1037] Romigh to Huntzinger, Denver, March 13, 1973.
[1038] Dale to Regional Director, Western Region, NPS, through General Superintendent, SOAR, NPS, Hereford, December 18, 1974.
[1039] Dale to General Superintendent, SOAR, December 18, 1974, WACC, Folder A 8215: Special Events F5.
[1040] David E. Gackenbach, Acting General Superintendent, SOAR, to Ronald Ruziska, Arizona State Land Department, Phoenix, January 25, 1989, WACC, Folder A 8215: Special Events F21.
[1041] The Coronado National Memorial Administrative Records, Western Archeological and Conservation Center, National Park Service, Tucson, Arizona (WACC) collection contains twenty-one files coded A 82 and A 8215. These files comprise thousands of pages of material on the Historical Pageants, generally segregated by year.

[1042] Coronado International Historical Pageant Meeting, May 16, 1984, Discussion Points and Resolutions, WACC, Folder A 8215: Special Events F16.
[1043] Theda Adcock, Festival Coordinator, to James E. Officer, Hereford, April 22, 1985, WACC, Folder A 8215: Special Events F17.
[1044] Coronado Superintendent Joseph L. Sewell to General Superintendent, SOAR, Hereford, April 18, 1988, WACC, Folder A 8215: Special Events F20.
[1045] Richard Byrd, "Coronado pageant may be in jeopardy due to personnel cuts," Sierra Vista Daily Herald-Dispatch, January 13, 1983, 1, WACC, Folder A 8215: Special Events F15; this articles says that these particular personnel cuts were the result of a request by an unnamed staff member that the Inspector General investigate Memorial staffing. In the same file is an unidentified, contemporary, editorial entitled "Get out, and enjoy," which added that "the National Park Service's budget is coming under close scrutiny. Without a good turn-out, this year's pageant, the eleventh, could be the last."
[1046] Clay to Officer, Phoenix, April 29, 1981, WACC, Folder A 8215: Special Events F14.
[1047] Adcock to Ken Ramsay, Sierra Vista Public Schools, Hereford, February 2, 1983
[1048] Comments Concerning Coronado Festival – Jim Officer, n.d., WACC, Folder A 8215: Special Events F16.
[1049] Coronado Pageant Evaluation....Jim Griffith, April 25, 1984, ibid.
[1050] Griffith to Adcock, Tucson, March 14, 1983, WACC, Folder A 8215: Special Events F15.
[1051] Coronado International Historical Pageant Meeting, May 16, 1984, Discussion Points and Resolutions.
[1052] Unidentified [illegible signature] to Ed Pilley, Interpretive Specialist, SOAR, April 21, 1986, WACC, Folder A 8215: Special Events F18.
[1053] Typed note, signed by Nick(?), March 26, 1986, WACC, Folder A 8215: Special Events F21.
[1054] Carlos Nagel to Pilley, Tucson, July 5, 1986, WACC, Folder A 8215: Special Events F19.
[1055] Proposal for Consultation Services to Carlos Nagel, n.d., ibid.
[1056] Dale to Ms. Mercedes Guererro, Hereford, September 16, 1986; Generic letter, Dale to (Group), Hereford, n.d., ibid.
[1057] Interpretive Media Specialist, SOAR, to Superintendent, Coronado National Memorial, Tucson, January 20, 1987, ibid.
[1058] Sewell to Acting General Superintendent, SOAR, Hereford, February 3, 1987, ibid.
[1059] Handwritten note, February 4, 1987, ibid.
[1060] Sewell to Superintendent, Tumacacori National Monument, Hereford, February 6, 1987, ibid.
[1061] Nagel to William Paleck, Acting General Superintendent, SOAR, February 7, 1987, ibid.
[1062] Typed note to Adcock, February 6, 1987, ibid.
[1063] Annual Statement for Interpretation and Visitor Services, July 8, 1987, WACC, Folder K 1817: Annual Statement for Interpretation F9.
[1064] Interpretive Media Specialist, SOAR, to Superintendent, Coronado National Memorial, Tucson, March 15, 1987, ibid.
[1065] Adcock to Officer, Hereford, May 13, 1987, ibid.
[1066] Sewell to General Superintendent, SOAR, Hereford, May 4, 1987, ibid.
[1067] Profesor Ricardo Montijo Castro to Sewell, Naco, Sonora, April 29, 1987, ibid.
[1068] Sewell to Richard Messick, Commander, Huachuca Company, Arizona Rangers, Hereford, April 28, 1987, ibid.
[1069] Sewell to General Superintendent, SOAR, Hereford, May 4, 1987.
[1070] Annual Statement for Interpretation and Visitor Services, July 8, 1987.
[1071] Adcock to Officer, Hereford, May 13, 1987, ibid.
[1072] Sewell to General Superintendent, SOAR, Hereford, May 4, 1987.
[1073] Coronado Superintendent Joseph L. Sewell to General Superintendent, SOAR, Hereford, April 18, 1988, WACC, Folder A 8215: Special Events F20.
[1074] Sewell to Acting General Superintendent, SOAR, Hereford, November 17, 1988, ibid.

[1075] Frank Sumrak, Interpretive Specialist, SOAR, through Operations Specialist, SOAR, to Acting General Superintendent, SOAR, December 8, 1988, WACC, Folder A 8215: Special Events F21.
[1076] Ibid.
[1077] Gackenbach to Ronald Ruziska, Arizona State Land Department, Phoenix, January 25, 1989, ibid.
[1078] Ruziska to Gackenbach, February 6, 1989, ibid.
[1079] Draft PSA, Rescheduling of the 1989 Coronado Borderlands Festival, March 15, 1989, ibid.
[1080] Sewell to Chief of Operations, SOAR, Hereford, April 27, 1989, ibid.
[1081] Sumrak to General Superintendent, SOAR, May 15, 1989, ibid.
[1082] Sewell to Chief of Operations, SOAR, Hereford, April 27, 1989.
[1083] Sumrak to General Superintendent, SOAR, May 15, 1989, ibid.
[1084] Ibid.
[1085] Ibid.
[1086] Draft PSA, Rescheduling of the 1989 Coronado Borderlands Festival, March 15, 1989.
[1087] Sumrak to General Superintendent, SOAR, May 15, 1989, ibid.
[1088] Interpretive Prospectus, State of Texas Mine Site, Coronado National Memorial, 1988, WACC, Folder K 18: Interpretive Prospectus F2.
[1089] Annual Statement for Interpretation and Visitor Services, Coronado National Memorial, 1988, WACC, Folder K 1817: Annual Statement for Interpretation F2.
[1090] Connie Toops, "Going to Bat for Bats," National Parks: The Magazine of the National Parks and Conservation Association, Vol. 75, No. 1-2 (January-February 2001), 31.
[1091] "Abandoned mines a danger to humans, a home to bats," CNN.com nature, August 28, 2000, http://www.cnn.com/2000/NATURE/08/28/mines.bats.ap/; David A. Saugey, "U.S. National Forests: Unsung Home to America's Bats," Bats, Vol. 9, No. 3 (Fall 1991), 3-6; National Park Service -- Mining and Minerals Branch, Coronado National Memorial, Abandoned Mine Closure project – Closure Proposals and Cost Estimates, March 1, 1993, CORO Files, provides some budgetary details on mine safing and bat habitat.
[1092] Draft Livestock Management Plan, Coronado National Memorial, Cochise County, Arizona, March 2000, II:14, CORO Files.
[1093] Ibid, IV:7.
[1094] Director, NPS, to Regional Director, Region Three, NPS, n.d. (November-December 1952), WACC, Folder H 14: Area & Service History 41-52 F3.
[1095] Grazing Preferences Involving Use of National Park Lands – 1955, WACC, Folder A 44: Memo of Agreement F18.
[1096] Master Plan Development Outline, Coronado National Memorial, Arizona, Forestry, July 1955, WACC, Folder D 18: Master Plan (Mission 66) F1.
[1097] Superintendent Philip Welles to Director, NPS, Hereford, July 30, 1961, WACC, Folder A 2615: Monthly Reports F6.
[1098] Draft Environmental Impact Statement, Proposed Resource Management Plan Applicable to Coronado National Memorial, September 10, 1973, WACC, Folder D 18: Resource Management Plan F13.
[1099] Denver Service Center, Planning Directive for Coronado National Memorial, January 1973, WACC, Folder D 18: Planning Directives F14.
[1100] final general management plan, September 1976, WACC, Folder D 18: General Management Plans F15.
[1101] Draft Livestock Management Plan, March 2000, I:4.
[1102] Annual Statement for Interpretation and Visitor Services, February 1988, WACC, Folder K 1817: Annual Statement for Interpretation F9.
[1103] Draft Livestock Management Plan, March 2000, I:4-5.
[1104] Master Plan Development Outline, Coronado National Memorial, Arizona, December 1961, WACC, Folder D 18: Master Plans (61,62,63) F5.

1105 Narrative Operating Program, Objectives 1964 Fiscal Year, n.d., WACC, Folder D 18: Master Plan (1964) F6.
1106 Environmental Assessment, Extension of the Arizona Trail, Coronado National Memorial, NPS, Arizona, July 15, 1994, CORO Files.
1107 Fact Sheet, Yaqui Ridge Trail, n.d., CORO Files.
1108 Statement for Management, Coronado National Memorial, Arizona, November 1980, WACC, Folder D 18: Planning Directives F14.
1109 Superintendent, Coronado National Memorial, to General Superintendent, SOAR, Hereford, August 22, 1973, WACC, Folder A 2615: Monthly Reports Daily Events F7.
1110 Coronado National Memorial Draft General Management Plan, July 1976, WACC, Folder D 18: General Management Plans F15.
1111 Draft Livestock Management Plan, March 2000, I:5.
1112 Establishment of the Coronado National Memorial (Name change from International Memorial), Arizona, By the President of the United States, A Proclamation (No. 2995), November 5, 1952, Intermountain Land Resources Program Center Files, NPS, Santa Fe, N.M.
1113 Summary of Federal Legeslation [sic] Which Amends the Establishment Act for Coronado National Memorial, n.d.; Senate Bill 2806, 86th Congress, 2nd Session (1960); Report No. 1654, to accompany Senate Bill 2806, 86th Congress, 2nd Session (1960); Memorandum, from Director, NPS, to Regional Director, Region Three, Subject: Proposed Legislation, Coronado National Memorial, August 20, 1958, Coronado National Memorial Administrative Records, Western Archeological and Conservation Center, NPS, Tucson, Arizona, Folder H 1415: Legislative History; NPS Boundary Status Report, Prepared August 7, 1956, Coronado National Memorial Administrative Records, Western Archeological and Conservation Center, NPS, Tucson, Arizona, Folder L 1417: Boundary Adjustments – Surveys & Reports.
1114 An Act to Provide for the establishment of the Coronado International Memorial, in the State of Arizona, approved August 18, 1941 (55 Stat. 630).
1115 Request for Transfer of Excess Real Property and Related Personal Property, from Director, NPS, to Commissioner, United States Section, International Boundary and Water Commission, February 1964; Letter, Donald E. Lee, Chief, Division of Land and Water Rights, NPS, to Bernard L. Boutin, Administrator, General Services Administration, March 5, 1964; Boundary Status Map, October 1958, Coronado National Memorial Administrative Records, Western Archeological and Conservation Center, NPS, Tucson, Arizona, Folder L 1417: Boundary Adjustments – Proposed/Enacted Legislation; Alphabetical listing by landowner's name, NPS Division of Land Acquisitions, July 10, 1979; Land Acquisition Plan, Coronado National Memorial, January 18, 1980 (and attached maps), Intermountain Land Resources Program Center Files, NPS, Santa Fe, N.M.; Land Ownership Record, NPS, September 2, 1960, Coronado National Memorial Administrative Records, Western Archeological and Conservation Center, NPS, Tucson, Arizona, Folder L 1425: Land Holdings – Sparkes & Acquisition.
1116 "Agreement: Coronado National Memorial, Cochise County, Arizona, and Coronado National Forest, Cochise County, Arizona," Signed October 16 and 19, 1979, Intermountain Land Resources Program Center Files, NPS, Santa Fe, N.M.
Slightly different, but not conflicting versions in the same files were used to add details.
1117 Boundary Status Map, October 1958; Alphabetical listing by landowner's name, July 10, 1979; Land Acquisition Plan, January 18, 1980 (and attached maps).
1118 Approval of field notes of Homestead Entry Survey No. 311, Office of the U.S. Surveyor General, Phoenix, Arizona, August 8, 1917, Coronado National Memorial Files
1119 Cochise Chapter of The Arizona Archeological Society, n.d.
1120 Bart Barbour, "Dude Ranches at Coronado National Memorial: A Brief History," Coronado National Memorial Files, from Tracking Book, Cochise County Assessor's Office, Bisbee, Arizona; Quit-Claim Deed, Frank Zaleski to Jose Zaleski, Signed January 3, 1956, Cochise

County Recorder's Office, Bisbee, Arizona, Deeds of Real Estate, Docket 142, pages 239-241.

[1121] Warranty Deed, Joe Zaleski, aka José, and wife Lucy, to John A. and Inez Z. Jones, Signed April 19, 1957, Cochise County Recorder's Office, Bisbee, Arizona, Deeds of Real Estate, Docket 166, pages 587-588.

[1122] Warranty Deed, Southwestern Monuments Association to United States of America, Recorded May 14, 1962, Intermountain Land Resources Program Center Files, NPS, Santa Fe, N.M.

[1123] Deed of Gift, John A. and Inez Z. Jones, of Santa Cruz County, Arizona, to John Z. and Lawrence D. Jones, Signed April 24, 1962, Cochise County Recorder's Office, Bisbee, Arizona, Deeds of Real Estate, Docket 300, pages 406-407.

[1124] Joint Tenancy Deed, John Z. Jones and Lawrence D. Jones to Everett Baumkirchner and Margaret E. Baumkirchner, husband and wife, an undivided half interest, Signed May 26, 1965, Cochise County Recorder's Office, Bisbee, Arizona, Deeds of Real Estate, Docket 389, page 21; Joint Tenancy Deed, John Z. Jones and Lawrence D. Jones to Fred and Mary Ann Baumkirchner, husband and wife, an undivided half interest, Signed May 26, 1965, Cochise County Recorder's Office, Bisbee, Arizona, Deeds of Real Estate, Docket 389, page 22; Realty Mortgage, Everett Baumkirchner and Margaret E. Baumkirchner, his wife, and Fred Baumkirchner and Mary Ann Baumkirchner, his wife, with John Z. Jones and Lawrence D. Jones, Signed June 1, 1965, Cochise County Recorder's Office, Bisbee, Arizona, Deeds of Real Estate, Docket 389, page 23.

[1125] Warranty Deed, Fred E. Baumkirchner and Mary Ann Baumkirchner, husband and wife, and Everett M. Baumkirchner and Margaret E. Baumkirchner, husband and wife, to Transamerica Title Insurance Company, as Trustee, Signed March 11, 1972, Cochise County Recorder's Office, Bisbee, Arizona, Deeds of Real Estate, Docket 841, pages 215-216; Warranty Deed, Transamerica Title Insurance Company to United States of America, Signed March 1, 1973, Cochise County Recorder's Office, Bisbee, Arizona, Deeds of Real Estate, Docket 841, page 218.

[1126] Request for bids for appraisal of properties by A.W. Gray, Division of Land Acquisition, Western Region, NPS, May 4, 1979, Intermountain Land Resources Program Center Files, NPS, Santa Fe, N.M.

[1127] Transamerica Title Insurance Company Preliminary Report, n.d., Intermountain Land Resources Program Center Files, NPS, Santa Fe, N.M.

[1128] Ibid.

[1129] Ibid.

[1130] Ibid.

[1131] Ibid.

[1132] Grant Deed, Fred E. Baumkirchner and Mary Ann Baumkirchner, his wife, as joint tenants, and Everett M. Baumkirchner and Margaret E. Baumkirchner, his wife, as joint tenants, to NPS, Signed March 20, 1980, Intermountain Land Resources Program Center Files, NPS, Santa Fe, N.M.

[1133] Request for bids for appraisal of properties by A.W. Gray, May 4, 1979.

[1134] Transamerica Title Insurance Company Preliminary Report, n.d.

[1135] Warranty Deed, Fred E. Baumkirchner and Mary Ann Baumkirchner, Husband and Wife; and Everett M Baumkirchner and Margaret E. Baumkirchner, Husband and Wife, to James M. Tyra and Billie Jean Tyra, Husband and Wife, Signed March 25, 1980, Cochise County Recorder's Office, Bisbee, Arizona, Deeds of Real Estate, Docket 1413, pages 456-457.

[1136] Warranty Deed, Fred E. Baumkirchner and Mary Ann Baumkirchner, husband and wife, and Everett M. Baumkirchner and Margaret E. Baumkirchner, husband and wife, to Lawrence Edward Ray, an unmarried man, Signed July 21, 1967, Cochise County Recorder's Office, Bisbee, Arizona, Deeds of Real Estate, Docket 491, page 525.

1137 Real Estate Mortgage for Arizona, Lawrence Edward Ray and Farmers Home Administration of the United States Department of Agriculture, September 27, 1967, Cochise County Recorder's Office, Bisbee, Arizona, Deeds of Real Estate, Docket 502, pages 478-479.

1138 Joint Tenancy Deed, Lawrence Edward Ray, husband of Maria T. Ray, as his sole and separate property, to James M. Tyra and Billie Jean Tyra, his wife, Signed August 13, 1971, Cochise County Recorder's Office, Bisbee, Arizona, Deeds of Real Estate, Docket 713, page 392.

1139 Warranty Deed, Fred E. and Mary Ann Baumkirchner, and Everett M. and Margaret E. Baumkirchner, to James M. and Billie Jean Tyra, March 25, 1980.

1140 Transamerica Title Insurance Company Preliminary Report, n.d.

1141 Warranty Deed, Fred E. and Mary Ann Baumkirchner, and Everett M. and Margaret E. Baumkirchner, to James M. and Billie Jean Tyra, March 25, 1980.

1142 Joint Tenancy Deed, Fred E. Baumkirchner and Mary Ann Baumkirchner, his wife, an undivided half interest, and Everett M. Baumkirchner and Margaret E. Baumkirchner, his wife, an undivided half interest, to James M. Tyra and Billie Jean Tyra, his wife, Signed September 30, 1971, Cochise County Recorder's Office, Bisbee, Arizona, Deeds of Real Estate, Docket 1221, page 457.

1143 Warranty Deed, Fred E. and Mary Ann Baumkirchner, and Everett M. and Margaret E. Baumkirchner, to James M. and Billie Jean Tyra, March 25, 1980.

1144 Grant Deed, James M. Tyra and Billie Jean Tyra, his wife, as joint tenants, to NPS, March 25, 1980, Intermountain Land Resources Program Center Files, NPS, Santa Fe, N.M.

1145 Warranty Deed, Fred E. and Mary Ann Baumkirchner, and Everett M. and Margaret E. Baumkirchner, to James M. and Billie Jean Tyra, March 25, 1980.

1146 Listing shows two properties of equal value belonging to the Greens; Sam R. Clark, Assessor, Cochise County, Arizona, to Alvin H. Reynolds, Chief Appraiser, Western Region, NPS, March 18, 1974, Intermountain Land Resources Program Center Files, NPS, Santa Fe, N.M.

1147 Transamerica Title Insurance Company Preliminary Report, n.d.

1148 Joint Tenancy Deed, Fred E. Baumkirchner and Mary Ann Baumkirchner, his wife, an undivided ½ interest, and Everett M. Baumkirchner and Margaret E. Baumkirchner, his wife, an undivided ½ interest, to Dewitt Green and Doretta Ruth Green, his wife, Signed August 23, 1971, Cochise County Recorder's Office, Bisbee, Arizona, Deeds of Real Estate, Docket 862, pages 10-11.

1149 Request for bids for appraisal of properties by A.W. Gray, May 4, 1979.

1150 Joint Tenancy Deed, Fred E. and Mary Ann Baumkirchner, and Everett M. and Margaret E. Baumkirchner, to Dewitt and Doretta Ruth Green, August 23, 1971.

1151 Grant Deed, Dewitt Green and Doretta Ruth Green, his wife, as joint tenants, to NPS, April 3, 1980, Intermountain Land Resources Program Center Files, NPS, Santa Fe, N.M.

1152 Sam R. Clark to Alvin H. Reynolds, March 18, 1974.

1153 Transamerica Title Insurance Company Preliminary Report, n.d.

1154 Warranty Deed, Robert G. Chavez and Betty J. Chavez, husband and wife, to Eileen G. Owens, Signed April 28, 1978, Cochise County Recorder's Office, Bisbee, Arizona, Deeds of Real Estate, Docket 1250, page 147.

1155 Request for bids for appraisal of properties by A.W. Gray, May 4, 1979.

1156 Warranty Deed, Fred E. Baumkirchner and Mary Ann Baumkirchner, husband and wife, and Everett M. Baumkirchner and Margaret E. Baumkirchner, husband and wife, to William Arthur Archie and Eloise Archie, husband and wife, Signed July 21, 1967, Cochise County Recorder's Office, Bisbee, Arizona, Deeds of Real Estate, Docket 493, page 280.

1157 Warranty Deed, William A. Archie and Eloise Archie, his wife, to Robert G. Chavez and Betty J. Chavez, his wife, Signed November 17, 1972, Cochise County Recorder's Office, Bisbee, Arizona, Deeds of Real Estate, Docket 831, page 427.

1158 Warranty Deed, Robert G. Chavez and Betty J. Chavez, husband and wife, to Eileen G. Owens, an unmarried woman, Signed April 28, 1978, Cochise County Recorder's Office, Bisbee, Arizona, Deeds of Real Estate, Docket 1250, page 147.

1159 Joint Tenancy Deed, Eileen G. Owens, an unmarried woman, to Allan Cerkowniak and Leona Cerkowniak, husband and wife, Signed January 4, 1985, Cochise County Recorder's Office, Bisbee, Arizona, Deeds of Real Estate, Listing number 860406690.

1160 Listing shows two properties of equal value belonging to the Greens; Sam R. Clark to Alvin H. Reynolds, March 18, 1974.

1161 Transamerica Title Insurance Company Preliminary Report, n.d.

1162 Joint Tenancy Deed, Fred E. Baumkirchner and Mary Ann Baumkirchner, his wife, an undivided ½ interest, and Everett M. Baumkirchner and Margaret E. Baumkirchner, his wife, an undivided ½ interest, to Dewitt Green and Doretta Ruth Green, his wife, Signed August 23, 1971, Cochise County Recorder's Office, Bisbee, Arizona, Deeds of Real Estate, Docket 862, pages 10-11.

1163 Request for bids for appraisal of properties by A.W. Gray, May 4, 1979.

1164 Joint Tenancy Deed, Fred E. and Mary Ann Baumkirchner, and Everett M. and Margaret E. Baumkirchner, to Dewitt and Doretta Ruth Green, August 23, 1971.

1165 Grant Deed, Dewitt Green and Doretta Ruth Green, his wife, as joint tenants, to NPS, April 3, 1980, Intermountain Land Resources Program Center Files, NPS, Santa Fe, N.M.

1166 Sam R. Clark to Alvin H. Reynolds, March 18, 1974.

1167 Transamerica Title Insurance Company Preliminary Report, n.d.

1168 Joint Tenancy Deed, Fred E. Baumkirchner and Mary Ann Baumkirchner, husband and wife, and Everett M. Baumkirchner and Margaret E. Baumkirchner, husband and wife, to Calvin R. Teague and Esther Teague, Signed September 30, 1966, Cochise County Recorder's Office, Bisbee, Arizona, Deeds of Real Estate, Docket 456, page 215.

1169 Request for bids for appraisal of properties by A.W. Gray, May 4, 1979.

1170 Joint Tenancy Deed, Fred E. and Mary Ann Baumkirchner, and Everett M. and Margaret E. Baumkirchner, to Calvin R. and Esther Teague, Signed September 30, 1966.

1171 Warranty Deed, Calvin R. Teague and Esther Teague, his wife, to William L. Cashman and Ramona E. Cashman, his wife, Signed April 29, 1971, Cochise County Recorder's Office, Bisbee, Arizona, Deeds of Real Estate, Docket 767, page 168.

1172 Transamerica Title Insurance Company Preliminary Report, n.d.

1173 Warranty Deed, Fred E. Baumkirchner and Mary Ann Baumkirchner, husband and wife, and Everett M. Baumkirchner and Margaret E. Baumkirchner, husband and wife, to Everett M. Baumkirchner Jr., a single man, Signed March 19, 1980, Cochise County Recorder's Office, Bisbee, Arizona, Deeds of Real Estate, Docket 1410, page 2.

1174 Request for bids for appraisal of properties by A.W. Gray, May 4, 1979.

1175 Warranty Deed, Fred E. Baumkirchner and Mary Ann Baumkirchner, husband and wife, and Everett M. Baumkirchner and Margaret E. Baumkirchner, husband and wife, to Everett M. Baumkirchner Jr., Signed October 11, 1971, Cochise County Recorder's Office, Bisbee, Arizona, Deeds of Real Estate, Docket 940, page 71; Agreement, Fred E. Baumkirchner and Mary Ann Baumkirchner, his wife, as to an undivided ½ interest; and Everett M. Baumkirchner and Margaret E. Baumkirchner, his wife, as to an undivided ½ interest, and Everett M. Baumkirchner Jr., a single man, Signed October 11, 1971, Cochise County Recorder's Office, Bisbee, Arizona, Deeds of Real Estate, Docket 732, page 107.

1176 Grant Deed, Everett M. Baumkirchner Jr., to NPS, Signed March 19, 1980, Intermountain Land Resources Program Center Files, NPS, Santa Fe, N.M.

1177 Warranty Deed, Fred E. and Mary Ann Baumkirchner, and Everett M. and Margaret E. Baumkirchner, to Everett M. Baumkirchner Jr., Signed March 19, 1980, CCR, Deeds of Real Estate, Docket 1410, page 2.

1178 Approval of field notes of Homestead Entry Survey No. 310, Office of the U.S. Surveyor General, Phoenix, Az., August 8, 1917, Coronado National Memorial Files.

1179 Cochise Chapter of The Arizona Archeological Society, n.d.
1180 Barbour, "Dude Ranches," from Tracking Book, Cochise County Assessor's Office, Bisbee, Arizona; Quit-Claim Deed, Frank Zaleski to Jose Zaleski, Signed January 3, 1956, Cochise County Recorder's Office, Bisbee, Arizona, Deeds of Real Estate, Docket 142, pages 239-241.
1181 Warranty Deed, Joe Zaleski, aka José, and wife Lucy, to John A. and Inez Z. Jones, Signed April 19, 1957, Cochise County Recorder's Office, Bisbee, Arizona, Deeds of Real Estate, Docket 166, pages 587-588.
1182 Deed, John A. and Inez Z. Jones to Southwestern Monuments Association, Signed and recorded May 22, 1959, Cochise County Recorder's Office, Bisbee, Arizona, Deeds of Real Estate, Docket 217, pages 129-130.
1183 Warranty Deed, Southwestern Monuments Association to United States of America, Recorded May 14, 1962.
1184 Deed of Gift, John A. and Inez Z. Jones, of Santa Cruz County, Arizona, to John Z. and Lawrence D. Jones, Signed April 24, 1962.
1185 Joint Tenancy Deed, John Z. and Lawrence D. Jones to Everett and Margaret E. Baumkirchner, Signed May 26, 1965; Joint Tenancy Deed, John Z. and Lawrence D. Jones to Fred and Mary Ann Baumkirchner, Signed May 26, 1965; Realty Mortgage, Everett and Margaret E. Baumkirchner, and Fred and Mary Ann Baumkirchner, with John Z. and Lawrence D. Jones, Signed June 1, 1965.
1186 Warranty Deed, Fred E. and Mary Ann Baumkirchner, and Everett M. and Margaret E. Baumkirchner, to Transamerica Title Insurance Company, as Trustee, Signed March 11, 1972; Warranty Deed, Transamerica Title Insurance Company to United States of America, Signed March 1, 1973.
1187 Thomas J. Allen, Regional Director, Southwest Region, NPS, to Fred Kennedy, Regional Forester, U.S. Forest Service, February 18, 1963, Intermountain Land Resources Program Center Files, Santa Fe, N.M.
1188 Letter, Office of the Acting Secretary of Agriculture to Office of the Secretary of the Interior, December 27, 1913, Coronado National Memorial Administrative Records, Western Archeological and Conservation Center, NPS, Tucson, Arizona, Folder L 1425: Land Holdings – Pyeatt.
1189 Application for Amendment, Cornelius N. Driscoll, September 23, 1914, Coronado National Memorial Administrative Records, Western Archeological and Conservation Center, NPS, Tucson, Arizona, Folder L 1425: Land Holdings – Driscoll.
1190 Testimonies of Witnesses Zeno Aston and Robert Fourr, Homestead Entry, Final Proof, April 14, 1921, Coronado National Memorial Administrative Records, Western Archeological and Conservation Center, NPS, Tucson, Arizona; Homestead Entry Application, John Pyeatt, Received U.S. Land Office, Phoenix, Arizona, Coronado National Memorial Administrative Records, Western Archeological and Conservation Center, NPS, Tucson, Arizona, Folder L 1425: Land Holdings – Pyeatt.
1191 Final Certificate, Homestead, John Pyeatt, Approved June 29, 1921, Coronado National Memorial Administrative Records, Western Archeological and Conservation Center, NPS, Tucson, Arizona, Folder L 1425: Land Holdings – Pyeatt; Barbour, "Dude Ranches."
1192 Barbour, "Dude Ranches;" George Brown 1998.
1193 George Brown 1998; Barbour, "Dude Ranches".
1194 Barbour, "Dude Ranches"; George Brown 1998; Bisbee Daily Review on June 18, 1950, Coronado National Memorial Files; Pete Van Cleve, "List of Classified Structures, CCC/WPA, Coronado Establishment and Land Acquisitions," 1996, Coronado National Memorial Files.
1195 Joint Tenancy Deed, George H. Howe and Martha J. Howe, his wife, to George F. Weick and Elsie R. Weick, his wife, Wood Dale, Illinois, Recorded April 27, 1973, Cochise County

Recorder's Office, Bisbee, Arizona, Deeds of Real Estate, Docket 853, page 84; George Brown 1998; Bart Barbour, "Dude Ranches".

[1196] Sam R. Clark to Alvin H. Reynolds, March 18, 1974.
[1197] Transamerica Title Insurance Company Preliminary Report, n.d.
[1198] Request for bids for appraisal of properties by A.W. Gray, May 4, 1979.
[1199] NPS Property Inspection Certificate, ca. May 25, 1979, Intermountain Land Resources Program Center Files, NPS, Santa Fe, N.M.
[1200] George Brown 1998.
[1201] Transamerica Title Insurance Company Preliminary Report, n.d.
[1202] Joint Tenancy Deed, Howe to Weick, April 27, 1973.
[1203] Clark to Reynolds, March 18, 1974.
[1204] Barbour, "Dude Ranching".
[1205] Transamerica Title Insurance Company Preliminary Report, n.d.
[1206] Sample letter to landowners by A.W. Gray, Chief, Division of Land Acquisition, Western Region, NPS, re: appraisal and land acquisition, May 3, 1979, Intermountain Land Resources Program Center Files, NPS, Santa Fe, N.M.
[1207] A.W. Gray, Chief, Division of Land Acquisition, Western Region, NPS, to Robert F. Temple, June 8, 1979, Intermountain Land Resources Program Center Files, NPS, Santa Fe, N.M.
[1208] NPS Property Inspection Certificate, ca. May 25, 1979.
[1209] Alphabetical listing by landowner's name, NPS Division of Land Acquisitions, July 10, 1979, Intermountain Land Resources Program Center Files, NPS, Santa Fe, N.M.
[1210] Master Deed Listing, NPS Division of Land Acquisitions, March 17, 1980, Intermountain Land Resources Program Center Files, NPS, Santa Fe, N.M.
[1211] Master Deed Listing, NPS Division of Land Acquisitions, April 11, 1980, Intermountain Land Resources Program Center Files, NPS, Santa Fe, N.M.
[1212] Paul R. Thompson, Acting Superintendent, Coronado National Memorial, to Director, Washington Office, NPS, July 30, 1979, Intermountain Land Resources Program Center Files, NPS, Santa Fe, N.M.
[1213] Handwritten note re: telephone call, Leland Auslander [sic] to Bob Gibbons, September 24, 1979, Intermountain Land Resources Program Center Files, NPS, Santa Fe, N.M.
[1214] Handwritten note re: telephone call, Auslender to Bob Gibbons, September 24, 1979.
[1215] Master Deed Listing, NPS Division of Land Acquisitions, March 31, 1980, Intermountain Land Resources Program Center Files, NPS, Santa Fe, N.M.
[1216] Memorandum, from Division of Land Acquisition, Western Region, to Chief, Coordination and Control Branch, Washington Office, NPS, May 12, 1980, Intermountain Land Resources Program Center Files, NPS, Santa Fe, N.M.
[1217] Master Deed Listing, March 31, 1980.
[1218] Memorandum, from Division of Land Acquisition, May 12, 1980.
[1219] Grant Deed, Leland I. Auslender to NPS, April 21, 1980, Intermountain Land Resources Program Center Files, NPS, Santa Fe, N.M.
[1220] Memorandum, from Division of Land Acquisition, May 12, 1980.
[1221] Grant Deed, Auslender to NPS, April 21, 1980.
[1222] Untitled map of Coronado National Memorial, July 1982, Intermountain Land Resources Program Center Files, NPS, Santa Fe, N.M.; Laurel W. Dale, Superintendent, Coronado National Memorial, to Chief, Energy, Mining and Minerals Division, NPS, Minerals Overview Report and Map, March 20, 1986, Intermountain Land Resources Program Center Files, NPS, Santa Fe, N.M.
[1223] Untitled map of Coronado National Memorial, July 1982; Minerals Overview Report and Map, March 20, 1986.
[1224] Grant Deed, Richard B. Richards and Cheryl Richards to NPS, December 15, 1981, Intermountain Land Resources Program Center Files, NPS, Santa Fe, N.M.
[1225] Grant Deed, Richards and Richards to NPS, December 15, 1981.

[1226] Untitled map of Coronado National Memorial, July 1982.
[1227] Minerals Overview Report and Map, March 20, 1986.
[1228] Grant Deed, Richard Richards and Cheryl Richards to NPS, scenic easement, February 4, 1985, Intermountain Land Resources Program Center Files, NPS, Santa Fe, N.M.
[1229] Ibid.
[1230] Memorandum, Joseph L. Sewell, Superintendent, Coronado National Memorial, to Regional Director, Western Region, NPS, May 3, 1988, Coronado National Memorial Files; Memorandum, Joseph L. Sewell, Superintendent, Coronado National Memorial, to Regional Director, Western Region, NPS, March 7, 1989, Coronado National Memorial Files.
[1231] Ed Lopez, "Montezuma Ranch Acquisition Process Briefing Paper," n.d., Coronado National Memorial Files.
[1232] Dale A. Anderson, Manager, Hazardous Waste Inspection Unit, Office of Waste Programs, Arizona Department of Environmental Quality, to Bob Cousins, Regional Director, Western Region, NPS, August 16, 1990, Coronado National Memorial Files.
[1233] Memorandum, Clay Cunningham, General Superintendent, Southern Arizona Group, NPS, to Regional Director, Western Region, NPS, July 31, 1990, Coronado National Memorial Files.
[1234] Addendum to the Land Protection Plan for Coronado national Memorial, October 26, 1988, Intermountain Land Resources Program Center Files, NPS, Santa Fe, N.M.; Memorandum, Clay Cunningham, General Superintendent, Southern Arizona Group, NPS, to Regional Director, Western Region, NPS, July 18, 1990, Coronado National Memorial Files.
[1235] Clay Cunningham to Regional Director, Western Region, July 18, 1990; Memorandum, Edward Lopez, Superintendent, Coronado National Memorial, to Regional Director, Western Region, August 15, 1990, Coronado National Memorial Files.
[1236] Draft Memorandum, Director, NPS, to Regional Director, Western Region, NPS, n.d., Intermountain Land Resources Program Center Files, NPS, Santa Fe, N.M.
[1237] Memorandum, Acting Director, NPS, to Regional Director, Western Region, NPS, October 31, 1990, Coronado National Memorial Files.
[1238] Lopez, "Montezuma Ranch Acquisition Process Briefing Paper," n.d.
[1239] Memorandum, Lewis S. Albert, Acting Regional Director, Western Region, NPS, to Associate Director, Operations, NPS, September 28, 1990; Lopez to Regional Director, Western Region, August 15, 1990; Lopez, "Montezuma Ranch Acquisition Process Briefing Paper," n.d.
[1240] Edward R. Haberlin, Chief, Division of Land Resources, Western Region, NPS, to Margo Martin, Chapter 13 Trustee, 14 January 1991, Coronado National Memorial Files.
[1241] Criminal Incident Record, Case/Incident Number 910056, filed by William R. Smith, July 29, 1991; Supplemental Criminal Incident Record, Case/Incident Number 910056, filed by Edward Lopez, July 29, 1991; Supplemental Criminal Incident Record, Case/Incident Number 910056, filed by William R. Smith, July 27, 1991; Supplemental Criminal Incident Record, Case/Incident Number 910056, filed by Michael D. Walden, July 26, 1991, Coronado National Memorial Files.
[1242] Lopez, "Montezuma Ranch Acquisition Process Briefing Paper," n.d.
[1243] Complaint for Forfeiture, United States District Court, District of Arizona, United States of America, Plaintiff vs. 82.5 acres of real property located in Cochise County, Arizona and known as the Montezuma Ranch, DBA The Sunrise Farms, Inc. with all improvements, fixtures and appurtenances thereto and thereon; Defendant, August 16, 1991, Coronado National Memorial Files.
[1244] Lopez, "Montezuma Ranch Acquisition Process Briefing Paper," n.d.
[1245] Ibid.
[1246] Edward R. Haberlin, Chief, Division of Land Resources, Western Region, NPS, to Linda A. Akers, United States Attorney, Department of Justice, District of Arizona, May 26, 1992, Coronado National Memorial Files.

[1247] Lopez, "Montezuma Ranch Acquisition Process Briefing Paper," n.d.; c.c. mail, Bob Cousins to Harlan Hobbs, Edward A. Lopez, and Sondra S. Humphries, Subject: CORO acquisitions, August 12, 1996, Coronado National Memorial Files.

[1248] Cindy K. Jorgenson, Assistant U.S. Attorney, Department of Justice, District of Arizona, to Melinda S. Barnett of James S. Marlar, P.C., and Jeffrey A. Bernick of Ridenour, Swenson, Cleer & Evans, August 16, 1993, Coronado National Memorial Files.

[1249] Cousins to Hobbs, Lopez, and Humphries, August 12, 1996.

[1250] Notice of Trustee's Sale, filed by Melinda S. Barnett of James S. Marlar, P.C., September 30, 1992, Cochise County, Arizona, Coronado National Memorial Files.

[1251] Jim Walters, Southwest Hazardous Waste Program Agent, to Southwest Land Resources Program Center, April 3, 1997, Coronado National Memorial Files.

[1252] Montezuma Ranch Update, probably written by Edward Lopez, July 1, 1997, Coronado National Memorial Files; Proposal for Clean-up, Eads Construction Redi-Mix, Inc., Bisbee, Arizona, September 16, 1997, Coronado National Memorial Files; Proposal for Clean-up, B-R Constructors, Inc., Huachuca City, Arizona, September 18, 1997, Coronado National Memorial Files.

[1253] Minerals Overview Report and Map, March 20, 1986.

[1254] Grant Deed, Richard B. Richards and Cheryl Richards to NPS, August 3, 1982, Intermountain Land Resources Program Center Files, NPS, Santa Fe, N.M.

[1255] Ibid.

[1256] Grant Deed, Western Farm Credit Bank to NPS, June 3, 1996, Coronado National Memorial Files.

[1257] Notice of Trustee's Sale, September 30, 1992; Cousins to Hobbs, Lopez, and Humphries, August 12, 1996.

[1258] Sondra S. Humphries, Chief, Division of Land Resources, Western Region, NPS, to Gary L. Buntrock, Garmar Enterprises, Inc., December 13, 1994, Coronado National Memorial Files.

[1259] c.c. mail, Jim Walters to Edward A. Lopez and Bob Cousins, April 22, 1996, Coronado National Memorial Files.

[1260] Sondra S. Humphries, Chief, Pacific Land Resources Program Center, NPS, to Michael Morris, Western Farm Credit Bank, May 22, 1996, Coronado National Memorial Files.

[1261] U.S. Department of the Interior Certificate of Inspection and Possession, Tract 101-39, filed by Edward Lopez, June 17, 1996, Coronado National Memorial Files.

[1262] Grant Deed, Western Farm Credit Bank to NPS, June 3, 1996.

[1263] Notification of Closing, Tract 101-39, May 22, 1997, Coronado National Memorial Files.

[1264] Description of Tract No. 101-40, Faxed from Julian Trujillo to Phil Young, November 19, 1997, Coronado National Memorial Files.

[1265] Notice of Trustee's Sale, filed by Ronald M. Horowitz of Anderson, Brody, Levinson, Weiser & Horwitz, P.A., April 21, 1994, Cochise County, Arizona, Coronado National Memorial Files; Cousins to Hobbs, Lopez, and Humphries, August 12, 1996.

[1266] Assignment of Beneficial Interest Under Deed of Trust to Elsie Weick, from Citibank (Arizona), Trustee, as successor to United Bank of Arizona, March 26, 1997, Coronado National Memorial Files.

[1267] Ethan Steele, Attorney at Law for Richard Richards, to Janet Martin, Office of United States Attorney, June 23, 1997, Coronado National Memorial Files.

[1268] Description of Tract No. 101-40, November 19, 1997; Montezuma Ranch Update, July 1, 1997; Proposal for Clean-up, Eads Construction Redi-Mix, Inc., September 16, 1997; Proposal for Clean-up, B-R Constructors, Inc., September 18, 1997.

[1269] Grant Deed, Elsie Weick to Sunrise, A Trust, February 5, 1998, Coronado National Memorial Files.

[1270] Handwritten note, re: Tract 101-40, September 13, 1999, Coronado National Memorial Files.

1271 c.c.mail, Julian Trujillo, Southwest Regional Office, NPS, to William Smith, Coronado National Memorial, June 9, 1998, Coronado National Memorial Files.

1272 Administrative Waiver, signed by Jim Bellamy, Superintendent, Coronado National Memorial, February 17, 1999, Coronado National Memorial Files.

1273 Complaint Form, Cochise County Zoning Regulations, Cochise County Planning Department, Building & Zoning Division, filed by Jim Bellamy, Superintendent, Coronado National Memorial, May 25, 1999, Coronado National Memorial Files.

1274 Memorandum, Jim Bellamy, Superintendent, Coronado National Memorial, to Regional Director, Intermountain Region, NPS, May 27, 1999, Coronado National Memorial Files.

1275 Robert Wierzal, Scottsdale, Arizona, to Jim Bellamy, Superintendent, Coronado National Memorial, October 7, 1999, Coronado National Memorial Files; Jim Bellamy, Superintendent, Coronado National Memorial, to Robert Wierzal, Scottsdale, Arizona, October 18, 1999, Coronado National Memorial Files; Memorandum, Barbara A. Sulhoff, Chief, Land Resources Program Center, Intermountain Region, NPS, to Field Solicitor, Santa Fe, New Mexico, NPS, November 30, 1999, Coronado National Memorial Files.

1276 Bellamy to Joseph P. Sánchez, Spanish Colonial Research Center (SPCO), NPS, Hereford, July 27, 2001, SPCO Files.

1277 Forfeiture Judgement as to Claimant Elsie Weick, United States District Court, District of Arizona, United States of America, Plaintiff vs. 82.5 acres of real property located in Cochise County, Arizona and known as the Montezuma Ranch, DBA The Sunrise Farms, Inc., with all improvements, fixtures and appurtenances thereto and thereon; Defendant, January 6, 1996, Coronado National Memorial Files.

1278 Lopez, "Montezuma Ranch Acquisition Process Briefing Paper," n.d.; Cousins to Hobbs, Lopez, and Humphries, August 12, 1996.

1279 Forfeiture Judgement as to Claimant Elsie Weick, January 6, 1996.

1280 Ethan Steele, Attorney at Law, Tucson, Arizona, to Paul Tatham, I.R.P. District Headquarters, Sierra Vista, Arizona, April 19, 1996, Coronado National Memorial Files.

1281 U.S. Department of the Interior Certificate of Inspection and Possession, Tract 101-40, signed by Edward Lopez, January 13, 1998, Coronado National Memorial Files.

1282 United States Marshal's Special Warranty Deed, Alfred E. Madrid, United States Marshal for the District of Arizona, to The United States of America for the United States Department of the Interior, National Park Service, January 3, 1998, Intermountain Land Resources Program Center Files, NPS, Santa Fe, N.M.

1283 Notification of Closing, Tract 101-41, February 2, 1998, Coronado National Memorial Files.

1284 Field Notes, Coronado National Forest, Elmer L. Hertel, March 3, 1915, Coronado National Memorial Administrative Records, Western Archeological and Conservation Center, NPS, Tucson, Arizona, Folder L 1425: Land Holdings – Kudzmi.

1285 Notice of Publication, Simon Kudzmi, August 29, 1929; Testimony of Claimant, Simon Kudzmi, Final Proof, December 28, 1929; Testimonies of Witnesses William Norick and Joseph Zaleski, Homestead Entry, Final Proof, December 28, 1929, Coronado National Memorial Administrative Records, Western Archeological and Conservation Center, NPS, Tucson, Arizona, Folder L 1425: Land Holdings – Kudzmi.

1286 Barbour, "Dude Ranches," from Tracking Book, Cochise County Assessor's Office, Bisbee, Arizona; Quit-Claim Deed, Frank Zaleski to Jose Zaleski, Signed January 3, 1956, Cochise County Recorder's Office, Bisbee, Arizona, Deeds of Real Estate, Docket 142, pages 239-241.

1287 Warranty Deed, Joe Zaleski, aka José, and wife Lucy, to John A. and Inez Z. Jones, Signed April 19, 1957, Cochise County Recorder's Office, Bisbee, Arizona, Deeds of Real Estate, Docket 166, pages 587-588.

[1288] Deed of Gift, John A. and Inez Z. Jones, of Santa Cruz County, Arizona, to John Z. and Lawrence D. Jones, Signed April 24, 1962, Cochise County Recorder's Office, Bisbee, Arizona, Deeds of Real Estate, Docket 300, pages 406-407.

[1289] Joint Tenancy Deed, John Z. Jones and Lawrence D. Jones to Everett Baumkirchner and Margaret E. Baumkirchner, husband and wife, an undivided half interest, Signed May 26, 1965, Cochise County Recorder's Office, Bisbee, Arizona, Deeds of Real Estate, Docket 389, page 21; Joint Tenancy Deed, John Z. Jones and Lawrence D. Jones to Fred and Mary Ann Baumkirchner, husband and wife, an undivided half interest, Signed May 26, 1965, Cochise County Recorder's Office, Bisbee, Arizona, Deeds of Real Estate, Docket 389, page 22; Realty Mortgage, Everett Baumkirchner and Margaret E. Baumkirchner, his wife, and Fred Baumkirchner and Mary Ann Baumkirchner, his wife, with John Z. Jones and Lawrence D. Jones, Signed June 1, 1965, Cochise County Recorder's Office, Bisbee, Arizona, Deeds of Real Estate, Docket 389, page 23.

[1290] Warranty Deed, Fred E. Baumkirchner and Mary Ann Baumkirchner, husband and wife, and Everett M. Baumkirchner and Margaret E. Baumkirchner, husband and wife, to Transamerica Title Insurance Company, as Trustee, Signed March 11, 1972, Cochise County Recorder's Office, Bisbee, Arizona, Deeds of Real Estate, Docket 841, pages 215-216; Warranty Deed, Transamerica Title Insurance Company to United States of America, Signed March 1, 1973, Cochise County Recorder's Office, Bisbee, Arizona, Deeds of Real Estate, Docket 841, page 218.

[1291] Peter M. Van Cleve, "History of Mining in the Coronado National Memorial" (1997), pp. 2-8, Coronado National Memorial Files.

[1292] "A Summary of the Abandoned Mineral Lands (AML) on the Coronado National Memorial," April 19, 1996, Coronado National Memorial Files.

[1293] Baron claim, 1/1/1889, and Baron claim papers, 4/4/1898, from Geoffrey T. Bohrer, "Siamese Triplets: Grace Sparkes, The State of Texas Mine, and the Coronado National Memorial," (National Park Service, 1993), pp. 1-2.

[1294] Van Cleve, "History of Mining," pp. 3-4.

[1295] Bohrer, "Siamese Triplets," pp. 1-2.

[1296] Van Cleve, "History of Mining," p. 5; Bohrer calls it the Mitchell Development Company, Bohrer, "Siamese Triplets, p. 2.

[1297] Van Cleve, "History of Mining," pp. 5-6.

[1298] Van Cleve, "History of Mining," pp. 6-7.

[1299] Sale Agreement, Nathan L. and Estelle D. Amster to T.J. Sparkes and Burdett Moody, September 1, 1926, Sparkes Collection, Box 12, Folder 464, Arizona Historical Society; Mining Deed, Nathan L. and Estelle D. Amster to T.J. Sparkes and Burdett Moody, September 27, 1926, The Grace M. Sparkes Collection (Ms. Collection 0752), Arizona Historical Society, Tucson, Arizona, Box 12, Folder 470.

[1300] Letter, Grace Sparkes, Prescott, Az., to Burdett Moody, c/o The Bureau Light, Water and Power, Los Angeles, Ca., January 30, 1939, The Grace M. Sparkes Collection (Ms. Collection 0752), Arizona Historical Society, Tucson, Arizona, Box 7, Folder 294.

[1301] Mining Deed, Burdett and Sarah C. Moody sell and quit claim to Grace Sparkes, June 9, 1942, The Grace M. Sparkes Collection (Ms. Collection 0752), Arizona Historical Society, Tucson, Arizona, Box 12, Folder 470; also see Folder 468.

[1302] Mining Deed, Thomas J. Sparkes Jr. and wife Maybelle; Charity S. and Perry L. Bones; and Genevieve Sparkes, widow of John G. Sparkes; all of Yavapai County, sell and quit claim all of the mine claims to Grace Sparkes, September 21, 1942, The Grace M. Sparkes Collection (Ms. Collection 0752), Arizona Historical Society, Tucson, Arizona, Box 12, Folder 470.

[1303] Letter, Sarah Moody to Grace Sparkes, 1946, The Grace M. Sparkes Collection (Ms. Collection 0752), Arizona Historical Society, Tucson, Arizona, Box 7, Folder 299.

[1304] Land Ownership Record, NPS, September 2, 1960.

1305 Gentry, McNulty & Tori, Attorneys at Law, Bisbee, Arizona, to Acting Superintendent, Coronado National Memorial, October 14, 1965, Coronado National Memorial Administrative Records, Western Archeological and Conservation Center, NPS, Tucson, Arizona, Folder L 1425: Land Holdings – Sparkes & Acquisition; also see other memos and letters in the same folder for improvements and sales prospects.

1306 Request for bids for appraisal of properties by A.W. Gray, May 4, 1979.

1307 Transamerica Title Insurance Company Preliminary Report, n.d.

1308 Ibid.

1309 Request for bids for appraisal of properties by A.W. Gray, May 4, 1979.

1310 Transamerica Title Insurance Company Preliminary Report, n.d.

1311 Quit Claim Deed, Charles J. Sparkes, Jack M. Sparkes, and Thomas F. Sparkes, to William J. Sparkes, Dated April 9, 1980, Intermountain Land Resources Program Center Files, NPS, Santa Fe, N.M.

1312 Request for bids for appraisal of properties by A.W. Gray, May 4, 1979.

1313 Transamerica Title Insurance Company Preliminary Report, n.d.

1314 Ibid.

1315 Ibid.

1316 "His aunt helped build park that could dispossess him," The Arizona Daily Star, September 13, 1979, D:1.

1317 Memorandum, Regional Director, Western Region, to Associate Director, Management and Operations, NPS, Subject: Legislative Cost Estimate, Coronado National Memorial, April 1, 1980, Intermountain Land Resources Program Center Files, NPS, Santa Fe, N.M.

1318 Grant Deed, William J. and Patricia M. Sparkes, to NPS, Signed December 29, 1986, Intermountain Land Resources Program Center Files, NPS, Santa Fe, N.M.

1319 "A Summary of the Abandoned Mineral Lands;" "Abandoned Mineral Lands (AML) and Related List of Classified Structure (LCS)," n.d., Coronado National Memorial Files.

1320 "A Summary of the Abandoned Mineral Lands."

1321 "A Summary of the Abandoned Mineral Lands."

1322 Superintendent, Coronado National Memorial, to Thomas Mulhern, February 23, 1976.

1323 Warranty Deed, Ruth M. Clark, a widow, and Charles A. Smith and Paquita C. Smith, his wife, to Coronado Investment Company, a partnership comprised of Peter G. Wray and H. Wayne Pruett, co-partners, Recorded July 2, 1970, Deeds of Real Estate, Cochise County Recorder's Office, Bisbee, Arizona, Docket 645, pages 543-545.

1324 Warranty Deed, Coronado Investment Company to Pruett-Wray Cattle Company, Signed May 1, 1973, Deeds of Real Estate, Cochise County Recorder's Office, Bisbee, Arizona, Docket 871, pages 481-483.

1325 Deed (Joint Tenancy), The Victorio Company, an Arizona Corporation; formerly Victorio Land and Cattle Company, an Arizona Corporation; formerly Pruett-Wray Cattle Company, an Arizona Corporation, to James J. Wardle and Jacqueline S. Wardle, husband and wife, Signed December 18, 1979, Cochise County Recorder's Office, Bisbee, Arizona, Deeds of Real Estate, Docket 1388, pages 333-334.

1326 Ibid.

1327 Transamerica Title Insurance Company Preliminary Report, n.d.

1328 Request for bids for appraisal of properties by A.W. Gray, May 4, 1979.

1329 Grant Deed, The Victorio Company, an Arizona Corporation which acquired title as Pruett-Wray Cattle Company, an Arizona Corporation, to NPS, Executed March 26, 1980, Intermountain Land Resources Program Center Files, NPS, Santa Fe, N.M.

1330 Ibid.

1331 Transamerica Title Insurance Company Preliminary Report, n.d.

1332 Ibid.

1333 Request for bids for appraisal of properties by A.W. Gray, May 4, 1979.

1334 Grant Deed, The Victorio Company, to NPS, Executed March 26, 1980.

[1335] Ibid.
[1336] Memorandum, Division of Land Acquisitioin, Western Region, NPS, to Chief, Coordination and Control Branch, Washington Office, NPS, May 12, 1980, Intermountain Land Resources Program Center Files, NPS, Santa Fe, N.M.
[1337] Deed (Joint Tenancy), The Victorio Company, to James J. and Jacqueline S. Wardle, Signed December 18, 1979.
[1338] Ibid.
[1339] Laurel W. Dale to Chief, Energy, Mining and Minerals Division, Minerals Overview Report and Map, March 20, 1986.
[1340] Joint Tenancy Deed, James J. Wardle and Jacqueline Wardle (aka Jacqueline S. Wardle), husband and wife, to Richard D. Compton and Judy L. Compton, husband and wife, Signed August 29, 1983, Cochise County Recorder's Office, Bisbee, Arizona, Deeds of Real Estate, Docket 1700, pages 285-286.
[1341] Grant Deed, Richard D. Compton and Judy L. Compton, husband and wife, to NPS, February 12, 1985, Intermountain Land Resources Program Center Files, NPS, Santa Fe, N.M.
[1342] Joint Tenancy Deed, James J. and Jacqueline Wardle, to Richard D. and Judy L. Compton, Signed August 29, 1983.
[1343] Grant Deed, Richard D. and Judy L. Compton, to NPS, February 12, 1985.
[1344] All-Inclusive Agreement, James J. Wardle and Jacqueline S. Wardle, husband and wife, to Jacques O'Keefe and Audrey C. O'Keefe, husband and wife, Signed January 5, 1980, Cochise County Recorder's Office, Bisbee, Arizona, Deeds of Real Estate, Docket 1395, pages 484-487.
[1345] Laurel W. Dale to Chief, Energy, Mining and Minerals Division, Minerals Overview Report and Map, March 20, 1986.
[1346] Grant Deed, Richard D. Compton and Judy L. Compton, husband and wife, to NPS, Signed February 12, 1985, Intermountain Land Resources Program Center Files, NPS, Santa Fe, N.M.
[1347] All-Inclusive Agreement, James J. and Jacqueline S. Wardle, to Jacques and Audrey C. O'Keefe, Signed January 5, 1980.
[1348] Joint Tenancy Deed, Jacques O'Keefe and Audrey O'Keefe, husband and wife, to Richard D. Compton and Judy L. Compton, husband and wife, Signed December 28, 1983, Cochise County Recorder's Office, Bisbee, Arizona, Deeds of Real Estate, Docket 1730, pages 579-580.
[1349] Grant Deed, Richard D. and Judy L. Compton, to NPS, Signed February 12, 1985.
[1350] Laurel W. Dale to Chief, Energy, Mining and Minerals Division, Minerals Overview Report and Map, March 20, 1986.
[1351] Grant Deed, Paul E. Froelich and Laurel A. Froelich, his wife, to NPS, Signed July 5, 1985, Intermountain Land Resources Program Center Files, NPS, Santa Fe, N.M.
[1352] All-Inclusive Agreement, James J. and Jacqueline S. Wardle, to Jacques and Audrey C. O'Keefe, Signed January 5, 1980.
[1353] Warranty Deed, James J. Wardle and Jacqueline S. Wardle, husband and wife, to Jacques O'Keefe and Audrey C. O'Keefe, husband and wife, Signed April 8, 1983, and recorded April 29, 1983, Cochise County Recorder's Office, Bisbee, Arizona, Deeds of Real Estate, Docket 1671, page 162; Joint Tenancy Deed, Jacques O'Keefe and Audrey C. O'Keefe, husband and wife, to Paul E. Froelich and Laurel A. Froelich, husband and wife, Signed April 8, 1983, Cochise County Recorder's Office, Bisbee, Arizona, Deeds of Real Estate, Docket 1671, pages 164-166.
[1354] Grant Deed, Paul E. and Laurel A. Froelich, to NPS, Signed July 5, 1985.
[1355] Laurel W. Dale to Chief, Energy, Mining and Minerals Division, Minerals Overview Report and Map, March 20, 1986.

1356 Grant Deed, Valentin Castro III and Deborah Castro, husband and wife, to NPS, Signed February 25, 1985, Intermountain Land Resources Program Center Files, NPS, Santa Fe, N.M.

1357 All-Inclusive Agreement, James J. and Jacqueline S. Wardle, to Jacques and Audrey C. O'Keefe, Signed January 5, 1980.

1358 Joint Tenancy Deed, Jacques O'Keefe and Audrey C. O'Keefe, husband and wife, to Valentin Castro III and Deborah Castro, husband and wife, Signed August 29, 1983, Cochise County Recorder's Office, Bisbee, Arizona, Deeds of Real Estate, Docket 1708, pages 40-43.

1359 Grant Deed, Valentin Castro III and Deborah Castro, to NPS, Signed February 25, 1985.

1360 Laurel W. Dale to Chief, Energy, Mining and Minerals Division, Minerals Overview Report and Map, March 20, 1986.

1361 Grant Deed, James J. Wardle and Jacqueline S. Wardle, his wife, to NPS, Signed February 6, 1985, Intermountain Land Resources Program Center Files, NPS, Santa Fe, N.M.

1362 Ibid.

1363 Frank C.W. Pooler to Chief, Forest Service, Albuquerque, New Mexico, April 5, 1940. Hayden Papers, AC, ASU, Box 591, folder 2., p. 2.

1364 An Act to Provide for the establishment of the Coronado International Memorial, in the State of Arizona, approved August 18, 1941 (55 Stat. 630), ILRPC Files.

1365 An Act To amend the Act entitled "An Act to provide for the establishment of the Coronado International Memorial, in the State of Arizona," approved August 18, 1941 (55 Stat. 630), approved July 9, 1952 (66 Stat. 510. Establishment of the Coronado National Memorial (Name change from International Memorial), Arizona, By the President of the United States, A Proclamation (No. 2995), November 5, 1952, ILRPC Files.

1366 Director, NPS, to Regional Director, Region Three, NPS, n.d. (November-December 1952), WACC, Folder H 14: Area & Service History 41-52 F 3, and other letters in the same folder.

1367 WACC, Folder A 44: Memo of Agreement F 18. Other agreemwnts in this file relate to recreational development, a water transmission line for CORO, fire control, and the Hereford Soil Conservation District.

1368 Master Plan, May 1957, p. 4. Soil and Moister Conservation (S&MC) section, p. 2

1369 WACC, Folder A 44: Memo of Agreement F 18.

1370 Grazing Preferences Involving Use of National Park Lands – 1955, WACC, Folder A 44: Memo of Agreement F 18.

1371 Master Plan Development Outline, Coronado National Memorial, Arizona, Forestry, July 1955, WACC, Folder D 18: Master Plan (Mission 66) F 1.

1372 Master Plan for the Conservation and Use of Coronado National Memorial (1961), "Objectives and Policies", Vol. I, Chapter 1, p. 6.

1373 Superintendent Philip Welles, Coronado National Memorial, to Director, NPS, Subject: July 1961, Monthly Narrative Report for Coronado National Memorial, Hereford, July 30, 1961, WACC, Folder A 2615: Monthly Reports F 6.

1374 Master Plan Development Outline, Coronado National Memorial, Arizona, Forestry, July 1955, pp. 4-5, WACC, Folder D 18: Master Plan (Mission 66) F 1. Each Master Plan has sections on resource management, including grazing and mining.

1375 Superintendent Lawrewnce D. Roush and Supervisory Park Ranger Ernest W. Kuncl, Coronado National Memorial, to Fred E. Baumkirchner; Memorandum of Understanding, signed by Superintendent Hugo Huntzinger, Coronado National Memorial 2-25-72, a representative of Coronado National Forest (signature illegible) 3-6-72, and Fred E. Baumkirchner, Permittee, Montezuma Grazing Allotment 3-16-72, WACC, Folder A 44: Memo of Agreement F 18.

1376 Draft Environmental Impact Statement, Proposed Resource Management Plan Applicable to Coronado National Memorial, September 10, 1973, WACC, Folder D 18: Resource Management Plan F 13.

[1377] Denver Service Center, Planning Directive for Coronado National Memorial, January 1973, WACC, Folder D 18: Planning Directives F 14.
[1378] Superintendent, CORO, to Deputy Director, NPS, Subject: Superintendent's Annual Report for Calendar Year 1773, Hereford, January 23, 1974, WACC, Folder A 2621: Annual Reports F 11.
[1379] Superintendent, CORO, to Regional Director, Western Region, Subject: Superintendents' Annual Report for Calendar Year 1974, Hereford, February 20, 1975, WACC, Folder A 2621: Annual Reports F 11
[1380] Final general management plan, September 1976, p. 10, WACC, Folder D 18: General Management Plans F 15.
[1381] Ibid, following p. 20.
[1382] Environmental Review, Final General Management Plan, September 1976, p. 7, WACC, Folder D 18: Resource Management Plan F 13.
[1383] "Boundary Adjustment – a Radical Proposal," n.d., WACC, Folder L 1417: Boundary Adjustments – Surveys & Reports F 1.
[1384] "Agreement: Coronado National Memorial, Cochise County, Arizona, and Coronado National Forest, Cochise County, Arizona," Signed October 16 and 19, 1979, ILRPC Files,
[1385] General Superintendent, Southern Arizona Group, to Associate Regional Director, Management and Operations, Western Region, Subject: Meeting With Southwest Regional Forester, Phoenix, October 6, 1986, WACC, Folder A 40: Conferences F 16.
[1386] Annual Statement for Interpretation and Visitor Services, 1986, , pp. 14-16, WACC, Folder K 1817: Annual Statement Interpretation F 9.
[1387] Superintendent, CORO, to Regional Director, Western Region, Subject: Superintendent's Annual Report for Calendar Year 1986, Hereford, February 23, 1987, WACC, Folder A 2621: Annual Reports F 11.
[1388] Superintendent, CORO, to General Superintendent, Southern Arizona Group, Subject: Briefing Statements FY 88 Congressional Hearings, Hereford, January 14, 1987, Issue: Grazing Management, WACC, Folder A 2623: Situation Reports F 12.
[1389] WACC, Folder A 44: Memo of Agreement F 18. This file also includes several letters, aggreements, and other assorted documentation regarding recreational development, a water transmission line for CORO, fire control, and the Hereford Soil Conservation District.
[1390] Freeman L. Nelson, Acting General Superintendent, Southern Arizona Group, to Regional Director, Western Region, NPS, Phoenix, September 21, 1987, ibid.
[1391] Annual Statement for Interpretation and Visitor Services, February 1988, pp. 16-17, WACC, Folder K 1817: Annual Statement for Interpretation F 9.
[1392] Draft Livestock Management Plan, Coronado National Memorial, Cochise County, Arizona, March 2000, pp. I:4-5, II:14, IV:7, CORO Files.
[1393] M.W. Merrill, Arizona Small Miners Association, to Charles F. Willis, Bisbee, May 2, 1940, WACC, Folder H 14: Area & Service History 1940 F 2.
[1394] An Act to Provide for the establishment of the Coronado International Memorial, in the State of Arizona, approved August 18, 1941 (55 Stat. 630), ILRPC Files.
[1395] Acting Regional Director, Region Three P.P. Patraw, to Director, NPS, Subject: Proposed Grazing and Mining Regulations, Santa Fe, March 5, 1953, WACC, Folder L 3023: Mining General F 39.
[1396] Superintendent Jack E. Stark, CORO, to Director, Southwest Region, NPS, Hereford, October 2, 1966, Subject: Report on Mining Activity in the United States, Mining. Mining Activities at Coronado National Memorial, ibid.
[1397] Superintendent Lawrence D. Roush, CORO, to Regional Director, Southwest Region, Hereford, May 15, 1969, and related letters and maps, ibid.
[1398] CORO Memorandum, Erny to Hugo [Huntzinger], Hereford, April 14, 1970, ibid. This file contains documents relating to mine claims around the Memorial.

[1399] Acting Director Carl O. Walker, Southwest Region, to Southwest Region Superintendents, Santa Fe, June 1971, ibid.

[1400] Department of the Interior, Draft Environmental Statement, Proposed Amendment of Act of August 18, 1941, Coronado National Memorial, Arizona, Prepared by Western Region, NPS (Handwritten: Preliminary Draft 1-8-73), WACC, Folder L 3023: Mining State of Texas F 41.

[1401] Acting Director John E. Cook, Western Region, to State Director, Arizona, Subject: Mining Claims within Coronado National Memorial, San Francisco, February 15, 1973, and related letters, etc., WACC, Folder L 3023: Mining General F 39.

[1402] Superintendent Hugo Huntzinger, Coronado National Memorial, to Deputy Director, NPS, Subject: Superintendent's Annual Report for Calendar Year 1773, Hereford, January 23, 1974, WACC Folder A 2621: Annual Reports F 11.

[1403] An Act to provide for the regulation of mining activity within, and to repeal the application of mining laws to, areas of the National Park System, and for other purposes. P.L. 94-429, September 28, 1976, WACC, Folder L 3023: Witkopp Tako F 40.

[1404] Unidentified memo, no names or dates attached, WACC, Folder L 3023: Mining General F 39.

[1405] Environmental Review, Final General Management Plan, September 1976, p. 32, WACC, Folder D 18: Resource Management Plan F 13.

[1406] "Agreement: Coronado National Memorial, Cochise County, Arizona, and Coronado National Forest, Cochise County, Arizona," Signed October 16 and 19, 1979, ILRPC Files.

[1407] See Chapter IX for narrative and sources; and WACC, Folder L 3023: Witkopp Tako F 40, passim.

[1408] Superintendent Joseph L. Sewell to Superintendent, Death Valley National Monument, Subject: Mine Closures, Hereford, November 17, 1987; Archeologist, Division of Archeology, WACC, Subject: Trip Report, Coronado Mine Safety Project, Tucson, January 12, 1988, WACC, Folder L 3023: Mining General F 39.

[1409] Ron Cron, Resource Maintenance Work Leader, Death Valley National Monument, to Superintendent, Coronado National Memorial, Subject: Coronado Mine Safing Project – 9/12/88 – 10/1/88, Death Valley, November 21, 1988; David L. Sharrow, Environmental Protection Specialist, Mining and Minerals Branch, to Chief, Environmental Assessment Section, Mining and Minerals Branch, Land Resources Division, Subject: Trip Report for Abandoned Mineral Lands Trip to Arizona, Denver, November 29, 1988, ibid. Also see associated letters and maps in the same file.

[1410] Peter M. Van Cleve, "History of Mining in the Coronado National Memorial" (1997), pp. 2-8, CORO Files.

[1411] "A Summary of the Abandoned Mineral Lands (AML) on the Coronado National Memorial," April 19, 1996, CORO Files.

[1412] Baron claim, 1/1/1889, and Baron claim papers, 4/4/1898, from Geoffrey T. Bohrer, "Siamese Triplets: Grace Sparkes, The State of Texas Mine, and the Coronado National Monument," (National Park Service, 1993), pp. 1-2.

[1413] Van Cleve, "History of Mining," pp. 3-4.

[1414] Bohrer, "Siamese Triplets," pp. 1-2.

[1415] Gerdes identified his former partner as "August Barron of Tombstone." Letter, Charles Gerdes, Gleeson, Arizona, to Mssrs. Sparks (sic) and Moody, Los Angeles, California, 4/15/39, The Grace M. Sparkes Collection (Ms. Collection 0752), Arizona Historical Society, Tucson, Arizona, Box 7, Folder 294.

[1416] Robert D. O'Brien, "Appraisal of Mineral Interests Inherent in the State of Texas Mine Tracts No. 101-06, 101-07, 101-08 Coronado National Monument," (San Francisco: National Park Service, Western Region, 1979), p. 3, ILRPC Files.

[1417] Van Cleve, "History of Mining," p. 5; Bohrer calls it the Mitchell Development Company, Bohrer, "Siamese Triplets, p. 2.

[1418] Van Cleve, "History of Mining," pp. 5-6.
[1419] O'Brien, "Appraisal of Mineral Interests," p. 4.
[1420] Van Cleve, "History of Mining," pp. 6-7.
[1421] Sale Agreement, Nathan L. and Estelle D. Amster to T.J. Sparkes and Burdett Moody, September 1, 1926, Sparkes Collection, Box 12, Folder 464, Arizona Historical Society; Mining Deed, Nathan L. and Estelle D. Amster to T.J. Sparkes and Burdett Moody, September 27, 1926, The Grace M. Sparkes Collection (Ms. Collection 0752), Arizona Historical Society, Tucson, Arizona, Box 12, Folder 470.
[1422] Van Cleve, "History of Mining," p. 8.
[1423] Letter, Grace Sparkes, Prescott, Az., to Burdett Moody, c/o The Bureau Light, Water and Power, Los Angeles, Ca., January 30, 1939, The Grace M. Sparkes Collection (Ms. Collection 0752), Arizona Historical Society, Tucson, Arizona, Box 7, Folder 294.
[1424] Burdett Moody to Grace M. Sparkes, February 1, 1939, Burdett Moody to Grace M. Sparkes, May 4, 1939, Ibid. The Sparkes papers contain sales contracts, never executed, from this period that confirm that the property was in negotiation for sale. See especially Box 12, Folders 465-467.
[1425] Van Cleve, "History of Mining," p. 7.
[1426] Burdett Moody to Grace M. Sparkes, August 1, 1941, The Grace M. Sparkes Collection (Ms. Collection 0752), Arizona Historical Society, Tucson, Arizona, Box 7, Folder 296, and others in the same folder.
[1427] See, in particular, Sparkes Collection, Box 7, Folder 294, Arizona Historical Society.
[1428] Mining Deed, Burdett and Sarah C. Moody sell and quit claim to Grace Sparkes, June 9, 1942, The Grace M. Sparkes Collection (Ms. Collection 0752), Arizona Historical Society, Tucson, Arizona, Box 12, Folder 470; also see Folder 468.
[1429] Mining Deed, Thomas J. Sparkes Jr. and wife Maybelle; Charity S. and Perry L. Bones; and Genevieve Sparkes, widow of John G. Sparkes; all of Yavapai County, sell and quit claim all of the mine claims to Grace Sparkes, September 21, 1942, The Grace M. Sparkes Collection (Ms. Collection 0752), Arizona Historical Society, Tucson, Arizona, Box 12, Folder 470.
[1430] Van Cleve, "History of Mining," p. 8.
[1431] Letter, Sarah Moody to Grace Sparkes, 1946, The Grace M. Sparkes Collection (Ms. Collection 0752), Arizona Historical Society, Tucson, Arizona, Box 7, Folder 299.
[1432] Land Ownership Record, NPS, September 2, 1960, NPS, September 2, 1960, WACC, Folder L 1425: Land Holdings – Sparkes & Acquisition F17.
[1433] Gentry, McNulty & Tori, Attorneys at Law, Bisbee, Arizona, to Acting Superintendent, Coronado National Memorial, October 14, 1965, Coronado National Memorial Administrative Records, Western Archeological and Conservation Center, NPS, Tucson, Arizona, Folder L 1425: Land Holdings – Sparkes & Acquisition; also see other memos and letters in the same folder for improvements and sales prospects.
[1434] Interpretive Prospectus, State of Texas Mine Site, prepared by Theda Adcock, Park Ranger, Coronado National Memorial, Hereford, February 16, 1988, WACC Folder K 18: Interpretive Prospectus F 2.
[1435] "A Summary of the Abandoned Mineral Lands;" "Abandoned Mineral Lands (AML) and Related List of Classified Structure (LCS)," n.d., Coronado National Memorial Files.
[1436] "A Summary of the Abandoned Mineral Lands."
[1437] Memorandum, Superintendent, Coronado National Memorial, to Thomas Mulhern, Historic Preservation, Western Regional Office, Subject: Historic Structures at Coronado National Memorial, February 23, 1976, Coronado National Memorial Files. George Brown is given as the main source for this report.
[1438] Robert D. O'Brien, "Mineral Tract No. 101-05 and 101-09, Coronado National Monument, Cochise County, Arizona" (San Francisco: National Park Service, Western Region, 1979), p. 2, WACC, Folder L 3023: Mining Minerals F 38.
[1439] "A Summary of the Abandoned Mineral Lands."

[1440] Superintendent, Coronado National Memorial, to Thomas Mulhern, February 23, 1976.
[1441] Land Ownership Record, NPS, September 2, 1960, NPS, September 2, 1960, WACC, Folder L 1425: Land Holdings – Sparkes & Acquisition F17.
[1442] Warranty Deed, Ruth M. Clark, a widow, and Charles A. Smith and Paquita C. Smith, his wife, to Coronado Investment Company, a partnership comprised of Peter G. Wray and H. Wayne Pruett, co-partners, Recorded July 2, 1970, Deeds of Real Estate, Cochise County Recorder's Office, Bisbee, Arizona, Docket 645, pages 543-545.
[1443] Warranty Deed, Coronado Investment Company to Pruett-Wray Cattle Company, Signed May 1, 1973, Deeds of Real Estate, Cochise County Recorder's Office, Bisbee, Arizona, Docket 871, pages 481-483.
[1444] Deed (Joint Tenancy), The Victorio Company, an Arizona Corporation; formerly Victorio Land and Cattle Company, an Arizona Corporation; formerly Pruett-Wray Cattle Company, an Arizona Corporation, to James J. Wardle and Jacqueline S. Wardle, husband and wife, Signed December 18, 1979, Cochise County Recorder's Office, Bisbee, Arizona, Deeds of Real Estate, Docket 1388, pages 333-334.

Index

A

Act of August 18, 1941 23, 37-38, 40, 47-51, 57-58, 77, 85, 136, 218, 252
Act to Provide for the Regulation of Mining Activity 158
Adams, John A. 13
Adcock, Theda 206, 208-209
Agua Prieta 38, 52, 72, 169, 200
Aguilar, Lic. Silverstre 42
Albert, Lewis S. 163, 234
Alberts, William 19, 22
Aleman Valdis, President (Miguel) 54-56
Allison, James 106
Allison, Mrs. James 86
Amster, Estelle D. 134, 241, 258
Amster, Nathan L. 134, 241, 258
Anaconda Copper Company 49
Anderson, Congressman Clinton P. 1, 5-6, 10, 12-13, 16, 18, 27, 62, 85, 104
Antelope Pass 31, 35
Aranda, Rigoberto 188
Aravaipa Creek 32-33
Archie, Eloise 144, 225
Archie, William 144, 225
Arellano, Ing. Luis Macias 48, 53
Arizona Cattle Growers' Association 18-20, 71, 101, 103
Arizona Coronado International Memorial Commission 2, 23, 45-46, 51, 53, 55, 59, 77
Arizona Daily Star 20, 102, 154
Arizona Department of Environmental Quality 162, 233
Arizona Game and Fish Department 147
Arizona Highways 28, 89
Arizona Historic Memorials Association 100
Arizona Mining Journal 133, 258
Arizona Republic 109, 175
Arizona Small Mine Operators Association 18, 22, 256
Arizona Trail 190, 214
Arizpe, Sonora 127, 204
Arnberger, Leslie P. 83
Arnold, Ben 51-52, 106
Arrowhood, Al 123
Arroyo de las Nutrias 126
Art Festival 200
Auslender, Leland I. 160-161, 230-231
Avery, Ben 109-110

B

Babbitt, Secretary Bruce 188, 190
Baicatcan 32
Bailey, Stuart M. 10, 22, 100
Baldi, Mary Lou 203
Ball, John 98, 100-101, 103
Banco Nacional de Crédito Ejidal 73
Barnett, Melinda S. 234
Baron, August 133-134, 240, 258
Barry, Laura 203
Baumkirchner, Everett M. Jr. 143-144, 222, 226
Baumkirchner, Fred E. 143-144, 160, 221-222, 228, 240, 254
Baumkirchner, Margaret E. 222
Baumkirchner, Mary Ann 222

Becker, Julius 100
Becker, Rudy 131
Beddome, C.C. 22
Bellamy, Jim 166-167, 177, 238
Benson, Arizona 26, 34-35, 52
Big Bend National Park 42, 44, 52
Billy Boy Mine 141, 218, 241, 259
Bimson, Walter R. 100
Biosphere Reserve Concept 185
Bisbee, Arizona 8, 13, 22, 26, 35, 39, 44, 46-47, 52, 57, 59, 63, 78, 81, 84, 86, 94-95, 97-101, 103, 105-107, 133, 192, 200-201, 222, 229, 240, 258
Bisbee Chamber of Commerce 22, 28, 41, 47, 52, 54, 69-72, 75, 87, 98, 101-103, 105-106
Bisbee Daily Review 61, 176-177
Bledsoe, F.C. 98
Blunt, Arthur 106
Bohrer, Geoffrey T. 133, 240, 258
Bolton, Dr. Herbert Eugene 7-8, 26-30, 34-35, 38, 99, 101
Bones, Perry 104
Bonita Mine 133-134, 240-241, 258-259
Boquillas Land and Cattle Company 128
Borderlands Symposium 110, 201
Border Guest Ranch 13, 131
Border Industrialization Program (BIP) 171
Bracero program 171
Bribiesca, Dr. Sergio 110, 200
Brooks, Don 106, 132, 229
Brophy, James E. 52, 105, 107
Brown, Bill 191, 197
Brown, George 129, 131-132, 229
Brubaker, George A. 59
Bureau of Land Management (BLM) 79-80, 87, 141, 158-159, 177, 190, 221-227, 241-242, 244-246, 249-251, 257
Burge, Moris 52
Burlew, E.K. 10, 191
Burroughs, Carroll A. 77, 79-81, 84, 86-87, 89, 106, 192
Busey, Mayor Ray 45, 105
Butler, G.M. 1, 11, 22

C

Cabrillo, Juan Rodríguez x, 29
Caldwell, John 106
Caley, Mayor W.K. 22, 101

Calles, Plutarco Elías 64
Camacho, President Manuel Avila 38
Cammerer, Arno B. 10, 14-15, 17-18
Cananea Cattle Company 38-39, 43-46, 48, 50-53, 55, 62, 65, 69-72, 182
Cananea Consolidated Copper Company 49, 63
Cananea Mountains 14
Canon City, Colorado 133, 258
Carabias, Julia 189-190
Cárdenas, Cuauhtémoc 74
Cárdenas, President Lázaro 64-65, 74
Carlson, Alvar W. 180
Carroll, Tom 204
Carter, Rosalynn 110
Casa Grande 31
Cashman, Jean 144, 160
Cashman, Ramona E. 144, 226
Cashman, William L. 144, 160, 226
Castañeda, Pedro de x, 32
Castro, Deborah 156-157, 251
Castro, Governor Raul H. 109
Castro, I.J. 42
Castro, Valentin III 156-157, 251
Catalina Highway Bill 11
Cave Creek Canyon 132
Cerkowniak, Allan 160
Cerkowniak, Allan and Leona 225
Cerkowniak, Leona 160, 225
Chapman, Secretary Oscar L. 6, 54
Chavez, Betty J. 144, 225
Chavez, Robert G. 144, 225
Chicago Mine 133, 240, 258
Chichilticale (also Chichilticalli) 31-33
Chief Mine 135-136, 154, 243-244, 259-260
Chihuahuan Desert 187-188, 190
Chiricahua National Monument 185-186
Church, Congressman 23
Cíbola, Seven Cities of ix, xi, xii, 27, 32, 34-35
Citibank 164-165, 234-235, 238
Ciudad Juarez 169, 172
Civilian Conservation Corps (CCC) 5, 104, 135
Clark, Bill 136, 143, 243, 260
Clark, Maurice 134, 241, 258
Clark, Ruth M. 143, 243, 260
Clark, W.E. 18-19, 22, 100, 103
Clay, John 152
Cochise County, Arizona 18-19, 22, 87-88, 97, 100, 109, 123, 130-133, 163,

166, 176-177, 187, 199-200, 203, 215, 221-227, 229, 231, 234-242, 244-251, 258
Cochise County Planning Department 166, 238
Cochise culture 124
Comité de Veteranos de la Revolución, campesinos y gambusinos de Cananea 67
Committee on Public Lands and Surveys 18, 22
Compostela ix, x, 26-27, 30, 34, 108
Compton, Judy L. 156, 246, 248, 250
Compton, Richard D. 156, 246, 248, 250
Confederación de Trabajadores de México, CTM 66
Confederación Nacional Campesina, CNC 66-69
Connor, Peter (also Conner) 133, 240, 258
Contreras, Mary 51
Control of Traffic in Wild Species of Flora and Fauna 181
Convention for the Protection of Migratory Birds and Mammals 180
Convention on Nature Protection and Wildlife Preservation in the Western Hemisphere 180
Convention on Wetlands of International Importance Especially as Waterfowl Habitat 180
Cook, John 77, 94, 185
Copper Canyon 15
Copper Company 48
Coro, Captain 126
Corona, Ing. Juan Manuel 38
Coronado, Francisco Vázquez de ix, xi, 2, 29, 35, 191
Coronado Cuarto Centennial Commission ix, xii, 2-4, 10, 12, 18, 26, 43, 71, 99-100, 102
Coronado International Memorial 2, 23, 26, 28, 37-39, 41-45, 47-53, 55-56, 58-59, 62, 72, 74, 89, 99, 252, 256
Coronado International Monument 6-7, 13-15, 17-19, 22, 27, 46, 57-58, 71, 78, 108
Coronado International Park 19
Coronado Investment Company 143, 243, 260, 292
Coronado National Memorial xii, 2, 28-29, 35, 36, 37, 47, 57, 58, 59, 60, 74, 75, 77-86, 89-94, 96, 98, 102-103, 107,
110-111, 123-124, 130, 132, 134-138, 142-145, 148, 151, 153, 157, 159-161, 165,-169, 176-177, 179, 182-183, 185-188, 190-194, 198, 202-204, 209, 212-215, 217-219
Coronado Peak 27, 52, 60, 78, 81, 83, 87, 90-91, 148, 194-195, 198-199, 204-205, 214
Cousins, Bob 155, 165, 233, 236, 238-239
Cox, Harlie 98
Culiacán ix, 34
Cultural Exchange Service of Tucson 207
Cunningham, M.J. 22, 98, 101, 103, 106

D

D'Albini, Alex 13, 19-22, 86-87, 102, 106, 213, 252-253
D'Albini, Fred 86
Dale, Laurel W. 109, 153, 155-156, 200-201, 203-204, 206
Daniels, Ambassador Josephus 4, 10, 17
Danzós Palomino, Ramón 67
Davidson, Assistant Secretary of Interior 44
Davis, John M. 83-84
Davis, Rev. James P. 98, 101, 103
Day, A. Grove 28-30, 34
Departamento de Asuntos Agrarias y Colonización 73
Diario Official 42
Díaz, Melchior 33
Díaz, Porfirio 63
Dickens, G.C. 5, 10, 12
DiPeso, Charles 30-33, 35, 124-126
Dirección General de Conservación y Aprovechamiento Ecológico de México 180
Division of Mining and Minerals 154, 243
Doredor, Bruce 135, 243, 259-260
Doredor Mine 135, 143, 154-157, 220, 243-245, 248-251, 259-260
Doty, Dale E. 54
Douglas, Gordon 151
Driscoll, Cornelius N. 130, 228
Drury, National Parks Service Director 39

E

Eaton, Paul 47, 51, 53, 55
Eidsvik, Harold 181
Ejidal Bank 73, 109

Ejidos 67-68, 73, 108-109, 170, 189
Elías, Rafael 127-128
Emanuel, A.W. 133, 240, 258
Erickson, Jacob 88
Espinosa, J. Manuel 27
Ewing, Dr. Russell 7
Extension Mine 133-134, 240-241, 258-259

F

Farmers Home Administration 144, 223
Faye, Jean 132
Federación de Trabajadores del Estado de Sonora 67
Fergusson, Erna 104
Fernández Delgado, Ing. Jesus Merino 42
Fernández McGregor, Ing. Rafael 38
Finch, John W. 4
Flippen, L.B. 49
Flores, Cesar 207
Fontana, Bernard 109-110
Fort Huachuca 87, 98, 101, 105, 132, 138, 192-193, 199, 203
Fraction Mine 135-136, 154, 243-244, 259-260
Fray Marcos de Niza Monument 22, 99
French, Dr. Alfred R. 110
Froelich, Laurel A. 156-157, 250
Froelich, Paul E. 156-157, 250
Fuente, Ing. Luis de la 42

G

Gadsden Purchase Treaty 127-128
Galiuro Mountains 35
Garcia Martínez, Ing. José 38
Garreau, Joel 169
Garvey, Governor Dan E. 45-46, 85, 105-106
Garza, Ing. Eulogia de la 48, 53
Garza, Nazario Ortiz 42
Gastellum, Luis 79-81, 83
Gatlin, John C. 53
General Agreement on Tariffs and Trade (GATT) 173
Gentry, J.T. 103
Gerdes, Charles 133, 258
Gibbons, Robert D. (Bob) 160, 230
Gila River 31, 35, 129, 187
Gladwin, Harold Sterling 124
Globe, Arizona 79-80, 95

Goldwater, Senator Barry 84, 86, 157
Gómez, Marte R. 38
Gómez y Gutierrez, Ing. Agustín 38
Goyette, C. Edgar 47
Graf, William 133, 240, 258
Grand Canyon 5
Gray, A.W. 148
Gray, Douglas 134, 241, 258
Gray Metals Company 133-134, 240-241, 258
Green, Dewitt 144, 160, 224-225
Green, Doretta Ruth 144, 160, 224-225
Greene, Colonel William Cornell 48-49, 53, 62, 70, 128
Greene, Frank T. 53, 55, 58, 69-70
Greene-Cananea Copper Company 48
Greene Cattle Company 47-49, 52, 182
Griffith, Jim 207
Gross, Cecilia 203
Grubb Stake Mine 9, 13, 213, 252
Grub Stake No. 2 Mine 135-136, 154, 243-244, 259-260
Grub Stake No. 3 Mine 135, 154, 243-244, 259-260
Guerra Limón, José María 185
Guirey, Fred 101
Gutierrez Roldán, Ing. Emilio 39-40
Gutmacher, Carl 49

H

Hall, Nick 100
Halseth, Odd S. 2, 38, 40-41, 43-45, 51-53, 55, 57, 59, 74, 78, 86, 100, 105-106, 108
Hammond, George P. 7
Hardy, Colonel E.N. 107
Hargis, Robert 106
Harris, John L. 133, 240, 258
Hartford Mining District 134, 143, 241-246, 249-251, 258, 260
Hathaway, W.H. 22
Haury, Dr. Emil 6
Hawikuh 5, 35
Hayden, Senator Carl 1, 3-4, 6, 9-10, 14-22, 39-41, 43-46, 50-59, 62, 71-74, 78-79, 84-87, 97, 104
Hearst, Senator George 128
Hearst, William Randolph 128
Heatwole, D.A. 148
Hereford Soil Conservation District 94

Hermandad del Santísimo Sacramento de la Caridad xi
Hermosillo 5, 66, 68, 128
Herrera Jordán, Ing. David 42, 48, 53
Herschede, W. Foy 107
Hertel, Elmer L. 131, 240
Historical Pageant 201
Historic Memorials Association 100
Hodge, Frederick W. 31
Homestead Entry Survey 310 (H.E.S. 310) 129, 140, 143, 145, 149, 217-218, 220-221, 226-228, 240
Homestead Entry Survey 311 (H.E.S. 311) 129, 143-145, 147, 149, 159160, 217, 220-228, 240
Houston, Congressman John M. 25-26
Howard, George Hill 128
Howard, Reverend John 106-107
Howe, George 138, 160, 229
Howe, Martha 160, 229
Huachuca Audubon Society 157
Huachuca Mountains 25, 36, 61, 64, 88, 97, 101, 103, 123-125, 127-129, 132, 135-136, 139-140, 143-145, 147, 151, 168, 176, 187, 192, 194-196, 198-199, 214-215
Hughes, Patricia H. 160, 229
Hull, Cordell 3-4, 17
Humphries, Sondra S. 165, 236
Huntzinger, Hugo 137, 146, 197-198, 204
Hutchison, Ira 156

I

Ickes, Harold L. 9-10
International Boundary and Water Commission 48, 52-53, 142, 147, 219-220
International Historical Pageant 200-201
International Park Commission of Mexico 40, 42, 44-45, 48, 52
International Plant Protection Convention 180
Ishpeming, Michigan 133, 240, 258
Islands in the Desert 132
Izábal, Governor Rafael 63

J

Jácome, Alex 45
Jaramillo, Juan de x, 32
Jay, Austin 107
Jeppson, Wayne 159
Joe's Spring allotment 214
Jones, Governor R.T. (Bob) 3-4, 100
Jones, Inez Z. 138, 143, 221, 227-228, 240
Jones, John A. 138, 140, 143, 213, 221, 227-228, 240
Jones, John Z. 143, 221, 240
Jones, Lawrence D. 143, 221, 228, 240
Josephine Mine 133-134, 240-241, 258-259

K

Keith, Mrs. J.M. 19, 21, 22, 26, 102-103
Kern County Land and Cattle Company 128
Kinnison, John 148
Kino, Father Eusebio Francisco 125
Klinck, Richard E. 89-90
Kudzmi, Simon 131, 240
Kudzmi Homestead 131, 138, 143, 145-147, 159, 217, 220-221, 227-228, 240

L

Lafora, Nicolás de 126-127
Lamoreaux, D. Tenny 108
Lawson, Lawrence M. 52
La Compañia Ganadora de Cananea, S.A. 49
La Crónica de Hoy 188
La Paz Agreement on Cooperation for the Protection and Improvement of the Environment in the Border Area 180
Lee, Henry Davis 13, 19-22, 102-103, 213, 252-253
Lee, R.L. 60
Lena Mine 132, 240, 258
Lime Peak 28
Limón, Guerra 186
Lindh, C. Otto 52
Livericio, Felix 135, 243, 259
Lochiel, Arizona 22, 32, 98-99, 126
Lone Mountain allotment 13, 213
Lone Mountain Ranch 21
Lookout Peak 27
Lopez, Edward 161, 163-166, 233-234, 236, 239
López, Jacinto 67-68
López Mateos, President Adolfo 61, 68
Lyons, D.M. 47

M

Macia, Ethel M. (Mrs. J.H.) 98, 100-101
Madrid, Alfred W. 166, 239
Mallory, L.D. 39
Manje, Captain Juan Mateo 125
Manson, Joni L. 33
Man in the Biosphere Programme 185
Maquiladoras 171-173
Marsh, Harold A. 81
Marsh, Howard 83
Master Plan 79
Master Plan Development Outline 93-94, 252
Master Plan for Coronado National Memorial 36, 81
Master Plan for the Conservation and Use of Coronado National Memorial: Mission 66 Edition 90
Master Plan for the Preservation and Use of Coronado National Memorial 94
Matamoros 172
Mathews, William R. 45, 105
Matson, Andy 100
Maxwell, Ross 42
McCarroll, John H. 106, 108
McCool, Grace 123
McCroskey, Mona Lange 104
McFarland, Senator 52-53
McKinney, Fred 106-107
McLoughlin, Rev. Emmett 100
McPhee, James C. 107
McWilliams, Carey 169
Messersmith, George 39
Mexican Constitution of 1917 67
Mexican Coronado International Commission 38, 40
Mexico-U.S. Joint Committee on Wildlife and Plant Conservation 180
Michaels, Gus R. 28, 37, 41, 97-101, 103
Miller, Jerome C. 7
Milne, Robert C. 110
Mission 66 77, 89-92, 95-96, 253
Miss Stake Mine 135-136, 154, 243, 259-260
Mitchell Mining Company 133, 240, 258
Montezuma Canyon 78, 87-88, 99, 101, 103-106, 124, 128-130, 132-133, 135-136, 138, 140, 142-143, 145-147, 149, 151, 159-160, 168, 193, 196-197, 205, 212-213, 215, 226, 240, 243, 258
Montezuma Estates 221
Montezuma Mountains 243
Montezuma Pass 52, 81, 89, 91, 95, 136, 145-146, 151, 153, 156, 158, 188, 194-196, 205, 213-214, 220, 254, 257, 281
Montezuma Peak xvi, 46, 52, 92
Montezuma Ranch 106, 129-132, 137-138, 145, 159-161, 164-167, 228, 229, 238
Moody, Burdett 97, 103, 134-135, 241, 258-259
Moore, Folsom 22, 86, 88, 98, 101, 103, 107
Moosman, Fred 177
Morgan, Congressman Charles M. 2, 26, 85, 100, 107, 109, 111, 148
Morgan, Lee 176
Mule Mountains 187, 192
Murdock, Congressman John Robert 2, 23, 25-28, 53
Murphy, Charles S. 59

N

Naco, Arizona 26-27, 29, 34-35, 64, 67, 94, 129, 131, 176, 189
Nagel, Carlos 207
National Parks and Conservation Association (NPCA) 148
National Peasant Confederation 66
Neasham, Dr. Aubrey 6-9, 11-12, 21, 28, 38, 55-56, 58, 75, 101
Nelms, Nancy Carter 106, 132, 137-138, 228-229
New York Mine 133-134, 240-241, 258-259
Niza, Fray Marcos de 31, 32, 98, 124
No. Two Mine 133-134, 154-156
Nogales 7-8, 21-22, 26-27, 44-45, 78, 84-86, 95, 99, 101, 105, 110, 139-140, 169, 172, 175
North American Free Trade Agreement (NAFTA) 173-174, 181
Nusbaum, Dr. Jesse L. 42, 52

O

O'Connell, Mrs. T.C. 100
O'Keefe, Audrey C. 155, 248-251
O'Keefe, Jacques 155, 248-251
Oblasser, O.F.M., Father Bonaventure 99
Obregón, President Alvaro 65

Officer, James 109, 111, 125, 206-208
Oñate, Juan de x
Organ Pipe Cactus National Monument 142, 184, 186, 190, 219
Ortega Cattaneo, Ing. Humberto 48, 53
Ortiz Noriega, Abel 67
Owens, Eileen 144, 160, 225
Owens, R.O. 106

P

Palominas, Arizona 27, 98, 203-204, 210
Palo Duro Canyon 5
Paring No. 1 Mine 135, 154-155, 243-245, 248-249, 251, 259-260
Paring No. 2 Mine 135, 154-156, 243-46, 248-251, 259-260
Paring No. 3 Mine 135, 154-156, 243-251, 259-260
Paring No. 4 Mine 135, 154-155, 243-244, 251, 259-260
Patagonia Range 14
Patten, Congressman 53
Paul Spur 94
Pecos Pueblo x
Pello, Manuel 55
Pérez, José Jesus 127
Perry, Don 55
Petersen, Harry H. 132
Petersen, Ruth Ethlyn 132
Peterson, Harry H. 228
Peterson, Ruth Ethlyn 228
Peterson, Thomas H. 108
Peterson-Stowe, Betty 130
Pimería Alta 110
Pinaleño Mountains 31
Pinkley, Frank (Boss) 97-98
Pooler, Frank C.W. 11-12, 15, 22
Porter, John T. 158
Presidio San Phelipe de Guevavi 126
Programa Nacional Fronterizo (PRONAF) 170
Pruett, H. Wayne 143, 243, 260
Pruett-Wray Cattle Company 143, 243, 246
Public Law 78 171
Pyeatt, John 129-130, 228
Pyeatt Homestead 131, 145, 147, 159, 217, 220, 227-229, 240
Pyle, Governor John Howard 45, 53-58, 78, 105-106

Q

Quiburi 32, 125-126
Quivira ix-x

R

Railroad Pass 31
Ranchos de Cananea 62
Rasking, George J. 133, 240, 258
Ratliff, Annie 129, 220, 226
Ratliff, Edward 129, 226
Ratliff, George 129, 220, 226
Ratliff, William 128-129, 217, 220, 226
Ray, Lawrence Edward 144, 160, 223
Reasonover, Olga M. 54
Relación del Suceso 34
Ren, D.B. 133, 240, 258
Research, Studies and Scientific Collection of Territorial and Aquatic Species of Wild Flora and Fauna 181
Reveley, Mr. 44
Richards, Cheryl A. 161, 231, 235, 238
Richards, Richard B. 145, 160-161, 163, 165, 229-231, 233-236, 238-239
Richey, Charles A. 44
Riley, Carroll L. 33
Riley, Peter 100
Riley, Samuel 158-159
Río Batepito 31
Río Bavispe 31
Río de San Joseph de Terrenate 125
Río San Bernardino 31
Ritchie, Mr. 12
Robins, Mayor James V. 45, 51, 85, 105
Roca, Paul 103
Rockwell, Margaret (Mrs. Foster) 38, 51, 52, 59, 78, 81, 86, 100, 103-106, 108, 135
Romero Quintana, Ing. Fernando 38, 40
Romo de Vivar, José 125
Ronstadt, Gilbert 109-110
Roosevelt, President Franklin D. 38
Rubio Mine 135-136, 154, 243-244, 259-260
Ruth, David 106

S

Saguaro National Monument 21, 252
Santa Cruz County Chamber of Commerce 21

Santa Cruz Valley 25, 27, 31
San Bernardino River Valley 30, 33
San Heronimo 82
San Ignacio del Babocomari Grant 128
San Joachín de Huachuca 125
San Juan de las Boquillas y Nogales Grant 127-128
San Pedro Grant 127-128
San Pedro Riparian National Conservation Area (NCA) 187-188
San Pedro River 27
San Pedro Valley 14, 25-28, 94, 101, 103, 124-125, 127-128, 132, 146, 168, 188, 192-193, 195-197
San Rafael del Valle Grant 127-128
San Rafael de la Zanja Grant 128
San Rafael Valley 14
Sauer, Carl 34-35
Saxon, Harry 106
Schroeder, Albert H. 32-33, 81
Scoyen, E.T. 39
Secretaría de Desarrollo Urbano y Ecología (SEDUE) 180-181
Secretaría de México, Ambiente, Recursos, Naturales y Pesca, SEMARNAP 185
SEDESOL 180
Segura, Emile 54, 58
Segura, Emilio, Jr. 53, 72
Sewell, Joseph L. 162, 208-209, 233
Shaken, Vice-Consul 66
Shattuck, Spencer S. 22, 98, 101, 103, 106
Shroeder, Al 83
Sierra del Pinacate 184
Sierra Vista, Arizona 131, 155, 158, 176, 193, 199-200, 203, 206, 215, 239, 257
Sierra Vista Herald 176-177
Simpson, Brig. General J.H. 31
Slaughter Ranch 31
Smith, Charles A. 106, 143, 243, 260
Smith, Don 21-22
Smith, George B. 106
Smith, Paquita C. 143, 243, 260
Smuggler's Pass 131
Sobaipuri 32-33, 125-126
Sonora 2, 14, 30-35, 38, 41-44, 46-47, 51, 53, 55, 57, 62-69, 72, 74-75, 85, 109-111, 127-128, 131, 170-171, 175, 179, 182, 187, 189, 190, 200, 202, 204, 206, 208, 215

Sonoran Desert 186, 190
Sonoran desert 182
Sonora Valley 14
Sorenson, Linda 163, 234
Soto, Hernando de x, 29
Souers, R.E. 100
Southern Arizona Group 152, 208, 210-211
Southwestern Minerals Exploration Association 147
Southwest Mission Research Center (SMRC) 201
Southwest Monuments Association (SMA) 140, 218, 221, 227
Southwest Parks and Monuments Association (SPMA) 140, 210-211, 227
Sparkes, Charles J. 154, 242
Sparkes, Grace M. 22, 38, 45-46, 48, 50-54, 56-61, 71-72, 74-75, 77-81, 86-87, 97, 103-109, 134-136, 138-139, 142-143, 153-154, 192, 195, 241-242, 259
Sparkes, Jack M. 154, 242
Sparkes, Patricia M. 154, 243
Sparkes, T.J. 134, 241, 258-259
Sparkes, Thomas Frederick 154, 242
Sparkes, William J. 152-154, 241-243
State of Texas Lode Mining Claim 153-154, 241-242
State of Texas Mine 9, 104, 107, 133-135, 138, 143, 148, 152-154, 192-193, 217, 220, 240-243, 254, 258-260
State of Texas No. 2 Mine 153, 241-242, 258
Steele, Ethan 166, 239
Steen, Charlie 31
Stevens Ranch 33
Stilwell, William H. 134, 241, 258
Sufea, Frank 100
Sulfur Springs Valley Electrical Cooperative 233
Sulphur Springs 124
Sumrak, Frank 211
Sunrise Farms 161, 231
Szekely, Alberto 181

T

Tako Mining 158
Tamaulipas 171
Tatham, Paul 239
Teague, Calvin R. 144, 226

Teague, Esther 144, 226
Temple, Robert F. 154, 242
Tenneco, Inc. 128, 215
Thomas, Georgia 100
Thompson, Paul R. 229
Thompson, Rufus M. 130
Thurston, Ambassador Walter P. 42
Tiguex Pueblo x, xii, 5
Tijuana 169, 172-173
Tillotson, Miner R. 38, 42, 46, 48-50, 52, 57, 60, 71-72, 78, 105
Tolson, Hillory A. 11-13, 15, 17, 20, 26, 37-48, 51-59, 69, 71-72, 78, 81, 84-86
Tombstone Epitaph 123
Truman, President Harry 59
Tumacacori National Historical Park 187
Tumacacori National Monument 201
Tunnelsite Mine 135-136, 154, 243-244, 259-260
Tyra, Billie Jean 144, 160, 223
Tyra, James M. 144, 160, 223

U

U.S. Federal Register 42, 158
U.S. Fish and Wildlife Service 180
Ullrich, William P. 151, 153
Undreiner, George J. 32-33
UNESCO Man and the Biosphere Programme 185
Unión General de Obreros y Campesinos Méxicanos, UGOCM 66-69
United States-Mexico Integrated Border Environmental Plan 181
United States Coronado Exposition Commission 4

V

Van Cleve, Peter M. 133, 240, 258
Van Dorn, Richard C. 133, 240, 258
Victorio Company 135, 141, 143, 148, 155-156, 217-218, 243-246, 260
Victorio Land and Cattle Company 243
Villas Pérez, Ing. Carlos 38-43
Vucinich, Marko 129, 220, 226

W

Wagstaff, R.M. 35
Wardle, Jacqueline S. 154, 157, 243, 245-246, 248-249, 252
Wardle, James J. 154, 157, 243, 245-246, 248-249, 252
Wardle Realty 155-156
Watkins, E.W. 191, 198
Watt, Secretary James 151
Watts, Rex 132
Weaver, Leo 100
Weick, Elsie R. 145, 160, 164-167, 229, 234-235, 238-239
Weick, George F. 145, 160, 229
Welles, Philip 88, 94, 108-110, 140, 143
Western Farm Credit Bank 164-165, 234, 236, 238
White, Colonel John R. 15, 21
Wickenburg Sun 108
Wilkins, Galvin 88
Willey, William E. 88
Williams, Arthur R. 38, 52-53
Willis, Charles F. 18, 22
Wilson, John 132
Winn, Fred 11, 17, 22
Winship, George P. 34
Wirth, Conrad L. 52, 60, 87, 92
Wirtz, A.J. 7
Wiswall, Charles E. 43, 45, 48-54, 56-57, 64, 69-73, 75, 123
Witkopp, Wilbert P. 158-159, 257
Wood, John 98, 100-101, 103, 105-106
Wray, Peter G. 143, 243, 260
Wright, Bassett T. 108
Wyllys, R.K. 27

Y

Yaqui Ridge Trail 214
Yavapai Associates 104
Yeager, W. Ward 7
Yocupicio Valenzuela, Román 65

Z

Z.T. Parker Mine 135-136, 141, 154, 218, 243, 244, 259-260
Zaleski, Frank 106, 131-132, 140, 228, 253
Zaleski, Joseph 13, 21- 22, 87, 93, 106, 130-132, 138, 140, 213, 220-221, 226-228, 240, 252
Zuni Pueblo x-xii, 31

about the authors

Dr. Joseph P. Sánchez is superintendent of Petroglyph National Monument and the Intermountain Spanish Colonial Research Center. Dr. Sánchez is also founder and editor of the *Colonial Latin American Historical Review* (CLAHR). Before his career with the National Park Service, Dr. Sánchez was a professor of Colonial Latin American history at the University of Arizona, Tucson. He has also taught at the University of New Mexico, Santa Ana College in Southern California and at the Universidad Autónoma de Guadalajara in Mexico. Throughout his career, he has researched archives in Spain, Mexico, France, Italy, and England, and has published several studies on the Spanish frontiers in California, Arizona, New Mexico, Texas, and Alaska. Dr. Sánchez has served as Acting Superintendent at Fort Davis National Historic Site and at Pecos National Historical Park. In April 2005, he was inducted into the prestigious Orden de Isabel la Católica as Knight Commander by King don Juan Carlos of Spain. In 2006 he was named to chair the History Commission of the Instituto Panamericano de Geografía e Historia which is headquartered in Mexico City and affiliated with the Organization of American States in Washington, D.C. Among his published books are: *The Rio Abajo Frontier, 1540-1692* (1987); *Pecos: Gateway to Pueblos and Plains* (Joseph P. Sánchez and John Bezy, coeditors; 1988); *Spanish Bluecoats: The Catalonian Volunteers in Northwestern New Spain, 1767-1810* (1990); *Gaspar Pérez de Villagrá's Historia de la Nueva México, 1610: A Critical and Annotated Spanish English Edition* (Joseph P. Sánchez, Alfredo Rodríguez, Miguel Encinias, co-editors; 1992); *The Aztec Chronicles: The True History of Christopher Columbus by Quilaztli of Texcoco* (1995); *Explorers, Traders, and Slavers: Forging the Old Spanish Trail, 1678-1850* (1997); *Don Fernando Duran y Chaves's Legacy: A History of the Atrisco Land Grant, 1693-1968* (1999); *Memorias del Coloquio Internacional El Camino Real de Tierra Adentro* (Joseph P. Sánchez and José de la Cruz Pacheco, co-editors; 2000); and *Exploradores, comerciantes y tratantes de esclavos: la forja de la Vieja Ruta Española, 1678-1850* (2001).

Dr. Bruce A. Erickson is assistant Professor of History at Le Moyne College in Syracuse, New York. Originally from Chicago, he has lived in Bisbee, Arizona, near Coronado National Memorial. In 1991, Dr. Erickson received his M.A. in Latin American Studies and, in 2001, his Ph.D. in Latin American History, both from the University of New Mexico. He has taught at Western New Mexico University and Eastern Michigan University. For eight years, he served as a research historian at the Intermountain Spanish Colonial Research Center. Dr. Erickson also served as a contract research historian for the National Park Service. His research interests cover a range of topics from gender on the Spanish Colonial frontier to historic trails dealing with the Spanish Colonial period. He has contributed to studies published by the National Park Service. Additionally, his research interests include contemporary efforts to sustain peace and guarantee Human Rights.

Dr. Jerry L. Gurulé is a historian-linguist for the National Park Service's Intermountain Spanish Colonial Research Center where he has worked since 1989. He received his Ph.D. in 1997 in Spanish Colonial Literature from the University of

New Mexico. Throughout his career, he has researched various archives in Spain and Mexico including the Archivo General de las Indias in Sevilla, the Archivo Historico Militar, Real Academia de la Historia, Museo Naval and the Biblioteca Nacional in Madrid, Spain, and the Archivo General de la Nación in Mexico City. Additionally, Dr. Gurulé serves on the editorial board of the *Colonial Latin American Historical Review* (CLAHR), a scholarly journal with a worldwide distribution. He is also on the editorial board of the *New Mexico Historical Review*. His research interests range widely from Spanish Colonial exploration and historical trails to Spanish shipwrecks, and nineteenth century Hispanic military units in Western United States. Among his publications are "The Shipwrecked Spanish Fleet of 1733" in CLAHR (1997), a study of the Spanish investigation of a shipwrecked convoy off the coast of Florida; and, "Franciso Vázquez de Coronado's Northward Trek Through Sonora" in Richard Flint and Shirley Cushing Flint, eds. *The Coronado Expedition to Tierra Nueva: The 1540-1542 Route Across the Southwest* (1997). His publications include co-authored bibliographical works such as *Bibliografia Colombina 1492-1990* on the Life and Times of Christopher Columbus, and *A Selected Bibliography of the Florida-Louisiana Frontier with References to the Caribbean, 1492-1819*. Additionallly, Dr. Gurulé is an accomplished Spanish language translator whose many translations are evident in many National Park Service and U.S. National Forest Service publications and exhibits.

other titles from rio grande books & lpd press

A Tapestry of Kinship: The Web of Influence among Escultores and Carpinteros in the Parish of Santa Fe, 1790-1860
by José Antonio Esquibel and Charles M. Carrillo

Archbishop Lamy: In His Own Words
edited and translated by Thomas J. Steele, S.J., Afterword by Archbishop Michael Sheehan

Atarque: Now All Is Silent…
by Pauline Chávez Bent

Avenging Victorio: A Novel of the Apache Insurgency in NM, 1881
by Dave DeWitt

Charlie Carrillo: Tradition & Soul/Tradición y Alma
by Barbe Awalt & Paul Rhetts

Dejad a los Niños: The History of the Guadalupe Parish
by John M. Taylor

Faces of Faith/Rostros de Fe
photos by Barbe Awalt; Foreword by Thomas J. Steele, S.J.

Frank Applegate of Santa Fe: Artist & Preservationist
by Daria Labinsky and Stan Hieronymus; Foreword by William Wroth

Holy Faith of Santa Fe: 1863-2000
by Stanford Lehmberg

Memories of Cíbola
by Abe Peña; Foreword by Marc Simmons

Navajo and Pueblo Earrings 1850 - 1945
Collected by Robert V. Gallegos
by Robert Bauver

New Mexico: A Biographical Dictionary, 1540-1980, Volume 1
by Don Bullis (**Volume II** will be published fall 2007)

New Mexico in 1876-1877: A Newspaperman's View,
The Travels and Reports of William D. Dawson
   by Robert J. Tórrez

Nicholas Herrera: Visiones de mi Corazón
   by Barbe Awalt & Paul Rhetts; Foreword by Cathy L. Wright

Our Saints Among Us: 400 Years of New Mexican Devotional Art
   by Barbe Awalt & Paul Rhetts

Portfolio of Spanish Colonial Design in New Mexico
   by E. Boyd Hall; Introduction by Barbe Awalt & Paul Rhetts

Religious Architecture of Hispano New Mexico
   by Thomas L. Lucero and Thomas J. Steele, S.J.

Saints of the Pueblos
   by Charles M. Carrillo; Foreword by Ron Solimon

Santos: Sacred Art of Colorado
   edited by Thomas J. Steele, S.J., Barbe Awalt & Paul Rhetts

Seeds of Struggle Harvest of Faith: History of the Catholic Church in New Mexico
   edited by Thomas J. Steele, S.J., Barbe Awalt & Paul Rhetts; Introduction by Archbishop Michael Sheehan

The Complete Sermons of Jean Baptiste Lamy:
Fifty Years of Sermons (1837-1886) (CD)
   edited and translated by Thomas J. Steele, S.J.

The Regis Santos: Thirty Years of Collecting 1966-1996
   by Thomas J. Steele, S.J., Barbe Awalt & Paul Rhetts

Tradición Revista: Southwest Art & Culture (Magazine)
   published by Barbe Awalt and Paul Rhetts

Villages & Villagers
   by Abe Peña; Foreword by Marc Simmons

Wake for a Fat Vicar: Father Juan Felipe Ortiz, Archbishop Lamy, and the New Mexican Catholic Church in the Middle of the Nineteenth Century
   by Fray Angélico Chávez and Thomas E. Chávez; Foreword by Bernard L. Fontana

Printed in the United States
75160LV00005B/7-72